Get the eBook FREE!

(PDF, ePub, Kindle, and liveBook all included)

We believe that once you buy a book from us, you should be able to read it in any format we have available. To get electronic versions of this book at no additional cost to you, purchase and then register this book at the Manning website.

Go to https://www.manning.com/freebook and follow the instructions to complete your pBook registration.

That's it!
Thanks from Manning!

Praise for the first edition

"The most readable and up-to-date treatment of Akka I have seen."

—Kevin Esler, TimeTrade Systems

"A great way to get started and go beyond the basics with Akka."

—Andy Hicks, London Scala Users Group

"A user's guide to Akka in the real world!"

—William E. Wheeler, TEKsystems

"A really useful book. Every chapter has working, real-world code that illustrates how to get things done using Akka."

—Iain Starks, Game Account Network

Akka in Action
Second Edition

Akka in Action

SECOND EDITION

FRANCISCO LOPEZ-SANCHO ABRAHAM

MANNING
SHELTER ISLAND

For online information and ordering of this and other Manning books, please visit
www.manning.com. The publisher offers discounts on this book when ordered in quantity.
For more information, please contact

    Special Sales Department
    Manning Publications Co.
    20 Baldwin Road
    PO Box 761
    Shelter Island, NY 11964
    Email: orders@manning.com

 Manning Publications Co.
20 Baldwin Road
PO Box 761
Shelter Island, NY 11964

Technical development editor:	Jean-François Morin
Development editors:	Kristin Watterson and Toni Arritola
Review editor:	Mihaela Batinic
Production editor:	Deirdre Hiam
Copy editor:	Tiffany Taylor
Proofreader:	Melody Dolab
Technical proofreader:	Ubaldo Pescatore
Typesetter and cover designer:	Marija Tudor

ISBN 9781617299216
Printed in the United States of America

To my brother Lorenzo,
who opened the door to software engineering for me
and to whom I owe my career.

brief contents

1 ▪ Introducing Akka   1

2 ▪ Up and running   27

3 ▪ One actor is no actor   44

4 ▪ Akka test kit   65

5 ▪ Fault tolerance   82

6 ▪ Discovery and routing   108

7 ▪ Configuration   126

8 ▪ Clustering   138

9 ▪ Sharding and persistence   171

10 ▪ Streams, persistence queries, and projections   192

11 ▪ Akka ports   217

12 ▪ Real-world example: An Akka betting house   238

13 ▪ Clustering, part 2   264

14 ▪ Connecting to systems with Alpakka   284

15 ▪ Akka betting house, part 2   306

16 ▪ Akka Streams, part 2   325

contents

preface xv
acknowledgments xvi
about this book xvii
about the author xx
about the cover illustration xxi

1   Introducing Akka   1

1.1   What is Akka?   2

1.2   Actors: A quick overview   4

1.3   Two approaches to scaling: Setting up the example   5

1.4   Traditional scaling   7

*Traditional scaling and durability: Moving everything
to the database 7 ▪ Traditional scaling and interactive use:
Polling 10 ▪ Traditional scaling: Transactions 11*

1.5   Scaling with Akka   12

*Scaling with Akka and durability: Sending and receiving
messages 13 ▪ Scaling with Akka and interactive use:
Pushing messages 15 ▪ Scaling with Akka and failure:
Asynchronous decoupling 16 ▪ The Akka approach: Sending
and receiving messages 16*

1.6   Actors: One programming model to rule up and out   18

An asynchronous model 18 ▪ Actor operations 19

1.7   Akka actors   22

ActorSystem   23 ▪ ActorRef, mailboxes, and actors   24
Dispatchers   24 ▪ Actors and the network   26

2 Up and running   27

2.1   Printing money   28

2.2   Starting to code   28

The protocol of the actor   28 ▪ Creating an application
and instantiating the actor   29 ▪ Sending messages   29
Implementing the actor: Receiving messages   30
Terminating the system   31 ▪ The application   31
The solution in Git   32 ▪ Running the app   32

2.3   Keeping state with a variable   33

2.4   Keeping state with behaviors   37

2.5   Scheduling a message   41

3 One actor is no actor   44

3.1   Simple parser example   45

Coding the app   46 ▪ Coding the guardian and spawning   47
Sending messages back and forth: Adapting responses   48
The protocol with the adapter's message   49 ▪ The adapter's
function   49 ▪ Delegating   49 ▪ A protocol with commands
and responses as traits   51 ▪ Coding the worker   51

3.2   Asking and expecting a reply   52

A simple question   53 ▪ Coding the manager   55 ▪ The
protocols   56 ▪ Asking   56 ▪ Coding the worker   58
Using context   59 ▪ Ask signature   59

3.3   Ask with a payload   61

4 Akka test kit   65

4.1   Testing approaches   66

4.2   Sync testing   67

Effects   67 ▪ More than one actor   70 ▪ Testing the logs   71

4.3   Async testing   72

Using probes   72 ▪ Fishing for messages   75 ▪ Logging   77
Log capturing   79

5 Fault tolerance   82

5.1   What fault tolerance is (and what it isn't)   83

Plain old objects and exceptions 85 ▪ Wrap it up and let it crash 89

    5.2   Actor lifecycle events: Signals 91

    5.3   Supervision strategies and signals 92

Uneventful resuming 92 ▪ Stopping and the PostStop signal 94 ▪ Restart and the PreRestart signal 95 Custom strategy 97

    5.4   Watching signals from an actor 98

    5.5   Back to the initial use case 100

Supervisor hierarchy initial design 100 ▪ Supervision hierarchy alternative design 101

6 Discovery and routing 108

    6.1   Discovery: The receptionist 109

    6.2   The built-in integration router pattern 112

    6.3   Balancing load using built-in routers 114

Akka pool router 116 ▪ Changing strategies 117 Akka group router 118 ▪ Consistent hashing strategy 120

    6.4   Implementing the router pattern using actors 123

Content-based routing 123 ▪ State-based routing 123

7 Configuration 126

    7.1   Trying out Akka configuration 127

Order 127 ▪ Subtrees 128 ▪ Substitutions 129 Using defaults 130

    7.2   Akka configuration 132

    7.3   Multiple systems 133

Lifting with Fallback 133

    7.4   Configuration in tests 135

Lifting in tests 135

8 Clustering 138

    8.1   On top of Akka Cluster 138

    8.2   Why use clustering? 140

Cluster membership: Joining a cluster 141 ▪ Minimal cluster example 143 ▪ Starting the cluster 145

Leaving the cluster   148 ▪ *Unreachable   150* ▪ *Downing
a reachable node   151*

8.3   Akka Management and the Cluster HTTP extension   153

Cluster subscriptions   156

8.4   Clustered job processing   157

In practice   159 ▪ *The code   160* ▪ *Work distribution
in the master   162* ▪ *Starting the cluster   166*

8.5   Resilient job   166

Serialization   167 ▪ *Testing is no different   168*

9   **Sharding and persistence   171**

9.1   Akka sharding and stateful systems   172

The big picture   172 ▪ *An example: A shipping
container   174* ▪ *The simplicity of the sharded
entities   176* ▪ *Rebalancing configuration   178*
Passivation   179 ▪ *Remembering entities   179*

9.2   Persistence   180

The ingredients   180 ▪ *Persistence combined with
sharding: A persistent entity   184* ▪ *Available
effects   184*

9.3   Customizing the persistent entity   186

Failure   186 ▪ *Recovery   186* ▪ *Snapshotting   187*
Tagging   188 ▪ *A peek at serialization and schema
evolution   188*

9.4   Running example   189

10   **Streams, persistence queries, and projections   192**

10.1   Akka Streams   193

Basic semantics   194 ▪ *Finite streams   194*
Source   194 ▪ *Flow   195* ▪ *Sink   195* ▪ *Blueprint   195*
Materialization   196 ▪ *Infinite streams   197*

10.2   Akka Persistence Query   198

Where the rubber meets the road   202

10.3   Projections   204

Reading   205 ▪ *Writing   205* ▪ *Putting everything
together   207* ▪ *The ShardedDaemonProcess   209* ▪ *Back to
the SPContainer projection   211* ▪ *All the main parts   212*

10.4   Projections in action   213

11 **Akka ports   217**

    11.1   Akka HTTP   217

Akka HTTP servers   218 ▪ *The path   218*
Directives   220 ▪ *Route directives   221* ▪ *Marshalling and unmarshalling   224* ▪ *Akka HTTP communicating with actors   225*

    11.2   Akka gRPC   228

The Protocol Buffers side   229 ▪ *The RPC side   229*
The plugin and the .proto file   229 ▪ *Akka gRPC in action   231* ▪ *Running the service   233* ▪ *Akka gRPC with an actor   233* ▪ *Running the example   236*

12 **Real-world example: An Akka betting house   238**

    12.1   The actors   239

The wallet   239 ▪ *The market   243* ▪ *The bet   248*

    12.2   The ports   259

The market   259

13 **Clustering, part 2   264**

    13.1   Akka Cluster Bootstrap   265

Clustering in local   265 ▪ *Cluster in action   267*

    13.2   Clustering with the Kubernetes API   269

Creating the Docker image   269 ▪ *Kubernetes deployment   271* ▪ *Optional: Setting Java options   274*
Kubernetes role and role binding   275 ▪ *Service account   276*

    13.3   Split Brain Resolver   277

An unreachable problem   277 ▪ *SBR strategies   280*

    13.4   Cluster singletons   281

14 **Connecting to systems with Alpakka   284**

    14.1   Alpakka Kafka   285

Consuming from Kafka in action   287 ▪ *Detecting consumer failures   290* ▪ *Auto-commit   290*
Committable sources   290

    14.2   Pushing to Kafka   293

At-most-once delivery guarantee   293 ▪ *At-least-once delivery guarantee   295*

    14.3   Effectively-once delivery   298

14.4 Alpakka CSV 300

Mapping by column 302 ▪ Reading and writing with FileIO 303

15 **Akka betting house, part 2 306**

15.1 Projections 307

Database projection 307 ▪ Kafka projection 312 The betting-house entry point 316

15.2 Configuration 317

Persistence 317 ▪ Cluster local 319 ▪ Cluster Kubernetes 319 Services, sharding, and projections 320

15.3 Deployment 321

Running local 321 ▪ Running in Kubernetes 322

16 **Akka Streams, part 2 325**

16.1 Processing elements through services 326

CPU-bounded services 326 ▪ Non-CPU bounded services 328

16.2 Connecting to an actor 334

16.3 Dealing with exceptions 337

Alternative 1: Deciders 338 ▪ Alternative 2: Modeling exceptions as data 339 ▪ divertTo 340 ▪ Restarting the source 341

16.4 Adding elements dynamically to a stream 346

appendix A *Setting up 350*

appendix B *Microservices and architectural principles 352*

index 365

preface

I joined Lightbend a little more than four years ago, and soon I began to visit customers and train them to build reactive architectures. I heard the same questions over and over again, and in trying to explain the principles, I learned much of what this book is about. But I wouldn't have written the book if it weren't for my friend Raymond Roestenburg.

The opportunity to write this edition of this book came to me by accident. I was working with Ray, and one day, he told me that he had written the previous edition. It was a bit outdated by then, and he thought it would make sense to have the next edition deal with the conversion from Akka Classic to Akka Typed. Writing a book is a lot of work, and he didn't have the time. I did, and I didn't lack motivation. I got in touch with Manning, and we made a plan. And here we are.

Since the first edition of this book, Akka has changed a lot, not only from untyped to typed actors but also to include some other abstractions—storing the state of actors with Akka Persistence, evenly distributing actors with Akka Sharding, creating views from an actor's history with Akka Projections, and more. Some of these abstractions were already there but were not used as often, and others are brand new.

This book's scope is due to my experience as a trainer for Lightbend. Akka has many modules, and for new users, it is difficult to know where to look. This book should give you enough breadth and depth to be sure you know the essentials of Akka as well as the tools you should know and will use often.

acknowledgments

Thanks especially to my good friend Raymond Roestenburg, who trusted me to maintain the high quality of the first edition of this book. Thanks also to Johan Andren, Patrik Nordwall, Enno Runne, and Renato Guerra Calvalcanti for helping me with many of my questions.

I thank my editors, especially Toni Arritola, who taught me—among many other things—the difference between writing down ideas and making them understandable. Thank you to technical proofreader Ubaldo Pescatore, technical development editor Jean-François Morin, review editor Mihaela Batinic, production editor Deirdre Hiam, copyeditor Tiffany Taylor, proofreader Melody Dolab, and, of course, Marjan Bace and Michael Stephens. And thanks to all the readers who helped me correct mistakes.

To all the reviewers: Akon Dey, Alessandro Campeis, Andrei Shpakau, Andres Sacco, Carlos Vilchez, Clifford Thurber, Daniel van Dorp, Gary Bake, Gilberto Taccari, Grahame Oakland, John Ackley, Keith Kim, Nathan B. Crocker, Nenko Ivanov Tabakov, Peter Pfister, Satej Kumar Sahu, Tim van Deurzen, Todd Cook, Vincent Theron, William E. Wheeler, and Yogesh Shetty, your suggestions helped make this a better book.

Last but not least, I want to thank my family, who have always been there for me every step of the way.

about this book

Akka in Action, Second Edition is a book about the Akka basics: most of the primitives Akka provides so that you can build Akka microservices alongside traditional Akka applications in a professional context. It focuses on each topic and goes into examples that are simple at the beginning and more complex later, building on the previous chapters. This way, you end up with a complete application that resembles what you'll find in practice.

Who should read this book

A minimally qualified reader is a developer with two to three years of experience as a developer, preferably in Java or Scala. You are familiar with object-oriented ideas such as methods, classes, and inheritance. You are also at least aware of the principles of functional programming. Finally, the idea of threads and the complexity of concurrent, distributed programming are not foreign to you, but previous experience solving those problems is not required.

How this book is organized: A roadmap

The book includes 16 chapters and 2 appendixes:

- Chapter 1 introduces Akka actors. You learn how the actor programming model solves a number of problems that have traditionally made scaling applications difficult.
- Chapter 2 looks at a few minimal examples of how to create an Akka application with only one actor to send messages to.
- Chapter 3 shows how to create a more realistic scenario with multiple actors sending messages back and forth.

- Chapter 4 is about unit tests for actors with ScalaTest and the `akka-testkit` module.
- Chapter 5 explains how supervision and monitoring enable the construction of reliable, fault-tolerant systems with multiple actors.
- Chapter 6 explores how actors can communicate when they are not in a parent-child relationship, with the receptionist and with routers.
- Chapter 7 explains how to use the Typesafe Config Library to configure Akka and your own application components.
- Chapter 8 examines how clustering in Akka is necessary to create distributed applications. It also discusses internals such as the lifecycle of a node in relation to the cluster.
- Chapter 9 shows how to use Akka Sharding and Akka Persistence to distribute actors in the cluster and keep their state in durable storage.
- Chapter 10 covers the basics of creating streams with Akka Streams, querying the history of persistent actors with Akka Persistence Query, and creating views from this history with Akka Projections.
- Chapter 11 is about creating Akka servers to make your actors accessible through HTTP and gRPC endpoints.
- Chapter 12 summarizes most of what you've learned so far in a real-world example of a betting house, using Akka Persistence to build the actors: a bet, a market, and a wallet.
- Chapter 13 expands your knowledge of clustering so that you can create clusters without knowing the IP addresses of your nodes in advance. After that, you learn how to deploy clusters in Kubernetes.
- Chapter 14 introduces Alpakka as the umbrella project for all connectors in Akka that you can use to connect external services such as databases, Kafka, and files to your actors. This chapter covers Kafka and files.
- Chapter 15 dives deep into the betting-house application, adding Akka endpoints to the application and projections from database to database and Kafka.
- Chapter 16 covers Akka Streams: they are a fundamental part of many modules in Akka, and almost every application has a streaming element these days.
- Appendix A shows you the tools you need to run all the examples.
- Appendix B explores microservices and how their basic features are present in Akka.

About the code

This book contains many examples of source code both in numbered listings and in line with normal text. In both cases, source code is formatted in a `fixed-width font like this` to separate it from ordinary text. Sometimes code is also **in bold** to highlight code that has changed from previous steps in the chapter, such as when a new feature adds to an existing line of code.

In many cases, the original source code has been reformatted; we've added line breaks and reworked indentation to accommodate the available page space in the book. In rare cases, even this was not enough, and listings include line-continuation markers (➡). Additionally, comments in the source code have often been removed from the listings when the code is described in the text. Code annotations accompany many of the listings, highlighting important concepts.

You can get executable snippets of code from the liveBook (online) version of this book at https://livebook.manning.com/book/akka-in-action-second-edition. The complete code for the examples in the book is available for download from GitHub at https://github.com/franciscolopezsancho/akka-topics, and from the Manning website at www.manning.com.

liveBook discussion forum

Purchase of *Akka in Action, Second Edition* includes free access to liveBook, Manning's online reading platform. Using liveBook's exclusive discussion features, you can attach comments to the book globally or to specific sections or paragraphs. It's a snap to make notes for yourself, ask and answer technical questions, and receive help from the author and other users. To access the forum, go to https://livebook.manning.com/book/akka-in-action-second-edition/discussion. You can also learn more about Manning's forums and the rules of conduct at https://livebook.manning.com/discussion.

Manning's commitment to our readers is to provide a venue where a meaningful dialogue between individual readers and between readers and the author can take place. It is not a commitment to any specific amount of participation on the part of the author, whose contribution to the forum remains voluntary (and unpaid). We suggest you try asking the author some challenging questions lest their interest stray! The forum and the archives of previous discussions will be accessible from the publisher's website for as long as the book is in print.

about the author

FRANCISCO LOPEZ-SANCHO ABRAHAM is an experienced software engineer and part of the Akka team. He has been a consultant for many years, from Japan to the United States and a few countries in between. Twenty years ago, he started his career in Spain, then moved to the UK, and for the last six years he has lived out and about, doing what he loves: programming and traveling.

Authors of the previous edition

RAYMOND ROESTENBURG is an experienced software craftsman, polyglot programmer, and software architect. He has been a production user, contributor, and evangelist of Akka since 2010. He is an honorary member of the Akka core team.

ROB BAKKER is an experienced architect/team lead in different environments and has also worked as a complete DevOps developer. Rob has developed applications in different languages like Scala, Java, and Go, running on different OS platforms. In recent years, he has been involved in AI/ML, Reactive, and IOT systems, all based on container technology. Dealing with security, concurrency, and system integration has always been an important part of these systems.

ROB WILLIAMS is the founder of ontometrics, a practice focused on Java solutions that include machine learning. He first used actor-based programming a decade ago and has used it for several projects since.

about the cover illustration

The figure on the cover of *Akka in Action, Second Edition,* is taken from a book by Thomas Jefferys, published between 1757 and 1772.

In those days, it was easy to identify where people lived and what their trade or station in life was just by their dress. Manning celebrates the inventiveness and initiative of the computer business with book covers based on the rich diversity of regional culture centuries ago, brought back to life by pictures from collections such as this one.

Introducing Akka

In this book, you learn how the Akka toolkit provides a single simple programming model for coding concurrent and distributed applications: the *actor programming model*. Actors are nothing new in and of themselves. What's unique is the way actors are provided in Akka to scale applications both up and out on the Java virtual machine (JVM). As you'll see, Akka uses resources efficiently and makes it possible to keep complexity relatively low while an application scales.

Akka's primary goal is to make it simpler to build applications that are deployed in the cloud or run on devices with many cores and that efficiently take advantage of the full capacity of the computing power available. It's a toolkit that provides the actor programming model, a runtime, and the necessary tools for building scalable applications. This chapter discusses the context in which Akka was created, the problem it is designed to solve, and its key architectural components.

1.1   *What is Akka?*

Until the middle of the 1990s, just before the internet revolution, it was usual to build applications that only ever ran on a single computer (a single CPU). If an application wasn't fast enough, the standard response was to wait for faster CPUs to be developed; there was no need to change the code. Problem solved. Programmers worldwide got a free lunch, and life was good.

> **NOTE** In 2005, Herb Sutter wrote in *Dr. Dobb's Journal* about the need for a fundamental change (http://www.gotw.ca/publications/concurrency-ddj .htm): he said that the limit of increasing CPU clock speeds had been reached, and the free lunch was over.

Around 2005, when Herb Sutter wrote his excellent article, companies ran applications on clustered multiprocessor servers (often no more than two or three—the spare was in case one of them crashed). Support for concurrency in programming languages was available but limited and was considered black magic by many mere mortal programmers. Sutter predicted that "programming languages . . . will increasingly be forced to deal well with concurrency."

Let's see what has changed since then. Fast-forward to today, and applications run on large numbers of servers in the cloud; many systems are integrated across many data centers. The ever-increasing demands of end users push the performance and stability requirements for the systems you build. Concurrency is prevalent, and it is here to stay.

But support for concurrency in most programming languages has hardly changed, especially on a JVM. Although the implementation details of concurrency APIs have improved, you still have to work with low-level constructs like threads and locks or fibers. Threads are notoriously difficult to work with, and fibers (lightweight threads) force you to think in terms of other low-level constructs like await, interrupt, and join.

Concurrency is a means to achieve scalability: the premise is that, if needed, more CPUs can be added to servers, which the application then automatically starts using. It's the next best thing to a free lunch. *Scalability* is how a system adapts to a change in demand for resources without negatively affecting performance.

Unlike *scaling up* (increasing resources: for example, CPUs on existing servers), *scaling out* refers to dynamically adding more servers to a cluster. Not much has changed since the 1990s in terms of how programming languages support networking—many technologies still use remote procedure calls (RPCs) to communicate over the network.

In the meantime, advances in cloud computing services and multicore CPU architecture have made computing resources ever more abundant. Platform as a Service (PaaS) offerings have simplified the provisioning and deployment of very large distributed applications, once the domain of only the largest players in the IT industry.

Cloud services like Amazon Web Services Elastic Compute Cloud (AWS EC2) and Google Compute Engine allow you to spin up thousands of servers in minutes, while tools like Docker and Kubernetes make it easier to package and manage applications on virtual servers.

The number of CPU cores in devices is also ever-increasing: even mobile phones and tablets have multiple CPU cores today. But that doesn't mean you can afford to throw any number of resources at any problem. In the end, everything is about cost and efficiency: effectively scaling applications to get more bang for your buck. Just as you'd never use a sorting algorithm with exponential time complexity, it makes sense to think about the cost of scaling.

You should have two expectations when scaling an application:

- The ability to handle any demand increase with finite resources is unrealistic. So, ideally, you want the resources to increase slowly when demand grows: a linear relationship or better. Figure 1.1 shows the relationship between demand and required resources.

- If resources must be increased, ideally, you want the complexity of the application to stay the same or increase slowly. (Remember the good old free lunch when no added complexity was required for a faster application!) Figure 1.2 shows the relationship between resources and complexity.

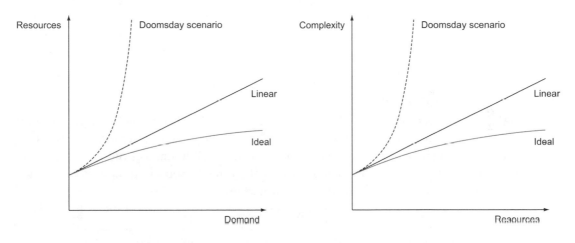

Figure 1.1 Demand vs. resources   **Figure 1.2 Complexity vs. resources**

Both the number of required resources and the complexity of the application contribute to the cost of scaling. I'm leaving many factors out of this back-of-the-envelope calculation, but it's easy to see that both rates have a significant effect on the total.

In one doomsday scenario, you have to pay increasingly more for underutilized resources. In another, the complexity of the application shoots through the roof when more resources are added. This leads to two goals: complexity stays as low as possible, and resources must be used efficiently while you scale the application.

Can you use today's common tools (threads or fibers and RPC) to satisfy these two goals? Scaling out with RPC and scaling up with low-level threading aren't good ideas. RPC pretends that a call over the network is no different from a local method call. Every RPC call, when synchronous, needs to block the current thread and wait for a response from the network for the local method call abstraction to work, which can be costly. This approach impedes the goal of using resources efficiently. When RPC is asynchronous, you are forced to pass a callback, which adds complexity. You may end up in the infamous *callback hell*: a callback that generates a callback that generates another, and so on, making the logic of the code hard to follow.

Another problem with this approach is knowing exactly where to scale up or scale out. Multithreaded programming and RPC-based network programming are like apples and pears: they run in different contexts, use different semantics, and run on different levels of abstraction. You end up hardcoding which parts of your application use threads for scaling up and which parts use RPC for scaling out.

Complexity increases significantly when you hardcode methods that work on different levels of abstraction. Quick—what's simpler, coding with two entangled programming constructs (RPC and threads) or using just one programming construct? This multipronged approach to scaling applications is more complicated than necessary to adapt flexibly to changes in demand.

Spinning up thousands of servers is simple today, but as you'll see in this chapter, the same can't be said for programming them. Akka gives you a single abstraction to deal with concurrency and scalability: the actor model, which provides coherent semantics that let you work on your business logic without worrying about whether your program needs to run on a thousand servers or just one.

1.2   Actors: A quick overview

Akka is centered on actors. Most of the components in Akka provide support in some way for using actors, whether for configuring actors, connecting actors to the network, scheduling actors, or building a cluster out of actors. What makes Akka unique is how effortlessly it provides support and additional tooling for building actor-based applications so you can focus on thinking and programming in actors.

Briefly, *actors* are a lot like message queues without the configuration and message-broker-installation overhead. They're like programmable message queues shrunk to micro size—you can easily create thousands or even millions of them. They don't "do" anything unless they're sent a message.

Messages are simple data structures that can't be changed after they've been created: they're *immutable*. Actors receive messages one at a time and execute some behavior whenever a message is received. Unlike queues, they can also send messages (to other actors).

Everything an actor does is executed asynchronously, meaning you can send a message to an actor without waiting for a response. Actors aren't like threads, but messages sent to them are pushed through on a thread at some point. How actors are connected to threads is configurable, as you'll see later; for now, just know that this is not a hardwired relationship.

We'll get a lot deeper into exactly what an actor is. At this point, the most important aspect of actors is that you build applications by sending and receiving messages. A message can be processed locally on an available thread or remotely on another server. You can decide later where the message is processed and where the actor lives, which is very different than when you're hardcoding threads or using RPC-style networking. Actors make it easy to build an application out of small parts that resemble networked services but have a much smaller footprint and less administrative overhead.

The Akka team took some of the foundational ideas about actors and, in collaboration with other industry leaders working on how to build better systems, synthesized their knowledge into the Reactive Manifesto.

> **The Reactive Manifesto**
>
> The Reactive Manifesto (www.reactivemanifesto.org) is an initiative to push for the design of systems that are more robust, more resilient, more flexible, and better positioned to meet modern demands. The Akka team has been involved in writing the Reactive Manifesto from the beginning, and Akka is a product of the ideas expressed in the manifesto.
>
> Efficient resource usage and an opportunity for applications to automatically scale (also called *elasticity*) are the drivers for much of the manifesto:
>
> - Blocking I/O limits opportunities for parallelism, so nonblocking I/O is preferred.
> - Synchronous interaction limits opportunities for parallelism, so asynchronous interaction is preferred.
> - Polling reduces the opportunity to use fewer resources, so an event-driven style is preferred.
>
> If one node can bring down all other nodes, that's a waste of resources. So you need isolation of errors (resilience) to avoid losing all your work.
>
> Systems need to be elastic: if there's less demand, you want to use fewer resources. If there's more demand, use more resources, but never more than required.
>
> Complexity is a big part of cost. So if you can't easily test your system, change it, or add new features, you've got a big problem.

1.3 Two approaches to scaling: Setting up the example

The rest of this chapter looks at a business chat application and the challenges when it has to scale to a large number of servers (and handle millions of simultaneous events). We'll look at the *traditional approach*, a method you're probably familiar with for building such an application (using threads and locks, RPC, and the like), and compare it to Akka's approach.

The traditional approach starts with a simple in-memory application that turns into an application that relies completely on a database for both concurrency and mutating state. Once the application needs to be more interactive, you have no choice but to poll the database. When more network services are added, the combination of working with the database and the RPC-based network increases complexity significantly. Isolating failure in this application becomes very hard as you go along. You'll probably recognize a lot of this discussion.

We'll then look at how the actor programming model simplifies the application and how Akka makes it possible to write the application once and scale it to any demand (thereby handling concurrency problems on any scale needed). Table 1.1 highlights the differences between the two approaches. As we discuss these items in the following sections, keep this overview in mind.

Table 1.1   Differences between the traditional approach and the Akka approach

Objective	Traditional method	Akka method
Scaling	Uses a mix of threads, shared mutable state in a database (create, insert, update, delete), and web service RPC calls	Actors send and receive messages. No shared mutable state. Log of immutable events.
Providing interactive information	Polls for current information	Event-driven: pushes when the event occurs
Scaling out on the network	Synchronous RPC, blocking I/O	Asynchronous messaging, nonblocking I/O
Handling failures	Handles all exceptions; continues only if everything works	Lets the application crash. Isolates the failure, and continues without the failing parts.

Imagine that you have plans to conquer the world with a state-of-the-art chat application that will revolutionize the online collaboration space. It's focused on business users to help teams easily find each other and work together. You probably have many ideas about how this interactive application can connect to project management tools and integrate with existing communication services.

In good lean startup spirit, you start with a minimal viable product (MVP) of the chat application to learn as much as possible from your prospective users about what they need. If this ever takes off, you could potentially have millions of users (who doesn't chat or work together in teams?). But two forces can slow your progress to a grinding halt:

- *Complexity*—The application becomes too complex to add any new features. Even the simplest change takes a huge amount of effort, and it gets harder to test the application properly, causing ongoing worry: What will fail this time?
- *Inflexibility*—The application isn't adaptive. With every big jump in the number of users, the application has to be rewritten from scratch. Each rewrite takes a

long time and is complex. You have more users than you can handle, and you're split between keeping the existing application running and rewriting it to support more users.

Let's say you have been building applications for a while and choose to build this one the way you have in the past, taking the traditional approach: using low-level threads, locks, and RPCs; blocking I/O; and—first on the menu, in the next section—mutating state in a database.

1.4   Traditional scaling

You start on one server. You set out to build the first version of the chat application and come up with a data-model design, shown in figure 1.3. For now, you keep these objects in memory.

A `Team` object is a group of `Users`, and many `Users` can be part of a `Conversation`. `Conversation` objects are collections of `Messages`. So far, so good.

You flesh out the application's behavior and build a web-based user interface (UI). You're at the point where you can show the application to prospective users and give demos. The code is

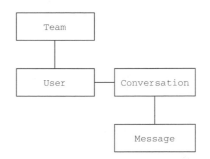

Figure 1.3   Data model design

simple and easy to manage. But so far, the application only runs in memory, so whenever it's restarted, all conversations are lost. It can also only run on one server. Your web app UI built with [insert shiny new JavaScript library] is so impressive that stakeholders want to immediately go live, even though you repeatedly warn that it's just for demo purposes. Time to move to more servers and set up a production environment.

1.4.1   Traditional scaling and durability: Moving everything to the database

You decide to add a database to the equation. You have plans to run the web application on two front-end web servers for availability, with a load balancer in front of the application. Figure 1.4 shows the new setup.

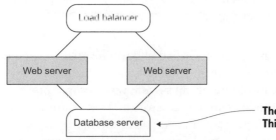

The database might be clustered for failover.
This detail is not important for the example.

Figure 1.4   Load balancer/failover

The code is becoming more complex: you can't just work with in-memory objects anymore, because how would you keep the objects consistent on the two servers? Someone on your team says, "We need to go stateless!" You remove all feature-rich objects and replace them with database code.

The state of the objects no longer resides in memory on the web servers, which means the methods on the objects can't work on the state directly; essentially, all important logic moves to database statements. The change is shown in figure 1.5.

DAOs convert the database representations back and forth to the `Team`, `User`, `Conversation`, and `Message` objects.

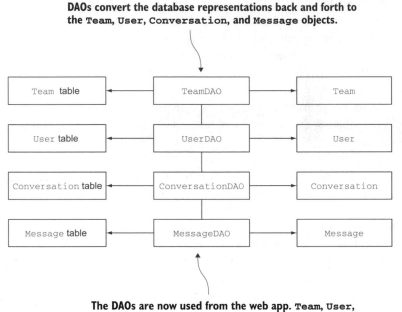

The DAOs are now used from the web app. `Team`, `User`, `Conversation`, and `Message` only contain data.

Figure 1.5   Data access objects

This move to statelessness leads to you replacing the objects with a database access abstraction. For this example, it's irrelevant which one; let's say you feel retro and use data access objects (DAOs, which execute database statements) that are later used by controllers that define the business logic.

Many things change:

- You no longer have the same guarantees you had when you, for instance, called a method on a `Conversation` object to add a `Message`. Before, you were guaranteed that `addMessage` would never fail since it was a simple operation on an in-memory list (barring the exceptional case of the JVM running out of memory). Now, the database might return an error at any `addMessage` call. The insert might fail, or the database might not be available because the database server crashed or due to a network problem.

- The in-memory version had a sprinkling of locks to ensure that the data wouldn't get corrupted by concurrent users. Now that you're using "Database X," you have to handle that problem and make sure you don't end up with duplicate records or other inconsistent data. You need to find out how to do that with the Database X library. All simple method calls to objects effectively become database operations, some of which must work in concert. Starting a conversation, for instance, requires at least an insert of a row in the `Conversation` and `Message` tables.
- The in-memory version was easy to test, and unit tests ran fast. Now you run Database X locally for the tests and add database test utilities to isolate tests. Unit tests run a lot slower. But you tell yourself, "At least I'm also testing the Database X operations," which were not as intuitive as you expected—they're very different from previous databases you've worked with.

You run into performance problems when you're porting the in-memory code directly to database calls since every call now has network overhead. So, to optimize query performance, you design specific database structures that are specific to your choice of database (SQL or NoSQL, it doesn't matter). The objects are anemic shadows of their former selves, merely holding data; all the interesting code has moved to the DAOs and the components of your web application. The saddest part of this situation is that you can reuse almost none of the earlier code; the structure of the code has completely changed.

The "controllers" in your web application combine DAO methods to achieve changes in the data (`findConversations`, `insertMessage`, and so on). This combination of methods results in an interaction with the database that you can't easily predict; the controllers are free to combine the database operations in any way, as illustrated in figure 1.6.

The figure shows one possible flow through the code to add a message to a conversation. You can imagine numerous variations of database access flows using DAOs.

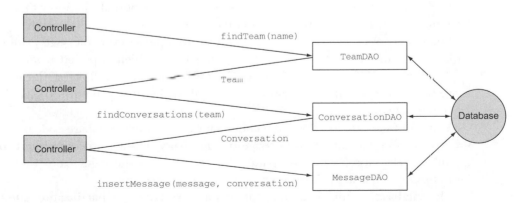

Figure 1.6   DAO interactions

Allowing any party to mutate or query records at any time can lead to performance trouble that you can't predict, like deadlocks and other problems. It's exactly the kind of complexity you want to avoid.

The database calls are essentially RPCs, and almost all standard database drivers (say, JDBC) use blocking I/O. So you're already in the state described earlier, using threads and RPCs together. The memory locks that synchronize threads and the database locks that protect against mutation of table records are not the same thing, and you have to take great care when combining them.

You went from one programming model to two that are interwoven. Your first rewrite of the application took a lot longer than expected.

> **This is a dramatization**
>
> The traditional approach to building the team chat app goes sour in a catastrophic way. Although the example is exaggerated, you've probably seen projects run into at least some of these problems (I have seen similar cases first-hand). To quote Dean Wampler from his presentation "Reactive Design, Languages, and Paradigms" (http://mng.bz/1q7n), "In reality, good people can make almost any approach work, even if the approach is suboptimal."

So, is this example project impossible to complete with the traditional approach? No, but it's suboptimal. It will be very hard to keep complexity low and flexibility high while the application scales.

1.4.2 *Traditional scaling and interactive use: Polling*

You run in this configuration for a while, and the number of users increases. The web application servers aren't using many resources; most are spent on (de-)serializing requests and responses. Most of the processing time is spent in the database. The code on the web server is mostly waiting for a response from the database driver.

You want to build more interactive features now that you have the basics covered. Users are used to Facebook and Twitter and want to be notified whenever their name is mentioned in a team conversation so they can chime in.

You decide to build a `Mentions` component that parses every message written and adds the mentioned contacts to a notification table, which is polled from the web application to notify mentioned users. The web application polls other information more often to reflect changes to users more quickly because you want to give them a truly interactive experience.

You don't want to slow down the conversations by adding database code directly to the application, so you add a message queue. Every message written is sent to this queue asynchronously, and a separate process receives messages from the queue, looks up the users, and writes a record in a notifications table.

The database is getting hammered at this point. You find out that the automated polling of the database and the `Mentions` component are causing database performance problems. You separate the `Mentions` component as a service and give it its own database, which contains the notifications table and a copy of the users table; these tables are kept up to date with a database synchronization job, as shown in figure 1.7.

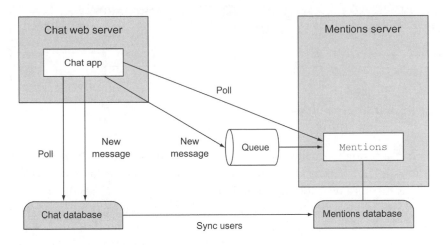

Figure 1.7   Service component

The complexity has increased again, and it's becoming more difficult to add new interactive features. Polling the database wasn't such a great idea for this kind of application, but there are no other real options because all the logic is in the DAOs, and Database X can't "push" anything into the web server.

You've also added more complexity to the application by adding a message queue: it has to be installed and configured, and code must be deployed. The message queue has its own semantics and context to work in; it's not the same as the database RPC calls or the in-memory threading code. Fusing all this code responsibly will be, once again, more complex.

1.4.3   *Traditional scaling: Transactions*

Users start to give feedback that they would love a way to find contacts using *typeahead* (the application gives suggestions while the user types part of a contact's name) and automatically receive suggestions for teams and current conversations based on their recent email conversations. You build a `TeamFinder` object that calls out to several web services like the Google Contacts API and Microsoft Outlook.com API. You build these web service clients and incorporate the finding of contacts, as shown in figure 1.8.

Then you find out that one of the services often fails in the worst possible way: you get long timeouts, or traffic slows to only a few bytes per minute. And because the web services are accessed one after the other, the `TeamFinder`—waiting for the response—fails the lookup after a long time even though the service that worked fine could have made many valid suggestions to the user.

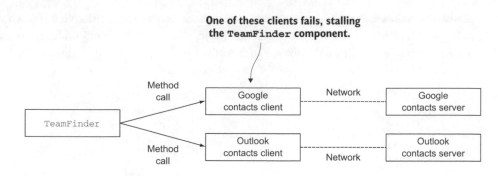

Figure 1.8 `TeamFinder` component

Even worse, although you have collected your database methods in DAOs and the contact lookup in a `TeamFinder` object, the controllers call these methods like any others. This means a user lookup sometimes happens between two database methods, keeping connections open longer than you want and eating up database resources. If the `TeamFinder` fails, everything else that's part of the same flow in the application also fails. The controller throws an exception and can't continue. How do you safely separate the `TeamFinder` from the rest of the code?

It's time for another rewrite, and it doesn't look like the complexity is improving. You're now using four programming models: one for in-memory threads, one for database operations, one for the `Mentions` message queue, and one for the contacts web services.

How do you move from 3 servers to, say, 10, and then to 100 servers if need be? Obviously, this approach doesn't scale well: you have to change direction with every new challenge. In the next section, you'll find out if there's a design strategy that doesn't require you to constantly change direction.

1.5   *Scaling with Akka*

Let's see if it's possible to deliver on the promise to use only actors to meet the application's scaling requirements. Since it's probably still unclear to you what actors are, I'll use the terms *objects* and *actors* interchangeably and focus on the conceptual differences between this approach and the traditional one. Table 1.2 shows this difference in approaches.

Table 1.2   Actors compared to the traditional approach

Goal	Traditional approach	Akka approach (actors)
Make conversation data durable, even if the application restarts or crashes.	Rewrite code into DAOs. Use the database as one big shared mutable state where all parties create, update, insert, and query the data.	Continue to use the in-memory state. Send changes to the state as messages to a log. This log is reread only if the application restarts.

Table 1.2   Actors compared to the traditional approach *(continued)*

Goal	Traditional approach	Akka approach (actors)
Provide interactive features (mentions).	Poll the database. Polling uses many resources even if there's no change in the data.	Push events to interested parties. The objects notify interested parties only when there's a significant event, reducing overhead.
Decouple services. The mentions and chat features shouldn't interfere with each other.	Add a message queue for asynchronous processing.	No need to add a message queue; actors are asynchronous by definition. No extra complexity; you're familiar with sending and receiving messages.
Prevent failure of the entire system when critical services fail or behave outside of specified performance parameters for any given time.	Try to prevent any error from happening by predicting all failure scenarios and catching exceptions for these scenarios.	Send messages asynchronously. If a message isn't handled by a crashed component, the crash has no effect on the stability of the other components.

It would be great if you could write the application code once and then scale it any way you like. You want to avoid radically changing the application's main objects: for example, the way you had to replace all logic in the in-memory objects with DAOs in section 1.4.1.

The first challenge you wanted to solve was to safekeep conversation data. Coding directly to the database moved you away from one simple in-memory model. Methods that were once straightforward turned into database RPC commands, leaving you with a mixed programming model. You must find another way to ensure that the conversations aren't lost while keeping things simple.

1.5.1 Scaling with Akka and durability: Sending and receiving messages

Let's first solve the initial problem of making conversations durable. The application objects must somehow save conversations. The conversations must be recovered when the application restarts. Figure 1.9 shows how a `Conversation` actor sends a `Message-Added` event to the database log for every message that's added in memory. The conversation can be rebuilt from these objects stored in the database whenever the web server (re)starts, as shown in figure 1.10.

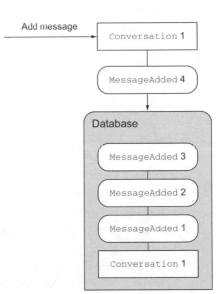

Figure 1.9   Persisting conversations

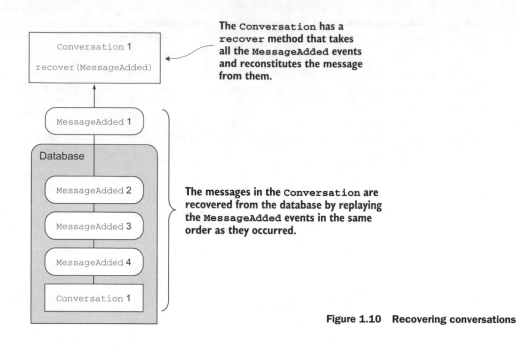

Figure 1.10   **Recovering conversations**

You'll learn how this process works in chapter 9. But as you can see, you only use the database to recover the messages in the conversation. You don't use it to express your code in database operations. The Conversation actor sends messages to the log and receives them again on startup. You don't have to learn anything new; you're just sending and receiving messages.

KEEPING CHANGES AS A SEQUENCE OF EVENTS

All changes are kept as a sequence of events—in this case, MessageAdded events. The current state of the Conversation can be rebuilt by replaying the events in the in-memory Conversation so it can continue where it left off. This type of database is often called a *journal*, and the technique is known as *event sourcing*. There's more to event sourcing, but this definition will do for now.

What's important to note here is that the journal has become a uniform service. All it needs to do is store all events in sequence and make it possible to retrieve the events in the same sequence as they were written to the journal. (We'll ignore some details for now, like serialization—if you can't wait, look at chapter 9.)

SPREADING OUT THE DATA: SHARDING CONVERSATIONS

The next problem is that you're still putting all your eggs in one server. The server restarts, reads all conversations in memory, and continues to operate. The main reason for going stateless in the traditional approach is that it's hard to imagine how you would keep the conversations consistent across many servers. And what would happen if there were too many conversations to fit on one server?

A solution is to divide the conversations over the servers in a predictable way or keep track of where every conversation lives. This is called *sharding* or *partitioning.* Figure 1.11 shows some conversations in shards across two servers.

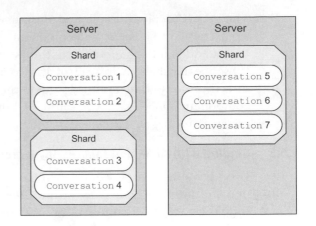

You can keep using the simple in-memory model of conversations if you have a generic event-sourced journal and a way to indicate how conversations should be partitioned. Many details about

Figure 1.11 Sharding

these two capabilities are covered in chapters 9 and 15. For now, let's assume that you can use these services.

1.5.2 Scaling with Akka and interactive use: Pushing messages

Instead of polling the database for every web application user, you can notify the user of an important change (an event) by directly sending messages to the user's web browser. The application can also send event messages internally as signals to execute particular tasks. Every object in the application sends an event when something interesting occurs. Other objects in the application can decide whether an event is interesting and take action on it, as shown in figure 1.12.

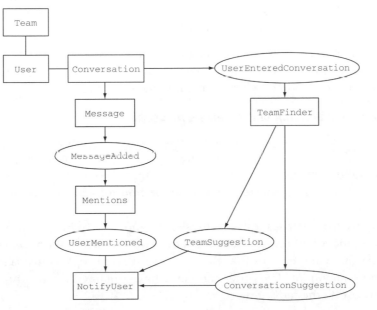

Figure 1.12 Events

The events (depicted as ellipses) decouple the system where there used to be undesired coupling between the components. The `Conversation` actor only publishes that it added a `Message` and continues its work. Events are sent through a publish-subscribe mechanism instead of the components communicating with each other directly. An event will eventually get to the subscribers: in this case, to the `Mentions` component. Once again, you can model the solution to this problem by sending and receiving messages.

1.5.3   Scaling with Akka and failure: Asynchronous decoupling

Users should be able to continue to have conversations even if the `Mentions` component crashes. The same goes for the `TeamFinder` component: existing conversations should be able to continue. Conversations can continue to publish events while subscribers—like the `Mentions` component and the `TeamFinder` object—crash and restart. The `NotifyUser` component can keep track of connected web browsers and send `UserMentioned` messages directly to the browser when they occur, relieving the application from polling.

   This event-driven approach has a few advantages:

- It minimizes direct dependencies between components. The `Conversation` actor doesn't know about the Mentions object and could not care less about what happens with the event. The `Conversation` can continue to operate when the `Mentions` object crashes.
- The components of the application are loosely coupled in time. It doesn't matter if the `Mentions` object gets the events a little later as long as it gets them eventually.
- The components are decoupled in terms of location. The `Conversation` and `Mentions` objects can reside on different servers; the events are just messages that can be transmitted over the network.

The event-driven approach solves the polling problem with the `Mentions` object and the direct coupling with the `TeamFinder` object. You can once again model the solution to this problem by sending and receiving messages.

1.5.4   The Akka approach: Sending and receiving messages

Let's recap what you've changed so far: `Conversations` are now stateful in-memory objects (actors) that store their internal state, recover from events, are partitioned across servers, and send and receive messages. You've seen how communicating between objects with messages instead of calling methods directly is a winning design strategy.

   A core requirement is that messages are sent to and received from every actor in order, one at a time, when one event is dependent on the next: otherwise, you'd get unexpected results. This requires that the `Conversation` keeps its messages secret from any other component. The order can never be maintained if any other component can interact with the messages.

It shouldn't matter if you send a message locally on one server or remotely to another. So you need a service that takes care of sending messages to actors on other servers if necessary. It must also keep track of where actors live and provide references so other servers can communicate with the actors. Akka does this for you, as you'll soon see. Chapter 8 discusses the basics of distributed Akka applications, and chapter 13 looks at clustered Akka applications (groups of distributed actors).

The Conversation actor doesn't care what happens with the Mentions component; but on the application level, you need to know when the Mentions component stops working so you can show users that it's temporarily offline, among other things. For this reason, you need to be able to monitor actors and reboot them if necessary. This monitoring should work across servers as well as locally on one server, so it must also send and receive messages. A possible high-level structure for the application is shown in figure 1.13.

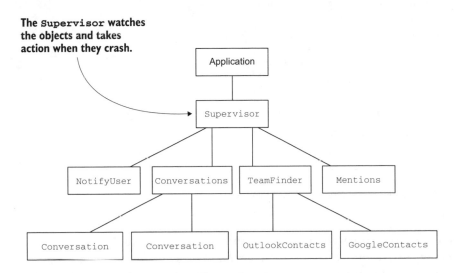

The Supervisor watches the objects and takes action when they crash.

Figure 1.13 High-level application structure

The Supervisor watches over the components and takes action when they crash. For example, it can decide to continue running when the Mentions component or the TeamFinder doesn't work. If both Conversation and NotifyUser stop working, the Supervisor can decide to restart or stop the application since there's no reason to continue. A component can send a message to the Supervisor when it fails, and the Supervisor can send a message to a component to stop or try to restart. As you'll see, this is conceptually how Akka provides error recovery, as discussed in chapter 4.

In the next section, you'll learn first about actors in general and then about Akka actors.

1.6   *Actors: One programming model to rule up and out*

Most general-purpose programming languages are written in sequence (Scala and Java are no exception to the rule). A concurrent programming model is required to bridge the gap between sequential definition and parallel execution.

Whereas parallelization is all about executing processes simultaneously, concurrency concerns itself with defining processes that *can* function simultaneously or overlap in time but don't necessarily *need* to run simultaneously. A concurrent system is not, by definition, a parallel system. Concurrent processes can, for example, be executed on one CPU using time slicing, where every process gets a certain amount of time to run on the CPU, one after another.

The JVM has a standard concurrent programming model (see figure 1.14) where, roughly speaking, processes are expressed in objects and methods, which are executed on threads. Threads can be executed on many CPUs in parallel or using a sharing mechanism like time slicing on one CPU. As discussed earlier, threads can't be applied directly to scaling out, only to scaling up.

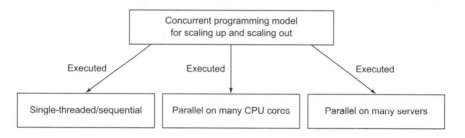

Figure 1.14   Concurrent programming model

The concurrent programming model that you're after should function for one CPU or many and for one server or many servers. The actor model chooses the abstraction of sending and receiving messages to decouple from the number of threads or servers being used.

1.6.1   *An asynchronous model*

If you want the application to scale to many servers, there's an important requirement for the programming model: it must be *asynchronous*, allowing components to continue working while others haven't responded yet, as in the chat application.

Figure 1.15 shows a possible configuration of the chat application, scaled to five servers. The Supervisor is responsible for creating and monitoring the rest of the application. The Supervisor now has to communicate over the network, which might fail, and every server could crash. If the Supervisor used synchronous communication, waiting for every response from every component, you could get into a problematic situation where one of the components didn't respond, blocking all other calls from happening. For instance, what would happen if the `Conversation` server was restarting and not responding to the network interface when the `Supervisor` wanted to send messages to all components?

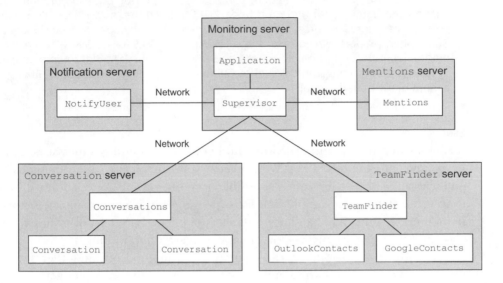

Figure 1.15   Scaled-out application

1.6.2   Actor operations

Actors are the primary building blocks in the actor model. All the components in the example application are actors, shown in figure 1.16. An actor is a lightweight process with only four core operations: create, send, designate the next behavior, and supervise. All of these operations are asynchronous.

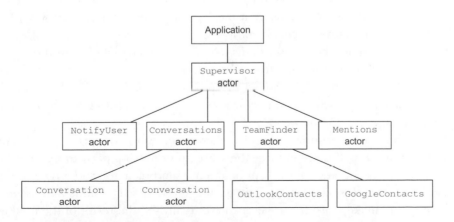

Figure 1.16   Application components

> ## The actor model—not new
>
> The actor model has been around for quite a while; the idea was introduced in 1973 by Carl Hewitt, Peter Bishop, and Richard Steiger. The Erlang language and its Open Telecom Platform (OTP) middleware libraries, developed by Ericsson around 1986, support the actor model and have been used to build massively scalable systems with requirements for high availability. An example of the success of Erlang is the AXD 301 switch product, which achieves a reliability of 99.9999999%, also known as *nine nines* reliability. The actor model implementation in Akka differs in a couple of details from the Erlang implementation but has been heavily influenced by Erlang and shares many of its concepts.

SEND

An actor can only communicate with another actor by sending it messages. This takes *encapsulation* to the next level. With objects, you can specify which methods can be publicly called and which state is accessible from the outside. Actors don't allow access to internal state (for example, the list of messages in a conversation). Actors can't share mutable state; they can't, for instance, point to a shared list of conversation messages and change the conversation in parallel at any point in time.

The `Conversation` actor can't simply call a method on any other actor, since doing so could lead to sharing mutable state. It has to send the other actor a message. Sending messages is always asynchronous in what is called a *fire-and-forget* style. If it's important to know that another actor received the message, the receiving actor should send back an acknowledgment message.

The `Conversation` actor doesn't have to wait and see what happens with a message to the `Mentions` actor; it can send a message and continue its work. Asynchronous messaging helps the chat application decouple the components; this is one reason you used a message queue for the `Mentions` object, which is now unnecessary.

The messages need to be immutable, meaning they can't be changed once they're created. This makes it impossible for two actors to change the same message by mistake or for a single actor to change a message twice but in different ways, both of which could result in unexpected behavior.

So what do you do when a user wants to edit a message in a conversation? You can send an `EditMessage` message to the conversation. The `EditMessage` contains a modified copy of the message instead of updating the message in place in a shared messages list. The `Conversation` actor receives the `EditMessage` and replaces the existing message with the new copy.

Immutability is an absolute necessity when it comes to concurrency. It is another restriction that simplifies life because there are fewer moving parts to manage.

The order of sent messages is kept between a sending actor and a receiving actor. An actor receives messages one at a time. Imagine that a user edits a message many times; it would make sense for the user to eventually see the result of the final edit of the message. The order of messages is only guaranteed per sending actor, so if many

users edit the same message in a conversation, the final result can vary depending on
how the messages are interleaved over time.

CREATE

An actor can create other actors. Figure 1.17 shows how the
Supervisor actor creates a Conversations actor. As you can see,
this action automatically creates a hierarchy of actors. The chat
application first creates the Supervisor actor, which in turn creates all other actors in the application. The Conversations actor
recovers all Conversations from the journal. It then creates a
Conversation actor for every Conversation that recovers itself
from the journal.

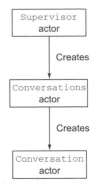

**Figure 1.17
Creating actors**

DESIGNING THE NEXT BEHAVIOR

State machines are a great tool for ensuring that a system executes
particular actions only when it's in a specific state. Actors receive
messages one at a time, which is a convenient property for implementing state machines. An actor can change how it handles incom-
ing messages by swapping out its behavior. An actor must designate the behavior to be
used for the next message it receives.

Imagine that users want to be able to close a Conversation. The Conversation
starts in a started state and becomes closed when a CloseConversation is received. Any
message that's sent to the closed Conversation can be ignored. The Conversation
swaps its behavior from adding messages to itself to ignoring all messages.

SUPERVISE

An actor needs to supervise the actors that it creates. The Supervisor in the chat
application can keep track of what's happening to the main components, as shown in
figure 1.18.

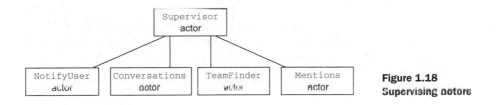

**Figure 1.18
Supervising actors**

The Supervisor decides what should happen when components fail in the system.
For example, it can decide that the chat application continues when the Mentions
component and the NotifyUser actor have crashed since they're not critical components. The Supervisor is notified with special messages that indicate which actor has
crashed and for what reason. The Supervisor can decide to restart an actor or take
the actor out of service.

Any actor can be a supervisor, but only for the actors it creates. In figure 1.19, the `TeamFinder` actor supervises the two connectors for looking up contacts. In this case, it could take the `OutlookContacts` actor out of service because it failed too often. The `TeamFinder` would then continue looking up contacts from Google only.

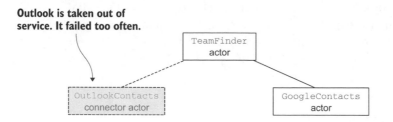

Figure 1.19   `TeamFinder` supervising contacts actors

Actors: Decoupled on three levels

Another way to look at actors is how they're decoupled for scaling on three levels: space/location, time, and interface. Actors can run simultaneously if there are enough CPUs or run one after the other if not. Actors can be co-located or far apart; and in a failure scenario, actors may receive messages they can't handle.

Decoupling on these three levels is important because this is exactly the flexibility required for scaling:

- *Space*—An actor gives no guarantee and has no expectations about where another actor is located.
- *Time*—An actor gives no guarantee and has no expectations about when its work will be done.
- *Interface*—An actor has no defined interface. Nothing is shared between actors; actors never point to or use a shared piece of information that changes in place. Information is passed in messages.

Coupling components in location, time, and interface is the biggest impediment to building applications that can recover from failure and scale according to demand. A system built out of components that are coupled on all three can only exist on one runtime and will fail completely if one of its components fails.

Now that you've looked at the operations an actor can perform, let's look at how Akka supports actors and what's required to make them process messages.

1.7   *Akka actors*

So far, you've learned about the actor programming model from a conceptual perspective and seen why you may want to use it. Let's look at how Akka implements the actor model and get closer to where the rubber meets the road. This section examines how everything connects—which Akka components do what—beginning with actor creation.

1.7.1 ActorSystem

The first thing we'll look at is how actors are created. Actors can create other actors, but what creates the first one?

All the actors shown in figure 1.20 are part of the same chat application. The application's first actor is the Supervisor. How do you make actors part of one bigger whole? The answer Akka provides is the ActorSystem. The first thing every Akka application does is create an ActorSystem. The ActorSystem can create so-called top-level actors, and it's a common pattern to create only one top-level actor for all actors in the application—in this case, the Supervisor actor that monitors everything.

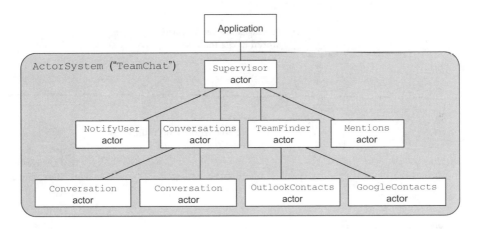

Figure 1.20 TeamChat ActorSystem

We've touched on the fact that you need support capabilities for actors, like remoting and a journal for durability. The ActorSystem is also the nexus for these support capabilities. Most capabilities are provided as *Akka extensions*: modules that can be configured specifically for the ActorSystem in question. A simple example of a support capability is the scheduler, which can send messages to actors according to a specific schedule.

An ActorSystem returns an address to the created top-level actor instead of the actor itself. This address is called an ActorRef. The ActorRef can be used to send messages to the actor. This makes sense when you think about the fact that the actor could be on another server.

Sometimes you'd like to look up an actor in the actor system. This is where Actor-Paths come in. You can compare the hierarchy of actors to a URL path structure. Every actor has a name. This name needs to be unique per level in the hierarchy: two sibling actors can't have the same name (if you don't provide a name, Akka can generate one for you, but it's a good idea to name all your actors). All actor references can be located directly by an actor path, which can be absolute or relative.

1.7.2 *ActorRef, mailboxes, and actors*

Messages are sent to the actor's `ActorRef`. Every actor has a mailbox—it's a lot like a queue. Messages sent to the `ActorRef` are temporarily stored in the mailbox to be processed later, one at a time, in the order they arrived. Figure 1.21 shows the relationship between the `ActorRef`, the mailbox, and the actor. How the actor processes the messages is described in the next section.

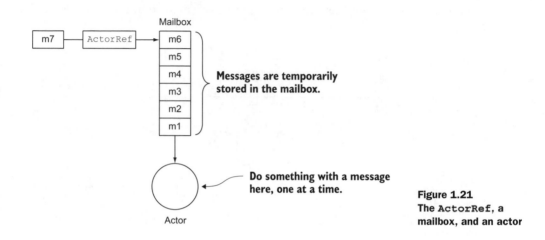

Messages are temporarily stored in the mailbox.

Do something with a message here, one at a time.

**Figure 1.21
The `ActorRef`, a mailbox, and an actor**

1.7.3 *Dispatchers*

Actors are invoked at some point by a dispatcher. The dispatcher pushes the messages in the mailbox through the actors, so to speak. This is shown in figure 1.22.

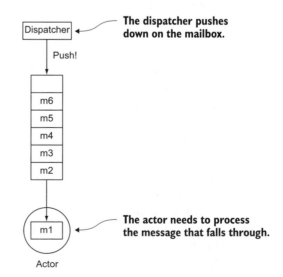

The dispatcher pushes down on the mailbox.

The actor needs to process the message that falls through.

Figure 1.22   The dispatcher pushes messages through the mailbox.

The type of dispatcher determines which threading model is used to push the messages through. Many actors can receive messages pushed through on several threads, as shown in figure 1.23.

Figure 1.23 shows the dispatcher pushing messages m1–m6 on threads 1 and 2 and messages x4–x9 on threads 3 and 4. This figure shouldn't make you think that you can or should control exactly which message will be pushed through on which thread. What's important is that you can configure the threading model quite extensively. All kinds of dispatchers can be configured in some way, and you can allocate a dispatcher to an actor, a specific group of actors, or all actors in the system.

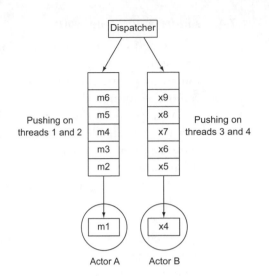

Figure 1.23 Dispatcher pushing messages through multiple actors

So when you send a message to an actor, you're really leaving a message behind in its mailbox. Eventually, a dispatcher will push the message through the actor. The actor, in turn, can leave a message behind for the next actor, and that message will be pushed through at some point.

Actors are lightweight because they run on top of dispatchers; the number of actors isn't necessarily directly proportional to the number of threads. Akka actors take a lot less space than threads: around 2.7 million actors can fit in 1 GB of memory. That's a big difference compared to 4096 threads for 1 GB of memory, so you can create different types of actors more freely than you could using threads directly.

You can choose different types of dispatchers that can be tuned to specific needs. Being able to configure and tune the dispatchers and mailboxes used throughout the application gives you a lot of flexibility when performance tuning.

Callback hell

A lot of frameworks provide asynchronous programming through callbacks. If you've used any of these frameworks, chances are good that you've been to a place called *callback hell*, where every callback calls another callback, which calls another callback, and so on.

Compare this approach to how the dispatcher chops up the messages in the mailbox and pushes them through on a given thread. Actors don't need to provide a callback in a callback, all the way down to some sulfur pit, which is good news. Actors drop off messages in a mailbox and let the dispatcher sort out the rest.

1.7.4   *Actors and the network*

How do Akka actors communicate with each other across the network? `ActorRefs` are essentially addresses to actors, so all you need to change is how the addresses are linked to actors. If the toolkit takes care of the fact that an address can be local or remote, you can scale the solution by configuring how the addresses are resolved.

Akka provides discovery out of the box—which you'll learn about in chapters 6 and 9—that enables the transparency you seek. Akka passes messages for a remote actor to a remote machine where the actor resides and passes the results back across the network.

The only thing that has to change is how references to remote actors are looked up; this can be achieved solely through configuration, as you'll see later. The code stays the same, so you can often transition from scaling up to scaling out without having to change a single line of code. The flexibility of resolving an address is heavily used in Akka, as you'll learn throughout this book. Remote actors, clustering, and even the test toolkit use this flexibility.

At this point, you should understand that actors can give you more flexibility at a decent level of complexity, making your application far easier to scale. But there's a lot more to be learned, and as always, the devil is in the details. Let's get up and running with actors in the next chapter!

Summary

- Scaling is traditionally hard to get right. Both inflexibility and complexity can quickly get out of control when scaling is required. Akka actors take advantage of key design decisions that provide more flexibility to scale.
- Actors are a programming model for scaling up and out, and everything revolves around sending and receiving messages. Although it's not a silver bullet for every problem, working with one programming model reduces some of the complexity of scaling.
- Akka is centered on actors. What makes Akka unique is how effortlessly it provides support and additional tooling for building actor-based applications so that you can focus on thinking about and programming actors.

Up and running 2

This chapter covers

- Defining an actor and its behavior
- Instantiating and sending messages to an actor
- Keeping state in the actor with a variable
- Keeping state in the actor with its behavior
- Scheduling sending a message

This chapter covers in practice the basic parts of Akka from the previous chapter: creating an actor, sending messages to actors, and setting actors' behavior. It also explains how to handle state and send messages with a scheduled delay.

Without further ado, let's start with a minimal Akka application: a wallet into which you can deposit money. This can be part of a larger application that handles betting on sports events with money from the wallet. You learn how to create such a betting application later in this book, but first you need to learn some basics.

> **NOTE** To run the examples in this book, follow the instructions in appendix A to install all the tools. When you've finished the installation, return here and get started.

In this chapter, you get to know different variants of such a wallet, which will guide you through some Akka primitives:

- At first, the wallet's only function is to print the deposited money to the console without keeping track of the total amount.
- Later, you learn how to store the money in a variable.
- Finally, you deactivate/activate the wallet.

NOTE The source code for this chapter is available at www.manning.com/ books/akka-in-action-second-edition or https://github.com/franciscolopez sancho/akka-topics/tree/main/chapter02. You can find the contents of any snippet or listing in the .scala file with the same name as the class or object. For example, you can find the snippet with `object Wallet` in the Wallet .scala file.

2.1 *Printing money*

In this chapter, you learn how to create an application and an actor and send two messages to the actor that will be output to the console. The following snippet shows the output of such an application: `Wallet$` is the class name of the actor, and the rest is what the actor logs, one line per message sent to the actor (recall that an actor acts as a message queue):

```
[Wallet$] – received '1' dollar(s)
[Wallet$] – received '10' dollar(s)
```

Now let's get right into the actor and the main class that make up the application.

2.2 *Starting to code*

When you create an actor, you must first specify the messages it can receive. It cannot receive just any type of message. You must define the actor's type, which in Akka terminology is called the actor's *protocol*.

2.2.1 *The protocol of the actor*

The Akka API specifies with `Behavior[Int]` that the behavior of the `Wallet` actor is such that it can receive messages of type `Int`. This is its protocol. In this example, the `Wallet` actor object has a protocol of type `Int` and is defined as follows:

```
import akka.actor.typed.Behavior

object Wallet {

  def apply(): Behavior[Int] = ...
}
```

The rest of the actor's code is not relevant at the moment. There could be many implementations, but the essential thing for the further development of the app is the definition of the messages the actor can receive.

2.2.2 Creating an application and instantiating the actor

Now that the protocol is set, you can create an application and add an actor using the `ActorSystem` you learned about in the previous chapter. An application is an executable program. You can create this application by defining an object that extends from `scala.App`:

```
object WalletApp extends App
```

This is a simple way to create a runnable class. At the end of the example, you learn how to run this class.

Next, let's focus on creating the actor in the signature of the `ActorSystem` constructor because the first parameter may not be clear. This is how you do it:

```
object WalletApp extends App {

  val guardian: ActorSystem[Int] = ActorSystem(Wallet(), "wallet")      ⟵┐
                                                                          │
}                                                    Instantiates an Akka │
                                                            application ──┘
```

In Scala, a generic type—equivalent to a Java generic—is identified by a letter in square brackets. The following snippet shows this generic type as `[T]` in the `ActorSystem` `apply` method, its constructor:

```
def apply[T](guardianBehavior: Behavior[T], name: String): ActorSystem[T]
```

> **NOTE** Every `object` in Scala—like the `ActorSystem`—is created via the `apply` method, but it can also be created via the object's name alone. For example, the constructor `ActorSystem(myParameters)` refers to `Actor-System.apply(myParameters)` under the covers. Another example is `Wallet()`, which references `Wallet.apply()`.

With this in mind, you can see how in `ActorSystem(Wallet(), "wallet")`, the first parameter refers to the wallet constructor, its `apply` method.

With this, you have an actor. Now let's send some messages to it.

2.2.3 Sending messages

Two things are worth noting. First, the `Wallet` actor is instantiated as an `Actor-System`, which is typed as `[Int]`. This signals what you already knew: that this actor can receive integers as messages only. Second, you may recall from chapter 1 that the `ActorSystem` is a reference to an actor, an `ActorRef`. This is the address you can use to send messages to the actor. To do this, you use the `tell` method, which is often represented with the bang operator (`!`). The following snippet means the numeral 1 is sent to the `myActorReference` address:

```
myActorReference ! 1
```

Combining all these ingredients, this snippet defines and instantiates the actor and sends two messages to it:

```
import akka.actor.typed.ActorSystem

object WalletApp extends App {                              ┐ Creates
                                                            │ the actor
  val guardian: ActorSystem[Int] = ActorSystem(Wallet(), "wallet")  ◁──┘
  guardian ! 1      │ Sends messages to the actor
  guardian ! 10
}
```

You send the actor first the integer 1 and then the integer 10. The type of the actor is
`Int`, as explicitly set in `ActorSystem[Int]`. But you can also verify this is the case
because the code compiles. In particular, the following lines compile:

```
guardian ! 1
guardian ! 10
```

If you send an `Int` to an actor that cannot receive `Int`, you get an error when compiling. The code will not compile, let alone run the application. This type checking—the
fact that the application will not compile if you try to send something other than its
message type—is one of the biggest improvements over previous versions of Akka.
Another advantage is that if you change the protocol of an actor while refactoring,
and the old protocol is still used elsewhere in the code, the compiler jumps to the res-
cue. The importance of this new feature can hardly be overestimated. Now let's look
at how an actor receives messages.

2.2.4   *Implementing the actor: Receiving messages*

As you've seen, the complete type of this actor is `Behavior[Int]`. Let's see how to
implement this behavior. To create a behavior, you use behavior factories. The
`Behaviors.receive` factory is a function with two inputs, `context` and `message`:
the context of the actor (`ActorContext`) and the message it receives (here, an `Int`).
The factory creates a `Behavior` as output. This is the factory's signature:

```
object Wallet {

  def apply(): Behavior[Int] =                          ┐ Signature of
    Behaviors.receive { (context, message) =>   ◁──┘ Behaviors.receive
      ...
    }
}
```

In this factory, you can use the message and the context to, for example, log the
received message. To do so, you can use `context` because one of the functions that
comes with the context is logging. You can add something like the following:

```
object Wallet {

  def apply(): Behavior[Int] =
    Behaviors.receive { (context, message) =>        ┐ Logs each
      context.log.info(s"received '$message' dollar(s)")  ◁──┘ received message
      ...
    }
}
```

Finally, you need to set the behavior for the next message. You can choose the same behavior using another behavior factory that you call with `Behaviors.same`. Together with the rest, you have the final implementation of the actor:

```
object Wallet {

  def apply(): Behavior[Int] =
    Behaviors.receive { (context, message) =>
      context.log.info(s"received '$message' dollar(s)")
      Behaviors.same
    }
}
```

← The next message will be processed by the same behavior.

Note that the `Behaviors` are nested like Russian dolls. Here the outer `def apply(): Behavior[Int]` is composed with a `Behaviors.receive` that contains a `Behaviors.same`. You'll see this pattern over and over.

2.2.5 Terminating the system

You should terminate the `ActorSystem` gracefully so the system can shut down all running modules that hold, for example, HTTP or database connections. To do so, you terminate the guardian (the `ActorSystem`) with `.terminate()`.

Because this example will run inside the sbt shell, you can add a hook to the shell to trigger the termination, such as listening for an Enter keystroke. You can do this with `scala.io.StdIn.readLine()`, which is triggered by pressing Enter:

```
object WalletApp extends App {
  ...
  println("Press ENTER to terminate")
  scala.io.StdIn.readLine()
  guardian.terminate()
}
```

The running code stops at `.readLine()` and waits. When you press Enter, the code continues and terminates the system.

> **NOTE** The sbt shell is the shell in which you can run sbt compiled programs. After you have installed sbt, typing `sbt` in your command line starts an sbt shell. In it, you can (among other things) compile, build, test, and run your Scala, Java, and C/C++ programs.

2.2.6 The application

With all this background, you can now understand the whole picture, as shown in the following listing.

Listing 2.1 Complete wallet code

```
object WalletApp extends App {

  val guardian: ActorSystem[Int] = ActorSystem(Wallet(), "wallet")   ←
  guardian ! 1
  guardian ! 10
```

Int-type messages sent to the actor

Instantiates an actor

```
    println("Press ENTER to terminate")
    scala.io.StdIn.readLine()
    guardian.terminate()
}

object Wallet {

    def apply(): Behavior.Receive[Int] =      ◁──┐ **Behavior that defines how the Wallet**
      Behaviors.receive { (context, message) =>     **actor responds to each message**
        context.log.info(s"received '$message' dollar(s)")
        Behaviors.same
      }
}
```

2.2.7   *The solution in Git*

This wallet is implemented in the akka-topics repository. If you have cloned the akka-topics project, you will find a build.sbt file in its root directory. sbt uses this file to compile, run, and test the project. The project has several subprojects, one per chapter, so you can run them, test them, and play around while reading the book. Each subproject consists of the following:

- *Name*—Defined by a `val`.
- *File location*—The name of the subproject's folder relative to the build.sbt file.
- *Scala version*—Once this is set, Scala will be automatically downloaded from sbt.
- *Library dependencies*—The libraries used in the subproject. They will also be automatically downloaded from sbt.

All examples in this chapter are implemented in the chapter02 subproject defined in the file build.sbt shown in the following snippet:

```
val chapter02 = project         ┌─ **Folder where the**
  .in(file("chapter02"))    ◁──┘   **project is located**
  .settings(
    scalaVersion := "2.13.1",     ◁──┤ **Scala version**
    libraryDependencies ++= Seq(
      "com.typesafe.akka" %% "akka-actor-typed" % "2.6.20",  ◁──┐ **Akka Typed**
      "ch.qos.logback" % "logback-classic" % "1.2.3"              **module**
      )
    )

...
```

This book is all about Akka Typed, and here you have the core module. This is where Akka Typed begins.

2.2.8   *Running the app*

To run the wallet app, you need to open the command line and start an sbt shell. To do this, go to the root directory of akka-topics and run the following:

```
$ sbt
```

You should see something like listing 2.2. Most of the output is irrelevant. The most important line is the first, which prints the sbt and Java versions. The next-most-important line is the last: it says the sbt server has been started, which means you are in the sbt shell.

Listing 2.2 Starting the sbt shell

```
[info] welcome to sbt 1.5.0 (AdoptOpenJDK Java 11.0.9)
[info] loading settings for project global-plugins from build.sbt ...
[info] loading global plugins from /Users/francisco/.sbt/1.0/plugins
[info] loading settings for project code-build from plugins.sbt ...
[info] loading project definition from /Users/francisco/AkkaBook/code/project
[info] loading settings for project code from build.sbt ...
[info] resolving key references (24537 settings) ...
[info] set current project to code (in build file:/Users/francisco/AkkaBook/
    code/)
[info] sbt server started at local:///Users/francisco/.sbt/1.0/server/
    347d55a887437ea58247/sock
[info] started sbt server
sbt:code>
```

sbt and Java versions →

Shows that the server has started

In the build.sbt file is the definition of the chapter02 subproject in GitHub at https://github.com/franciscolopezsancho/akka-topics/tree/main/chapter02. Therefore, the subproject can be referenced when you are in the sbt shell. You can use this reference to select the subproject and run it with the following command:

```
$ project chapter02
$ run
```

Your output should look like the following. It lists all the programs you can run in the current subproject (chapter02) and asks you to pick one.

Listing 2.3 Runnable apps in subproject chapter02

```
[info] compiling 13 Scala sources to
➥/Users/francisco/AkkaBook/code/chapter02/target/scala-2.13/classes ...
Multiple main classes detected. Select one to run:
 [1] com.manning.WalletApp
 [2] com.manning.WalletOnOffApp
 [3] com.manning.WalletStateApp
 [4] com.manning.WalletTimerApp

Enter number:
```

Enter 1 to select `WalletApp` and see the output of the running application.

2.3 *Keeping state with a variable*

Next, you'll learn how to add state to the wallet, which allows you to keep track of the total amount in the wallet. State management is one of the most important features of Akka. In a distributed and concurrent environment, managing state is a hard problem. With Akka, it's easier because you manage state sequentially, message by message, within the actor. Let's see how.

State can be implemented by behaviors: that is, functions. In this example, the wallet stores a value in `total` that can increase or decrease within certain limits. To keep things simple, the maximum value is set to 2 and the minimum value is set to 0 (zero). When the maximum/minimum values are exceeded, the wallet stops increasing/decreasing and the actor stops running, signaling that the wallet is in an unacceptable state.

You already know what a protocol is. But actors with integers as their protocol are used only for example purposes. Any real use-case protocol is implemented with several types belonging to a hierarchy with a sealed *trait* at the top.

> **DEFINITIONS**   *Traits* are like interfaces in Java. For more information, go to https://docs.scala-lang.org/tour/traits.html. A *sealed trait* is a trait that allows the compiler to check whether your pattern matching over its cases is exhaustive. When it is not exhaustive, the compiler raises a warning. For more information, go to the section "Sealed types" at http://mng.bz/Pz8v.

Instead of using `Behavior[Int]`, as in the previous wallet, this wallet has `Behavior[Command]`. Its protocol has two types of messages, `Increase(amount: Int)` and `Decrease(amount: Int)`, both belonging to the `Command` trait:

```
object WalletState {

  sealed trait Command
  final case class Increase(amount: Int) extends Command
  final case class Decrease(amount: Int) extends Command

  ...
}
```

You may wonder why the protocol type is now called `Command`. This is a common name that makes it easy to see which messages should request an action from the actor. Not all messages are meant to issue commands to the actor; you see some examples in the next chapter.

> **NOTE**   You may have noticed that you can use `Increase` with a negative number to decrease the total of the wallet. To avoid this, you can use a function that ensures that you always take the absolute value of the amount when reading it or raises an error.

The wallet has an initial value of 0 and a maximum value of 2. That's why you have `WalletState(0,2)` as a factory method in listing 2.4. The actor is created using input parameters (more on creation after the listing). Once you have created the wallet, you can send messages using its protocol. For simplicity, only the increment of the wallet is shown here.

Listing 2.4   Application that creates a wallet

```
object WalletStateApp extends App {

  val guardian: ActorSystem[WalletState.Command] =
    ActorSystem(WalletState(0, 2), "wallet-state")
  guardian ! WalletState.Increase
  guardian ! WalletState.Increase
  guardian ! WalletState.Increase


}
```

0 is the initial total, and 2 is its max.

Sends messages

To run the app, type the following into the command line as before

```
$ project chapter02
$ run
```

but select 3, `WalletStateApp`. Doing so generates the following output. The wallet logs the total up to the maximum value and then overloads:

```
INFO WalletState$ - increasing to 1
INFO WalletState$ - increasing to 2
INFO WalletState$ - I'm overloaded. Counting '3' while max is '2'. Stopping.
```

To store the total `amount` and the maximum value in the actor, you need to learn something new: how to create an actor while passing initial values to it. In the previous example, you created an actor without passing values during creation.

First, you need to add the two variables—the initial total and the maximum value—to the actor's constructor: that is, to the `def apply` method of the `Wallet` actor. Strictly speaking, they are not variables: in Scala they are called *values*—immutable variables. Adding these "variables" looks like this:

```
def apply(total: Int, max: Int): Behavior[Command]
```

Second, you must maintain the value of the two parameters from one call to the next (from one message to the next) in such a way that after the first increment, the `total` and `max` values are available when the next increment message arrives. To accomplish this, you need to refer to the same behavior in a way other than `Behaviors.same`. To keep both values, you call `apply(current, max)` directly and pass the new updated values (keep in mind that the wallet has more logic than is shown here—this snippet shows only the relevant parts needed to hold the state of the actor: `total` and `max`):

```
object WalletState {

  def apply(total: Int, max: Int): Behavior[Command] =
    Behavior.receive { (context, message) =>
      ...
      val current = total + 1
      ...
      apply(current, max)
    }

}
```

Input function

Increases the total

Output function designating the next behavior while keeping the new total and max

Because behaviors are functions, you can use their inputs and outputs to transfer state from one function to the next (from one behavior to the next). Here, by setting `apply(current, max)` at the end of `def apply(total: Int, max: Int)`, you handle the next message with the same apply function but with newly updated input parameters. The first time, `total` and `max` were set to 0 and 2 using `.apply(0,2)`—that is, `WalletState(0,2)`—thanks to Scala syntactic sugar. But after processing an `Increase` message, the next behavior will be `.apply(1,2)`. This way, the behavior has new input values, and the state is transferred from one message to the next.

Finally, when the max is reached, the actor stops by setting the next behavior as `Behaviors.stopped`.

> **NOTE** Once the actor stops, it cannot process any more messages. All messages remaining in its queue or new messages sent to its address are forwarded by the system to another actor named `deadLetters` (more about this in chapter 3). Bear in mind that `apply()` is not a recursive function but a factory that receives a function as input and outputs a `Behavior` (a function). The factory `Behaviors.receive` that defines the `apply` method receives a function of type `(context, message) => Behavior` and therefore outputs a `Behavior`. This is functional style, and there is no recursion.

Let's look at the wallet, its logging, and how it manages state when it receives `Increase`.

Listing 2.5 **`Wallet` actor with state**

```scala
import akka.actor.typed.Behavior
import akka.actor.typed.scaladsl.Behaviors

object WalletState {

  sealed trait Command
  final case class Increase(amount: Int) extends Command
  final case class Decrease(amount: Int) extends Command
                                                              Input, total, and max
                                                              representing the state
  def apply(total: Int, max: Int): Behavior[Command] =   ◁──┘
    Behaviors.receive { (context, message) =>
      message match {
        case Increase(amount) =>
          val current = total + amount
          if (current <= max) {
            context.log.info(s"increasing to $current")    Output as a behavior,
            apply(current, max)                        ◁──  not as a call to a method
          } else {
            context.log.info(
              s"I'm overloaded. Counting '$current' while
              ➥max is '$max'. Stopping")
            Behaviors.stopped
          }
          case Decrease(amount) =>           ◁──  The same as Increase, but
                                                  with the obvious differences
            ...
```

Stops the actor. Any message left in the mailbox will not reach the actor. (annotation pointing to `Behaviors.stopped`)

```
            }
        }
    }
```

Remember, when the wallet increases and the current value is less than the maximum value, the wallet is further increased by setting `WalletState.apply(current, max)` as the next behavior. From the first to the second message, the behaviors are first `.apply(0,2)` and then `.apply(0 + 1, 2)`.

Conversely, `Decrease` stops when the wallet value becomes negative. The code is practically the same, so we won't repeat it here. If you are curious, you can look at the code in the repo.

Note how the protocol is written within the actor. The messages of a protocol are always specific to an actor, and in this sense, they are not meant to be reused by other actors. They are the API of the actor and belong to it.

In this section, you have learned how to manage state as a value with an actor. You need to add the state in its constructor and pass it to the next behavior. But there is also another way to store state in an actor: with behaviors.

2.4   *Keeping state with behaviors*

Keeping state with different behaviors in an actor has a different purpose than storing state with variables. You use behaviors to represent that the actor reacts differently to the same messages. If you only want to change variables within the actor, don't use this method; use what you learned in the previous section.

Depending on the actor's state, the same message can do very different things. For example, an actor can act as a proxy and have two states: open and closed. When it is open, it forwards messages to another destination, as any proxy would. However, when it is closed, it does not forward messages: instead, it notifies a third party.

Let's implement another wallet. Similar to the previous variant, for the sake of simplicity, you can increase the amount but not decrease it. What is new is that this wallet has two states represented by two behaviors: activated and deactivated. If the wallet is activated, it responds as in the previous example and increases the total amount when it receives an `Increase`. On the other hand, if the wallet is deactivated, the total amount cannot be changed. If the actor receives an `Increase` in this state, it discards the `Increase` and reports that no change was made.

> **NOTE**   This feature makes this actor a finite state machine (FSM) because it reacts differently to the same input. Without going into too much detail, an FSM is a model that has a finite number of states. Depending on the state—also called a behavior—the same input can produce different results. Because actors are defined by behaviors, they are perfect for implementing this model.

For simplicity, the wallet now has neither a maximum value nor the ability to decrease, and it has a default value of zero as the initial `total`. The wallet has the following protocol available:

```
object WalletOnOff {

  sealed trait Command
  final case object Increase(amount: Int) extends Command
  final case object Activate extends Command
  final case object Deactivate extends Command

  ...
}
```

No input parameters are required to instantiate the wallet because it has no maximum value and zero is the default initial amount. You can instantiate it and send `Increase` messages in both states, deactivated and activated. Note that the default state is activated. The following snippet shows how to increase, deactivate, and activate the wallet:

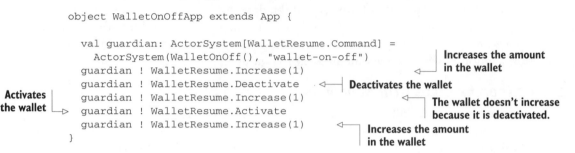

```
object WalletOnOffApp extends App {

  val guardian: ActorSystem[WalletResume.Command] =
    ActorSystem(WalletOnOff(), "wallet-on-off")
  guardian ! WalletResume.Increase(1)
  guardian ! WalletResume.Deactivate
  guardian ! WalletResume.Increase(1)
  guardian ! WalletResume.Activate
  guardian ! WalletResume.Increase(1)
}
```

Activates the wallet

Increases the amount in the wallet

Deactivates the wallet

The wallet doesn't increase because it is deactivated.

Increases the amount in the wallet

To run this app, select option 2 (`WalletOnOffApp`) in the sbt shell under the same subproject. The output is as follows:

```
INFO  [WalletOnOff$] - increasing to 1
INFO  [WalletOnOff$] - wallet is deactivated. Can't increase
INFO  [WalletOnOff$] - activating
INFO  [WalletOnOff$] - increasing to 2
```

You can provide this functionality with what you have already seen in this chapter. Creating more methods like `.apply` gives you multiple behaviors so you can refer from one to another.

To implement that the wallet has a default value of zero and its state is activated by default, you can do the following:

```
object WalletOnOff {

  ...

  def apply(): Behavior[Command] = activated(0)
    activated(0)

  ...
}
```

The `activated` behavior increments the total when an `Increment` message is processed and switches to the `deactivated` behavior when a `Deactivate` is processed.

The wallet defines the activated and deactivated behaviors. Let's start with activated.

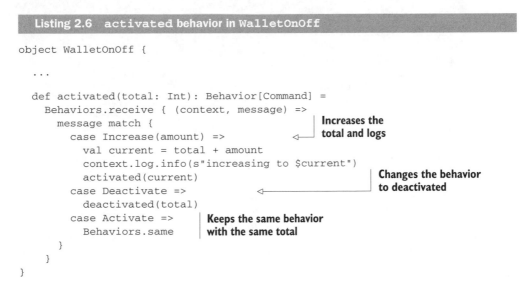

```
object WalletOnOff {

  ...

  def activated(total: Int): Behavior[Command] =
    Behaviors.receive { (context, message) =>
      message match {                                    Increases the
        case Increase(amount) =>                         total and logs
          val current = total + amount
          context.log.info(s"increasing to $current")
          activated(current)                             Changes the behavior
        case Deactivate =>                               to deactivated
          deactivated(total)
        case Activate =>            Keeps the same behavior
          Behaviors.same           with the same total
      }
    }
}
```

You may wonder why on Activate, the wallet uses Behavior.same and not activated(total). You can use Behavior.same because there is no incrementing, so the wallet is using the same behavior again. You don't need to pass a new total. (You could pass the same total, but it's easier to read Behavior.same.)

The deactivated behavior works as follows. It logs that it cannot increase when it receives an Increase message and returns to activated when it receives an Activate. When the wallet is deactivated, the total stays the same.

```
object WalletOnOff {

  ...

  def deactivated(total: Int): Behavior[Command] = {
    Behaviors.receive { (context, message) =>
      message match {                              Logs that it
        case Increase =>                           can't increase
          context.log.info(s"wallet is deactivated. Can't increase")
          Behaviors.same
        case Deactivate =>          Keeps the same behavior
          Behaviors.same            with the same total
        case Activate =>                        Changes to the activated
          context.log.info(s"activating")       behavior with the same total
          activated(total)
      }
    }
  }
}
```

The code for the entire actor now looks like the following listing.

Listing 2.8 `WalletOnOff` actor

```
object WalletOnOff {

  sealed trait Command
  final case class Increase(amount: Int) extends Command
  final case object Deactivate extends Command
  final case object Activate extends Command

  def apply(): Behavior[Command] = activated(0)        ⟵┐ Default
                                                          behavior

  def activated(total: Int): Behavior[Command] =       ⟵┐ Activated
    Behaviors.receive { (context, message) =>             behavior
      message match {
        case Increase(amount) =>
          val current = total + amount
          context.log.info(s"increasing to $current")
          resume(current)
        case Deactivate =>
          deactivated(total)
        case Activate =>
          Behaviors.same
      }
    }

  def deactivated(total: Int): Behavior[Command] = {   ⟵┐ Deactivated
    Behaviors.receive { (context, message) =>             behavior
      message match {
        case Increase =>
          context.log.info(s"wallet is deactivated. Can't increase")
          Behaviors.same
        case Deactivate =>
          Behaviors.same
        case Activate =>
          context.log.info(s"activating")
          activated(total)
      }
    }
  }
}
```

In this section, you have seen how to create an FSM in Akka Typed. The Akka primitives already have the semantics of an FSM; you could say that the axioms of the actor model contain these semantics. You saw this axiom in chapter 1: "An actor must designate the behavior to be used for the next message it receives." Because this axiom is implemented directly in Akka, you can create an FSM with nothing but its basic building blocks—its behaviors.

In a concurrent environment, thinking in terms of time is error-prone. Akka simplifies this task. Instead of making an actor wait (as you might know from threads), you can schedule messages to it.

2.5   *Scheduling a message*

Let's implement another wallet that is very similar to the previous one. Everything is the same except that with this wallet, you can send a deactivation message that deactivates the wallet for several seconds.

With this deactivation, a user of the wallet doesn't have to remember to send an activation message to reactivate the wallet. When deactivated, the wallet sends an activation message to itself after a few seconds. How long, exactly, is specified in the previous deactivation message, which now contains the deactivation duration. Bear in mind that there is no waiting on the actor's side—the actor keeps processing messages as usual. This scheduling doesn't include anything like blocking.

Here's how this is represented in the protocol:

```
object WalletTimer {

  sealed trait Command
  final case class Increase(amount: Int) extends Command
  final case class Deactivate(seconds: Int) extends Command
  private final case object Activate extends Command

  ...

}
```

Apart from the deactivation, which now has the duration as a parameter, `Activate` is marked as `private`, so it is impossible to activate the wallet from outside the actor. The wallet can only be reactivated by the actor. This new variant is called `Wallet-Timer`.

> **NOTE** Making the protocol private or public is a common pattern used in Akka. This allows you to provide both a public API, which is a set of messages that other actors can use, and a private API, which deals with the actor's internal functionality.

With this new wallet, you can create the application as follows:

```
object WalletTimerApp extends App {

  val guardian: ActorSystem[WalletTimer.Command] =
    ActorSystem(WalletTimer(), "wallet-timer")
  guardian ! WalletTimer.Increase(1)
  guardian ! WalletTimer.Deactivate(3)

}
```

To run this app, select option 4 (`WalletTimerApp`) in the sbt shell under the same subproject. The output is as follows:

```
10:10:49,896 INFO  [WalletTimer$] - increasing to 1    Resumes after
10:10:52,914 INFO  [WalletTimer$] - activating    ◁⎯⎤ 3 seconds
```

To implement scheduling an `Activate`, you need to use the factory `Behaviors` `.withTimers` to create a scheduler builder. With this builder, you can use

`.startSingleTimer` to create a timer that schedules a message once. These two parts are one `Behavior` that can be combined with the other `Behavior`s—activated and deactivated—just like any other.

The signature for creating a timer expects the message to be sent and the delay, as shown in the following code. `T` is the type of the actor's protocol, and `FiniteDuration` is the type of delay:

```
def startSingleTimer(msg: T, delay: FiniteDuration): Unit
```

An integer can be automatically converted to a `FiniteDuration`—for example, in seconds—by importing `scala.concurrent.duration._` and calling `.second` in the integer.

Listing 2.9   activated behavior from `WalletTimer`

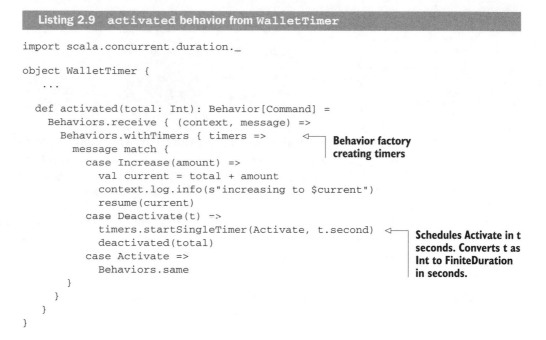

```
import scala.concurrent.duration._

object WalletTimer {
  ...

  def activated(total: Int): Behavior[Command] =
    Behaviors.receive { (context, message) =>
      Behaviors.withTimers { timers =>          ← Behavior factory
        message match {                           creating timers
          case Increase(amount) =>
            val current = total + amount
            context.log.info(s"increasing to $current")
            resume(current)
          case Deactivate(t) =>
            timers.startSingleTimer(Activate, t.second)   ← Schedules Activate in t
            deactivated(total)                              seconds. Converts t as
          case Activate =>                                  Int to FiniteDuration
            Behaviors.same                                  in seconds.
        }
      }
    }
}
```

The rest of the wallet can stay the same. With the message scheduling, you have added the new functionality. Pretty simple, isn't it?

Summary

- The `ActorSystem` is the first actor. At the same time, it represents the entire system.
- You should terminate the `ActorSystem` so the system can gracefully shut down all running modules that hold, for example, HTTP or DB connections.
- The operator `tell`—in its short form, the bang (`!`) operator—allows you to send messages to an actor.
- For each message that an actor processes, you need to define the behavior for the next message. Thanks to this abstraction, you only have to worry about

processing a single message at a time, eliminating a whole dimension of concurrency problems.

- Behaviors are nested to form the complete behavior of an actor just as functions are chained, where the output of one function is the input of the next.
- Multiple messages usually form the protocol of the actor. They are the actor's API and the only way another actor can communicate with it.
- An actor can store its state two ways: as a value in its constructor by adding a variable that can be updated when messages are received, or as a behavior by creating multiple behaviors that respond differently to the same messages. This arrangement is also called a finite state machine.
- `Behaviors.withTimers` allows you to schedule messages by specifying when and how often the message should be sent.

One actor is no actor

This chapter covers

- Actors as a hierarchy
- Creating more actors
- Sending messages back and forth and adapting responses
- Sending messages and waiting for a reply

A colony of ants is more than just an aggregate of insects that are living together. One ant is no ant. Two ants, and you begin to get something entirely new. Put a million together with the workers divided into different castes, each doing a different function—cutting the leaves, looking after the queen, taking care of the young, digging the nest out, and so on—and you've got an organism weighing about 11 kilograms [24 pounds], about the size of a dog, and dominating an area the size of a house.

—David Suzuki: *The Sacred Balance: Rediscovering Our Place in Nature*
(Greystone Books, 1997)

Actors are very much the same as ants—they come in organized groups. One actor is no actor; they come in systems. Let's see how.

One of the most compelling features of the actor model is that each actor makes local decisions. At the same time, actors belong to a hierarchy: a top-down relationship between parents and children. Each time an actor creates another actor, it becomes that actor's parent. These two properties—locality and hierarchy—allow the actor model to delegate easily. Traditional Akka applications are based on this delegation.

So far, you have learned how to create actors of the type `ActorSystem`, but this type of actor is unique. It is a singleton. Each `ActorSystem` has only one instance of this type, and this actor has a double task. It is the root of the hierarchy of all actors and the mechanism that controls the entire system. This chapter is about this hierarchy, why it is important, and how to implement it.

To learn this, you will see an application that parses text. It is modeled with a manager that delegates the parsing of each text to an actor: a parser. The manager specializes in creating parsers and delegating tasks to them, while the parsers do only one thing and do it well: process text. Let's put this into practice by creating a hierarchy of actors that together serve this one purpose.

NOTE The source code for this chapter is available at www.manning.com/ books/akka-in-action-second-edition or https://github.com/franciscolopcz sancho/akka-topics/tree/main/chapter03. You can find the contents of any snippet or listing in the .scala file with the same name as the class, object, or trait. For example, you can find the snippet with `object ErrorKernelApp` in the ErrorKernelApp.scala file.

3.1   Simple parser example

The actors in this application are a guardian, which creates a manager, which in turn creates several workers. The guardian passes the list of texts to be parsed to the manager, which passes them to the workers to parse. The hierarchical structure is shown in figure 3.1.

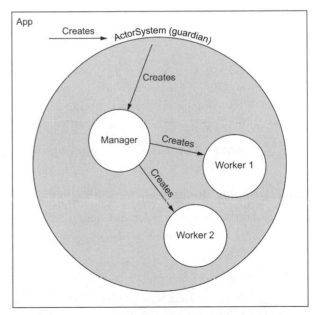

Figure 3.1   Top-down relationship of creation among actors, from the top `ActorSystem` to the bottom workers

The application passes the work—the list of strings representing texts—to the guardian, which sends the list down the chain. When the workers are finished parsing, they notify the manager. To understand this notification, the manager needs an adapter (more about the adapter in section 3.1.3). Figure 3.2 shows how the work is delegated and performed.

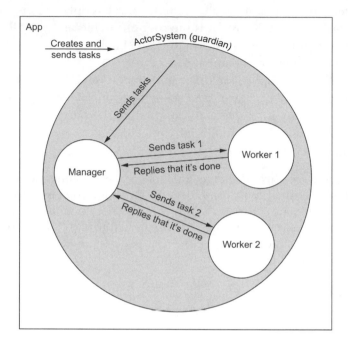

Figure 3.2   Direction of messages between the manager and the workers

Typically, you produce messages not at the app level, as in this example, but rather through endpoints like HTTP, gRPC, or something similar. How you create these entry points is covered in chapter 11. For now, we don't get into how to connect to an Akka app from the outside. Instead, we focus on the app itself.

> **NOTE** The examples for this section can be found in the `errorkernel` package.

3.1.1 Coding the app

To see how to implement figure 3.2, let's start at the top of the hierarchy (the guardian) with the input sent from the app to the guardian. The guardian's protocol is as follows:

```
object Guardian {

  sealed trait Command
  final case class Start(texts: List[String]) extends Command

  ...
}
```

`Start` contains the texts to parse, and it's used like this:

```
object ErrorKernelApp extends App {

  val guardian: ActorSystem[Guardian.Command] =
    ActorSystem(Guardian(), "error-kernel")
  Guardian ! Guardian.Start(List("-one-", "--two--"))
}
```

Texts to parse ← (annotation pointing to the `Guardian.Start` line)

When the guardian receives `Start`, it passes the list of texts to the manager, which splits the list and assigns one piece per worker. The application produces the following output:

```
INFO  [Guardian$] - setting up. Creating manager
INFO  [Manager$] - sending text '-one-' to worker
INFO  [Manager$] - sending text '--two--' to worker
INFO  [Worker$] - 'Actor[akka://error-kernel/user/manager-alpha/
➥worker-one-#1892512941]' DONE!. Parsed result: one
INFO  [Worker$] - 'Actor[akka://error-kernel/user/manager-alpha/
➥worker--two--#1275513111]' DONE!. Parsed result: two
INFO  [Manager$] - text '-one-' has been finished
INFO  [Manager$] - text '--two--' has been finished
```

Let's focus on the first three lines of this output: how the guardian creates the manager and the manager delegates tasks during setup. To do this, you need two new tools from the Akka toolkit:

- `Spawn`—To create actors from another actor, you use the context by using `context.spawn([someActorsApplyMethod], [someName])`. The signature is the same as that for the `ActorSystem` and creates an `ActorRef` to which you can send messages. In the next example, the spawning is done inside a `Behaviors.setup`.
- `Behaviors.setup`—This factory creates a behavior that is executed only once: when the actor is instantiated. It creates a behavior from a function with only one input parameter: the `context: ActorContext` used to spawn the manager.

Once the guardian is set up, it uses the manager to delegate the parsing of the texts in the `Start` message.

3.1.2 Coding the guardian and spawning

The following listing shows how the guardian creates the manager and delegates tasks to it.

Listing 3.1 Guardian

```
import akka.actor.typed.scaladsl.Behaviors
import akka.actor.typed.{ ActorRef, ActorSystem, Behavior }

object Guardian {

  sealed trait Command
  final case class Start(texts: List[String]) extends Command
```

Form input ← (annotation pointing to the `Start` case class line)

```
def apply(): Behavior[Command] =
  Behaviors.setup { context =>
    context.log.info("Setting up. Creating manager")
    val manager: ActorRef[Manager.Command] =
      context.spawn(Manager(), "manager-alpha")
    Behaviors.receiveMessage {
      case Start(texts) =>
        manager ! Manager.Delegate(texts)
        Behaviors.same
    }
  }
}
```

**Creates an actor
inside an actor**

**Texts
input**

**Delegates texts
to the manager**

Once the guardian and manager are created, the guardian can start processing messages. They are processed with the method `Behaviors.receiveMessage`, where the guardian delegates to the manager the test contained in `Start`. It wraps them in a `Delegate` message that the manager can understand and sends them with `tell` (that is, `!`). Next, let's look at the manager.

3.1.3   *Sending messages back and forth: Adapting responses*

The manager is responsible for creating one worker per text to be parsed and sending the worker the text. Sending a message from the manager to the worker works the same as before, but now the worker must reply to the manager. This is where a new concept comes into play: the *adapter*.

An adapter is needed for the worker's response because the response type belongs to the worker, not the manager. The worker uses its own protocol to respond, and that is a problem. Remember that each actor has its own protocol. That is the only protocol it understands, so in principle, the manager cannot understand the worker's answer.

For the manager to understand the worker's answer, you need two things: an adapter function and an adapter message. The adapter function is used to send a message to the worker, and the adapter message is used to receive a message from the worker.

The rest of the process—creating a worker—is the same as with the guardian. Spawning is all you need.

The manager consists of four parts:

- A message adapter in the protocol
- An adapter function
- Delegating (creating a worker per text and sending the text for parsing)
- Receiving the worker's response and logging its task completion

This is shown in the figure 3.3.

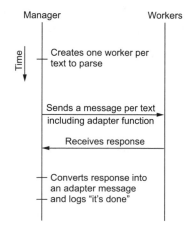

**Figure 3.3   Manager functionality
in chronological order**

3.1.4 The protocol with the adapter's message

The manager's protocol has `Delegate` to get the texts to be parsed and `Worker-DoneAdapter` (which is the adapter's message) to transform the worker's response:

```
object Manager {

    sealed trait Command
    final case class Delegate(forms: List[String]) extends Command
    private final case class WorkerDoneAdapter(response: Worker.Response)
        extends Command

    ...
}
```

It is worth noting that the modifier is `private`. This ensures that no actor other than the manager uses the message. Otherwise, the manager could receive this message from any actor confirming that a text has been parsed. Only the manager can convert a `Worker.Response` message into a `WorkerDoneAdapter` message.

3.1.5 The adapter's function

The adapter's function is an actor (an `ActorRef`) that lives between two worlds. It is an `ActorRef[Worker.Response]`, so it is a `Worker.Response` sharing the protocol of the worker (shown in the next section). It understands the worker responses. On the other hand, the adapter has a reference to the manager. And since the adapter's function has the worker protocol and the manager's reference, it can act as their intermediary:

```
object Manager {
    ...

    val adapter: ActorRef[Worker.Response] =
        context.messageAdapter(rsp => WorkerDoneAdapter(rsp))
}
```

.messageAdapter belongs to the context API (ActorContext).

The manager sends a request to the worker, and the worker responds to the adapter, which in turn wraps the worker's message into a `WorkerDone-Adapter` and sends it to the manager, as shown in figure 3.4.

You create the adapter function in `Behaviors.setup`, so it is created only once. This is shown in the following section.

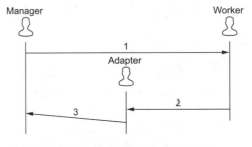
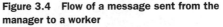

Figure 3.4 Flow of a message sent from the manager to a worker

3.1.6 Delegating

Delegating involves using the adapter function and the worker protocol to send texts from the manager to the workers. The worker protocol has two messages:

- Parse—Command containing the string to be parsed and a reference to the actor to reply to
- Done(text: String)—Response containing the parsed string so the manager can track what has been done

The worker protocol is as follows:

```
object Worker {

  sealed trait Command
  final case class Parse(replyTo: ActorRef[Worker.Response], text: String)
      extends Command                      ◁─┐  Command that the
                                              │  actor can receive
  sealed trait Response
  final case class Done(text: String) extends Response    ◁─┐  Response that the
                                                             │  actor can send
  ...
}
```

The adapter function, once created, is used directly. It is passed in the `replyTo` of the `Parse` message along with the data to be parsed:

```
object Manager {
  ...
  worker ! Worker.Parse(adapter, text)
  ...
}
```

Finally, the worker's response is translated by the intermediate adapter function into the adapter message. The manager receives the `Worker.Done` wrapped in the adapter message and looks inside it to print the parsed text to the console. The manager code in the following listing shows how its four parts come together (message adapter, adapter function, delegating, and receiving).

Listing 3.2   Manager behavior

```
object Manager {

  sealed trait Command
  final case class Delegate(texts: List[String]) extends Command      ┐ Adapter
  private case class WorkerDoneAdapter(response: Worker.Response)      │ message
      extends Command                                                 ┘

  def apply(): Behavior[Command] =
    Behaviors.setup { context =>
      val adapter: ActorRef[Worker.Response] =                        ┐ Adapter
        context.messageAdapter(response => WorkerDoneAdapter(response)) │ function

      Behaviors.receiveMessage { message =>
        message match {
          case Delegate(texts) =>
            forms.map { text =>
```

```
                          val worker: ActorRef[Worker.Command] =
  Spawns one    ┌──▷        context.spawn(Worker(), s"worker-$text")
  worker per text │         context.log.info(s"sending task '$text to $worker")
                │           worker ! Worker.Parse(adapter, form)
                  }
                  Behaviors.same                              │ Deals with the
                case WorkerDoneAdapter(Worker.Done(text)) =>  ◁─┘ worker's reply
                  context.log.info(s"form '$form' has been finished")
                  Behaviors.same
              }
            }
          }
      }
```

This is everything: the manager's protocol, the adapter message, and the delegate. The adapter function is used as an intermediary between the manager and the worker, and finally, the adapter message is used in the worker's response. Next, let's discuss the worker's protocol.

3.1.7 A protocol with commands and responses as traits

The worker's protocol is shown in the following snippet. You may be surprised to see two traits. Until now, you have only seen `Command`, but now you have `Response`. The type of actor is defined by the `Command` that defines the messages the actor exposes:

```
object Worker {

  sealed trait Command
  final case class Parse(replyTo: ActorRef[Worker.Response],     To be sent
  ➥text: String)                                                to the actor
      extends Command

  sealed trait Response                                          To be sent
  final case class Done(text: String) extends Response          by the actor
  ...
}
```

Messages of type `Response` cannot be sent to the actor. They do not belong to its type. They must be sent by the actor that defines them to another actor, which means this other actor is responsible for translating and adapting the message. To finish, let's look at the worker.

3.1.8 Coding the worker

The logic of the worker is as follows:

1 The worker receives the `Parse` message.
2 It parses the text by removing any hyphens. (This example uses a simple function so we don't get distracted by the business logic.)
3 It replies `Done` to the manager.
4 It stops, processes no further messages, and is removed from memory.

You've seen all this before, so here is the code without further explanation.

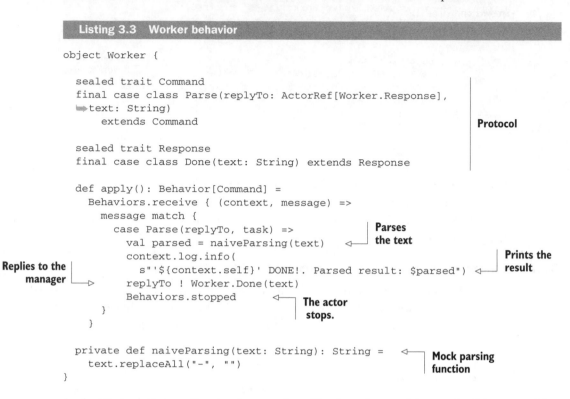

Listing 3.3   Worker behavior

```scala
object Worker {

  sealed trait Command
  final case class Parse(replyTo: ActorRef[Worker.Response],
  text: String)
      extends Command

  sealed trait Response
  final case class Done(text: String) extends Response

  def apply(): Behavior[Command] =
    Behaviors.receive { (context, message) =>
      message match {
        case Parse(replyTo, task) =>
          val parsed = naiveParsing(text)
          context.log.info(
            s"'${context.self}' DONE!. Parsed result: $parsed")
          replyTo ! Worker.Done(text)
          Behaviors.stopped
      }
    }

  private def naiveParsing(text: String): String =
    text.replaceAll("-", "")
}
```

Protocol

Parses the text

Prints the result

Replies to the manager

The actor stops.

Mock parsing function

And with that, the application is complete. You have learned how to build an app hierarchically, from the app to the worker, via the guardian and the manager. You also learned how to spawn actors and create adapters.

The next section deals with a different type of request/response. It is called `ask`, and it is a request that expects a response.

3.2   Asking and expecting a reply

In Akka, to *ask* means to send a message that includes a callback within a certain time. When an actor asks, two things can happen: it either receives a response indicating that the message has been processed or receives no response. If it doesn't get a response after waiting a certain amount of time, the actor has to decide what to do. This is the same as many other types of communication, such as sending an email. If you need an answer and don't get it, how long are you willing to wait before you take action?

In Akka, the answer is formulated in terms of time and two possible outcomes. When you ask for something, you have to specify how long you are willing to wait; to do so, you use the `Timeout` class. Because you may or may not receive a response, you check the two options: `Success` and `Failure`. These two options form the class `Try[T]`, where `T` is the type of the actor being asked, which you receive on a successful answer. Otherwise, T does not apply—if the actor does not answer, there is a failure, which does not have type T.

Following the same structure as in the previous example, you have an app, a guardian, a manager, and workers, but there are also a few differences. The manager no longer tells the worker what to do but asks them, imposing a time limit. The worker spends about 3 seconds parsing the text to simulate complex parsing.

Figure 3.5 shows how the manager asks a worker to parse and waits for the response. If the response comes quickly enough, the manager receives the response in a Success; otherwise, it receives an exception in a Failure.

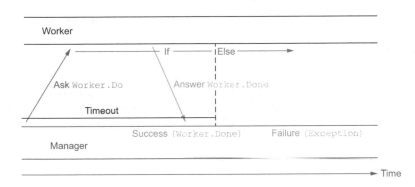

Figure 3.5   Possible outcomes for the manager when it asks the worker to parse a text

The entry point of the application and the guardian are the same as in the previous example and therefore are not covered in this section. As always, let's look at the running application before dealing with the code.

NOTE   The examples in this section can be found in the simplequestion package if no package is explicit in the snippet.

3.2.1   A simple question

If you run the SimpleQuestion app from the solutions repository, you can see two types of results. The order of parsing—and therefore the output—are not always the same, and neither are the results, but there are only two kinds of results. The first is the *happy path*, where everything is going well: each worker completes its task on time, and the manager registers that completion. This output shows a Success in response to each request to parse:

```
[Worker$]  - worker-text-c: done
[Manager$] - text-c parsed by worker-text-c
[Worker $] - worker-text-a: done
[Manager$] - text-a parsed by worker-text-a
[Worker $] - worker-file-b: done
[Manager$] - text-b parsed by worker-text-b
```

The second kind of result is the *unhappy path*, when parsing a text takes longer than is acceptable. In the following output, `text-c` takes more than 3 seconds, while the other two texts are processed in a timely manner:

```
[Worker $] - worker-text-a: DONE!
[Manager$] - text-a read by worker-text-a
[Worker $] - worker-text-b: DONE!
[Manager$] - text-b read by worker-text-b
[Manager$] - parsing text-c' has failed with [Ask timed out on
➡[Actor[akka://example-ask-without-content/user/manager-1/
➡worker-text-c#-1664156553]] after [3000 ms]. Message of type
➡[ask.simple.Worker$Parse]. A typical reason for
➡`AskTimeoutException` is that the recipient actor
➡didn't send a reply.
[Worker $] - worker-text-c: DONE!
[DeadLetterActorRef] - Message [ask.simple.Worker$Done$]
➡to Actor[akka://example-ask-without-content/deadLetters]
➡was not delivered. [1] dead letters encountered. If this is
➡not an expected behavior then
➡Actor[akka://example-ask-without-content/deadLetters] may have
➡terminated unexpectedly. This logging can be turned off or
➡adjusted with configuration settings 'akka.log-dead-letters'
➡and 'akka.log-dead-letters-during-shutdown'.
```

Texts processed on time

Late answer

If you look at the error in parsing `text-c`, you will see that three related things happened:

- The manager no longer waited for the response. It registered a failure and reported that the task was not completed:

```
[Manager$] - parsing 'text-c' has failed with [Ask timed out ...
```

- On the worker side, the worker completed the task and logged the fact that it completed the parsing. That's why you see the following message even though the parsing took longer than the manager was willing to wait:

```
[Worker$] - worker-text-c: DONE!
```

- The third point concerns the `deadLetters` actor mentioned in chapter 2. When the worker finished its task, it tried to send a response, but this message never reached the manager. This happened because asking goes through an intermediate actor, like the adapter from the previous example.

  An ephemeral actor is created that acts as a proxy between the manager and the worker responsible for the timeout. When the time is up, the proxy actor sends an error message to the manager and stops. Because the manager has stopped, the message from the worker to the proxy can no longer reach it. Then the `ActorSystem` takes over, and the message sent to this stopped actor is forwarded to the `deadLetters` actor.

Figure 3.6 represents both cases: success and failure.

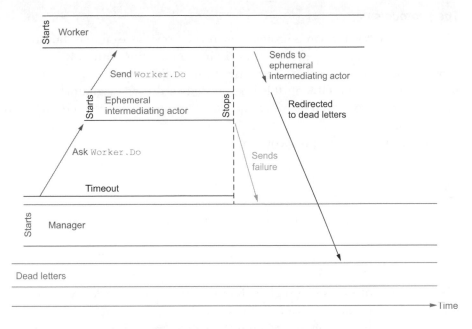

Figure 3.6   Ephemeral intermediate actor lifespan and duties after a timeout

If a message can reach its destination, you have some information about it. But this should be taken with a grain of salt; sending messages to the deadLetters actor guarantees only best effort—the delivery guarantee is at-most-once. This means each message is sent only once. Whether it reaches its destination does not matter to the sender, which does not wait for an acknowledgment.

If for some reason something goes wrong in the worker and it throws an exception, the manager receives a timeout. In such a scenario, no response is sent from the worker due to the exception; therefore, nothing ends up in dead letters.

3.2.2   *Coding the manager*

The manager does the following:

1 It creates a worker for each received text and asks it to Parse.
2 The ask specifies what to do with the response:
   – On a Success, the manager sends a Report message to itself containing the worker's name.
   – On a Failure, the manager wraps the exception message in a report, which it again sends to itself.
3 When the manager receives a report, whether success or failure, the content is printed.

3.2.3 *The protocols*

The manager has the same protocol as in the previous example, but instead of the adapter, it now has `Report`, which works in combination with `ask`. `Report` is necessary to deal with the worker's response. In the callback of `ask`, the manager has to send a message to itself, and this is expressed in the `ask` signature. Before we deal with that, let's look at the manager and worker protocols to see both sides of the communication.

Here is the manager protocol:

```
object Manager {

  sealed trait Command
  final case class Delegate(texts: List[String]) extends Command
  private case class Report(description: String) extends Command

  ...
}
```

The worker protocol is also slightly different from the previous example. The `Parse` message does not need to contain the text to be printed; now the text is passed to the worker as an input parameter when it is created. `Done` also does not contain a reference to the text to be parsed; the `Report` used in the `ask` contains that reference. Here is the worker protocol:

```
object Worker {

  sealed trait Command
  case class Parse(replyTo: ActorRef[Worker.Response]) extends Command   ⟵── Command that the
                                                                              actor can receive

  sealed trait Response
  case object Done extends Response   ⟵── Response that the
                                          actor can send

  ...
}
```

After defining both sides of the communication, let's see how `ask` works.

3.2.4 *Asking*

In the following snippet, the worker is created right before the `ask`. Then the `ask` uses the worker reference and `Worker.Parse` to send the request. Finally, the callback processes the responses for success and failure. It creates one report or another, depending on whether the response is a success or a failure:

```
object Manager {
    ...
```

Sends the message to the worker →
```
    val worker: ActorRef[Worker.Command] =
        context.spawn(Worker(file), s"worker-$text")        ← Creates a worker
    context.ask(worker, Worker.Parse) {
```

```
case Success(Worker.Done) =>
  Report(s"$text parsed by ${worker.path.name}")
case Failure(ex) =>
  Report(s"parsing '$text has failed with [${ex.getMessage()}")
```

Defines the callback over
the two possible outcomes

```
  ...
}
```

This snippet requires a timeout that specifies how long the manager will wait for the response. This is set with `timeout`:

```
implicit val timeout: Timeout = Timeout(3, SECONDS)
```

This implicit value is passed to the `ask` by Scala because `ask` has an implicit argument of this type, as you can see in this simplified version of its signature:

```
package akka.actor.typed.scaladsl

trait ActorContext ... {

  ...

  def ask(target: ... createRequest: ...)(implicit responseTimeout:
  ➥Timeout): Unit

  ...
}
```

> ### Scala implicits
>
> Scala implicits are a difficult subject. For now, here is a TL;DR version that is sufficient for you to understand this example.
>
> To fill implicit arguments like `responseTimeout`, Scala looks for compatible types marked as `implicit val`. The compiler looks for these values in the same class—among other places—and if it finds them, it uses them as input for the implicit arguments. And that's it; implicit arguments can be automatically filled with implicit values that appear in the same class.
>
> Therefore, it is enough to add the timeout in this class as an implicit value for the `ask` to be populated. The compiler determines that the timeout is the right argument for the `ask` method and uses it.

To repeat, `Worker.Parse` can be used in the manager as `context.ask(worker, Worker.Parse)`. Even if the signature is `Worker.Parse(replyTo: Actor-Ref[Worker.Response])`, you don't need to add the parameter `replyTo` when instantiating a `Worker.Parse`. This parameter is created and added for you by the `ActorSystem` and acts as the intermediate actor, just like the adapter in the previous section. When you put all these pieces together, you get the following manager.

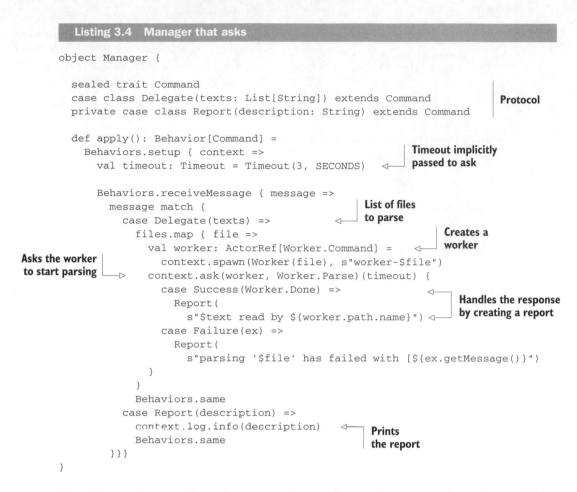

Listing 3.4 Manager that asks

```
object Manager {

  sealed trait Command
  case class Delegate(texts: List[String]) extends Command          Protocol
  private case class Report(description: String) extends Command

  def apply(): Behavior[Command] =
    Behaviors.setup { context =>                          Timeout implicitly
      val timeout: Timeout = Timeout(3, SECONDS)          passed to ask

      Behaviors.receiveMessage { message =>
        message match {                          List of files
          case Delegate(texts) =>                to parse
            files.map { file =>
              val worker: ActorRef[Worker.Command] =          Creates a
                context.spawn(Worker(file), s"worker-$file")    worker
              context.ask(worker, Worker.Parse)(timeout) {
                case Success(Worker.Done) =>
                  Report(                                 Handles the response
                    s"$text read by ${worker.path.name}")   by creating a report
                case Failure(ex) =>
                  Report(
                    s"parsing '$file' has failed with [${ex.getMessage()}")
              }
            }
            Behaviors.same
          case Report(description) =>
            context.log.info(description)          Prints
            Behaviors.same                         the report
        }}}
    }
}
```

Now that you've seen how the `ask` works, you know the manager's entire workflow.
The manager receives the text to parse, creates a worker for each text, and then asks
each worker to parse the text. Finally, depending on whether the answer arrives on
time, the manager creates a report of success or failure.

3.2.5   Coding the worker

The worker does the following:

1 When it is created, it receives the file that it must process.
2 After receiving `Parse` and the reference to which it should respond, it starts
   parsing the file. The parsing is a pseudo-parse whose only purpose is to introduce the duration. Once the worker is done, it responds with `Done`.
   – The fake parsing takes between 2 and 4 seconds to finish. This relates to
     the manager's timeout time of 3 seconds, so on average, half the requests
     time out.

The code for the worker is shown in the following listing.

Listing 3.5 Worker

```scala
object Worker {

  sealed trait Command
  final case class Parse(replyTo: ActorRef[Worker.Response]) extends Command

  sealed trait Response
  final case object Done extends Response

  def apply(text: String): Behavior[Command] =
    Behaviors.receive { (context, message) =>
      message match {
        case Parse(replyTo) =>
          fakeLengthyParsing(file)
          context.log.info(s"${context.self.path.name}: done")
          replyTo ! Worker.Done
          Behaviors.same
      }
    }

  private def fakeLengthyParsing(file: String): Unit = {
    val endTime = System.currentTimeMillis + Random.between(2000, 4000)
    while (endTime > System.currentTimeMillis) {}
  }
}
```

Protocol

Prints a message including the actor's name

Text to parse

Fake reading of the delegated task

Replies to whatever is asked

Now you have the whole picture and the details of this application for parsing text implemented with ask.

3.2.6 *Using context*

So far, you've seen how an actor can log, ask, spawn, and refer to itself using context. Using self is handy when you want to use the actor's path. You may remember from chapter 2 that the path is formed by the hierarchy of an actor's parents and children. Here is the path of one of the workers:

```
akka://example-ask-without-content/user/manager-1/worker-file-c#-1664156553
```

Before you move on to the next example, you need to understand how ask works under the covers if you want to use it when you send a message with a payload—for example, if you send the worker the message to parse along with the replyTo.

3.2.7 *Ask signature*

Previously, you learned that when you use ask with Parse(replyTo: Actor-Ref[Worker.Response]), the replyTo is added for you. To understand why this happens, let's look at the ask signature:

```
package akka.actor.typed.scaladsl
```

```
trait ActorContext ... {

  ...

    def ask[Req, Res](target: RecipientRef[Req], createRequest:
    ➥ActorRef[Res] => Req)(mapResponse: Try[Res] => T)(implicit
    ➥responseTimeout: Timeout, classTag: ClassTag[Res]): Unit

  ...
}
```

It may seem daunting, so let's take it step by step.

In the previous section, in `context.ask(worker, Worker.Parse)`, `worker` corresponds to the `target` parameter and the `Worker.Parse` corresponds to `create-Request`. The annotations `[Req, Res]` at the beginning of the method are placeholders for the types in this method. For example, for `Req`, the compiler can check whether the type you use in `target RecipientRef[Req]` is the same as the one in `createRequest: ActorRef[Res] => Req`. In this example and the previous one, `Req` is `Worker.Command`.

`Worker.Parse` may look like an object, but as you just saw, `createRequest` is a function with the signature `ActorRef[Res] => Req` and not an object. So the question is this: How is the `Worker.Parse` class used as a function? You saw a hint in the previous section, but let's be more explicit.

If you're not familiar with Scala, this is probably confusing. Classes and objects can be treated like functions if they have an `apply` method and a `case` class like the way `Worker.Parse` has the `apply` method under the hood:

```
object Worker {
  ...
  final case class Parse(replyTo: ActorRef[Worker.Response])
      extends Command
  ...
}
```

Thanks to the compiler, the `case` class `Worker.Parse(replyTo: Actor-Ref[Worker.Response])` creates a method like the following:

```
def apply(replyTo: ActorRef[Worker.Response]): Worker.Parse =
➥new Worker.Parse(replyTo)
```

Because this method is available, the compiler understands that this is what you mean when you put `Worker.Parse` in the `ask` method. The compiler concludes that you are referring to the `apply` function of this `case` class because that is the only thing that makes sense in the context of the `createRequest` signature.

And that's it: thanks to syntactic sugar and cleverness of the compiler, you pass `Worker.Parse.apply()` to this method using `Worker.Parse`, which is equivalent to `ActorRef[Worker.Response]) => Worker.Parse`. That brings us full circle to the `createRequest` signature in `ask`.

For completeness, here are the remaining parameters. Feel free to skip to the next section if you've had enough technical details and would rather get back to the example. The `mapResponse` defines the callback as `Success` or `Failure`, depending on whether the response arrives on time. You already know this, but let's take a closer look. `mapResponse: Try[Res] => T` reads as follows:

- `mapResponse` is a function that needs to define two functions: one with the input `Success[Res]` and the output `T`, and another with the input `Failure` and the output `T`.
- In this example, `Res` is `Worker.Done` and `T` is `Manager.Command`. The `Try[Res] => T` expresses that after receiving the `Worker.Done` (wrapped in a `Success` or a `Failure`), the callback produces a `Manager.Command`. This command is the message the callback sends back to the manager; here, it is a `Report`.
- The `implicit responseTimeout: Timeout` is the amount of time the request waits for a response.

As you now know, because it is an implicit argument, if there is an implicit value in the scope, it will be used without having to be passed explicitly. There are many scopes in Scala, but we won't go into that here. (For more info, see chapter 42 of *Get Programming with Scala* by Daniela Sfregola; Manning, 2021, www.manning.com/books/get-programming-with-scala.)

> **NOTE** You should not pay much attention to the `implicit classTag`. It is there for historical reasons and binary compatibility.

Now let's move on to the most common use of `ask`, which is a little different from what you've seen so far. There are two ways to use `ask`: the empty one you just saw, where the message sent as a question contains only a `replyTo`, and the loaded one, where the message sent contains additional information.

In the next section, you change your parsing worker; and instead of passing the text to be parsed when you create the worker, you pass the text in the message sent to the worker each time you ask it to parse. This way, the worker can process a different text each time.

3.3 Ask with a payload

To include the text to parse in the message, the protocol of the worker must be as follows:

```
object Worker {

  sealed trait Command
  final case class Parse(            Provides the
      text: String,            ◁──┘ text to parse
      replyTo: ActorRef[Worker.Response])
    extends Command
```

```
sealed trait Response
final case object Done extends Response

...

}
```

> **NOTE**   The examples for this section can be found in the questionwith-
> payload package if no package is explicit in the snippet.

When you specify the createRequest parameter for the request, you can't rely on
Worker.Parse.apply() as you did before. Remember that createRequest expects
a function with only one parameter so the system can pass the replyTo for you:

```
package akka.actor.typed.scaladsl

trait ActorContext ... {

  ...

  def ask[Req, Res](target: RecipientRef[Req], createRequest: ActorRef[Res]
  ➥=> Req)(...)
  ...
}
```

But if Worker.Parse.apply has two parameters, text and replyTo, you can't just
pass it to createRequest. You need to create a function that fills in the text parameter and leaves the replyTo parameter unfilled. Then you can pass this function to
createRequest. You can do this with a technique called *currying*.

   Currying allows you to pass some parameters to a function and leave others empty.
The result of currying is a function with fewer parameters than the original function.
For example, if you have the function multiplication(x: Int)(y: Int) = x * y,
you can curry it like multiplication(4): that is, you pass only the x, not the y. This
way, you get a new function, multiplicationCurried(z: Int) = 4 * z, and you
can use this function in your program: for example, multiplicationCurried(3),
which gives 12 as a result.

> **NOTE**   The name multiplicationCurried is fictitious. What you call it is
> your decision.

In Scala, you must explicitly specify when a function can be curried. You do this by
separating the individual input variables you want to pass with parentheses. For the
multiplication example, you would do so like this:

```
def multiplication(x: Int)(y: Int)
```

You can use the function partially as multiplication(4)_. (Note that the under-
score is necessary to signal that y is not passed.) This gives you back multiplication-
Curried, which you can use elsewhere in your program.

In the following snippet, a curried function gives the signature you need for the parsing worker:

```
object Manager {
  ...

  def auxCreateRequest(text: String)(replyTo: ActorRef[Worker.Response]):
  ➥Worker.Parse = Worker.Parse(text, replyTo)

  ...
}
```

For example, if you pass a `text` like "text-a" to this function, you will get back the function you need. That function matches the signature of `createRequest`: `ActorRef[Res] => Req`:

```
ActorRef[Worker.Response] => Worker.Parse("text-a", replyTo)
```

Once you have added this function to your manager, you can change the previous creation of the worker, shown again here:

```
package simplequestion

object Manager {
  ...

  val worker: ActorRef[Worker.Command] =
    context.spawn(Worker(text), s"worker-$text")        ◁┐  Passes the text
  context.ask(worker, Worker.Parse){                     │  on creation
  ...
}
```

Change it to the following implementation:

```
object Manager {
  ...

  val worker: ActorRef[Worker.Command] =
    context.spawn(Worker(), s"worker-$text")
  context.ask(worker, auxCreateRequest(text)){          ◁┐  Passes the
  ...                                                    │  text on ask
}
```

This change from passing `Worker.Parse` directly to creating `auxCreateRequest` and passing that curried function to the `ask` is what you need to enable passing a payload. With this, you have learned how to include a payload when asking an actor.

Summary

- Traditional Akka applications are built as a hierarchy of actors. The first actor is the `ActorSystem`, and below it are its children. The children created by the `ActorSystem` can create other children, and so on, creating the hierarchy of actors.

- When you send messages back and forth between two actors, you need the adapters to convert the response to the protocol of the receiving actor.
- You can create adapters with `context.messageAdapter`.
- Instead of `tell`, which is fire and forget, an actor can ask. The asking actor expects an answer within a certain time. Therefore, it must specify a timeout and a callback handling both cases: the possible `Success` and `Failure`.
- You can use currying in a function like `sum(Int: a, Int: b)` with `sum(Int: a)(Int: b)`. Currying allows you to create more complex adapters that you can use with `ask`.

Akka test kit

This chapter covers

- Testing actors with the Akka test kit
- Testing synchronous scenarios
- Testing asynchronous scenarios

When testing is limited to a single component, anyone can test quickly. But when testing includes integrations, ease and speed are usually lost. *Actors* provide an interesting solution to this problem for the following reasons:

- Actors fit in with Behavior Driven Development (BDD) because they embody behavior as a fundamental primitive.
- Actors come in systems and are therefore fundamentally built on integration.
- Actors are based on messaging, which has huge advantages for testing because you can simulate any behaviors by sending messages.

In this chapter, you learn two methods for testing actors. On the one hand, you learn how to stub the `ActorSystem` to test actors in isolation and with deterministic guarantees. You may remember from the previous chapters that the `ActorSystem` is the first actor, the parent of all the others, and also manages the application's resources.

On the other hand, you test actors in a real-world context where multiple actors interact with each other and messages arrive in an indeterminate order. Accordingly, you learn about testing in synchronous and asynchronous settings.

4.1   Testing approaches

To test actors—if they are written in Scala—you work with the ScalaTest framework. ScalaTest is an xUnit-style testing framework designed for readability, so it should be easy to read and understand the intent of the test. With this framework alone, testing actors can pose some difficulties:

- *Expected order*—Sending messages is asynchronous in a real scenario, which makes it difficult to specify the order in which the expected values should be asserted in the unit test.
- *Statelessness*—An actor hides its internal state and does not allow direct access to it. Access should be possible only through the `ActorRef`. Sending messages to an actor is our only way to know its internal state (which is limited to the state the actor had when it replied).
- *Collaboration/integration*—If you want to do an integration test for multiple actors, you need to eavesdrop on the actors to assert that the messages have the expected values. It is not immediately clear how to do this. You'll learn to do this with a probe.

Fortunately, Akka has the `akka-testkit` module, which contains a set of testing tools that make actor testing much easier. This module enables several types of testing:

- *Synchronous unit testing*—An actor instance is not directly accessible. To solve this problem, the test kit provides a `BehaviorTestKit` you can use to access the effects resulting from what is executed in the actor instance. Another tool is the `TestInbox`, which you can use to instantiate an `ActorRef` that serves as a probe.
- *Asynchronous unit testing*—The `akka-testkit` module provides `ActorTestKit` and `TestProbe`, which are similar to their synchronous counterparts. However, they have important differences: they create complete `ActorSystems` and are therefore indeterministic.
- *Multiple JVM and node testing*— Akka provides tools for testing clusters, but that is not covered in this book. You can learn more at http://mng.bz/Jg8a.

The option closest to running your code in production is the asynchronous style, which is tested using the `ActorTestKit` class. In this book, the focus is on asynchronous testing because it can reveal problems in the code that would not be noticed in a stubbed-sync environment. This is usually the safest choice. It also probably won't surprise you that I recommend a classic unit-testing approach instead of mocking.

The classic approach tests that you get certain outputs from certain inputs to make sure your code works properly. This is called testing the *external behavior*. In mocking, on the other hand, you test the *internal behavior*: that is, the specific implementation. For example, you can test that your `insertClient` method calls the correct validation method and the DB method of your repository. A significant disadvantage of mocking is that if you now want to change the `insertClient` implementation—for example, to call a web service instead of the DB—you also have to change the tests. Not ideal.

In the following sections, you use the `akka-testkit` module to test some basic scenarios. You learn the main options to test the specific sync and async contexts.

> **NOTE** The source code for this chapter is available at www.manning.com/ books/akka-in-action-second-edition or https://github.com/franciscolopez-sancho/akka-topics/tree/main/chapter04. You can find the contents of any snippet or listing in the .scala file with the same name as the class, object, or trait. For example, you can find the snippet with `object Simplified-Worker` in the SimplifiedWorker.scala file.

4.2 Sync testing

Sync testing is intended to test an actor in isolation to check its internal logic in a white-box style. It is sequential and therefore not suitable for testing asynchronous calls that are part of the actor's logic or for testing interaction with the real implementation with other actors. Timers and the scheduler also cannot be tested this way. Using this toolkit, you can test three things: effects, reception of messages, and logs.

4.2.1 Effects

Actor *effects* are most of the methods that can be executed in an actor via the `ActorContext`. For example, the actor has been spawned, has been stopped, or has no effect yet. There are about a dozen types of `akka.actor.testkit.typed` `.Effect` (see http://mng.bz/WAl1). Let's test `Spawned` and `NoEffect`.

Here you have the same scenario as in the previous chapter where you created workers from the manager so they can parse a text. For simplicity, let's look at the parts that show you how to test an effect: in this case, the creation of the worker.

This simplified scenario has two actors, one creating the other. One of the actors—the worker—is of type `String` and ignores all messages it receives. Similar to `Behavior.same`, `Behaviors.ignore` provides the `ignore` function. This is the actor's protocol:

```scala
object SimplifiedWorker {
    def apply() = Behaviors.ignore[String]
}
```

The next actor protocol—the manager—is as follows:

```scala
object SimplifiedManager {

  sealed trait Command
  final case class CreateChild(name: String) extends Command

  ...
}
```

This actor creates a `SimplifiedWorker` for each `CreateChild` message:

```
object SimplifiedManager {

    ...                            <—| Protocol

    def apply(): Behaviors.Receive[Command] =
        Behaviors.receive { (context, message) =>
            message match {
                case CreateChild(name) =>                        Spawns
                    context.spawn(SimplifiedWorker(), name)  <—| the actor
                    Behaviors.same
}
```

Now let's focus on testing:

1 Create the test kit with `BehaviorTestKit(initialBehavior: Behavior [T])` so that `initialBehavior` is the actor you can test.
2 Test the expected effect with `testkit.expectedEffect(effect: Effect)`.
3 To send messages to the actor (`initialBehavior`), you can use `testkit.run(message: T)`: in this case, `CreateChild`.

The following listing uses the `BehaviorTestKit` to test whether an actor has been spawned. It proves that you don't get any effect before you send the message to the actor and that you get the spawned effect afterward.

Listing 4.1 Simplified manager testing spawning

```
import akka.actor.testkit.typed.scaladsl.BehaviorTestKit
import akka.actor.testkit.typed.Effect.{ NoEffects, Scheduled, Spawned }
import org.scalatest.wordspec.AnyWordSpec
import org.scalatest.matchers.should.Matchers

class SyncTestingSpec extends AnyWordSpec with Matchers {

    "Typed actor synchronous testing" must {

        "spawning takes place" in {
            val testKit = BehaviorTestKit(SimplifiedManager())        Empty list
            testKit.expectEffect(NoEffects)                    <—|    of effects
            testKit.run(SimplifiedManager.CreateChild("adan"))   <—
            testKit.expectEffect(Spawned(SimplifiedWorker(), "adan"))
        }                                                            Sends a CreateChild
    }                                                                message to the manager
}
```

Checks the effect (annotation pointing to `testKit.expectEffect(Spawned(SimplifiedWorker(), "adan"))`)

You can run this test—along with the code in the rest of the section—by executing the following command in the repository's root directory:

```
sbt "chapter04/testOnly *SyncTestingSpec"
```

This test outputs the following:

```
[info] SyncTestingSpec:
[info] Typed actor synchronous testing
[info] - must record spawning
```

You can see how this output corresponds to the code defining the test:

```
class SyncTestingSpec ...

  "Typed actor synchronous testing" must {

    "record spawning" in {...}

  ...
}
```

> **NOTE** This definition of the test is not Akka-specific. It corresponds to the ScalaTest semantics.

On the Akka side, we can see how `BehaviorTestKit` is used to create a test kit that you use as an interface to interact with the actor. For each assertion with `expect-Effect`, you can check whether an effect exists by polling from a queue in the test kit's stubbed context. This mechanism enables determinism—a stubbed context with a queue.

This type of testing is about stubbing. There is no real `ActorSystem` but only a dummy `ActorSystemStub`. When you use `Spawn` or any other action that belongs to the actor's context, an effect representing this action is created and stored in a queue that you can later retrieve with `testKit.expectEffect`.

The context itself (`ActorContext`) is a `StubbedActorContext` that mocks methods such as `spawn`, `stop`, and `scheduleOnce` and stubs values such as `Children`, `Self`, and `System`. All of this is available after the creation of the `BehaviorTestKit`. This process is illustrated in figure 4.1.

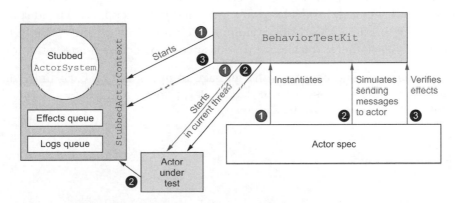

Figure 4.1 Testing the components of the `BehaviorTestKit`

In addition to the methods related to the context, the `BehaviorTestKit` provides methods such as `childInbox`, `childTestKit`, and `logEntries`, as well as methods to clear the child inbox or log entries. In this chapter, you learn more about `logEntries`.

4.2.2 *More than one actor*

As before, let's simplify the example where the manager and the workers parse the text and look at the part where the manager passes the text to the workers so they can parse it. Here, the manager (`SimplifiedManager`) acts as a proxy for another actor, and it has the following protocol

```
object SimplifiedManager {

  sealed trait Command
  final case class Forward(message: String, sendTo: ActorRef[String])
    extends Command

  ...
}
```

which is used like this:

```
object SimplifiedManager {

    ...

    def apply(): Behaviors.Receive[Command] =
      Behaviors.receive { (context, message) =>
        message match {
            ...
          case Forward(text, sendTo) =>
            sendTo ! text
            Behaviors.same
}
```

How can you prove that the simplified manager forwards the message? To prove this, you need `TestInbox[T]`. With it, you create a probe that is a fake actor—here, a fake worker—and a queue where it keeps received messages (its inbox). The idea is to test whether the forwarding works by examining the probe's inbox and seeing if the forwarded message is there. You check this with `probe.expectMessage(message: T)`.

> **NOTE** This method consumes the message from the inbox. Each time you call `probe.expectMessage(message:  T)`, a message—if any—is fetched and removed from the probe's inbox.

The test is as follows:

```
class SyncTestingSpec ...

  ...

  "actor gets forwarded message from manager" in {
    val testKit = BehaviorTestKit(SimplifiedManager())
```

```
        val probe = TestInbox[String]()
        testKit.run(SimplifiedManager.Forward("hello", probe.ref))
        probe.expectMessage("hello")
    }
    ...
}
```

Probe with a stubbed actor
ref and a queue as an inbox

Asserting could poll
messages from the queue.

4.2.3 Testing the logs

Logging is an essential part of any program, and as such, it is included in the manager/workers parsing application from the previous chapter. With the `BehaviorTestKit`, you can check whether logging works as expected. The underlying mechanism is the same as for effects or messages. The logs are stored in a queue, and you can retrieve them to check your expectations.

Let's use the same `SimplifiedManager` actor as in the previous examples and add logging, first to the protocol and then to the actor:

```
object SimplifiedManager {

    sealed trait Command             Protocol
    case object Log extends Command
    ...

    def apply(): Behaviors.Receive[Command] =
      Behaviors.receive { (context, message) =>
        message match {
              ...
          case Log =>
            context.log.info(s"it's done")      Logging
            Behaviors.same
        }
      }
}
```

You need to know two things to check the logging:

- The log entries are accessible via `testKit.logEntries`.
- These entries are wrapped in the `CapturedLogEvent(level: Level, message: String)` class.

You can verify that the simplified manager is logging as it should as follows:

```
class SyncTestingSpec ...

    ...
    "record the log" in {
        val testKit = BehaviorTestKit(SimplifiedManager())
        testKit.run(SimplifiedManager.Log)
        testKit.logEntries() shouldBe Seq(             Proves
          CapturedLogEvent(Level.INFO, "it's done"))   expectations
    }
    ...
}
```

The log events are of type `CapturedLogEvent` because the `BehaviorTestKit` maps all real log events to this type. Otherwise, you would have to check a specific implementation, depending on your chosen logging.

Although the `BehaviorTestKit` is useful in certain scenarios, it cannot test scheduled messages or multiple actors. And because one actor is not really an actor, as you learned in the previous chapter, you naturally focus on group interactions in asynchronous environments. Let's look at how you can test in these circumstances.

4.3   Async testing

Asynchronous testing works with a real `ActorSystem` with parallel executions, where you have no guarantee about the order in which messages arrive. This is a black-box testing style.

To create this type of test, you use the `ActorTestKit` instead of the `Behavior-TestKit`. The `ActorTestKit` creates a real `ActorSystem`, where each actor has a full `ActorContext` rather than the previous stubbed context. Instead of the `Test-Inbox`, you now have a `TestProbe` that you use similarly, although it has a richer API. This section looks at some of these new methods, like awaiting an assert, fishing for messages of specific types, and passing code to be executed within a certain time.

Figure 4.2 shows how the `ActorTestKit` is typically used for testing. The actor spec creates a real `ActorSystem` with its usual hierarchy containing the actor under test and a test probe. The test probe acts as a monitor that eventually receives messages as effects of the messages sent to the actor.

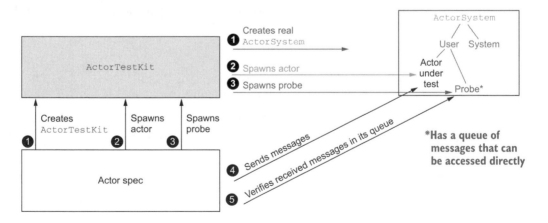

Figure 4.2   Testing components of the `ActorTestKit`

4.3.1   Using probes

Let's start with the similarities to testing the forwarding of a message from one actor to another, as in the example in the previous section. This is similar to sync testing, so let's test the same actor:

```
object SimplifiedManager {

  sealed trait Command
  final case class Forward(message: String, sendTo: ActorRef[String])
      extends Command

    def apply(): Behaviors.Receive[Command] =
      Behaviors.receive { (context, message) =>
        message match {
            ...
          case Forward(text, sendTo) =>
            sendTo ! text
            Behaviors.same
}
```

The test is the same when you test the probe—that is, `probe.expectMessage`—but there are a few differences:

- To create an instance of the actor under test, you use `testKit.spawn`.
- To create the probe, you use `testKit.createTestProbe`.
- The `ActorTestKit` is created only once for the entire spec, and you need to shut down its `ActorSystem` after all the tests are complete. To do this, you add the `BeforeAndAfterAll` trait and override the `afterAll` method. It makes sense to have only one `ActorTestKit` and shut it down at the end because creating and shutting down an `ActorSystem` takes time, and you don't want to do that for every test in your suite.

This listing shows how everything plays together.

Listing 4.2 Essential parts of an async test

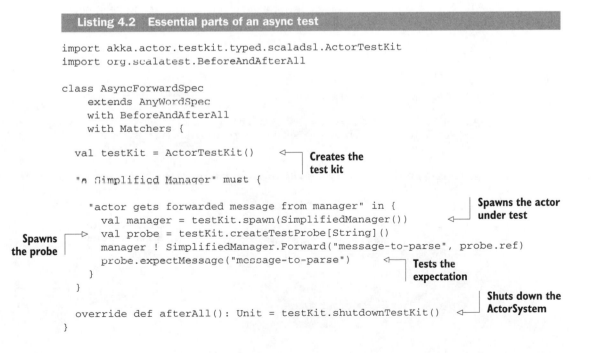

```
import akka.actor.testkit.typed.scaladsl.ActorTestKit
import org.scalatest.BeforeAndAfterAll

class AsyncForwardSpec
    extends AnyWordSpec
    with BeforeAndAfterAll
    with Matchers {

  val testKit = ActorTestKit()                    <─┐ Creates the
                                                     │ test kit
  "a Simplified Manager" must {

    "actor gets forwarded message from manager" in {        ┌─ Spawns the actor
      val manager = testKit.spawn(SimplifiedManager())   <──┘  under test
      val probe = testKit.createTestProbe[String]()
      manager ! SimplifiedManager.Forward("message-to-parse", probe.ref)
      probe.expectMessage("message-to-parse")       <─┐ Tests the
    }                                                  │ expectation
  }
                                                      ┌─ Shuts down the
  override def afterAll(): Unit = testKit.shutdownTestKit()  <──┘  ActorSystem
}
```

Spawns the probe

At the moment, this test is very similar to the sync examples, with one big difference: you are forced to shut down the `ActorSystem`.

Monitoring

Before you read the next section, you need to learn how to monitor an actor. Monitoring uses a probe to check whether a real actor receives a message. This is often necessary when you send a message to an actor that triggers a cascade of messages to that actor or another actor. You need to verify that this stream of messages is as expected.

So far, you've only used a probe to check whether a message was forwarded to that probe by a real actor. For example, when you forwarded in `SimplifiedManager`,

```
case Forward(text, sendTo) =>
  sendTo ! text
```

`Forward` was the protocol of the real actor, and `sentTo` was the probe. You sent a message to the real actor and checked with the probe to see if the message was finally forwarded.

The idea now is to place a probe in front of the actor under test so that the probe receives the message and then passes it to the actor behind it. Although the protocol is from the behavior under test, you interact with this monitor as if it were the actor under test. This is done with the following `monitor` method from the `Behaviors` factory:

```
def monitor(monitor: ActorRef[T], behavior: Behavior[T]): Behavior[T]
```

Here, `T` is the protocol of the actor under test, and `monitor` is the probe—`probe.ref`, of type `ActorRef`. You can see this in practice in the following simple test:

```
class AsyncForwardSpec ...
  ...

  "a monitor" must {

    "intercept the messages" in {

      val probe = createTestProbe[String]
      val behaviorUnderTest = Behaviors.receiveMessage[String] { _ =>
        Behaviors.ignore
      }
      val behaviorMonitored = Behaviors.monitor(probe.ref,
          behaviorUnderTest)              ◁——
      val actor = testkit.spawn(behaviorMonitored)

      actor ! "checking"                   Creates a behavior
      probe.expectMessage("checking")      with a monitor probe

    }
  }
  ...
}
```

Once the probe and the behavior under test are defined, you can create a monitor with them and spawn it. This monitor actor has the probe that intercepts any message sent to the behavior, and the behavior under test. Every time you send a message to the monitor, the probe intercepts the message and forwards it to the behavior. This way, you can prove that the actor under test receives the message by testing its probe.

4.3.2 Fishing for messages

Let's say you have a counter that can pause for a few seconds and then resume automatically. During the pause, the counter can't be incremented, as shown in this listing.

Listing 4.3 Fishing for messages in a counter

```
object CounterTimer {

  sealed trait Command
  final case object Increase extends Command
  final case class Pause(seconds: Int) extends Command
  private[fishing] final case object Resume extends Command

  def apply(): Behavior[Command] =
    resume(0)

  def resume(count: Int): Behavior[Command] =
    Behaviors.receive { (context, message) =>
      Behaviors.withTimers { timers =>
        message match {
          ...
          case Pause(t) =>
            timers.startSingleTimer(Resume, t.second)      ◁─┐ You get a resume t
            pause(count)                                       seconds after the
  }}}                                                          Pause message.

  def pause(count: Int): Behavior[Command] = {
    Behaviors.receive { (context, message) =>
      message match {
        ...
        case Resume =>
          context.log.info(s"resuming")
          resume(count)
  }}}
}
```

Now you can test that you get a resume message by using the fishing capabilities of the probe in the `ActorTestKit`. This works as follows.

You must develop a strategy for each possible message the probe encounters during the test. During this time, you can explicitly stop fishing—because the probe receives the expected message—or let the time run out until the test fails. There are four strategies for fishing for messages (figure 4.3):

- Keep the message and complete the testing.
- Keep the message and continue testing.
- Discard the message and continue testing.
- Disregard any previous catches and fail.

If you complete the test without it failing, you can use the messages the probe received and assert on them. Figure 4.3 describes these strategies. Note that the message types are fictitious.

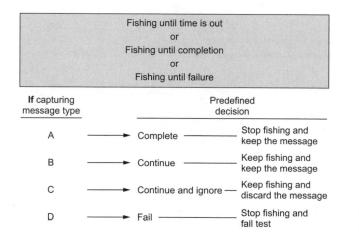

Figure 4.3   Possible fishing strategies

To prove that the counter resumes after a pause, you need to set the test to complete when the probe receives a Resume message. The wait time must be set greater than the seconds in Pause(seconds: Int). Let's see this in action.

Listing 4.4   Fishing for the right message

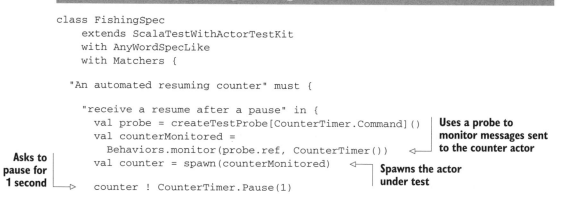

```scala
class FishingSpec
    extends ScalaTestWithActorTestKit
    with AnyWordSpecLike
    with Matchers {

  "An automated resuming counter" must {

    "receive a resume after a pause" in {
      val probe = createTestProbe[CounterTimer.Command]()
      val counterMonitored =
        Behaviors.monitor(probe.ref, CounterTimer())
      val counter = spawn(counterMonitored)

      counter ! CounterTimer.Pause(1)
```

Uses a probe to monitor messages sent to the counter actor

Spawns the actor under test

Asks to pause for 1 second

```
probe.fishForMessage(3.seconds) {
  case CounterTimer.Increase =>
    FishingOutcomes.continueAndIgnore
  case CounterTimer.Pause(_) =>
    FishingOutcomes.continueAndIgnore
  case CounterTimer.Resume => FishingOutcomes.complete
      }
    }
  }
}
```

◁──┐ **Fishes, with a**
    patience of 3 seconds

◁── **Completes**
     with success

To skip some work, you can extend from `ScalaTestWithActorTestKit`—as the previous listing does—to avoid creating the `ActorTestKit` and terminating the `ActorSystem` by yourself. Without the reference to the `ActorTestKit`, you can use `spawn` and `createTestProbe` directly instead of `testKit.spawn` and `testKit.createTestProbe` as before. This is possible because the `testKit` is implicitly available within the `ScalaTestWithActorTestKit`.

4.3.3 Logging

Log testing is similar in an asynchronous environment, although there are a couple of differences. Instead of looking at a queue of logs, you need to intercept them. To do so, you use the `LoggingTestKit`. The other difference is that `LoggingTestKit` doesn't wrap the logging events in a `CaptureLogEvent` like `BehaviorTestKit` does.

Logback dependency

`LoggingTestKit` requires logback dependency. This means adding the following to your build.sbt file:

```
val LogbackVersion = "1.2.3"
libraryDependencies += "ch.qos.logback" % "logback-classic" %
  ➥LogbackVersion
```

Let's test the same logging feature of the simplified manager that was tested in the synchronous version:

```
object SimplifiedManager {

  sealed trait Command                        Protocol
  case object Log extends Command

  def apply(): Behaviors.Receive[Command] =
    Behaviors.receive { (context, message) =>
      message match {
          ...
        case Log =>
          context.log.info(s"it's done")      ◁── Logging
          Behaviors.same
      }
    }
}
```

To use the `LoggingTestKit`, you need to set two things:

- The expectation
- The trigger that causes logging

For example, you can set the expectation to catch "it's done" in the logs and trigger it by sending a `Log` message to the simplified manager:

```
class AsyncLogSpec ...
  ...

  LoggingTestKit.info("it's done").expect {
        manager ! SimplifiedManager.Log
  }
  ...
}
```

The entire test is shown in the next listing.

Listing 4.5   Using `LoggingTestKit` and `ScalaTestWithActorTestKit`

```
import akka.actor.testkit.typed.scaladsl.ScalaTestWithActorTestKit
import akka.actor.testkit.typed.scaladsl.LoggingTestKit

class AsyncLogSpec
    extends ScalaTestWithActorTestKit          ◁──   Delegates the creation
    with AnyWordSpecLike                               and termination of
    with Matchers {                                    the ActorTestKit

  "a Simplified Manager" must {                       The test kit comes from
                                                      ScalaTestWithActorTestKit.
    "be able to log 'it's done'" in {
      val manager = testKit.spawn(SimplifiedManager(), "manager")   ◁──

      LoggingTestKit.info("it's done").expect {
         manager ! SimplifiedManager.Log          ◁──   Sets the code to
      }                                                  trigger the logging
    }
  }
}
```

Sets the expectation ──▷ (points to `LoggingTestKit.info("it's done").expect {`)

Note that there is no indication of which actor is logging what. The only assertion this test makes is that at the end, the text "it's done" is logged in the `INFO` level. The expectation applies to the entire `ActorSystem`, unlike with the synchronous test kit, which applies only to an actor created with the `BehaviorTestKit`.

You may remember `deadLetters` from chapter 3: messages whose address no longer exists because their destination—the `ActorRef`—no longer exists. With the `LoggingTestKit`, you can easily catch the logging generated in `deadLetters` by using a regular expression that matches the logging event.

To re-create this scenario, all you need is a stopped actor, which you can create using the `Behaviors.stopped` factory:

```
val behavior: Behavior[String] = Behaviors.stopped
```

Sending a message to this stopped actor redirects it to `deadLetters`. You can test this with the `LoggingTestKit.empty` constructor by adding the desired `.withLog-Level` and the regular expression via `.withMessageRegex`.

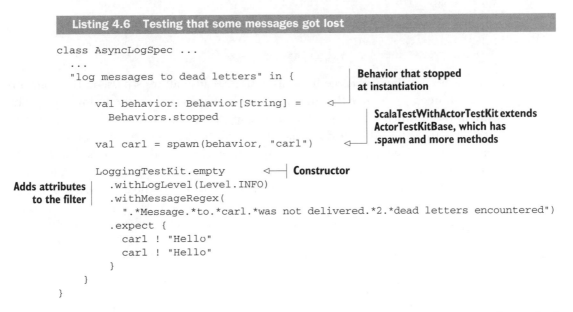

Listing 4.6 Testing that some messages got lost

```
class AsyncLogSpec ...
  ...
  "log messages to dead letters" in {          Behavior that stopped
                                               at instantiation
      val behavior: Behavior[String] =  ◄──┘
        Behaviors.stopped                      ScalaTestWithActorTestKit extends
                                               ActorTestKitBase, which has
      val carl = spawn(behavior, "carl")  ◄──┘ .spawn and more methods

      LoggingTestKit.empty         ◄──┤ Constructor
        .withLogLevel(Level.INFO)
        .withMessageRegex(
          ".*Message.*to.*carl.*was not delivered.*2.*dead letters encountered")
        .expect {
          carl ! "Hello"
          carl ! "Hello"
        }
    }
}
```

Adds attributes to the filter

This simple example proves that two messages were sent to `deadLetters` instead of the original `carl` actor.

In this section, you have seen how asynchronous testing is similar to synchronous testing. However, there are some important differences, such as the creation of the `ActorSystem`, testing real actors, and the ability to schedule messages. Next, let's look at some unique features of the `ActorTestKit`.

4.3.4 Log capturing

Logging is essential to any application, but reading the logs generally is not useful when testing—at least, not if all the tests are successful. Log statements become noise in these circumstances.

Let's see this in action by running the `AsyncLogSpec` test from listing 4.3. All you need to remember is that this spec proves that a `SimplifiedManager` logs "it's done" when it receives a `SimplifiedManager.Log` message. You can run the test by executing the following:

```
sbt "chapter04/testOnly **.AsyncLogSpec"
```

This produces the following output:

```
10:42:13.844 DEBUG AsyncLogSpec - Starting ActorTestKit
10:42:13.964 INFO logging.SimplifiedManager$ - it's done
10:42:14.094 INFO akka.actor.CoordinatedShutdown -
Running CoordinatedShutdown with reason [ActorSystemTerminateReason]
```

Noise

```
[info] AsyncLogSpec:
[info] a Simplified Manager
[info] - must be able to log 'it's done'
[info] Run completed in 740 milliseconds.
[info] Total number of tests run: 1
[info] Suites: completed 1, aborted 0
[info] Tests: succeeded 1, failed 0, canceled 0, ignored 0, pending 0
[info] All tests passed.
[success] Total time: 1 s, completed
```

In this scenario, the first three lines are noise because all tests passed. To avoid this noise, you need to capture the logs. You can do that by adding the following logging configuration, which includes a `CapturingAppender` and a `CapturingAppender-Delegate` from the Akka test kit and the usual `ConsoleAppender` you can use in every JVM application. The `CapturingAppender` captures the test logs. If a test fails, the `CapturingAppenderDelegate` flushes the captured logs into its `appender-ref` (here, `STDOUT`), which is output to the console according to the `ConsoleAppender`:

```xml
<?xml version="1.0" encoding="UTF-8"?>
<configuration>

    <appender name="STDOUT" class="ch.qos.logback.core.ConsoleAppender">
        <encoder>
            <pattern>[%date{ISO8601}] [%level] [%logger] [%marker]
            ➥[%thread] - %msg</pattern>
        </encoder>
    </appender>

    <appender name="CapturingAppender"
    ➥class="akka.actor.testkit.typed.internal.CapturingAppender"/>

    <logger
     name="akka.actor.testkit.typed.internal.CapturingAppenderDelegate">
      <appender-ref ref="STDOUT"/>
    </logger>

    <root level="DEBUG">
        <appender-ref ref="CapturingAppender"/>
    </root>
</configuration>
```

With the previous configuration, you don't get the noisy log statements. However, to get the logs when the tests fail, you need to add the `LogCapturing` property to your spec, as follows:

```
class AsyncLogSpec
    extends ScalaTestWithActorTestKit
    with AnyWordSpecLike
    with Matchers                        Adds the LogCapturing trait to
    with LogCapturing           ◁──────  print the logs when the test fails
```

With these two things in place, if all the tests pass, you get nothing but the result of the tests. And if a test fails, you get all the logs.

Summary

- The `BehaviorTestKit` can test an actor in isolation, but it cannot test scheduling or asynchronous calls in code. It is built by mocking an `ActorSystem` by creating queues to store the effects of messages sent to the actor. This allows you to implement a white-box testing style.

- With the `ActorTestKit`, there are no restrictions for testing scheduled messages or asynchronous calls. It creates a real `ActorSystem`. Messages sent to an actor can run in parallel and arrive in an undetermined order. This allows you to implement a black-box testing style.

- You can extend your test class with `ScalaTestWithActorTestKit` to avoid creating the `ActorTestKit` and shutting down the `ActorSystem` after all tests.

- `Behaviors.monitor` lets you monitor a real actor with a probe. Every message sent to the actor is also sent to the probe, which you can use to test expectations.

- To determine whether your actor received a particular message, you can fish for message types using a probe from the `ActorTestKit`. This way, you can determine what to do depending on the captured message: keep or discard the message, continue or stop fishing, or fail the test.

- To avoid noise, you can mute the logging messages on successful tests by adding a `CapturingAppender` to the logback.xml configuration. To print the log messages again on failed tests, add the `CapturingAppenderDelegate` to the logback.xml configuration and extend your test with `LogCapturing`.

Fault tolerance

This chapter covers

- Self-healing systems and the let-it-crash principle
- The actor lifecycle signals
- Supervising strategies and their signals
- Monitoring and watching

This chapter covers Akka's tools for making applications more resilient. These tools, which follow the *let-it-crash* principle, are supervision, monitoring, and the actor lifecycle features. We look at examples that show how to apply them to typical failure scenarios.

> **NOTE** The source code for this chapter is available at www.manning.com/ books/akka-in-action-second-edition or https://github.com/franciscolo pezsancho/akka-topics/tree/main/chapter05. You can find the contents of any snippet or listing in the .scala file with the same name as the class, object, or trait.

5.1 *What fault tolerance is (and what it isn't)*

Let's start with a definition of what we refer to here as a *fault-tolerant* system and why you'd write code to embrace the notion of failure. In an ideal world, a system is always available and can guarantee that it will be successful with each undertaken action. The only two paths to this ideal are using components that can never fail or accounting for every possible fault by providing a recovery action, which is also assured of success. In most architectures, what you have instead is a catch-all mechanism that terminates as soon as an uncaught failure arises.

Even if an application attempts to provide recovery strategies, testing them is hard, and ensuring that the recovery strategies work adds another layer of complexity. In the procedural world, each attempt to do something requires a return code that is checked against a list of possible faults. Exception handling has become a fixture of modern languages, promising a less onerous path to providing the various required means of recovery. Although it has succeeded in yielding code that doesn't need fault checks on every line, the propagation of faults to ready handlers hasn't improved significantly.

The idea of a system that's free of faults sounds great in theory, but the sad fact is that building a system that's also highly available and distributed is not possible for a nontrivial system. The main reason is that large parts of any nontrivial system aren't under your control, and these parts can break. Then there's the prevalent problem of responsibility: as collaborators interact, often using shared components, it's not clear who's responsible for which possible faults.

A good example of potentially unavailable resources is the network: it can go awry at any time or be partly available. If you want to continue operation, you have to find another way to communicate or disable communication for a while. You may depend on third-party services that can misbehave, fail, or be sporadically unavailable. The servers your software runs on can fail, be unavailable, or experience total hardware failure. You obviously can't magically make a server reappear out of its ashes or automatically fix a broken disk to guarantee writing to it. This is why *let it crash* was born in the rack-and-stack world of the telcos, where failed machines were common enough to make their availability goals impossible without a plan that accounted for them.

Because you can't prevent all failures from happening, you have to adopt a strategy that keeps the following in mind:

- Things break. The system needs to be *fault tolerant* so it can stay available and continue to run. Recoverable faults shouldn't trigger catastrophic failures.
- In some cases, it's acceptable if the most important features of the system stay available as long as possible while failing parts are stopped and cut off from the system so they can't interfere with the rest of the system and produce unpredictable results.

- In other cases, certain components are so important that they need active back-ups (probably on a different server or using different resources) that can kick in when the main component fails to quickly remedy the unavailability.
- A failure in certain parts of the system shouldn't crash the entire system, so you need a way to isolate particular failures that you can deal with later.

Of course, the Akka toolkit doesn't include a fault-tolerance silver bullet. You still have to handle specific failures, but you can do so in a cleaner, more application-specific way. The Akka features in table 5.1 enable you to build the fault-tolerant behavior you need.

Table 5.1 Fault-avoidance strategies

Strategy	Description
Fault containment or isolation	A fault should be contained within a part of the system and not escalate to a total crash.
Structure	Isolating a faulty component means a structure must exist to isolate the component from the rest of the system. The system needs a defined structure in which active parts can be isolated.
Redundancy	A backup component should be able to take over when a component fails.
Replacement	If a faulty component can be isolated, you can replace it in the structure. The other parts of the system should be able to communicate with the replaced component just as they did with the failed component.
Reboot	If a component gets into an incorrect state, you need the ability to get it back to a defined initial state. The incorrect state may be the reason for the fault, and it may not be possible to predict all the incorrect states the component can get into because of dependencies outside of your control.
Component lifecycle	A faulty component needs to be isolated. If it can't recover, it should be terminated and removed from the system or reinitialized with a correct starting state. A defined lifecycle must exist to start, restart, and terminate the component.
Suspend	When a component fails, all calls to the component should be suspended until the component is fixed or replaced so the new component can continue the work without dropping a beat. The call handled at the time of failure also should not disappear—it could be critical to recovery. Further, it may contain information critical to understanding why the component failed. You may want to retry the call when you're sure there was another reason for the fault.
Separation of concerns	It's great if the fault-recovery code can be separated from the normal processing code. Fault recovery is a cross-cutting concern in the normal flow. A clear separation between normal flow and recovery flow simplifies the work that needs to be done. Changing the way the application recovers from faults is simpler if you achieve this clean separation.

"But wait a minute," you may say. "Why can't you use plain old objects and exceptions to recover from failures?" Normally, exceptions are used to back out of a series of actions to prevent an inconsistent state rather than to recover from a failure in the sense we have been discussing. In the next section, let's see how hard it would be to add fault recovery using exception handling and plain old objects.

> **NOTE** This chapter does not cover the tooling for recovering from catastrophic failure. If a computer bursts into flames, you need to have an Akka cluster in place. Chapter 8 dives into that topic.

5.1.1 Plain old objects and exceptions

Let's look at an example of an application that receives logs from multiple threads, parses interesting information out of the files into row objects, and writes these rows into a database. A file-watcher process keeps track of added files and informs many threads in some way to process them. Figure 5.1 depicts an overview of the application and highlights the parts we'll zoom in on (those that are *in scope*).

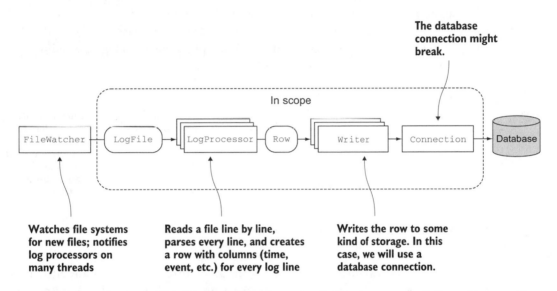

Figure 5.1 Processing logs from the `FileWatcher`, to the `LogProcessor`, to the `Writer`, and to the database

If the database connection breaks, you want to be able to create a new connection to another database and continue writing instead of backing out. If the connection starts to malfunction, you may want to shut it down so that no part of the application uses it anymore. In some cases, you need to reboot the connection to get rid of a temporary bad state. Let's look at the case of using a new connection to the same database with standard exception handling; we'll use pseudocode to illustrate the potential problem areas.

First you set up all the objects that will be used from the threads. After setup, they will be used to process the new files that the file watcher finds. You also set up a database writer that uses a connection (see figure 5.2).

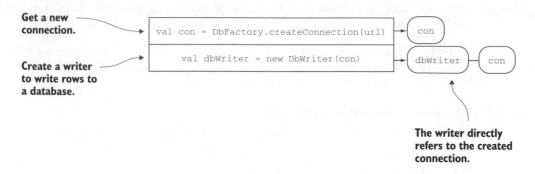

Figure 5.2   Create a writer with a connection.

The dependencies for the writer are passed to the constructor, as you'd expect. The database factory settings, including the different URLs, are passed in from the thread that creates the writer. Next you set up some log processors; each gets a reference to a writer to store rows, as shown in figure 5.3.

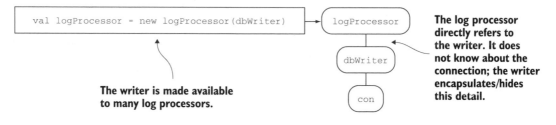

Figure 5.3   Create a log processor using the writer.

The flow shown in figure 5.3 is called from many threads to simultaneously process files found by the file watcher. Figure 5.4 shows a call stack where a DbBroken-ConnectionException is thrown, indicating that you should switch to another connection. The details of every method are omitted; the diagram shows only where an object eventually calls another object.

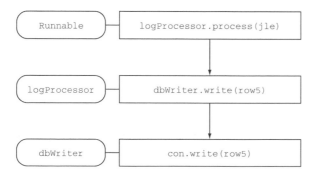

The diagram only shows where each object (on the left) eventually calls another object down the call stack. The other details of the method are omitted.

Figure 5.4   Call stack diagram from the runnable to the log processor to the write

Instead of throwing the exception up the stack, you'd like to recover from the DbBrokenConnectionException and replace the broken connection with a working one. The first problem you face is that it's hard to add the code to recover the connection in a way that doesn't break the design. Also, you don't have enough information to re-create the connection: you don't know which lines in the file have already been processed successfully and which line was being processed when the exception occurred. Figure 5.5 shows the difficulties of communication failures among different parts of the stack. Notice that the flow in this image is from top to bottom on the left side and bottom to top on the right side, moving down into the call stack and back when an error occurs.

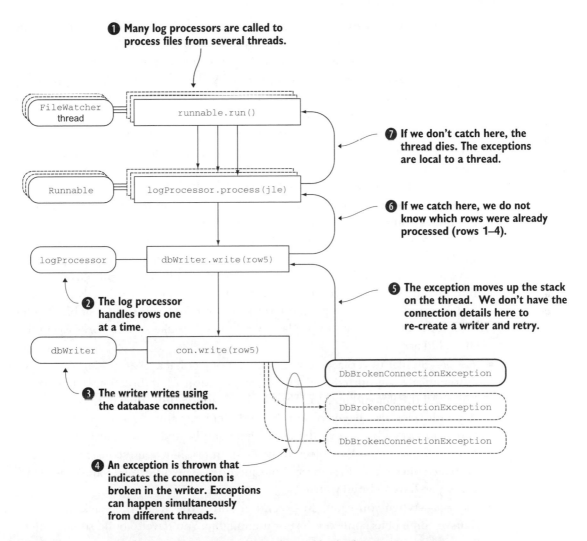

Figure 5.5   Call stack from the file watcher to the writer and back when an error occurs

Making both the processed lines and the connection information available to all objects would break your simple design and violate basic best practices like encapsulation, inversion of control, and single responsibility, to name a few. (Good luck at the next code peer review with your clean-coding colleagues!) You want the faulty component replaced. Adding recovery code directly into the exception handling will entangle the functionality of processing log files with database connection recovery logic. Even if you found a spot to re-create the connection, you'd have to be very careful that other threads didn't use the faulty connection while you were trying to replace it with a new one; otherwise, some rows would be lost.

Also, communicating exceptions between threads isn't a standard feature; you have to build this yourself, which isn't trivial. Let's look at the fault-tolerance requirements to see if this approach stands a chance:

- *Fault isolation*—Isolation is made difficult by the fact that many threads can throw exceptions at the same time. You have to add a locking mechanism. It's hard to remove the faulty connection from the chain of objects: the application would have to be rewritten to get this to work. There's no standard support for cutting off the use of the connection in the future, so this needs to be built into the objects manually with some level of indirection.
- *Structure*—The structure that exists between objects is simple and direct. Every object possibly refers to other objects, forming a graph; you can't replace an object in the graph at runtime. You have to create a more involved structure (again, with a level of indirection between the objects).
- *Redundancy*—When an exception is thrown, it goes up the call stack. You may miss the context for deciding which redundant component to use or lose the context of which input data to continue with, as seen in the preceding example.
- *Replacement*—There's no default strategy to replace an object in a call stack; you have to find a way to do it yourself. There are dependency injection frameworks that provide some features to do this, but if any object refers directly to the old instance instead of through the level of indirection, you're in trouble. If you intend to change an object in place, you'd better make sure it works for multithreaded access.
- *Reboot*—Similar to replacement, getting an object back to an initial state is not automatically supported and takes another level of indirection you have to build. All the dependencies of the object must be reintroduced as well. If these dependencies also need to be rebooted (let's say the log processor can also throw a recoverable error), things can get complicated with regard to ordering.
- *Component lifecycle*—An object only exists after it's been constructed or is garbage-collected and removed from memory. Any other mechanism is something you have to build yourself.
- *Suspend*—When you catch an exception and throw it up the stack, the input data or some of its context is lost or unavailable. You have to build something to

buffer the incoming calls while the error is unresolved. If the code is called from many threads, you need to add locks to prevent multiple exceptions from happening at the same time. And you have to find a way to store the associated input data to retry later.

- *Separation of concerns*—The exception-handling code is interwoven with the processing code and can't be defined independently of the processing code.

That doesn't look promising: getting everything to work correctly would be complex and a real pain. It looks like some fundamental features are missing for easily adding fault tolerance to the application:

- Re-creating objects and their dependencies and replacing these in the application structure isn't available as a first-class feature.
- Objects communicate with each other directly, so it's hard to isolate them.
- The fault-recovery code and the functional code are tangled with each other.

Luckily, we have a simpler solution. You've already seen some actor features that can help with these problems. Actors can be (re-)created from `Behaviors` functions and communicate through actor references instead of direct references. In the next section, we look at how actors provide a way to untangle the functional code from the fault-recovery code and how the actor lifecycle makes it possible to suspend and restart actors (without invoking the wrath of the concurrency gods) in the course of recovering from faults.

5.1.2 *Wrap it up and let it crash*

In the previous section, you saw that building a fault-tolerant application with plain old objects and exception handling is complex. Let's look at how actors simplify this task. What should happen when an actor processes a message and encounters an exception? We have discussed why you don't want to graft recovery code into the operational flow, so catching the exception where the business logic resides is not an option.

Instead of catching exceptions in an actor, you let the actor crash. The actor code for handling messages contains only happy-path processing logic and no error handling or fault recovery logic, so it's effectively independent of the recovery process, which keeps things much clearer. The mailbox for a failing actor is suspended until the supervising behavior in the recovery flow has decided what to do with the exception. Messages can still be sent to the mailbox, but they will be stashed.

Figure 5.6 shows a supervisor behavior that takes care of only the recovery actions and an actor that takes care of the domain logic. The two can be mixed by wrapping the actor behavior in the supervisor behavior.

A supervisor not only catches exceptions but also uses the exception to decide what to do with the faulty actors it supervises. The supervising behavior does not attempt to repair the actor's state; it decides what to do with the faulty actor by triggering a

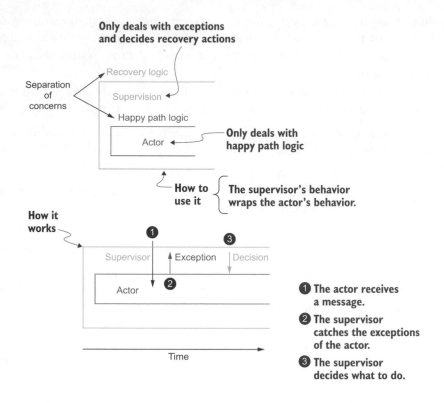

Figure 5.6   Supervisor wrapping an actor's behavior and deciding on a recovery action after an exception

predefined strategy. The supervisor has three options for deciding what to do with the actor:

- *Restart*—The actor must be re-created. After the restart (or reboot, if you will), the actor continues to process messages. The rest of the application uses an `ActorRef[T]` to communicate with the actor and continues to use the same reference and, with it, the same mailbox from which the new actor instance will automatically read new messages.

- *Resume*—The same actor instance should continue to process messages. The exception that would cause the actor to crash is logged only by the supervisor.

- *Stop*—The actor must be terminated. It no longer participates in the processing of messages.

You need to take some special steps to recover the failed message, as you learn later when we look at implementing a restart. Suffice it to say that in most cases, you shouldn't reprocess a message because it probably caused the error in the first place.

An example is the case where the `LogProcessor` encounters a corrupted file or an unparseable line. Reprocessing corrupted files can end up in a so-called *poisoned mailbox*—no other message is ever processed because the corrupted message keeps failing. For this reason, Akka chooses not to leave the failed message in the mailbox after throwing an exception; you can do this yourself if you are absolutely sure the message did not cause the error, as you learn later.

Let's recap the benefits of the let-it-crash approach:

- *Fault isolation*—A supervisor can decide to terminate an actor. The actor is removed from the `ActorSystem`.
- *Structure*—The `ActorSystem` hierarchy of actor references makes it possible to replace actor instances without other actors being affected.
- *Redundancy*—An actor can be replaced by another. In the example of the broken database connection, the fresh actor instance can connect to a different database. The supervisor can also decide to stop the faulty actor and create another type instead. Another option would be to route messages in a load-balanced fashion to many actors, as discussed in chapter 6.
- *Replacement*—An actor can always be re-created from its `Behavior`. A supervisor can decide to replace a faulty actor instance with a fresh one without knowing any details about re-creating the actor.
- *Reboot*—This can be done through a restart.
- *Component lifecycle*—An actor is an active component. It can be started, stopped, and restarted. The next section examines how the actor goes through its lifecycle.
- *Suspend*—When an actor crashes, its mailbox is suspended until the supervisor decides what should happen with the actor.
- *Separation of concerns*—The normal actor message-processing and supervision fault-recovery flows are orthogonal. They can be defined and evolve completely independently of each other.

Remember that the most dangerous actors (actors most likely to crash) should be as far down the hierarchy as possible. Faults that occur far down the hierarchy can be handled or monitored by more actors than faults that occur higher up the hierarchy. If a fault occurs at the top level of the `ActorSystem`, it can lead to a restart of all top-level actors or even to a shutdown of the `ActorSystem`. In the following sections, you learn the coding details of the actor lifecycle and supervision strategies.

5.2 Actor lifecycle events: Signals

An actor as an individual entity is spawned, lives for a while, and eventually stops. In the previous chapters, you have seen examples of how actors start or are initialized. If an actor contains a `Behavior.setup`, its code is executed immediately after spawning. This is its first event in life.

During an actor's lifetime, failures can trigger a restart before the actor finally stops. Regardless of whether an actor is forced to restart or stop due to a failure, it receives a message beforehand: a warning that one of these two actions is imminent.

This is where the `ActorSystem` comes into play, sending these cautionary messages called *signals.* Depending on whether the strategy is a restart or a stop, the system sends a `PreRestart` or `PostStop` signal.

In Akka Typed, an actor not only understands its protocol (its explicit type) but also can deal with signal-type messages. They are an essential part of the `Actor-System`, as they provide a way to deal with failures in the lifecycle of the actor and its children. From now on, let's distinguish between messages and signals. *Messages* refer to the protocol you've seen so far: command/event, request/response. On the other hand, a *signal* refers only to objects of the type `Signal`.

An actor affects its children when it is stopped or restarted. Its children are forced to stop in both cases because by default, the actor's supervision is set to stop. This behavior can be changed through configuration. Examples can be found at the end of the section.

Also be aware that it is not only the parents that influence their children or the supervisor that decides the next behavior of its inner actor. It is also possible for each actor to establish a relationship with another actor by observing when that actor is terminated or fails. This is called *watching*.

Let's go through how supervision deals with the actor's lifecycle and its signals under different strategies.

5.3 Supervision strategies and signals

Certain signals are subproducts of a supervision strategy. `Supervision-Strategy.stop` and `.restart` are intertwined with the signals `PostStop` and `Pre-Restart`.

5.3.1 Uneventful resuming

When a message is processed and throws an exception, the simplest way to deal with it is to resume. With this strategy, the exception is logged, and the message from the mailbox is lost forever.

> **NOTE** It is possible to keep this message, but then you must fix the error by catching both the exception and the message. With this approach, you leave the Akka monitoring model and return to an imperative `try/catch`.

Let's look at how things play out in figure 5.7 if an exception to message X occurs with a resume strategy.

The first part—the initialization you have already seen—is a `Behavior.setup`. This behavior wraps the actor's behavior and provides an initialization that is executed when the actor is spawned.

Figure 5.7 shows that when the actor processes message X, it raises an exception X that is forwarded to its supervisor, which is also a behavior. This exception X has no consequences for the actor because the supervisor applies the resume strategy and therefore selects a `Behavior.same` as the next behavior for the actor.

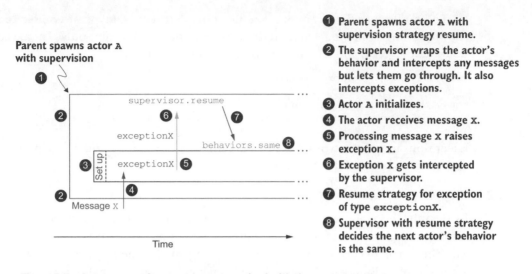

Figure 5.7 Actor processing messages supervised with the resume strategy

This mechanism is another example of how one behavior is composed with another, like matryoshka dolls: the supervisor is nothing more than a wrapping behavior on top of the actor's behavior. It intercepts all messages sent to the actor and wraps them in a try/catch before passing them on, which allows the actor's exceptions to be intercepted. This approach not only takes care of its exceptions but also overrides the return behavior of its inner actor: in figure 5.7, the Behavior.same in step 8.

Overriding the actor's next behavior is necessary because if an exception is thrown within the actor, execution terminates at that point, and the original next behavior of the actor can no longer be reached. You can supervise someBehavior using Behaviors.supervise(someBehavior).

Then you need to add the supervision strategy to use with .onFailure. If you want the actor to maintain the same state it had before the exception was thrown, you must use resume. If you use restart instead, the actor loses its previous state.

The following snippet is an example of how to use the resume strategy:

```
val behavior: Behavior[Command] = ...    ⟵┤ Actor's behavior
```

```
Behaviors.supervise(behavior).onFailure(SupervisorStrategy.resume)
```
Supervision strategy

In this setting, every exception is treated the same. Any throwable exception that is not fatal is handled with the resume strategy. However, if an error is thrown, such as a ThreadDeath or an OutOfMemoryError, the ActorSystem is terminated ungracefully by the JVM. Alternatively, you can set akka.jvm-exit-on-fatal-error = off in the configuration to try to exit the ActorSystem gracefully before terminating the JVM. Chapter 7 covers how configuration works.

To handle specific exceptions, you need to add them as a type of `.onFailure`, as shown in the following snippet. In this example, you catch only `IndexOutOf-BoundException` and its subtypes using a resume strategy:

```
val behavior: Behavior[Command] = ...

Behaviors.supervise(behavior)
    .onFailure[IndexOutOfBoundException](SupervisorStrategy.resume)
```

Exceptions not of this type or its descendants are not caught by this strategy and result in the termination of the actor.

5.3.2 *Stopping and the PostStop signal*

By default, this is the actor supervisor strategy: if you don't explicitly set a supervision strategy, one will be set for you. Stopping is the safest choice because you never know why the error occurred. Was there something in the message combined with the actor's application logic? Could it have been a call to an external service? In previous versions of Akka, restart was a default strategy, but that was too optimistic. After a failure, it is safer to assume that the exception will not go away but will persist.

This strategy has `PostStop` as an associated signal that the actor can use to respond before it is finally stopped. Figure 5.8 shows what happens with the default supervision strategy after a failed message, along with the `PostStop` signal sent to the actor.

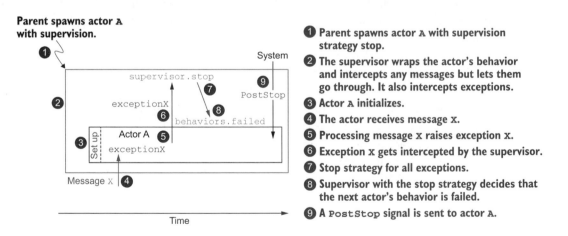

Figure 5.8   An actor with a default supervision strategy is stopped.

In this illustration, the message X in the actor raises an exception X that the supervisor catches. The strategy decides to set `Behaviors.failed` on the actor, and the system sends a `PostStop` signal to the actor to give it one last chance to clean up anything that needs to be closed, such as open connections, files, and expiring resources.

In the following snippet, the `.receiveSignal` method lets you access the `PostStop` signal sent to the actor:

```
import akka.actor.typed.{ Behavior, PostStop }
import akka.actor.typed.scaladsl.Behaviors

object SupervisionExample {

  def apply(): Behavior[String] =
    Behaviors
      .receivePartial[String] {
        ...
      }
      .receiveSignal {
        case (context, PostStop) =>
          context.log.info("about to stop")
          Behaviors.same
      }
}
```

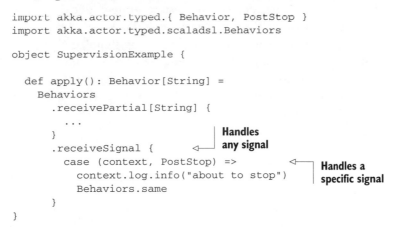

In this example, you can see how the protocol and signals are handled. Signals are handled by

```
def receiveSignal(ctx: TypedActorContext[T], msg: Signal): Behavior[T]
```

which has a very similar signature to

```
def receive(ctx: TypedActorContext[T], msg: T): Behavior[T]
```

which you've already seen for normal messages. The obvious difference is the type of `msg`, but it's also important to note that signals can only be sent from the underlying system to an actor. You can't send a signal to the actor because the signal doesn't belong to its type.

With the stop strategy, no more messages from the mailbox are processed because the next behavior is set to `Behavior.stopped`. After processing the `PostStop` signal, the mailbox and the supervisor are deleted together with the actor. You can set this strategy as follows:

```
val behavior: Behavior[Command] = ...

Behaviors.supervise(behavior).onFailure(SupervisorStrategy.stop)
```

5.3.3   Restart and the PreRestart signal

This strategy creates a new incarnation of the same actor definition after a failed message. The process is transparent to the entire system, as the `ActorRef[T]` used as a facade to communicate with the actor is still valid. Any message sent to this actor is stashed and eventually processed by the new instance of an equivalently functioning actor.

Before it is removed, the supervisor sets the actor's next behavior to `Behavior.failed`, which prevents further messages from being processed. The system notifies the actor with a `PreRestart` signal.

Figure 5.9 shows the process from the receipt of the message that raises the exception to the reincarnation of the actor. Here, actor `A` receives message `X` and raises an exception `X` that the supervisor catches. The restart strategy decides on `Behavior .failed` as the next behavior for the actor, and the system sends `PreRestart` before removing the actor. This signal is similar to the `PostStop` signal, giving you some leeway before the stop. Once this signal is processed, the actor is stopped while its mailbox continues to operate as usual, at least as far as receiving messages is concerned. Immediately after the actor is spawned, if it has a `Behavior.setup`, the code in this method is executed before a new message is processed.

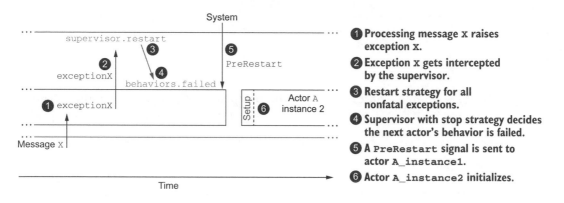

Figure 5.9   Actor with a restart supervision strategy

To make a long story short, the faulty actor receives a `PreRestart` signal and is re-created and reinitialized. For the rest of the system, everything remains the same.

It is important to note that at this point, any state of the actor is lost, at least for a standard actor. Chapter 9 looks at persistent actors that can maintain their state in this and even more difficult scenarios.

Setting up this strategy is as simple as any other:

```
Behaviors.supervise(behavior).onFailure[IndexOutOfBoundException]
➥(SupervisorStrategy.restart)
```

In addition to this strategy, a common configuration is added when monitoring the restart: `.restartWithBackoff`. In situations where the exception is thrown by an external component, such as an HTTP server or a database, it makes sense not to try to reconnect every millisecond. A backoff restart configuration waits a certain amount of time ranging from a minimum to a maximum and increases the waiting exponentially each time it receives an exception.

You also want to avoid stress on the external service when it comes back online. When many actors restart, too many connections can be requested almost simultaneously—even with a backoff strategy—resulting in a load spike for the resource. To avoid this, a randomizer parameter is added to this configuration. The signature is as follows, and an example is shown at the end of the next section:

```
def restartWithBackoff(minBackoff: FiniteDuration, maxBackoff:
    FiniteDuration,
      randomFactor: Double): BackoffSupervisorStrategy
```

You can mix these strategies to create a custom strategy: a combination of multiple supervisions depending on the catch exceptions.

5.3.4 *Custom strategy*

You've seen the basics, but usually you don't want to handle all exceptions with the same strategy. The following snippet shows a more realistic scenario that combines different strategies depending on the exception. These exceptions are handled by different supervision strategies. To combine these strategies, you use the composition principle you've already seen, with one behavior inside the other:

```
Behavior.supervise(
  Behavior.supervise(
    Behaviors.supervise(         Behavior[T]
      behavior              ⟵⎯  goes here.
    ).onFailure[ExceptionX](SupervisorStrategy.resume)
  ).onFailure[ExceptionY](SupervisorStrategy.restart)
).onFailure[ExceptionZ](SupervisorStrategy.stop)
```

If you think you're better off without handling exception Z, you're right. SupervisorStrategy.stop is by default the strategy that handles every nonfatal exception.

For readability, you can create a single function to use with your behavior with all these strategies (backoff included):

```
package faulttolerance3

object DbWriter {
  ...

  def supervisorStrategy(behavior: Behavior[Command]): Behavior[Command] =
    Behaviors
      .supervise {
        Behaviors
          .supervise(behavior)
          .onFailure[UnexpectedColumnsException]
          .SupervisorStrategy.resume
      }
      .onFailure[DbBrokenConnectionException](SupervisorStrategy
        .restartWithBackoff(minBackoff = 3, maxBackoff = 30, randomFactor =
          0.1)
        .withResetBackoffAfter(15))

}
```

You use the function like this: supervisorStrategy(someBehavior).

5.4   *Watching signals from an actor*

An actor can watch another actor and be notified when the observed actor stops. The signals a watching actor can receive are `Terminated`, its subclass `ChildFailed`, or a custom class. A custom class is equivalent to `Terminated` but contains more information that may be relevant to the listener. `Terminated` or `ChildFailed` messages contain only the `ActorRef` of the watched actor.

A stopped actor sends the `Terminated` signal if it was not stopped directly due to an exception; otherwise, it sends `ChildFailed`. Note that `ChildFailed` is a subtype of `Terminated`, so the order is important when pattern matching. You must match the `ChildFailed` subtype first; otherwise, the `ChildFailed` signal would also match `Terminated`.

Let's relate this to the logging application at the beginning of the chapter. A file-monitoring (file watcher) process tracks the added files and tells another component to process them, as shown in figure 5.10.

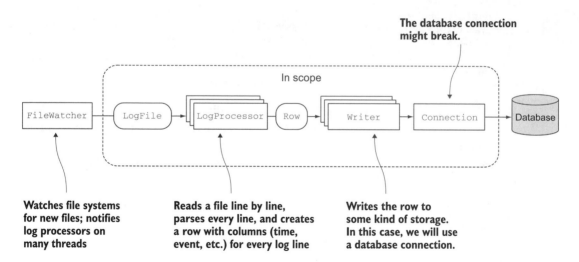

Figure 5.10   Processing logs from the file watcher, to the log processor, to the writer, and to the database

Let's write a much simpler version of file watcher to see how watching and signals go together. This `SimplifiedFileWatcher` logs a `Terminated` message when the log processor explicitly stops, not because of an exception. The file watcher can watch any actor included in the `Watch` message and receives the `Terminated` signal if a watched actor stops.

```
import akka.actor.typed.{ ActorRef, Behavior, ChildFailed, Terminated }
import akka.actor.typed.scaladsl.{ Behaviors }
```

```
object SimplifiedFileWatcher {

  sealed trait Command
  final case class Watch(ref: ActorRef[String]) extends Command

  def apply(): Behavior[Command] =
    Behaviors
      .receive[Command] { (context, message) =>
        message match {
          case Watch(ref) =>
            context.watch(ref)          ◁──┐  Watches any actor,
            Behaviors.same                  │  whether a child or not
        }
      }
      .receiveSignal {
        case (context, Terminated(ref)) =>     ◁──┐  Deals with the situation when
          context.log.info("terminated")          │  the watched actor stops
          Behaviors.same
      }
}
```

You can prove that this works as expected with the following test. To do so, you define a log processor that stops when it receives a "stop" message and treats any other string message as unhandled, which returns `Behavior.same` and logs that the message was not handled. This is done with `.receiveMessagePartial`:

```
Class MonitoringExample ... {

  "Among two actors, NO parent/child related, the watcher" must {
    "be able to be notified with Terminated when watched actor stops" in {
      val watcher = spawn(SimplifiedFileWatcher())
      val logprocessor = spawn(Behaviors.receiveMessagePartial[String] {
        case "stop" =>
          Behaviors.stopped                        Watches the log
      })                                           processor actor

      watcher.ref ! SimplifiedFileWatcher.Watch(logprocessor.ref)   ◁──┘

      LoggingTestKit.info("terminated").expect {   ◁──┐  Proves the message "terminated"
        logprocessor ! "stop"   ◁──┐  Sends "stop"     │  is logged by the watcher
      }                            │  to the actor
    }

  ...
}
```

Here, the simplified actor representing the log processor is watched by including it in the `Watch` message when it is sent to the watcher. Then a "stop" message is sent to the log processor, which triggers the `Terminated` signal to the watcher and thus the logging of "terminated".

The last important thing you need to know is that if an actor is watching another actor but has not implemented a `receiveSignal`, it produces a `DeathPact-Exception` if the watched actor terminates or fails. There are two possibilities: either you forgot to take care of this situation or you did it on purpose. If you decide not to handle the signal, you implicitly associate the monitored actor's termination/failure event with the monitoring actor's strategy, allowing the exception to bubble up.

5.5   *Back to the initial use case*

With all these ideas and techniques for monitoring and supervision, let's return to the previous log-processing application. We look at two possible designs for this application and an implementation sketch.

5.5.1   *Supervisor hierarchy initial design*

In this first design, the initial actor, the guardian—called `LogProcessing-Guardian`—creates all the actors in the application and connects them directly to each other via `ActorRefs`. This is shown in figure 5.11.

> **NOTE**   The classes and objects for this section can be found in the `fault-tolerance1` package.

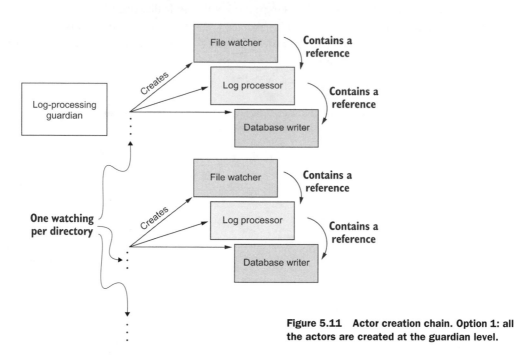

Figure 5.11   Actor creation chain. Option 1: all the actors are created at the guardian level.

Each type of actor knows the `ActorRef` of the next actor to which it sends messages. The file watcher knows about the log processor, which in turn knows about the database writer. Each actor must remain alive and always refer to the next actor in the chain. If an actor in this chain stops, the actor that references it will start sending messages to `deadLetters`, breaking the application. The stop strategy is not an option here; a restart must be used so the same `ActorRef` can be used repeatedly. Actors must be monitored and respawned as needed. Figure 5.12 shows how things are arranged in this setup.

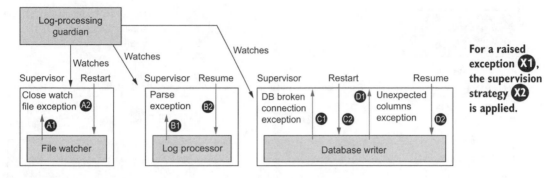

Figure 5.12   **Supervision and monitoring for the Akka logging app with creation option 1**

A disadvantage is that the guardian must collect the knowledge of the entire application. Monitoring the file watcher and the database writer means the `LogProcessing-Guardian` must contain the logic to respond to their signals. If the file watcher is stopped on an unexpected exception, the log processor and the database writer are not stopped because they are not children in the file watcher hierarchy. Let's try again with a different design.

5.5.2   *Supervision hierarchy alternative design*

Figure 5.13 shows a different approach, a simpler one. The `LogProcessingGuardian` does not create all actors; the file watcher creates one log processor per directory, and the log processor creates a database writer.

> **NOTE**   The classes and objects for this section can be found in the `fault-tolerance2` package.

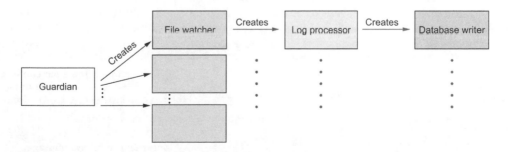

Figure 5.13   **Actor creation chain. Option 2: the guardian only creates the file watcher.**

The normal and recovery processes are still defined separately. The difference is that the file watcher and log processor now also create actors, while the process of messages remains the same (see figure 5.14).

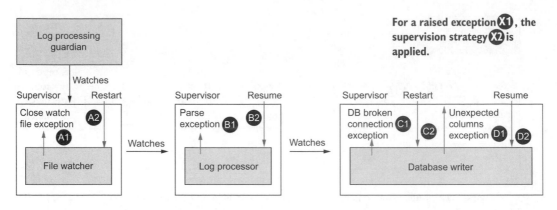

Figure 5.14   Supervision and monitoring for the Akka logging app with creation option 2

The advantage of this approach is that the log processor can now watch the database writer and decide what to do when it receives a `Terminated` or `ChildFailed` signal. It can make an informed decision and, for example, create a new database writer with an alternative URL to a completely different database node.

The `LogProcessingGuardian` no longer has to monitor the entire application, only the `FileWatcher` actors. If the `LogProcessingGuardian` monitors both the file watcher and the database writer, you must distinguish between the signals of a terminated file watcher and a database writer, resulting in less isolated code to handle problems of the different components.

SKETCHING THE DESIGN

Let's sketch this design—the better one—in an implementation that compiles. Listing 5.2 shows the `App` and `LogProcessingGuardian`. This design follows creation chain option 2: the guardian creates one file watcher per directory. Each file watcher creates one log processor per file, and each log processor processes one file. The first actor is the `LogProcessingGuardian`, to which `App` passes the directories to be processed.

```
Listing 5.2   Building the supervisor hierarchy
```

Input. These directories could come from args using **Main** instead of extending from **App.**

```
object LogProcessingImprovedDesign extends App {

  val directories = Vector("file:///source1/", "file:///source2/")

  val guardian = ActorSystem[Nothing](
    LogProcessingGuardian(directories),
    "log-processing-app")
}
```

Not meant to receive messages. There's a Nothing protocol.

```
object LogProcessingGuardian {

  def apply(directories: Vector[String]) =
    Behaviors
      .setup[Nothing] { context =>                    ◁─── Not meant to receive messages.
        directories.foreach { directory =>                 There's a Nothing protocol.

          val fileWatcher: ActorRef[FileWatcher.Command] =
            context.spawnAnonymous(FileWatcher(directory))
          context.watch(fileWatcher)              ◁─── Monitors each
        }                                              file watcher
        Behaviors
          .receiveMessage[Nothing] {
            case _: Any =>
              Behaviors.ignore
          }
          .receiveSignal {
            case (context, Terminated(actorRef)) =>
              ...                    ◁─── Checks that not all file watchers
              Behaviors.same              are terminated. If no file watchers
          }                               are left, shuts down the system.
      }
}
```

NOTE In this example, you create an actor with spawnAnonymous. This method is the same as spawn, but you don't need to give the actor a name since a random name is created for you. For modeling, this is a good option because it is simpler. However, in a project that will be deployed and used, it is recommended to use spawn and give the actor a name so you can make sense of it when debugging the application.

Before we look at the FileWatcher implementation, here are the various exceptions that this application considers.

Listing 5.3 Exceptions in the log-processing application

```
@SerialVersionUID(1L)
class ClosedWatchServiceException(msg: String)     ◁─── FileWatcherCapabilities
    extends Exception(msg)                               exception
    with Serializable

@SerialVersionUID(1L)
class ParseException(msg: String, val file: File)  ◁─── LogProcessor's
    extends Exception(msg)                               parser exception
    with Serializable

@SerialVersionUID(1L)
class DbBrokenConnectionException(msg: String)     ◁─── DbWriter's
    extends Exception(msg)                               connector exceptions
    with Serializable

@SerialVersionUID(1L)
class UnexpectedColumnsException(msg: String)      ◁─── LogProcessor's specific
    extends Exception(msg)                               parser exception
    with Serializable
```

These exceptions must be serializable because they must be sent over the wire. It is useful to note that all actors must also be serializable, but you don't have to take care of it. Akka does it for you.

Listing 5.4 shows the file watcher with the proposed design that starts monitoring the directory at initialization—using `FileWatchingAbilities`. It creates and monitors a log processor that simplifies monitoring and provides the ability to interrupt the cascade of failures. This solves both disadvantages mentioned in the initial design.

The file watcher extends `FileListeningAbilities`, which takes care of the specifics of a file-listening API, such as listening to a directory and registering the files in it. This provides more freedom in composition, code isolation, and testability.

Another important feature is that the file watcher restarts and creates a new instance of the actor if file listening fails. However, if another exception occurs, it stops not only itself but also its children: that is, its child log processor and its grandchild database writer.

Listing 5.4 File watcher sketch implementation

```
object FileWatcher extends FileListeningAbilities {

  sealed trait Command
  final case class NewFile(file: File, timeAdded: Long) extends Command
  final case class FileModified(file: File, timeAdded: Long) extends Command

  def apply(directory: String): Behavior[Command] =
    Behaviors
      .supervise {
        Behaviors.setup[Command] { context =>        Starts listening to the directory,
          ...                                        spawns, and watches a log processor
          ...
          ...              When a new file is in the
          Behaviors        directory, receives NewFile
            .receiveMessage[Command] {
              case NewFile(file, _) => ...           Sends a file to
              ...                                    the log processor
              case FileModified(file, _) => ...
              ...              Sends an event to
            }                  the log processor
            .receiveSignal {
              case (_, Terminated(ref)) => ...
              ...              Stop itself as the log processor
            }                  will be unresumable
        }
      }
      .onFailure[ClosedWatchServiceException](SupervisorStrategy.restart)
}

trait FileListeningAbilities {        Provides the file
                                      listing API
  def register(uri: String) = ...
}
```

When a modified file is in the directory, receives FileModified

Supervision restart. After restart, work can be duplicated; deduplication is out of the scope.

The log processor in listing 5.5 creates a database writer and monitors it as it parses files. The supervision ignores exceptions of type `ParseException` by resuming when a line in the file cannot be parsed.

When the log processor receives a termination message, it may attempt to point to another URL to re-create a database writer. This actor may find that all of its available URLs have failed and stop itself when it runs out of options.

Listing 5.5   Log processor sketch implementation

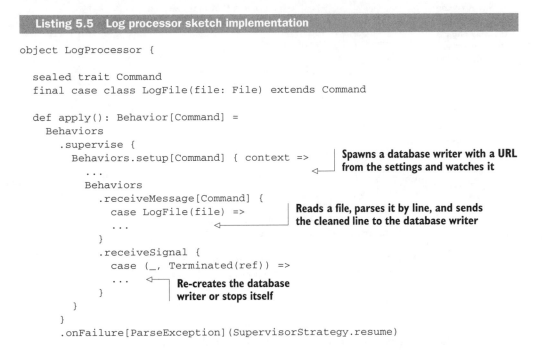

```
object LogProcessor {

  sealed trait Command
  final case class LogFile(file: File) extends Command

  def apply(): Behavior[Command] =
    Behaviors
      .supervise {
        Behaviors.setup[Command] { context =>       Spawns a database writer with a URL
          ...                                        from the settings and watches it
          Behaviors
            .receiveMessage[Command] {
              case LogFile(file) =>                  Reads a file, parses it by line, and sends
                ...                                  the cleaned line to the database writer
            }
            .receiveSignal {
              case (_, Terminated(ref)) =>
                ...          Re-creates the database
            }                writer or stops itself
        }
      }
      .onFailure[ParseException](SupervisorStrategy.resume)
```

The log processor is created from each file that the file watcher finds in each directory. This log processor is now responsible for creating a database writer, monitoring it, and re-creating it as needed.

Finally, listing 5.6 shows the `DbWriter` actor, the last chain of the hierarchy. This actor receives a parsed row and converts it into the schema required by the database. In case of a restart or stop, it closes its connection to avoid resource leaking. Depending on which exception `UnexpectedColumnsException` or `DbBrokenConnectionException` throws, the actor resumes or restarts. Both strategies are combined in a single function for better readability.

Listing 5.6   `DbWriter` sketch implementation

```
object DbWriter {

  sealed trait Command
  final case class Line(time: Long, message: String, messageType: String)
    extends Command
```

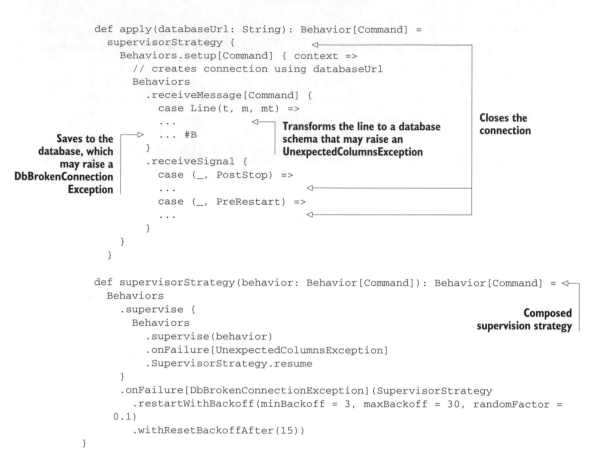

```
def apply(databaseUrl: String): Behavior[Command] =
  supervisorStrategy {                        ⟵──────────────────────┐
    Behaviors.setup[Command] { context =>                           │
      // creates connection using databaseUrl                       │
      Behaviors                                                     │
        .receiveMessage[Command] {                                  │
          case Line(t, m, mt) =>                                    │
            ...                        ⟵──┐                          │
            ... #B                        │                          │
        }                                 │                          │
        .receiveSignal {                                            │
          case (_, PostStop) =>                                     │
            ...                               ⟵──────────────┐       │
          case (_, PreRestart) =>                            │       │
            ...                                 ⟵─────────────┘       │
        }
    }
  }

def supervisorStrategy(behavior: Behavior[Command]): Behavior[Command] = ⟵─┐
  Behaviors                                                                │
    .supervise {                                                           │
      Behaviors                                                            │
        .supervise(behavior)                                               │
        .onFailure[UnexpectedColumnsException]                             │
        .SupervisorStrategy.resume                                         │
    }                                                                      │
    .onFailure[DbBrokenConnectionException](SupervisorStrategy             │
      .restartWithBackoff(minBackoff = 3, maxBackoff = 30, randomFactor =
  0.1)
      .withResetBackoffAfter(15))
}
```

Saves to the database, which may raise a DbBrokenConnection Exception

Transforms the line to a database schema that may raise an UnexpectedColumnsException

Closes the connection

Composed supervision strategy

If the database connection breaks, the database writer is re-created. The database writer creates a new connection in `.setup` using the `databaseUrl`. The restart waits a few seconds to avoid any database writer accessing the database when the database is unresponsive and probably overloaded. For the same reason, the backoff strategy waits a bit longer at each restart until the maximum waiting time is reached. There is also some randomness to prevent all database writers from performing a backoff at the same time. If no backoff has occurred after 15 seconds, the next backoff returns to the minimum.

The processed `Line` may throw an `UnexpectedColumnsException`, but this failure is related to the data, not the actor's state or context. The actor ignores this failure and logs some information about it, while the behavior remains the same. In short, the database writer logs and resumes.

Summary

- Fault tolerance is one of the most exciting aspects of Akka, and it's a critical component in the toolkit's approach to concurrency.
- The philosophy of "let it crash" is not a doctrine of ignoring the possible malfunctions that may occur or the toolkit swooping in and healing any faults.

- You need to anticipate recovery requirements, but the tools to deliver them without meeting a catastrophic end (or having to write a ton of code) are unparalleled.
- Because the actor model is built on messages, even when an actor goes away, the rest can continue to function.
- Supervisor strategies can resume, stop, or restart; the choice is yours, given the requirements in each case. The default is the stop strategy.
- Fault tolerance is incomplete if you don't have clustering. Otherwise, you have no protection against catastrophic failures.

Discovery and routing 6

In this chapter, you learn how an actor can find another actor that is not its child. For example, suppose a manager creates workers to parse files, and later you develop a statistics collector that is only concerned with how many workers there are and how much work they do. If the collector is not embedded when the workers are created, how can it find the workers to request the information it needs? In other words, how can you add this new collector without tangling it up with the manager/worker part?

In Akka Typed, this problem has been solved with the *receptionist*. The idea is simple: the receptionist registers and subscribes actors to a specific key. Thus, all subscribers to that key are notified when a registration occurs.

You also learn how to send messages to actors behind a proxy, called *routers*. Akka has two built-in routers, but you don't always have to use them. In some cases, the best choice is to use simple actors as intermediaries.

> **NOTE** The source code for this chapter is available at www.manning.com/
> books/akka-in-action-second-edition or https://github.com/franciscolopezsan
> cho/akka-topics/tree/main/chapter06. You can find the contents of any snip-
> pet or listing in the .scala file with the same name as the class, object, or trait.

6.1 Discovery: The receptionist

The receptionist is an extension, meaning it is a class with only one instance in the
`ActorSystem`. The receptionist is the mechanism that allows actors to register for
a specific key so that any actor can request notifications for that key. For the key,
you need to define the `ServiceKey`; and to request notifications, you need the
`context.system.receptionist.Receptionist`.

Let's say you have an application that lets you register customers in a hotel, and
you want to inform the hotel concierges about high-end registrations so they can pre-
pare for VIP clients. This is implemented with a `HotelConcierge` actor subscribing
to a key called `goldenKey`. VIP guests register for this key when they reach the hotel,
and the subscribed `HotelConcierge` receives the list of registered guests and—to
simplify the example—prints in the console only the guest's name.

The concierge `goldenKey` is a `ServiceKey`. This is a kind of key specific to the
receptionist API, and it needs a name (`concierge-key`), as you can see in the following snippet. This name, in combination with its type, makes the service key unique.
That is, two service keys with the same type but different names are two different keys
for the receptionist:

```
import akka.actor.typed.receptionist.ServiceKey
...
object HotelConcierge {

  val goldenKey = ServiceKey[VIPGuest.Command]("concierge-key")    ⟵  Key name that makes
  ...                                                                  the key unique
}
```

When a VIP guest registers at the hotel, the person at the front desk enters the guest's
data into the hotel app. This creates the actor representing the guest and sends
the `EnterHotel` message to that actor, which triggers its registration to the concierge `goldenKey` by sending a `Register` message to the `context.system`
`.receptionist`, as shown in the following snippet. Note that the `Register` message
requires a `ServiceKey` and the reference to the actor to be registered:

```
import akka.actor.typed.scaladsl.Behaviors
import akka.actor.typed.receptionist.{ Receptionist, ServiceKey }

object VIPGuest {

  sealed trait Command
  final case object EnterHotel extends Command
```

```
def apply() = Behaviors.receive[Command] { (context, message) =>
  message match {
    case EnterHotel =>
      context.system.receptionist ! Receptionist
        .Register(HotelConcierge.goldenKey, context.self)
      Behaviors.same
  }
}}
```

Registers to HotelConcierge .goldenKey on entering

On the other hand, the concierge actor subscribes to the key instead of registering, but it needs an adapter because the notification it receives does not belong to its protocol. It belongs to the receptionist API and is an `akka.actor.typed.receptionist` `.Receptionist.Listing`. The adapter needs to wrap this message in the following protocol, which belongs to the concierge:

```
sealed trait Command
private final case class ListingResponse(listing: Receptionist.Listing)
    extends Command
```

Because `ListingResponse` contains only a `Receptionist.Listing`, you can directly use the `context.messageAdapter` to map the two:

```
val listingNotificationAdapter =
    context.messageAdapter[Receptionist.Listing](ListingResponse)
```

With the adapter, the concierge can now subscribe by sending a `Subscribe` message with the `goldenKey`:

```
context.system.receptionist ! Receptionist
  .Subscribe(goldenKey, listingNotificationAdapter)
```

Finally, when the concierge receives the registration list, it logs each guest's name. This happens every time a guest registers. You can see the whole actor in the following listing.

Listing 6.1   `HotelConcierge` actor

```
import akka.actor.typed.scaladsl.{ Behaviors }
import akka.actor.typed.receptionist.{ Receptionist, ServiceKey }

object HotelConcierge {

  val goldenKey = ServiceKey[VIPGuest.Command]("concierge-key")

  sealed trait Command
  private final case class ListingResponse(listing: Receptionist.Listing)
      extends Command

  def apply() = Behaviors.setup[Command] { context =>
    val listingNotificationAdapter =
      context.messageAdapter[Receptionist.Listing](ListingResponse)
```

The key, attached to the guest protocol

Adapter message to receive the message from the receptionist

Adapter function to translate the message from the receptionist

```
    context.system.receptionist ! Receptionist
      .Subscribe(goldenKey, listingNotificationAdapter)          ◁──┐ Subscription
                                                                     │ to the key
    Behaviors.receiveMessage {
      case ListingResponse(goldenKey.Listing(listings)) =>       ◁──┐ Message from
        listings.foreach { actor =>                                 │ the receptionist
          context.log.info(s"${actor.path.name} is in")
        }
        Behaviors.same
      }
    }
  }
```

Let's test that this works as expected. Each time a guest enters the hotel, the list of subscribed guests is sent to each concierge.

Listing 6.2   Using the receptionist

```
import org.scalatest.wordspec.AnyWordSpecLike
import org.scalatest.matchers.should.Matchers

class ReceptionistUsageSpec extends ScalaTestWithActorTestKit
    with AnyWordSpecLike with Matchers with LogCapturing {

  "An actor subscribed to a ServiceKey " should {
    "get notified about all the actors each time an actor registers" in {
      val guest = spawn(VIPGuest(), "Mr.Wick")
      spawn(HotelConcierge())
      LoggingTestKit.info("Mr.Wick is in").expect {
        guest ! VIPGuest.EnterHotel
      }
      val guest2 = spawn(VIPGuest (), "Ms.Perkins ")
      LoggingTestKit.info("Ms.Perkins is in").expect {
        LoggingTestKit.info("Mr.Wick is in").expect {
          guest2 ! Guest.EnterHotel
        }
      }
    }
  }
}
```

Subscribes to the key on creation → (points to `spawn(HotelConcierge())`)

Registers to the key when a guest enters the hotel (points to `guest ! VIPGuest.EnterHotel` and `guest2 ! Guest.EnterHotel`)

You can test this by running the following in the root directory of the Git repository:

```
$ sbt "chapter06/testOnly *ReceptionistUsageSpec"
```

The receptionist API allows you to `Find` registered actors as an active retrieval mechanism, not a passive one like the subscription you just saw. `Find` is a one-time message that returns all currently registered actors at that time. You use it in the same way as the subscription: you need an adapter and the service key. Using the same example, you can find the registered actors as follows:

```
context.system.receptionist ! Receptionist
  .Find(HotelConcierge.goldenKey, listingResponseAdapter)
```

You can deregister an actor by sending a `Deregister` message with the same signature. This way, you can deregister a guest when they leave the hotel:

```
object VIPGuest {

  sealed trait Command
  final case object EnterHotel extends Command
  final case object LeaveHotel extends Command

  def apply() = Behaviors.receive[Command] { (context, message) =>
    message match {
      case EnterHotel => ...

      case LeaveHotel =>
        context.system.receptionist ! Receptionist
          .Deregister(HotelDesk.goldenKey, context.self)     <── Actor requesting
        Behaviors.same                                           deregistration
}}}
```

When an actor stops, it is automatically deregistered. So if the actor no longer plays a role in your application after leaving the hotel, stopping will do. You can do the following:

```
object VIPGuest {

  ...

  def apply() = Behaviors.receiveMessage[Command] {
      case EnterHotel => ...
      case LeaveHotel => Behaviors.stopped
}}}
```

> **DEFINITION**   *Routers* are proxies that forward messages to actors.

Routers are essential to scale up or out: for example, if you want to scale up a task and create multiple instances of the same task. Routers help you do this by forwarding messages to these tasks and splitting the work. At the beginning of the next section, you learn three reasons to use routers to control message flow:

- Performance
- Message content
- State

Then you learn how to create routing processes for each of these patterns. If you need a routing solution for performance or scaling reasons, you should use Akka's built-in routers, because they are optimized.

6.2   *The built-in integration router pattern*

First, let's examine the integration router pattern in general—when it's applicable and how it works—before we get into individual router implementations. When you move on to the implementation, you start with the commonly known pattern for routing various messages through a necessary series of steps. Let's look at an example of a high-way speeding ticket.

In this example, a camera takes photos, a processor extracts data from them, and a validator notifies the highway patrol when the speed limit is exceeded. This flow is divided into three parts that represent different router patterns. Let's start with the camera. A camera takes photos and sends them in batches to multiple photo processors. This type of routing is all about performance. Figure 6.1 shows how the camera divides the work.

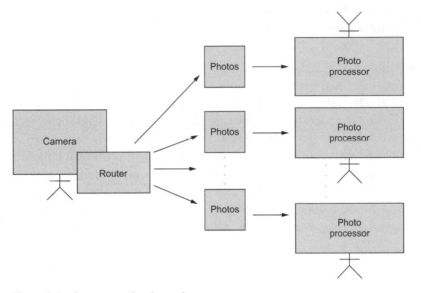

Figure 6.1   Camera routing for performance

Depending on whether a photo processor is busy, it processes the photos or sends a message to the camera to inform it that the photos could not be processed. If it is available, it analyses the photos and extracts the license plate, speed, and so on. Figure 6.2 shows how the photo processor reacts differently depending on its state. The reason for using this router is to control the state of the message flow.

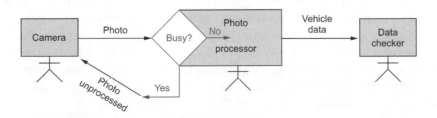

Figure 6.2   Photo processor routing based on state

Finally, the data checker checks the provided data and alerts the highway patrol if it detects a violation, such as excessive speed. Otherwise, it sends a message to the camera to delete the photos. This is *content-based routing* (figure 6.3).

As mentioned, there are three reasons to construct logic that controls message flow in your applications. Let's dig a little deeper into them:

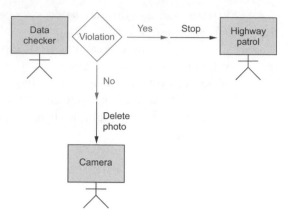

Figure 6.3   Data checker routing based on content

- *Performance*—If a task takes a lot of time and you have many such tasks, although they can be processed in parallel, they should be split between different instances. In the speeding ticket example, drivers can be evaluated in parallel because all the processing logic is contained exclusively in each recorded case.
- *Content of the received message*—The message has an attribute (in this example, speed). Depending on its value, the message should go to one task or another.
- *State of the router*—For example, if the photo processor is busy, all new messages must be sent back to the camera; otherwise, they should be processed normally.

In all cases, the application must decide based on a certain logic which task (actor) it should send a message to. The possible actors a router can choose from are called *routees* in Akka.

In this chapter, you learn about various approaches to routing messages and some other Akka mechanisms that are useful for implementing routers and your own processes. One example is processing messages differently depending on the state of an actor that receives them. The next section covers routing by message content or the actor state.

6.3   *Balancing load using built-in routers*

One of the reasons for using an integration router is to distribute the load among different actors and improve system performance when many messages are being processed. These can be local actors (scale up) or actors on remote servers (scale out). A key Akka argument for using scaling is the ease of routing.

In the camera example, the detection step—analyzing the photo—takes a relatively long time to process. To be able to parallelize this task, you use a router. In figure 6.1 (reproduced here for you as figure 6.4), you see that the camera—as a router—can send the message to one of the photo processors.

When the camera receives a message, it decides which photo processors it should send the batch of photos to. This decision is based on a *routing strategy*.

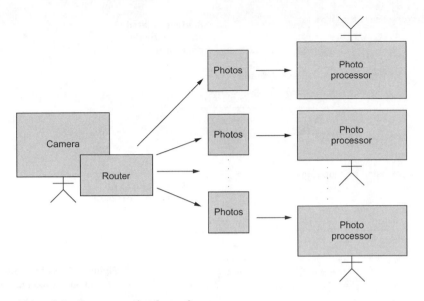

Figure 6.4 Camera routing for performance

DEFINITION A *routing strategy* is the logic that selects the final destination of a sent message.

You can use Akka's built-in router functionality to implement this type of router. In Akka, a separation is made between the router, which contains the routing logic, and the actor, which represents the router. The router logic decides which routee is selected and can be used within an actor to make a selection. The router actor is self-contained and uses the routing logic to manage the routees.

The built-in routers are available in two variants:

- *Pool*—These routers manage the routees. They are responsible for creating routees and removing them from the list when they stop. A pool can be used when all routees are created in place and do not yet exist. It is important to know that—like any other actor—a routee is stopped by default, but usually it is better to set it to restart.
- *Group*—The group routers do not create routees. The routees must be created somewhere in the application, and the group router uses the receptionist to find them. A group router can be used if you need to control the lifecycles of the routees, meaning where and how they are instantiated.

Figure 6.5 shows the actor hierarchy of routees and the differences between using a pool and a group router. With a pool, the routees are children of the router, whereas with a group router, routees can be children of any other actor. They only need to be up and running.

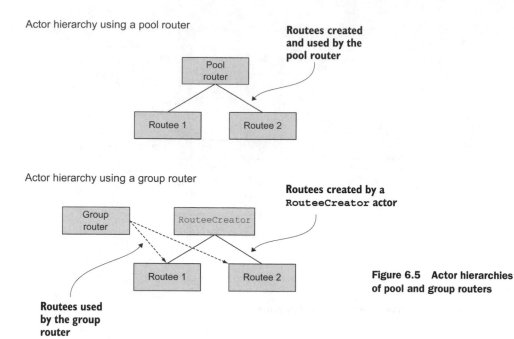

Figure 6.5 Actor hierarchies of pool and group routers

Akka built-in routers have different routing strategies, summarized in table 6.1.

Table 6.1 Router logic options

Logic	Description
RoundRobinRouting	The first received message goes to the first routee, the next message goes to the second routee, and so on. When all routees have received a message, everything starts again from the beginning.
RandomRouting	Each received message goes to a randomly selected routee.
ConsistentHashing	A consistent hashing is applied to the message to select a routee. This algorithm is especially useful for distributing the work evenly among routees whose number may change over time.
withBroadcastPredicate	A message is sent to all routees that satisfy a predicate function T => Boolean, where T is the type of message sent.

In sections 6.3.2 and 6.3.4, you learn more about the options and how to use them. These options are used in pool routers and group routers.

6.3.1 *Akka pool router*

The pool router creates and manages routees for you. You do not have to explicitly create the actors to which it forwards messages. A pool can be used if all routees exist only in the router's domain and no further interaction with them is expected. For simple routees, a pool is a good choice.

To define a pool, you specify the number of instances and the behavior the pool needs to instantiate. Then you `.spawn` the pool like any other actor. It is an `Actor-Ref` you can send messages to, as you can see in the following example (note that the type of the router must be the same as its routees):

```scala
import akka.actor.typed.scaladsl.{ PoolRouter, Routers }

object Manager {

  def apply(behavior: Behavior[String]) =
    Behaviors.setup[Unit] { context =>
      val routingBehavior: Behavior[String] =
          Routers.pool(poolSize = 4)(behavior)
      val router: ActorRef[String] =
          context.spawn(routingBehavior, "test-pool")

    (0 to 10).foreach { n =>
      router ! "hi"
    }
  }
}
```

Sets the pool size and the behavior to instantiate

Spawns the pool

Sends messages to the router and thus to its routees

This example is tested in `PoolRoutersSpec.scala` in a test called "send messages in a round-robin fashion," if you want to play around with it.

Remember that the router can send a message to a child that has stopped. When a router's child stops, a `Terminated(child)` message is sent to its router. But before this signal arrives, the router may already be sending a message to that child. In this case, the message is forwarded to `deadLetters`.

When the pool router is terminated, all routees are also terminated due to the parent-child relationship. Conversely, when all the children stop, the router also stops.

It is good practice to provide a restart strategy for the routees used by a pool router. When a routee fails, it is stopped by default, which causes the pool router to reduce its performance. The pool router creates the routees but cannot recover them after a failure.

6.3.2 Changing strategies

The default strategy of a pool is round-robin. To change to a random strategy, add `withRandomRouting()`:

```scala
val routingBehavior: PoolRouter[String] =
    Routers
        .pool(poolSize = poolSize)(behavior)
        .withRandomRouting()
```

Strategy setting

To select broadcasting, for example, for messages of a certain importance, you need the following:

```scala
val routingBehavior: PoolRouter[String] =
    Routers
        .pool(poolSize = poolSize)(behavior)
        .withBroadcastPredicate(violation => violation.level > 5)
```

Strategy selection

This can be used by the data checker when it detects a serious violation by a driver that you want to broadcast to all highway patrol officers.

Instead of filtering by a property of the message content, you can also filter by the message type, provided there is a behavior like the following:

```
object HighWayPatrol {
  sealed trait Command
  final case class Violation(plateNumber: String) extends Command
  final case class WithinLimits(plateNumber: String) extends Command    Protocol

  ...
}
```

You can broadcast each violation message to all patrol officers as follows:

```
object BroadcastingChecker {
  ...
  val dataCheckerRouter: PoolRouter[HighWayPatrol.Command] =
      Routers
        .pool(poolSize = 4)(behavior)
        .withBroadcastPredicate(msg =>              Message
          msg.isInstanceOf[HighWayPatrol.Violation])    type filter

  ...
}
```

Pool routers are easy to use, but sometimes they are too limiting and you want more flexibility and control over when and where routees are created. The alternative is to create the routees yourself and assign them to a group router.

6.3.3   *Akka group router*

A group router is (in some ways) the same as a pool router. It forwards messages to the routees just like a pool router does. The difference lies in the relation with its routees: you instantiate the routees outside the router and register them to the receptionist with a service key. Then, to create a group router, you only need to use the routees' service key. This way, the router can find the routees via the receptionist and send messages. By default, the strategy in a group router is `withRandomRouting`.

Creating a group router is easier than creating a pool router. You just need to pass the `ServiceKey` of the routees. You don't have to specify the number of routees because that is defined by the routees registered with that key.

Let's say you have a photo processor like the following:

```
object PhotoProcessor {
  val key = ServiceKey[String]("photo-processor-key")
  def apply(): Behavior[String] = ...
}
```

You can create a camera that can send the content of its photos to a pool of Photo-Processors like this:

```
object Camera {
```

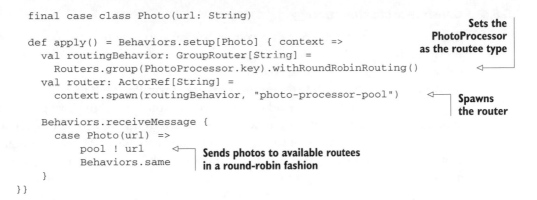

```
final case class Photo(url: String)

def apply() = Behaviors.setup[Photo] { context =>        Sets the
  val routingBehavior: GroupRouter[String] =             PhotoProcessor
    Routers.group(PhotoProcessor.key).withRoundRobinRouting()   as the routee type
  val router: ActorRef[String] =
    context.spawn(routingBehavior, "photo-processor-pool")    Spawns
                                                              the router
  Behaviors.receiveMessage {
    case Photo(url) =>
        pool ! url        Sends photos to available routees
        Behaviors.same    in a round-robin fashion
  }
}}
```

Note that a photo's URL cannot reach a `PhotoProcessor` actor until at least one is registered.

You can put all this together and prove that a photo processor receives photos from a camera by running a test like the following.

Listing 6.3   Testing that the camera distributes the load evenly

```
class RoutingExamplesSpec
  extends ScalaTestWithActorTestKit
  with AnyWordSpecLike
  with Matchers
  with LogCapturing {

"a group router" should {
    "send messages to all photo processors registered" in {
      val photoProcessor1 = TestProbe[String]
      val pp1Monitor = Behaviors.monitor(
          photoProcessor1.ref, PhotoProcessor())

      val photoProcessor2 = TestProbe[String]          Intercepts messages to
      val pp2Monitor = Behaviors.monitor(              the photo processor
          photoProcessor2.ref, PhotoProcessor())

      system.receptionist ! Receptionist.Register(PhotoProcessor.Key,
      ➥spawn(pp1Monitor))
      system.receptionist ! Receptionist.Register(PhotoProcessor.Key,
      ➥spawn(pp2Monitor))

      val camera = spawn(Camera())
      camera ! Camera.Photo("A")    Sends photos
      camera ! Camera.Photo("B")

      photoProcessor1.receiveMessages(1)    Each photo processor
      photoProcessor2.receiveMessages(1)    receives a message
    }
```

The group router with a round-robin strategy ensures that each photo processor receives its fair share of messages.

6.3.4   *Consistent hashing strategy*

The previous section showed that routers are an easy way to scale up and out. But there can be a problem with sending messages to different routees. For example, consider the following common scenario.

A manager splits work between two workers in parallel. One type of worker obfuscates sensitive data, while the other type enriches the data with third-party vendors. When these two actors finish their tasks, they have to send the product to a final actor that aggregates both pieces of work; let's call it the aggregator. However, the message from the data obfuscator and the data enricher can be sent to the wrong aggregator, as figure 6.6 shows. The problem is ensuring that the manager's original message, which was split between the workers, ends up being merged back into the same aggregator. It would not be surprising if workers sent their finished work from the same message to different aggregators if you used the strategies seen so far. In figure 6.6, aggregator Y may not be able to merge the two parts—or, worse, it may merge them incorrectly, and the error may go unnoticed.

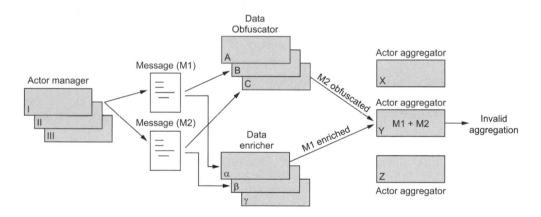

Figure 6.6   Distributing and aggregating messages

To solve this problem—among others—the *consistent hashing* strategy was introduced. Consistent hashing is an algorithm that solves a more general problem than this and is widely used in the industry to partition data. Examples include Cassandra, DynamoDB, Couchbase, GlusterFS, and many more. The history of the algorithm goes back to trying to balance the load on cache servers on the internet, taking into account that servers go down and new ones come in, and some servers can handle a larger load than others. This is one of the reasons why in Akka, *consistent hashing* is usually used with the group router and not with the pool router. The routees in a group router are meant to increase or decrease, register or deregister, but the same is not true in a pool router.

Returning to the previous example, to send messages generated from the same original message to the same aggregator, you can use a router with consistent hashing in the data-obfuscator and data-enricher actors. An instance of this router in each worker sends similar messages to the same routee and to the same aggregator, allowing the pieces to fit together properly.

For this to work, the router must detect when two messages are similar. This is done by the hash created from each message's string. There are several steps to assigning a message to a routee, as shown in figure 6.7. (These are Akka internals that are not visible to normal users.)

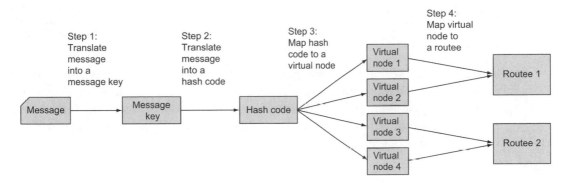

Figure 6.7   Steps the consistent hashing router follows to decide which routee to select

In step 1, the message is translated into the message key of type `String`. Similar joinable messages have the same key: for example, the message ID. It does not matter how this key is constructed; the only restriction is that the key is always the same for similar messages. The extraction of this message key is different for each type of message and must be implemented. Therefore, a router with the constant hashing strategy requires the definition of this mapping function.

In step 2, a hash code is created from this message key. This hash code is used to select a virtual node (step 3). Step 4 is to select the routee that handles all messages for this virtual node.

The first thing you may notice is the use of virtual nodes. Can't you assign a hash code directly to a routee and forget about virtual nodes? Well, virtual nodes are the secret sauce of constant hashing. They are used for two reasons:

- To give a greater chance of distributing all messages evenly across routes
- To allow for the removal and addition of routes

The number of virtual nodes served by a routee must be configured when using a consistent hashing strategy by specifying the factor multiplied by the number of routees, as in the definition of `withConsistentHashingRouting` in the snippet after next.

Besides using a `ServiceKey` for a group router, you also need to provide the hashing function: the mapping from message to message key. The following snippet has both, along with the protocol for the aggregator:

```
object Aggregator {

  sealed trait Command {
    def id: String
  }
  final case class Obfuscated(id: String, content: String) extends Command
  final case class Enriched(id: String, metadata: String) extends Command

  val serviceKey = ServiceKey[Aggregator.Command]("agg-key")

  def mapping(command: Command) = command.id
  ...
}
```

ID that allows the different parts of the same message to be forwarded to the same aggregator

Service key to allow a group router to find registered aggregators

Function from message to message key

These are the key and the mapping function that the data obfuscator and data enricher need to route the messages. With them, they can create a group router, as shown in the following snippet. With this strategy, two messages with the same ID have the same hash and, thus, the same routee. Note that to spawn the router, the actor uses `.spawnAnonymous`:

```
object DataEnricher {
  ...

  def apply() = Behaviors.setup[Command] { context =>

    val router = context.spawnAnonymous {
      Routers
        .group(Aggregator.serviceKey)
        .withConsistentHashingRouting(10, Aggregator.mapping)
    }
    ...
}
```

Points to the service key to find registered aggregators

Uses factor 10 to spread the load more evenly on the aggregators. Uses a mapping function to allow the creation of a hash.

It is a good practice to name actors for debugging purposes, but this is just a small example chosen here for simplicity. If you look at the Akka source code, many specs use this kind of spawning for this reason.

> **NOTE**   The specific logic of how the aggregate merges the messages has little to do with routing. If you are interested, you can find the code in the RoutingExamplesSpec.scala file, which also contains tests.

The data enricher and the obfuscator have very similar logic. Here is the rest of the enricher, which gives a complete view of how the actor uses the router:

```
object DataEnricher {
  sealed trait Command
  final case class Message(id: String, content: String) extends Command
```

```
def apply() = Behaviors.setup[Command] { context =>
  val router = ...

  Behaviors.receiveMessage[Command] {
    case Message(id, content) =>
      router ! Aggregator.Enriched(id, content + ":metadata")
      Behaviors.same
  }
}}
```

The router uses the ID that comes from the original message to calculate the hash. The same is true for the router from the obfuscator, so the aggregator receives both processing parts of the same message.

In this section, you learned how to use Akka routers, which are used for performance reasons, but remember that routers are also used based on the content of a message or the state of the actor. The next section examines the content- and state-based routing approaches.

6.4 Implementing the router pattern using actors

To route in Akka, you are not always required to implement a pool or group router. If the router's decision is based on the message or the state of the actor, it is easier to implement it in a normal actor with the behaviors API.

This section looks at some ideas for the router pattern with normal actors. We start with a message-based router and follow it with a state-based router. We explored both ideas previously in chapters 2 and 3.

6.4.1 Content-based routing

The most common routing pattern in a system is based on the messages. In the speed limit ticket example, you saw a message-based router. If the traveler's speed is below the speed limit, the photo is not needed and is deleted; but if the speed is higher, it is a violation, and processing should continue to alert highway patrol (figure 6.8).

A flow is selected based on the content of the message. In this example, you can route based on the value of the message or its type. You've already seen that with pattern matching on the message.

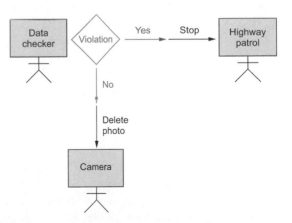

6.4.2 State-based routing

The state-based routing approach involves changing the routing behavior based on the state of the router, as you've seen in the photo

Figure 6.8 Routing based on message content

processor (figure 6.9). You can easily route depending on the state by using the finite state machine capabilities of any behavior.

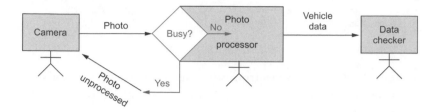

Figure 6.9   Photo processor routing depending on the state

The following is a sketch of the photo processor processing photos when it is available or sending them back to the camera when it is not:

```scala
object PhotoProcessorSketch {

  val key = ServiceKey[String]("photo-procesor-sketch-key")

  sealed trait Command
  final case class File(
      location: String,
      camera: ActorRef[Camera.Photo])
    extends Command
  final case object Done extends Command

  def apply(): Behavior[Command] = ready()

  private def ready() = Behaviors.receiveMessage {
    case f: File =>
      ...
      busy()            ◁──┐ Processes the photo; when finished, returns
  }                        │ to ready() by sending Done to itself

  private def busy() = Behaviors.receiveMessage {
    case File(location, camera) =>
      camera ! Camera.Photo(location)   ◁──┐ Can't process the file and sends
      Behaviors.same                       │ back the photo to the camera
    case Done =>
      ready()
  }
}
```

This plain actor can provide routing functionality by designating the next behavior to handle the next message—the most basic functionality of an actor.

In this chapter, you've learned how actors can find each other even if they are not in direct contact, thanks to the receptionist and built-in routers. With them, you're one step closer to creating distributed and fault-tolerant systems with actors.

To be fail-safe even if the racks catch fire, you need to distribute the `Actor-Systems` across multiple machines. That is, you need clusters—and to build them, you first need to learn about Akka configuration in chapter 7.

Summary

- The receptionist is used within an actor to find other actors that have not been spawned by this actor or passed by a message or initialization.
- Pool and group routers are built into Akka and can use multiple strategies to deliver to their routees. Pool routers spawn their own routees, while group routers do not and use the receptionist to find them.
- The available strategies are random, round-robin, consistent hashing, and broadcasting. Round-robin is a fair distribution: each routee gets a message until they all have one, and then the distribution starts over. Consistent hashing uses a hashing algorithm to deterministically forward messages to routees; this approach is useful when routees come and go. Broadcasting uses a predicate, and each message is sent to every routee that matches that predicate.
- You can use a simple actor to implement routers that route based on content, using pattern matching for the messages, or based on the state of the actor, by specifying the next behavior.

Configuration

Thus far, we've focused on creating actors and working with the `ActorSystem`. To create an application that can be run and is ready for deployment, you need to bundle several other things with it. First this chapter dives into how Akka supports configuration. Then we look at logging, including how you can use your own logging framework. Finally, we go through a deployment example.

> **NOTE** The source code for this chapter is available at www.manning.com/ books/akka-in-action-second-edition or https://github.com/franciscolo pezsancho/akka-topics/tree/main/chapter07. You can find the contents of any snippet or listing in the .scala file with the same name as the class, object, or trait.

Akka uses the Typesafe Config Library, which supports a state-of-the-art set of capabilities. The typical features are the ability to define properties in different ways and then reference them in the code (job one of configuration is to grant runtime flexibility by making it possible to use variables outside the code). There's also a sophisticated means of merging multiple configuration files based on simple conventions that determine how overrides occur. One of the most important requirements of a configuration system is providing a way to target multiple environments (such as development, testing, and production) without having to explode the bundle. This chapter shows how that's done, as well.

7.1 Trying out Akka configuration

Like other Akka libraries, the Typesafe Config library takes pains to minimize the dependencies that are needed; it has no dependencies on other libraries. Let's start with a quick tour of how to use the configuration library.

The library uses a hierarchy of properties. Figure 7.1 shows a possible configuration of an application defining four properties using a self-defined hierarchy. The properties are grouped within the MyApp1 node: version, name, and database (MyApp1 is also a property).

```
MyApp1   version = 10

         name - "My application"

         database   connect="jdbc:mysql://localhost/mydata"

                    user="me"
```

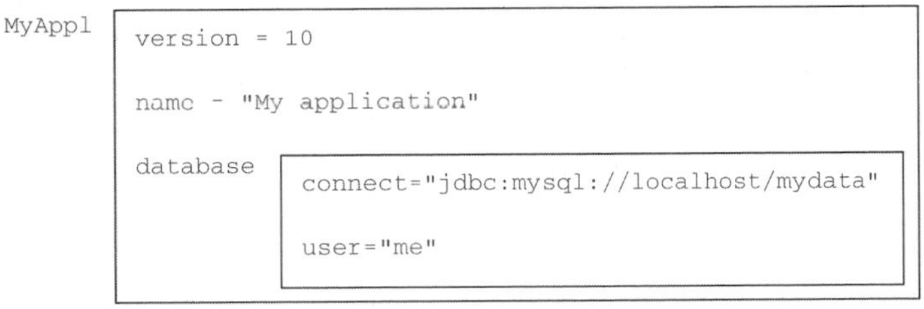

**Figure 7.1
Configuration example**

The ConfigFactory is used to get the configuration. This is often called within the Main class of your application. The library also supports the ability to specify which configuration file is used. The following sections cover the configuration files in more detail, but let's start by using the default:

```
import com.typesafe.config.ConfigFactory
import com.typesafe.config.Config

val config: Config = ConfigFactory.load()
```

7.1.1 Order

When using the default, the library tries to find the configuration file. Since the library supports several different configuration formats, it looks for different files in the following order:

- *application.properties*—This file should contain the configuration properties in the Java property file format.

- *application.json*—This file should contain the configuration properties in the JSON style.
- *application.conf*—This file should contain the configuration properties in the Human-Optimized Config Object Notation (HOCON) format. This format is based on JSON but is easier to read. (You can find more details on HOCON and the Typesafe Config library at https://github.com/typesafehub/config.)

It's possible to use all the different files in your project at the same time. Here's an example of an application.conf file:

```
MyAppl {
  version = 10
  description = "My application"          Nesting is done by
  database {                          ◄─┘ grouping with {}.
    connect="jdbc:mysql://localhost/mydata"
    user="me"
  }
}
```

For simple applications, this file often suffices. The format looks somewhat like JSON. The primary advantages are that it's more readable and it's easy to see how properties are grouped. JDBC is a perfect example of properties that most apps need and that are easier to manage when grouped. In the dependency injection world, you would group items like this by controlling the injection of the properties into objects (such as `DataSource`). This is a simpler approach. Let's look at how you can use these properties now that you have an initial understanding of them.

You can use several methods to get the values as different types, and the period (`.`) is used as the separator in the path of the property. The basic types are supported, and you can get lists of these types:

Gets the "MyAppl.version" value
from application.conf

```
val applicationVersion = config.getInt("MyAppl.version")        ◄──────
val databaseConnectString = config.getString("MyAppl.database.connect")  ◄──
```

Gets the "MyAppl.database.connect"
value from application.conf

7.1.2   Subtrees

Sometimes an object doesn't need much configuration. What if you have a class `DBaseConnection` that's creating the database connection? This class needs only the connect string and the `user` property. When you pass the full configuration to the `DBaseConnection` class, it needs to know the full path of the property. But when you want to reuse `DBaseConnection` in another application, a problem arises. The start of the path is `MyAppl`, but the other application probably has a different configuration root. So, the path to the property has changed. This can be solved by getting a subtree for your new configuration:

```
import com.typesafe.config.Config
```

Gets the subtree by name (used
in application-specific code)

```
val databaseCfg: Config = configuration.getConfig("MyAppl.database")   ◄──┘
```

```
val databaseConnectURL: String = databaseCfg.getString("connect")
```
        References the property relative to the subtree root (used in DBaseConnection)

Using this approach, instead of configuration, you give the `databaseCfg` to `DBase-Connection`. Now `DBaseConnection` doesn't need the full path of the property; it only needs the last part: the property's name. This means `DBaseConnection` can be reused without introducing path problems.

7.1.3 Substitutions

You can also perform substitutions when a property is used multiple times in your configuration, such as the hostname of the database `connect` string:

```
hostname="localhost"
MyApp1 {
    version = 10
    description = "My application"
    database {
        connect="jdbc:mysql://${hostname}/mydata"
        user="mc"
    }
}
```
`hostname="localhost"`   **Simple variable definition, no types needed (note quotes, though)**

`connect="jdbc:mysql://${hostname}/mydata"`   **Familiar ${} substitution syntax**

Config file variables are often used for things like the application name or version numbers since repeating them in many places in the file could potentially be dangerous. It's also possible to use system properties or environment variables in the substitutions:

```
hostname=${?HOST_NAME}
MyApp1 {
  version = 10
  description = "My application"
  database {
    connect="jdbc:mysql://${hostname}/mydata"
    user="me"
  }
}
```
`hostname=${?HOST_NAME}`   **Question mark (?) means optional**

The problem is that you never know for sure that these properties exist. To account for this, you can make use of the possibility that the redefinition of a property overrules the previous definition. And the substitution of a system property or environment variable definition vanishes if there's no value for the specified property `HOST_NAME`. Here's how to do this:

```
hostname="localhost"
hostname=${?HOST_NAME}
MyApp1 {
  version = 10
  description = "My application"
  database {
    connect="jdbc:mysql://${hostname}/mydata"
```
`hostname="localhost"`   **Defines the usual simple way**

`hostname=${?HOST_NAME}`   **If there's an environment variable, override; otherwise, leave the value you just assigned.**

```
        user="me"
    }
}
```

It's pretty easy to see what's going on. Defaults are important in configuration because you want to force the user to do as little configuration as possible. And often, apps should run with no configuration until they need to be pushed into a production environment; development can often be done with nothing but defaults.

7.1.4   *Using defaults*

Let's continue with our simple JDBC configuration. It's generally safe to assume developers will connect to a database instance on their machine, referenced as `localhost`. As soon as someone wants to see a demo, you'll be scrambling to get the app working on an instance that has different names, and the database will likely be on another machine.

The laziest thing you can do is make a copy of the config file, give it a different name, and include some logic in the app that says, "Use this file in this environment and the other file in the other environment." The problem is that now all your configuration is in two places. It makes more sense to override the two or three values that will be different in the new target environment, and the defaulting mechanism lets you do that easily. The configuration library contains a fallback mechanism; the defaults are placed into a configuration object that is then handed over to the configurator as the fallback configuration source. Figure 7.2 shows a simple example.

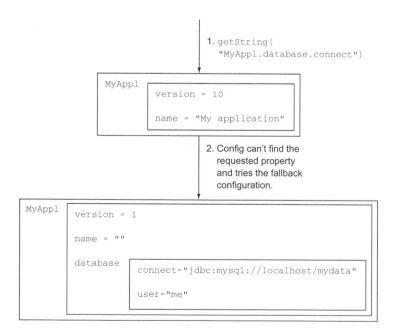

Figure 7.2   Configuration fallback

> **Preventing null properties**
>
> The defaulting mechanism prevents cases where values differ depending on where they're used. Given this principle, when a configuration property is read, the value should always be set. If the framework allowed the property to be empty, the code would behave differently based on how (and where) configuration was done. So, if you try to get a config value from the configuration that isn't set, an exception is thrown.

This fallback structure grants a lot of flexibility. But for it to provide the defaults you need, you have to know how to configure them. They're configured in the file reference.conf and placed in the root of the JAR file; the idea is that every library contains its own defaults. The configuration library finds all the reference.conf files and integrates these settings into the configuration fallback structure. This way, all the needed properties of a library always have a default, and the principle of always getting a value back is preserved. (Later, you see that you can explicitly stipulate defaults programmatically, as well.)

You already saw that the configuration library supports multiple formats: Java properties, JSON, and HOCON. Nothing is stopping you from using multiple formats in a single application. Each file can be used as the fallback of another file. And it supports the possibility of overruling properties with system properties, which is the higher-ranking configuration. The structure is always the same, so the relationships between defaults and overrides are always the same. Figure 7.3 shows the files the config library uses to build the complete tree in priority order.

Most applications use only one of these application file types. But if you want to provide a set of application defaults and then override some of them, as with the example JDBC settings, you can do so. When following this guide, keep in mind that the upper configuration files shown in figure 7.3 will overrule values defined in the lower files.

By default, the file application.{conf,json,properties} is used to read the configuration. There are two ways to change the name of the configuration file. The first option is to use an overloaded load function on the ConfigFactory. When loading the configuration, supply the name of the base:

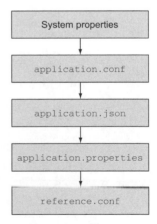

Figure 7.3   Priority of the configuration fallback structure. The highest priority is at the top and overrides definitions in lower files.

```
val config = ConfigFactory.load("myapp")
```

Requests that the configuration factory load the file myapp.{conf,json,properties}

This way, the configuration factory doesn't try to load application.{conf,json, properties}, but rather myapp.{conf,json,properties}. (This is required if you need multiple configurations in a single JVM.)

Another option is to use Java system properties. Sometimes this is the easiest approach because you can create a Bash script to run the application while setting a Java property pointing to the configuration of your choice instead of exploding JARs (that is, instead of providing the unzipped JAR structure with only the specific configuration for that environment).

System properties can be used for the name of the configuration file when you're using the `load` method without arguments—that is, `ConfigFactory.load()`. Setting system properties is as easy as adding the `-D` option. For example:

```
-Dconfig.file="config/myapp.conf"
```

when using the configuration file config/myapp.conf. When you use one of these properties, the default behavior of searching for the different .conf, .json, and .properties files is skipped.

You can use the following three system properties to control which configuration file the application reads:

- `config.resource` specifies a resource name, not a base name: for example, application.conf, not `application`.
- `config.file` specifies a file system path; again, it should include the extension.
- `config.url` specifies a URL.

7.2   *Akka configuration*

Okay, you've seen how you can use the configuration library for your application's properties, but what do you need to do when you want to change some of Akka's configuration options? How is Akka using this library? It's possible to have multiple `ActorSystems` with their own configuration. When no configuration is present at creation, the `ActorSystem` creates the configuration using the defaults:

```
val system = ActorSystem("mySystem")
```
ConfigFactory.load() is used internally to create a default config for the config argument that is omitted here.

But it's also possible (and useful) to supply the configuration while creating an `ActorSystem`. Here's a simple way to accomplish this:

```
val configuration = ConfigFactory.load("myapp")
val systemA = ActorSystem("mySystem",configuration)
```
Loads the configuration, providing a name

Passes it to the ActorSystem constructor

The configuration is within your application in the settings of the `ActorSystem`. This can be accessed within every actor. Here, the `applicationDescription` gets its value from the property `MyAppl.name`:

```
val mySystem = ActorSystem("myAppl")
val config = mySystem.settings.config
val applicationDescription = config.getString("MyAppl.name")
```

Once the ActorSystem is constructed, you can get the config by referencing it using this path.

Gets a property as usual

You've seen how you can use the configuration system for your properties and use the same system to configure the ActorSystem that's the backbone of Akka. The presumption in these sections has been that you have only one Akka app on a given system. The next section covers configuring multiple systems that share a single instance.

7.3   *Multiple systems*

Depending on your requirements, you may need different configurations—say, for multiple subsystems—on a single instance (or machine). Akka supports this in several ways. Let's start by looking at cases where you're using several JVMs, but they run in the same environment using the same files.

You already know the first option: use system properties. When a new process is started, a different configuration file is used. But usually, a lot of the configuration is the same for all the subsystems, and only a small part differs. This problem can be solved by using the include option.

Let's look at an example. Let's say you have this baseConfig.conf file:

```
MyAppl {
  version = 10
  description = "My application"
}
```

In this example, you start with this simple configuration root, which would most likely have one shared and one differing property; the version number is probably the same across subsystems, but you typically want different names and descriptions for each subsystem. For this, you can have another file named, for example, subAppl.conf:

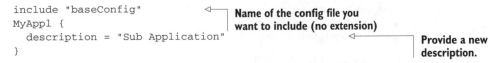

```
include "baseConfig"
MyAppl {
  description = "Sub Application"
}
```

Name of the config file you want to include (no extension)

Provide a new description.

Because the include is before the rest of the configuration, the value of description in the configuration is overridden just as it was in a single file. This way, you can have one basic configuration and put only the differences in the specific configuration files for each subsystem.

7.3.1   *Lifting with Fallback*

You can combine configurations that have some paths in common. Prioritize one of them—also called *lifting*—so it is selected over the fallback configuration.

This technique is often used in testing when you only need to override a few properties of the main configuration. For example, you can set `akka.loglevel` to `debug` instead of `info`.

Let's start with common paths in one file called combined.conf:

```
MyAppl {
  version = 10
  description = "My application"
}
subApplA {
  MyAppl {
    description = "Sub application"
  }
}
```

By lifting this, you get a shared property (version) and override description.

Here, you can lift the subtree within `subApplA` of the configuration to put it in front of the configuration chain. Figure 7.4 shows this lifting.

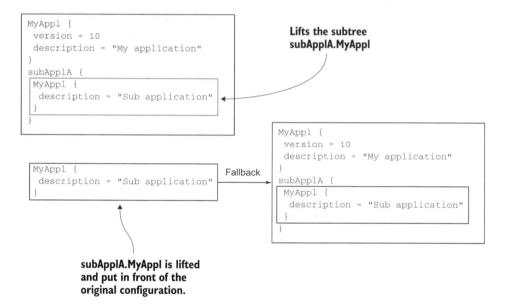

Figure 7.4   Lifting a configuration section

The next snippet shows how to do this. Load the configuration to have both the lift and the fallback. Note that the fallback is chained programmatically here (not relying on the file conventions covered earlier):

```
val configuration = ConfigFactory.load("combined")
val subApplACfg = configuration.getConfig("subApplA")
val config = subApplACfg.withFallback(configuration)
```

Selects the subtree subApplA

Adds a configuration as fallback

Now you can request the property `MyApp1.description` using `config.getString` (`"MyApp1.description"`) and get the result `"Sub application"` because the description configuration value is set in the configuration at the highest level (sub-App1A.MyApp1.description). However, when you ask for `MyApp1.version`, you get the value `10`: the version configuration value isn't defined in the higher configuration (subApp1A.MyApp1), so the normal fallback mechanism is used to provide the configuration value.

7.4 Configuration in tests

By default, the `ActorTestKit` loads the properties from the application-test.conf file if it exists in your project; otherwise, it follows the order you've already seen (shown again as figure 7.5). You can also directly use a string with `ConfigFactory.parseString` to describe the configuration to add or overwrite a property. This example overwrites `akka.loglevel`:

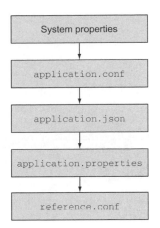

```
ConfigFactory.parseString("akka.loglevel = DEBUG")
```

These two approaches can also be mixed by lifting, using `.parseString` as the lifted configuration and then reverting to the default configuration: for example, application-test.conf, if it exists. If it does not, the `ActorTest-Kit` looks for application.conf, and so on. Here's how you lift with `.parseString` and fall back to the default configuration:

Figure 7.5 Priority of the configuration fallback structure. The highest priority is at the top, which overrides definitions in lower files.

```
val config: Config = ConfigFactory.parseString("""
  akka.loglevel = DEBUG
  akka.log-config-on-start = on
  """).withFallback(ConfigFactory.load())
```

The next section shows how this can be used in the `ScalaTestWithActorTestKit`.

7.4.1 Lifting in tests

You can add a configuration to a test via the `ScalaTestWithActorTestKit` using the test-kit constructor that accepts a `Config`. Here you can use all the options seen so far, with the `ConfigFactory.parseString` alone or any lifting.

For example, a specific configuration can connect to a local database to run tests. But you may want to modify some values for a specific test suite. Let's say you have the following in-memory.conf file:

```
akka.eventsourced-entity {
    journal-enabled = true
    read-journal = inmem-read-journal
}
...
```

You want to set `journal-enabled` to `false` in a specific test suite.

Let's create a test to see this in action. A property is defined with a string in the test itself that overrides a value from the configuration that came from a .conf file.

Listing 7.1   Using a value from the direct configuration

```
class AsyncLogConfigSpec
    extends ScalaTestWithActorTestKit(
      ConfigFactory
        .parseString("""akka.eventsourced-entity = false""")          Lifts the
        .withFallback(ConfigFactory.load("in-memory")))               configuration
    with AnyWordSpecLike                                              Falls back to the
    with Matchers {                                                   configuration
                                                                      in-memory.conf

  "Actor" must {

    "lift one property from conf" in {
      val inmemory = testKit.system.settings.config
      val journalenabled =
        inmemory.getString("akka.eventsourced-entity.journal-enabled")
      val readjournal =
        inmemory.getString("akka.eventsourced-entity.read-journal")

      val loggerBehavior: Behavior[String] = Behaviors.receive {          Actor that
        (context, message) =>                                              only logs
          message match {
            case message: String =>
              context.log.info(s"$journalenabled $readjournal")
              Behaviors.same
          }
      }

      val loggerActor = spawn(loggerBehavior)
      val message = "anymessage"

      LoggingTestKit
        .info("false inmem-read-journal")          Proves that only
        .expect {                                   journal-enabled has changed
          loggerActor.ref ! message
        }
    }
}}}
```

Retrieves values from the configuration (annotation for `val inmemory`/`val journalenabled`/`val readjournal` block)

The `journal-enabled` value is overwritten in the test, while `read-journal` remains the same. You can run this test by executing the following at the command line:

```
sbt chapter07/test
```

Configuration is a crucial part of delivering applications. Although it starts with meager requirements that are usually easily met, demands invariably appear that can complicate matters, and often the configuration layer of an application becomes tangled and complex. The Typesafe Config library provides a number of powerful tools to prevent this from happening:

- Easy defaulting based on convention (with overrides)
- Sophisticated defaulting that allows you to require the least amount of configuration necessary
- Several syntax options: traditional, Java, JSON, and HOCON

We haven't come near to exhausting this topic, but you've seen enough to deal with a broad range of typical requirements that will come up as you start to deploy Akka solutions.

Summary

- The Typesafe Config library reads a hierarchy of priorities, including system properties, application.conf, application.json, application.properties, and reference.conf.
- With the HOCON syntax, you can add a default value and an optional value read from the system properties. This way, you can use the default value in one environment—usually local—and override it in other environments, such as stage or production, by setting the system property.
- Combine several files to create your complete configuration. These files form a tree, and each branch or leaf can be assigned to a specific area in your application such as the database, servers, or business values.
- You can override values by setting them to higher branches. This way, you override lower branches of the configuration and fall back on the remaining properties for the rest of the values.

Clustering 8

This chapter covers

- Forming a cluster
- Cluster monitoring
- Building a clustered Akka app

An Akka cluster is a group of nodes that communicate peer to peer to form a whole. These nodes are `ActorSystems` that live in independent JVMs. Thanks to its decentralized structure, a cluster has no single point of failure, is fault-tolerant, and can dynamically increase and decrease the number of nodes.

Distributed applications run in environments that are not fully under your control, such as cloud computing platforms or remote data centers. The larger the cluster, the greater the ability to distribute the load, but the greater the risk of failure. In the event of this inevitable failure, Akka offers clustering and many extensions that provide solutions to common needs raised over the years. One of these requirements is the means to monitor and change the state of the cluster nodes.

8.1 On top of Akka Cluster

Akka Cluster gives rise to multiple tools. You learn about the first two modules in this book, and it may be useful to know that the others are available when you need them:

- *Cluster singleton*—An actor that has only one instance in the entire cluster and is relocated to another node in case of failure. More on this later in this chapter.
- *Cluster sharding*—Actors are automatically distributed to different nodes by a partition key, which is also used to communicate with the actors. This provides load balancing and resilience when the nodes leave the cluster. More about this in chapter 9.
- *Distributed data*—Distributed key-value objects are ultimately consistent and can be used by any actor in any node of the cluster. The values are conflict-free replicated data types.
- *Distributed publish-subscribe*—Actors can create, publish, and subscribe to topics.
- *Reliable delivery*—Instead of the default at-most-once delivery, this module offers at-least-once guarantees.
- *Multi-DC cluster*—You can deploy clusters in different data centers (DCs) to increase resilience.

In addition to this plethora of modules, several tools under the Akka Management umbrella are designed to interact with cluster nodes:

- *Core* (or *Management*)—Provides the basic functionality to interact with the cluster through HTTP, which forms the base for different modules in Akka Management.
- *Management Cluster HTTP*—Uses the core module to offer an endpoint to read and modify the state of the nodes in the cluster.
- *Cluster Bootstrap*—Automates the discovery of nodes in the network instead of using static configuration.
- *Discovery*—The basis for Cluster Bootstrap and many other Akka modules. It provides a lookup service for static configurations, as well as dynamic DNS, plus a specific implementation for Kubernetes, Amazon Web Services (AWS), Consul, or Marathon.

It is useful to have a mental model of these two major categories: `akka-cluster` with its modules and the `akka-management` core with its extensions. In this chapter, you learn about using `akka-cluster` to form a cluster and `akka-management` and `akka-management-cluster-http` to work on the nodes of the cluster over HTTP. The next section covers how a node becomes a member of the cluster, how to listen for membership events, and how to detect when nodes in the cluster have crashed.

NOTE The source code for this chapter is available at www.manning.com/ books/akka-in-action-second-edition or https://github.com/franciscolopez sancho/akka-topics/tree/main/chapter08a and https://github.com/francis colopezsancho/akka-topics/tree/main/chapter08b. You can find the contents of any snippet or listing in the .scala file with the same name as the class, object, or trait. The code in this chapter is grouped into two projects in the

Git repository with different executables and configurations. This separation helps you run them separately without much extra configuration and lets us map ideas from the chapter text to the projects. The simplest cluster application is in chapter08a, and a more complex example of a cluster with word-counting logic is in chapter08b. This grouping of projects based on executables and ideas will continue throughout the book.

8.2   *Why use clustering?*

A *cluster* is a dynamic group of nodes. On each node, an `ActorSystem` listens on the network. Clusters build on top of the `akka-remote` module, making location transparency possible in Akka. Whether an actor is in the same node or not, its location is abstracted, so it's transparent to deal with an actor despite its residence. Your code, the business logic, doesn't have to concern itself with this. Figure 8.1 shows a cluster of four nodes.

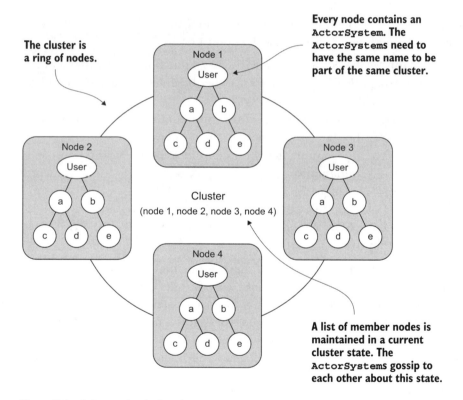

Figure 8.1   A four-node clustered `ActorSystem`

The cluster module's ultimate goal is to provide fully automated features for actor distribution and failover. Let's concentrate on the following features:

- *Cluster membership*—Fault-tolerant membership for `ActorSystem`s.

- *Partition points*—An ActorSystem can be partitioned into actor subtrees located on different nodes. We discuss this and roles later in the chapter.

A single-purpose data-processing application is a good example of a candidate application for using clusters: for example, data-processing tasks like image recognition and real-time analysis of social media. Nodes can be added or removed when more or less processing power is required. Processing jobs are supervised: if an actor fails, the job can be restarted and retried on the cluster until it succeeds or is abandoned.

Figure 8.2 shows an example, but don't worry about the details (once you learn the basic concepts of clustering, we'll look at an example in depth). The goal is to develop an app that counts words: how many occurrences of a word are in a series of texts.

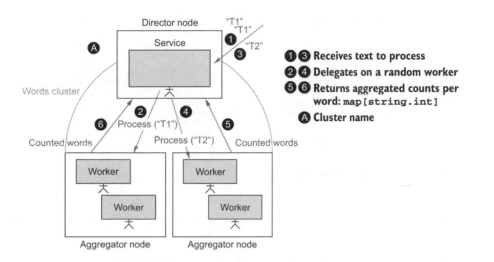

Figure 8.2 Sketch of an application that counts words

Before we get into the nitty-gritty of the application, you need to know how to create a cluster using seed nodes, how nodes become seed nodes, and how they can join and leave the cluster. In the following sections, you see how a cluster is formed and experiment with the REPL console to join and leave a simple cluster. Finally, you learn about the different states a member node can go through and how to receive notifications about those state changes.

8.2.1 Cluster membership: Joining a cluster

Like any group, a cluster needs a few "founders." Akka provides a seed node feature for this purpose. *Seed nodes* are the starting point of the cluster and serve as the first point of contact for other nodes. Nodes join the cluster by sending a JOIN message containing the joining node's unique address. The Cluster module ensures that this message is sent to one of the registered seed nodes.

A node doesn't need to contain actors other than the `ActorSystem`, so it is possible to use pure seed nodes. Figure 8.3 shows how a first seed node initializes a cluster and how other nodes join the cluster.

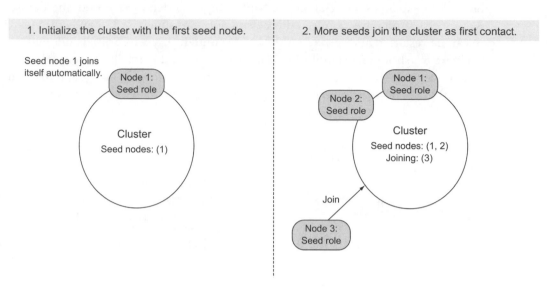

Figure 8.3   Initializing a cluster with seed nodes

Seed nodes can be defined in three ways. Note that these different methods must not be mixed:

- *Configuration*—Passing a configuration of initial node addresses, usually for local development or testing. Using them in production is not recommended.
- *Using Cluster Bootstrap*—Programmed to automatically find nodes in cloud environments such as Kubernetes, AWS, Google Cloud, Azure, and others. This is the recommended approach for use in such environments.
- *Programmatically*—If neither of the preceding is an option, you can add seed nodes using an implementation that you write yourself.

Because this is an introductory chapter about clustering, we only cover the definition of seed nodes through configuration. In this setting, you specify a list of seed nodes with a host and a port for each of them. The first one in the list plays a special role in forming the cluster; other seeds can join the cluster only if it is Up. This restriction was introduced to prevent individual clusters from forming while the seed nodes are starting up.

The seed nodes can all boot independently as long as the first seed node is started at a given time. Other nodes that are not seed nodes can join the cluster through one of the seed nodes after the first seed node is started and Up. Once the first seed node has formed the cluster and set all other seed nodes to Up, it can safely leave the cluster and pass its leadership to the next seed node in the list: that is, the one with the lowest IP address. Figure 8.4 shows the nodes in the cluster for the word-counting application.

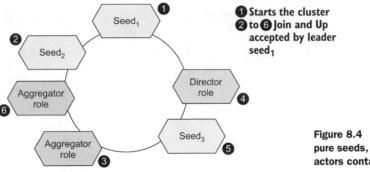

Figure 8.4 **Cluster formation from pure seeds, and joining of nodes with actors containing business logic**

8.2.2 *Minimal cluster example*

Let's start with creating seed nodes via the REPL console to give you better insight into how a cluster is formed. To be clear, you wouldn't perform these steps manually if you were setting up a cluster application; this example shows how to interact with the cluster at a low level to better understand the primitives.

The only things you need are an ActorSystem and some configuration. We begin with the configuration because in this case, the ActorSystem is created in the REPL.

The ActorSystem needs to be configured to use the cluster module. Listing 8.1 shows a minimal configuration setting the seed nodes. The configuration requires you to select the following:

- *The actor provider*—It can be a local or a cluster. The local option is used for applications that do not require distribution, such as a streaming processor or an HTTP server. Otherwise, you can choose the cluster provider to allow actors to be created in any node. To do this, set akka.actor.provider = cluster in the configuration.
- *The remote*—This is the internal mechanism through which actors on different nodes communicate with each other.
- *The seed nodes*—The list of hosts, ports, and ActorSystem names of the start nodes. Remember, seed nodes are not the only option, but let's focus on them for now.

Listing 8.1 Configuring the seed nodes in application.conf

```
akka {
  actor {
    provider = "cluster"        ◁── Initializes the
  }                                  cluster module
```

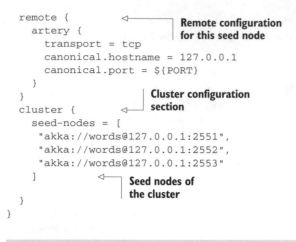

```
  remote {
    artery {
      transport = tcp
      canonical.hostname = 127.0.0.1
      canonical.port = ${PORT}
    }
  }
  cluster {
    seed-nodes = [
      "akka://words@127.0.0.1:2551",
      "akka://words@127.0.0.1:2552",
      "akka://words@127.0.0.1:2553"
    ]
  }
}
```

> ### Keeping the addresses exactly the same
>
> You see 127.0.0.1 and not `localhost` in listing 8.1 because the latter might resolve to a different IP address, depending on your setup, and Akka interprets the addresses literally. You can't depend on DNS resolution for the `akka.remote` `.artery.canonical.hostname` value that is used exactly for the system's address; no DNS resolution is done on it. The exact value of the address is used when actor references are serialized between Akka remote nodes. So, once you send a message to the remote actor referred to by such an actor reference, the remote actor will use that exact address to connect to the remote server.
>
> The primary reason not to use DNS resolution is performance. DNS resolution, if configured incorrectly, can take seconds—or minutes, in a particularly bad case. Determining that delays are caused by an incorrect DNS configuration is not easy, and the problem usually is not immediately apparent. Not using DNS resolution avoids this problem, but it means you have to be careful when configuring the addresses.

`remote.artery` refers to the remoting implementation: `artery` is a reimplementation of the classic Akka module for node intercommunication that provides, among other things, better performance and reliability. `artery.transport` provides three protocols:

- `tcp`—The default setting. It is based on Akka Streams TCP, which provides high throughput and low latency.
- `tls-tcp`–The same as `tcp` but with encryption using Akka Streams TLS.
- `aeron-udp`–Based on Aeron (UDP). Offers better performance than `tcp` in terms of throughput and latency but at the cost of CPU consumption—even if the application does not use the available message rates.

`artery.canonical.hostname` is a unique location defined by an address and a port. If multiple names refer to the same IP address, only one can be used. Consequently, 127.0.0.1:port can be used on local development but not across the network, because it is not unique.

artery.canonical.port is the port on which the ActorSystem should listen. It is selected automatically—and the value is chosen randomly between certain limits if it is set to 0.

To use this configuration, the project must include the following dependency in its build.sbt file:

```
val AkkaVersion = "2.6.20"
"com.typesafe.akka" %% "akka-cluster-typed" % AkkaVersion
```

With this configuration, you have everything you need to create a cluster.

8.2.3 Starting the cluster

Let's start the first node by accessing the sbt console and writing down the Actor-System. This is an alternative to writing a file with an App and an ActorSystem as you have done so far.

The previous configuration is in the book's Git repository in a project called chapter08a. Begin there with the sbt console so you have all the dependencies in place, and set the PORT variable used in the configuration file to 2551:

```
sbt -DPORT=2551 chapter08a/console
```

This produces the following output:

```
[info] Loading settings for project global-plugins from build.sbt ...
...
Type in expressions for evaluation. Or try :help.    REPL where you can
scala>                                          ⟵    write Scala code
```

From here, you need to create the ActorSystem. The easiest way is to paste the following in the console. Enter :paste and then copy the test:

```
scala> :paste
// Entering paste mode (ctrl-D to finish)
import akka.actor.typed.ActorSystem
import akka.actor.typed.scaladsl.Behaviors          Starts the ActorSystem
                                                      with the previous
 val guardian = ActorSystem(Behaviors.empty, "words")  ⟵  configuration
```

Behaviors.empty is enough to create the actor. As soon as you press Ctrl-D, you exit the insert mode, and the console interprets the code. The following listing shows the most important messages from the output of this execution.

Listing 8.2 Output of sbt

```
// Exiting paste mode, now interpreting.

INFO akka.remote.artery.tcp.ArteryTcpTransport - Remoting started with
➡transport [Artery tcp] ; listening on address
➡[akka://words@127.0.0.1:2551]     ⟵  Akka-Remote has started
    ...                                 with the TCP protocol and
                                        this canonical address.
```

**Node started successfully
in cluster mode**

**No automatic downing available for unreachable
nodes (more info about downing later)**

```
INFO akka.cluster.Cluster - Cluster Node [akka://words@127.0.0.1:2551] -
⇒Started up successful

INFO akka.cluster.Cluster - Cluster Node [akka://words@127.0.0.1:2551] -
⇒No downing-provider-class configured, manual cluster downing
⇒required                                                        ◄
...
     guardian: akka.actor.typed.ActorSystem[Any] = akka://words    ◄
...
```

**ActorSystem type and cluster name
taken from the ActorSystem**

Version from cluster.settings.app-version

```
INFO akka.cluster.Cluster - Cluster Node [akka://words@127.0.0.1:2551] -
⇒Node [akka://words@127.0.0.1:2551] is JOINING itself (with roles
⇒[seed, dc-default], version [0.0.0]) and forming
⇒new cluster
INFO akka.cluster.Cluster - Cluster Node [akka://words@127.0.0.1:2551] -
⇒is the new leader among reachable nodes
⇒(more leaders may exist)                                        ◄
INFO akka.cluster.Cluster - Cluster Node [akka://words@127.0.0.1:2551] -
⇒Leader is moving node [akka://words@127.0.0.1:2551] to [Up]
...
WARN akka.remote.artery.Association - Outbound control stream to
⇒[akka://words@127.0.0.1:2552] failed. Restarting it.
⇒akka.remote.artery.OutboundHandshake$HandshakeTimeoutException:
⇒Handshake with [akka://words@127.0.0.1:2552] did not complete within
⇒20000 ms                                  ◄
```

**Tried to connect to other seeds, failed,
and stopped trying after 20 seconds**

**Doesn't transition to Up until the leader is
elected and grants the transition**

You can interpret this output as shown in figure 8.5. The leader node has switched to Up and is ready to accept other nodes. The role of the leader node is to manage the convergence of the cluster and the membership transitions. Only one node can be the leader at any time, and any cluster node can become the leader.

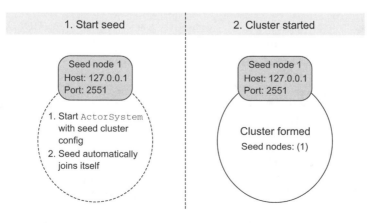

Figure 8.5 The initial
seed node joins itself
and forms the cluster.

You can now do the same thing to start two more nodes on two other terminals: just change the ports to 2552 and 2553. Adding a node on port 2552 looks like this:

```
sbt -DPORT=2552 chapter08a/console

scala> :paste
// Entering paste mode (ctrl-D to finish)
import akka.actor.typed.ActorSystem
import akka.actor.typed.scaladsl.Behaviors

val guardian = ActorSystem(Behaviors.empty, "words")
```

These nodes join the cluster, as shown in figure 8.6.

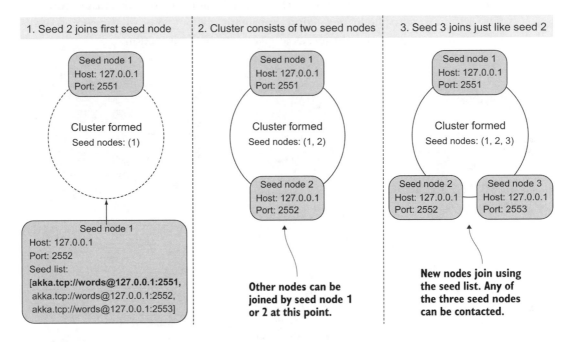

Figure 8.6 Start up the second seed node.

After you start nodes 2552 and 2553, you can see in their outputs the confirmation that the nodes have joined the cluster:

```
INFO akka.cluster.Cluster - Cluster Node [akka://words@127.0.0.1:2552] –
➥Welcome from [akka://words@127.0.0.1:2551]
```
          ◁─┐ **Accepted and gets**
             ack from the leader

The next snippet shows the output of the first seed node confirming that node 2 wants to join, is accepted, and is set to Up by the leader:

```
Cluster Node [akka://words@127.0.0.1:2551] - Sending InitJoinAck message
➥from node [akka://words@127.0.0.1:2551] to
➥[Actor[akka://words@127.0.0.1:2552/...
```
                                          Welcomes the = new
                             ◁────┘   **node on port 2552**

```
Cluster Node [akka://words@127.0.0.1:2551] - Node
[akka://words@127.0.0.1:2552] is JOINING, roles [seed, dc-default],
version [0.0.0]
Cluster Node [akka://words@127.0.0.1:2551] - Leader is moving node
[akka://words@127.0.0.1:2552] to [Up]
```

Initial node status ⟶

⟵ **Seed node 2 joins**

`. . .`   ⟵ **Equivalent console output for the node on port 2553**

Seed nodes 2 and 3 both request to join the cluster. The leader puts them in the Joining state and them into the Up state, making them part of the cluster. All three seed nodes have now successfully joined the cluster.

Figure 8.7 shows the different states of a node in the cluster, also known as the node's *lifecycle*. These states can be changed by leader actions or cluster commands. The system triggers the leader actions automatically, but you can also send Cluster-Command messages to the cluster, as discussed in the next section.

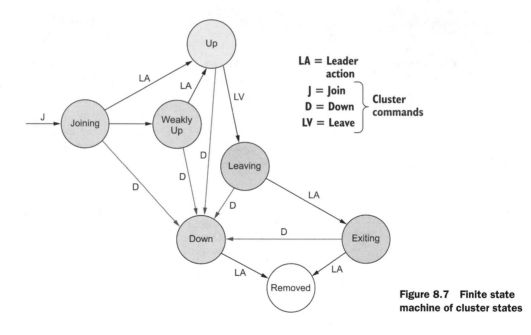

LA = Leader action
J = Join
D = Down   } Cluster commands
LV = Leave

Figure 8.7   Finite state machine of cluster states

8.2.4   *Leaving the cluster*

Let's send a ClusterCommand to make the leader (node 1) leave the cluster. When this happens, the next node—the one with the lowest IP address—takes over the role of leader. Press Enter to return to the sbt console, and in node 1's terminal, create an address to reference node 1 and send a Leave to the cluster manager:

```
scala> import akka.cluster.typed.{ Cluster, Leave }
```
Gets the address for this node

```
scala> val address = Cluster(guardian).selfMember.uniqueAddress.address
address: akka.actor.Address = akka://words@127.0.0.1:2551
```
⟵

**Forces seed node 1
to leave the cluster**

```
scala> Cluster(guardian).manager ! akka.cluster.typed.Leave(address)    ←
Cluster Node [akka://words@127.0.0.1:2551] - Marked address
➥[akka://words@127.0.0.1:2551] as [Leaving]        ←─┤ Marked as Leaving by itself
Cluster Node [akka://words@127.0.0.1:2551] - Leader is moving node
➥[akka://words@127.0.0.1:2551] to [Exiting]        ←
Cluster Node [akka://words@127.0.0.1:2551] - Shutting down... Cluster Node
➥[akka://words@127.0.0.1:2551] - Successfully shut down       Marked as
                                                              Exiting by itself
```

In the output, you can see that node 1 marks itself as `Leaving` and then `Exiting` while still being the leader. These state changes are propagated to all nodes in the cluster. Then the cluster node is shut down while the `ActorSystem` continues to run. This is shown in figure 8.8.

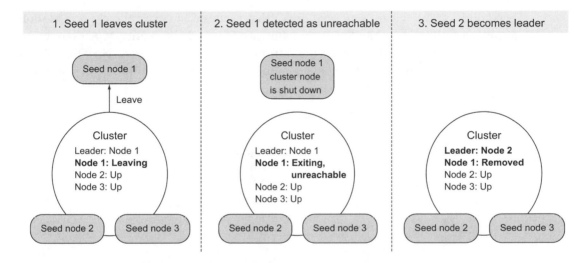

Figure 8.8   The first seed node leaves the cluster.

Looking at the terminal of node 2, you can see the confirmation of the exit and removal of the leader and the election of a new leader:

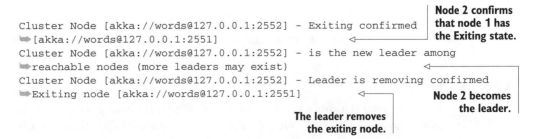

Gossip protocol

You may wonder how the seed nodes in the example know that the first seed node is leaving, exiting, and finally removed. Akka uses a *gossip* protocol to communicate the state of the cluster to all member nodes of the cluster.

Every node gossips to other nodes about its own state and the states it has seen (the gossip). The protocol makes it possible for all nodes in the cluster to eventually agree about the state of every node. This agreement is called *convergence*, which can occur over time while the nodes gossip to each other. To assist this convergence in the case of unreachable nodes, the Split Brain Resolver (SBR) was created.

A leader for the cluster can be determined after convergence. The first node (in sort order) that is Up or Leaving automatically becomes the leader. (The full remote address of the node is used to sort nodes, such as akka.tcp://words@ 127.0.0.1:2551.)

Seed nodes 2 and 3 learn that seed node 1 has requested to leave the cluster. As soon as node 1 transitions to the `Exiting` status, seed node 2 automatically takes over and changes the status of the leaving node from `Exiting` to `Removed`. Now the cluster has two seed nodes and is still fully functional. The transitions of node 1 in this example are shown in figure 8.9.

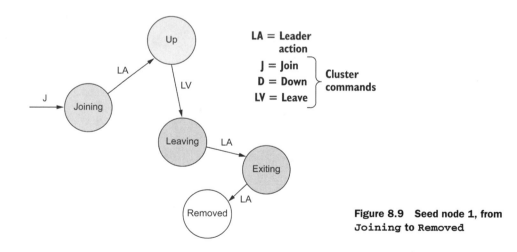

LA = Leader action
J = Join
D = Down   } **Cluster commands**
LV = Leave

Figure 8.9   Seed node 1, from `Joining` to `Removed`

Now let's look at a situation where the state is not represented. This is the case when a node is missing.

8.2.5   *Unreachable*

There are various reasons a node cannot be reached, including a network partition, a very long garbage collector (GC) pause, or an ungraceful shutdown. In these cases, the leader cannot fulfill its duties: that is, the nodes cannot be set to the `Leaving` or `Up` state. The only state you can set under these circumstances is `WeaklyUp`.

Let's see what happens if one of the seed nodes crashes without the possibility of shutting it down properly. This can be simulated by killing the process.

> **NOTE** Under Linux or macOS, you can kill a process with `kill -9 [PID]`. On Windows 10, you can use `taskkill /F /PID [pid_number]`. You can find this PID by searching a Java process with the parameters `-jar [.../.../]sbt -launch.jar` and `-DPORT=2551` if you try to kill node 1 of the previous example.

Here is the output of the terminal running seed node 2 when seed node 1 is abruptly terminated:

Seed node 1 becomes unreachable.

```
Cluster Node [akka://words@127.0.0.1:2552] - Marking node as UNREACHABLE
[Member(akka://words@127.0.0.1:2551, Up)].                          <-
Cluster Node [akka://words@127.0.0.1:2552] - is the new leader among
reachable nodes (more leaders may exist)   <-
```

Node 2 becomes the leader.

Seed node 1 is marked as `UNREACHABLE` by the cluster, thanks to a failure-detection mechanism that decides when a node should be considered unreachable.

The seed node was in an `Up` state when it crashed, but this can happen in any state. The node marked as `UNREACHABLE` must be shut down in this scenario because there is no way back. It cannot recover and return to the cluster; this is not allowed for security reasons.

To start the node again, you can run the `Main` class in chapter08a, which contains the same code you pasted to start the node:

```
import akka.actor.typed.ActorSystem
import akka.actor.typed.scaladsl.Behaviors

object Main extends App {

  ActorSystem(Behaviors.empty, "words")
}
```

To start a node with this `Main`, enter the following in the command line:

```
sbt -DPORT=2552 chapter08a/run
```

Note that the port here is 2552. Feel free to change it depending on what ports are available to you.

8.2.6 *Downing a reachable node*

It is possible to shut down a node from any node in the cluster by sending an `akka.cluster.type.Down` message. The following listing shows how to shut down node 1 from the REPL by creating the address that points to node 1 and sending a down message to the cluster manager.

Listing 8.3 Taking down seed node 1 manually

```
scala> import akka.actor.Address
scala> import akka.cluster.typed.{ Cluster, Down}
scala> val address = Address("akka", "words", "127.0.0.1",2551)
address: akka.actor.Address = akka://words@127.0.0.1:2551
scala> Cluster(guardian).manager ! Down(address)
Cluster Node [akka://words@127.0.0.1:2552] - Marking unreachable node
↪[akka://words@127.0.0.1:2551] as [Down]
Cluster Node [akka://words@127.0.0.1:2552] - Leader can perform its duties
↪again
Cluster Node [akka://words@127.0.0.1:2552] - Leader is removing unreachable
↪node [akka://words@127.0.0.1:2551]
Association to [akka://words@127.0.0.1:2551] with UID [3375074971115939575]
    is irrecoverably failed. UID is now quarantined and all messages to this
    UID will be delivered to dead letters. Remote ActorSystem must be
    restarted to recover from this situation. Reason: Cluster member
    removed, previous status [Down]
```

> Seed node 1 is set to Down.

> Seed node 1 is set to Removed.

> Seed node 1 is quarantined and removed.

> Seed node 2 can now set any member to Up, Down, Exiting, or Removed.

The output also shows that the `ActorSystem` of seed node 1 would have to reboot if it wanted to reconnect. Although an unreachable node can be configured via settings to shut down automatically after a certain time, this is not recommended. It is best to use the Akka SBR, which will automatically make this decision for you based on your configuration. You can set it by adding the following to your .conf:

```
akka.cluster.downing-provider-class =
↪"akka.cluster.sbr.SplitBrainResolverProvider"
```

This topic is discussed in more detail in chapter 13.

Failure detector

The cluster module uses an implementation of a φ *accrual failure detector* to detect unreachable nodes. The work is based on a paper by Naohiro Hayashibara, Xavier Défago, Rami Yared, and Takuya Katayama (https://ieeexplore.ieee.org/document/1353004). Detecting failures is a fundamental concern for fault tolerance in distributed systems.

The φ accrual failure detector calculates a value on a continuous scale (called a φ [phi] value) instead of determining a Boolean value indicating failure (if the node is reachable or not). From the referenced paper: "Roughly speaking, this value captures the degree of confidence that a corresponding monitored process has crashed. If the process crashes, the value is guaranteed to accrue over time and tend toward infinity, hence the name." This value is used as an indicator for suspecting that something is wrong (a suspicion level) instead of determining a hard-and-fast yes-or-no result.

The suspicion level concept makes the failure detector tunable and allows for a decoupling between application requirements and monitoring the environment. The cluster module provides settings for the failure detector that you can tune for your specific network environment in the `akka.cluster.failure-detector` section, including a threshold for the φ value at which a node is deemed unreachable.

Nodes are often deemed unreachable when they're in a *GC pause* state, which means it's taking far too long to finish garbage collection, and a JVM can't do anything else until garbage collection has completed.

In this example, you looked at the cluster logs to determine the cluster's state and see how to interact with it. You entered commands into the console to get nodes to leave the cluster or switch to the `Down` state. As mentioned earlier, this is not the approach you use in a real application—all these tasks are delegated to the SBR module.

A special module is available to interact with the cluster, check its status, and change it: Akka Management, particularly the Cluster HTTP submodule. Let's take a look at it.

8.3 *Akka Management and the Cluster HTTP extension*

Akka Management is a set of tools you can use to perform cluster operations. Many modules are built on top of it, but for now, we focus on `akka-management-cluster-http`. Its API lets you check the status of the cluster via HTTP calls and change it if the configuration allows.

To add this functionality, you need to include some library dependencies: `akka-management`, `akka-management-cluster`, and, to work around the transitive dependencies, `akka-cluster-sharding` and `akka-discovery`. Here's how:

```
val AkkaManagementVersion = "1.1.4"
val AkkaVersion = "2.6.20"

libraryDependencies ++= Seq(
"com.lightbend.akka.management" %% "akka-management" % AkkaManagementVersion,
"com.lightbend.akka.management" %% "akka-management-cluster-http" %
AkkaManagementVersion,
"com.typesafe.akka" %% "akka-cluster-sharding" % AkkaVersion,
"com.typesafe.akka" %% "akka-discovery" % AkkaVersion)
```

This gives you the following `akka-management` default configuration:

```
akka.management.http.hostname = "<hostname>"
akka.management.http.port = 8558
```

InetAddress.getLocalHost.get HostAddress is used if .hostname is "<hostname>" or empty.

Port pun: it "complements" 2552

That provides an HTTP endpoint at

```
[InetAddress.getLocalHost.getHostAddress]:8558
```

Something like 192.168.178.70:8558

Now you need to start the Akka Management server in each node:

```
import akka.management.scaladsl.AkkaManagement

AkkaManagement(system).start()
```

Adding this code to the `Main` in chapter08a starts the Akka Management server in each node when you run it. Such a `Main` looks like this:

```
import akka.actor.typed.ActorSystem
import akka.actor.typed.scaladsl.Behaviors
import akka.management.scaladsl.AkkaManagement

object Main extends App {

  ActorSystem(Behaviors.empty, "words")        ⟵┐ Starts the ActorSystem in cluster
  AkkaManagement(system).start()    ⟵┐           mode as per the configuration
                                      Starts the Akka
}                                     Management server
```

Remember, since this example is running on the same machine, you need to pay attention to the ports: not only `remote.canonical.port`, as before, but also `akka.management.http.port`, which must also be different from the default for all nodes except the first one that is running. Otherwise, you get

```
java.net.BindException: [xyz-address] Address already in use.
```

Do the following to start the first node:

```
$ sbt -DPORT=2551 \
-Dakka.management.http.port=8558 \
-Dakka.management.http.hostname=127.0.0.1 chapter08a/run
```

Then do the same in another terminal, setting ports 2552 and 8559 to start another node and add it to the cluster. Once node 1 is set up, you can manage the cluster with the now-added `akka-management`. The available operations are shown in table 8.1.

Table 8.1   Akka Management HTTP available paths

Path	HTTP method	Required form fields	Description
/cluster/members/	GET	None	Returns the status of the cluster in JSON format
/cluster/members/	POST	Address: {address}	Executes the `join` operation in the cluster for the provided {address}
/cluster/members/ {address}	GET	None	Returns the status of {address} in the cluster in JSON format
/cluster/members/ {address}	DELETE	None	Executes the `leave` operation in the cluster for the provided {address}
/cluster/members/ {address}	PUT	Operation: Down	Executes the `down` operation in the cluster for the provided {address}

Table 8.1 Akka Management HTTP available paths *(continued)*

Path	HTTP method	Required form fields	Description
/cluster/members/ {address}	PUT	Operation: Leave	Executes the leave operation in the cluster for the provided {address}
/cluster/shards/ {name}	GET	None	Returns shard info for the shard region with the provided {name}

By default, only the getters are available. All operations that have side effects—that is, that change the states of nodes—are available only if the following is set: `akka .management.http.route-providers-read-only` = `false`.

You can use the getter `127.0.0.1:8558/cluster/members` to get the status of your cluster. You should get something similar to the following listing.

Listing 8.4 Status of the cluster

```
{
  "leader": "akka://words@127.0.0.1:2551",        ⬅
  "members": [              ⬅─┐  List of members
    {
      "node": "akka://words@127.0.0.1:2551",
      "nodeUid": "-4766935219030085168",
      "roles": [
        "seed",
        "dc-default"
      ],
      "status": "Up"
    },
    {                                               The leader is
      "node": "akka://words@127.0.0.1:2552",        the oldest.
      "nodeUid": "-6827274415967400234",
      "roles": [
        "seed",
        "dc-default"
      ],
      "status": "Up"
    }
  ],
  "oldest": "akka://words@127.0.0.1:2551",         ⬅─┘
  "oldestPerRole": {
    "seed": "akka://words@127.0.0.1:2551",
    "dc-default": "akka://words@127.0.0.1:2551"
  },
  "selfNode": "akka://words@127.0.0.1:2551",
  "unreachable": []              ⬅─┐  Flagged as
}                                    unreachable
```

If `akka.management.http.route-providers-read-only` is set to `false`, you can force the node on port 2552 to leave by requesting

```
curl -XDELETE localhost:8558/cluster/members/akka://words@127.0.0.1:2552
```

The response is {"message":"Leaving akka://words@127.0.0.1:2552"}.

8.3.1 *Cluster subscriptions*

Another way to check the status of the cluster is subscription. Instead of making a synchronous HTTP call to the akka-management-cluster HTTP module, you can be notified with ClusterDomainEvent messages. You can subscribe an actor to these cluster events using the subscriptions method on the akka.cluster.typed .Cluster.

The word-counting application shows how the guardian subscribes to the cluster domain events to verify that the application is Up and ensure a minimum number of nodes in the cluster to which it can hand off work. You don't want to start processing text if there are no workers to do the counting. But before we get to that, let's look at how an actor can subscribe to lifecycle events and be notified.

NOTE   The source code for the following example is available at www.manning .com/books/akka-in-action-second-edition or https://github.com/franciscol opezsancho/akka-topics/tree/main/chapter08b. You can find the contents of any snippet or listing in the .scala file with the same name as the class, object, or trait.

The following listing shows how an actor subscribes to .setup, defines its behavior to handle these ClusterDomainEvents, and unsubscribes when it receives a PostStop signal.

Listing 8.5 Subscribing to cluster domain events

```scala
import akka.actor.typed.PostStop
import akka.actor.typed.scaladsl.Behaviors
import akka.cluster.typed.{ Cluster, Subscribe, Unsubscribe }
import akka.cluster.ClusterEvent._
import akka.cluster.MemberStatus

object ClusterDomainEventListener {

  def apply() = Behaviors.setup[ClusterDomainEvent] { context =>
    Cluster(context.system).subscriptions ! Subscribe(
      context.self,
      classOf[ClusterDomainEvent])          ⟵┐  Subscribes to the cluster domain
                                                events on actor creation
    Behaviors
      .receiveMessage[ClusterDomainEvent] {  ⟵  Listens for cluster
        case MemberUp(member) =>                 domain events
          context.log.info(s"$member UP.")
          Behaviors.same
        case MemberExited(member) =>
          context.log.info(s"$member EXITED.")
          Behaviors.same
        case MemberRemoved(m, previousState) =>
          if (previousState == MemberStatus.Exiting) {
            context.log.info(s"Member $m gracefully exited, REMOVED.")
```

```
      } else {
        context.log.info(s"$m downed after unreachable, REMOVED.")
      }
      Behaviors.same
    case UnreachableMember(m) =>
      context.log.info(s"$m UNREACHABLE")
      Behaviors.same
    case ReachableMember(m) =>
      context.log.info(s"$m REACHABLE")
      Behaviors.same
    case event =>
      context.log.info(s"not handling ${event.toString}")
      Behaviors.same

  }
  .receiveSignal {
    case (context, PostStop) =>
      Cluster(context.system).subscriptions ! Unsubscribe(
        context.self)                          ◁───  Unsubscribes after
      Behaviors.stopped                              receiving the stopped signal
  }
  }
}
```

Together with `Cluster.manager`, which is used to shut down or exit nodes in the cluster, `Cluster.subscriptions` completes the available API of `akka.cluster`
`.typed.Cluster`. While the former is used almost exclusively in Akka internals, the latter is used in applications.

With this understanding of the basics of an Akka cluster, let's dive into the details of a simple application and distinguish what belongs to the cluster functionality and what belongs to the application domain.

8.4   Clustered job processing

The following application uses two main types of actors: the master and the worker, each living in different nodes depending on whether the node has the role of director or aggregator. The master produces texts that need to be grouped and counted by words. To accomplish this, the master delegates the grouping and counting of each text to the workers while aggregating only the result of each worker's work.

Each text is sent from the master to a random worker, which processes it by counting the occurrences of each word in the text. The worker node processes each text asynchronously, resulting in faster processing, and sends the result of the count back to the master, which summarizes the work. The idea is to divide and conquer in the context of a resilient application. This is shown again in figure 8.10.

Depending on the node's role, a master is created on a director node, and the workers are created on the aggregator nodes. When a director node starts, it creates a master actor and a router that can communicate with each registered worker. The master uses this router to delegate each text to each worker. To simplify the example, the master produces a text every second instead of pulling data from a source such as a topic or a queue as it would in a real application.

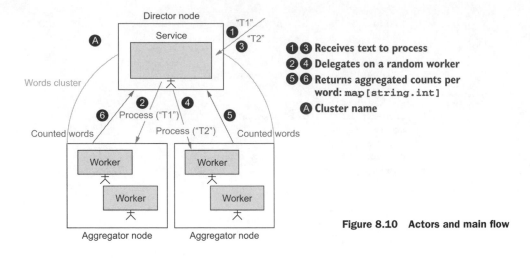

Figure 8.10   Actors and main flow

The master sends messages at the specified rate to a random worker and expects a response within three seconds. This response can be a `Success` with the aggregation of words or a `Failure` with the original message, which is then forwarded to a queue (called `lag`) for reprocessing. If successful, the master merges the aggregation with its current state and keeps the total sum of all aggregations received up to that time. Again, this is shown in figure 8.11.

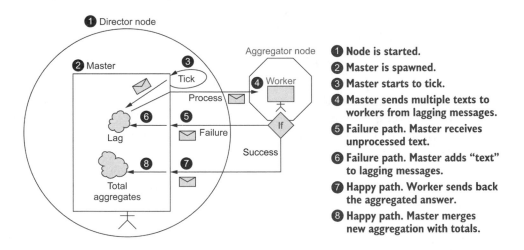

Figure 8.11   Flow of a master

When an aggregator node starts, it creates the number of workers specified in the configuration. These workers register during setup with a `Worker.RegistrationKey` so the master's router, which subscribes to that key, can find them and send them work.

From that point on, messages arrive at the workers and are processed, and the results are returned in the form of a `Map[String,Int]` indicating the frequency per word.

Figure 8.12 shows the business logic of a worker. The following sections cover the steps in detail, from starting the cluster to distributing the work to testing the application's resilience in case of a crashed aggregator node.

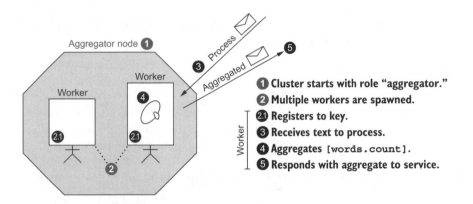

Figure 8.12 Worker business logic

> ## Some caveats for the example
>
> In this example, it is assumed that the error is due not to the content of the message but rather to the lack of communication. If a worker cannot process a message because of the content, the situation is handled by supervision—and that would not illustrate the main topic of this chapter. The troubleshooting we are concerned with here is resilience through clustering.

8.4.1 *In practice*

To see the logic between the master and the workers at runtime, let's look at the logs of the director node where the master is running. When the workers reach Up status, a master is created and sends them texts to process. Eventually, they respond, and the count is added to the master state. The following listing shows the output logging two types of variables from the master when running CounterApp: the lag and the current word count.

Listing 8.6 Aggregator output from the master actor with aggregator nodes

```
[17:50:14,499] [DEBUG]—receiving, current lag 0                          ◁──┐
[17:50:14,505] [DEBUG]—current count HashMap(this -> 16, a -> 32, very ->
 ▶16, simulates -> 16, simple -> 16, stream -> 32)
```
When text comes back and is merged over previous counts

When new text is ready to be sent to a worker

```
[17:50:14,505] [DEBUG]—current count HashMap(this -> 17, a -> 34, very ->
➡17, simulates -> 17, simple -> 17, stream -> 34)
[17:50:14,505] [DEBUG]—current count HashMap(this -> 18, a -> 36, very ->
➡18, simulates -> 18, simple -> 18, stream -> 36)
[17:50:14,505] [DEBUG]—current count HashMap(this -> 19, a -> 38, very ->
➡19, simulates -> 19, simple -> 19, stream -> 38)
[17:50:14,505] [DEBUG]—current count HashMap(this -> 20, a -> 40, very ->
➡20, simulates -> 20, simple -> 20, stream -> 40)
```

The lag is zero because the workers are available and all texts sent at this time are processed without any problems. Let's dive into the code.

8.4.2 *The code*

Part of the entry point for starting the application is shown in listing 8.7. Some of it is related to the `role` and `port` parameters specified at startup. If no parameters are passed, an aggregator is created with a random port for the `akka.remote` configuration. Otherwise, the parameters can specify the port and role of the node.

> **Listing 8.7 Entry point of the application**

```
import akka.cluster.Cluster
import akka.actor.typed.scaladsl.{ Behaviors, Routers }
import akka.actor.typed.{ ActorSystem, Behavior }
import com.typesafe.config.ConfigFactory

object CounterWordsApp {

  def main(args: Array[String]): Unit = {
    if (args.isEmpty) {
      startup("aggregator", 0)          ⟵┐ When no params are passed, spawns
    } else {                              │ an aggregator node in a random port
      require(
        args.size == 2,
        "Usage: two params required 'role' and 'port'")   ⟵┐ When params are
      startup(args(0), args(1).toInt)                      │ passed, two are required:
    }                                                      │ role and port
  }

  def startup(role: String, port: Int): Unit = {

    val config = ConfigFactory
      .parseString(s"""
      akka.remote.artery.canonical.port=$port
      akka.cluster.roles = [$role]
      """)                                              ┌ Adds role and port to the selected
      .withFallback(ConfigFactory.load("words"))   ⟵─┘ configuration file, words.conf

    ActorSystem[ClusterDomainEvent](ClusteredGuardian(), "WordsCluster",
    ➡config)                 ⟵┐ Starts
  }                            │ the cluster
         ┌ The file continues with the
  ...  ⟵┘ ClusteredGuardian definition.
```

These parameters can be the following:

```
sbt:chapter08b>runMain example.countwords.CounterApp seed 2551
sbt:chapter08b>runMain example.countwords.CounterApp director 2555
sbt:chapter08b>runMain example.countwords.CounterApp aggregator 2556
sbt:chapter08b>runMain example.countwords.CounterApp aggregator 2557
```

Executing each one from a different terminal would launch four application nodes: one seed node, one director, and two aggregators. Since the master can't do anything without the workers, it makes sense for the master to be moved to Up only when the cluster has a certain minimum number of worker nodes. You can use the configuration to set the minimum number of members with a particular role as a prerequisite for becoming Up. This configuration file defines a list of local seed nodes running on 127.0.0.1 and ports 2551, 2552, and 2553; since 2551 is the first seed node, this is sufficient to start the cluster.

Listing 8.8 Configuring the minimum number of worker nodes for `MemberUp`

```
...
cluster {
    seed-nodes = [
    "akka://WordsCluster@127.0.0.1:2551",
    "akka://WordsCluster@127.0.0.1:2552",
    "akka://WordsCluster@127.0.0.1:2553",
    ]
    role {
      seed.min-nr-of-members = 1            Number of node members required
      aggregator.min-nr-of-members = 2      for any node to be moved to Up
    }
}
example.countwords {          Number of workers in         Number of texts to be pulled
  workers-per-node = 5    ◁─┘ each aggregator node         from the lag queue and
  delegation-parallelism = 20              ◁────────────   distributed to the workers
}
...
```

This configuration specifies that at least two aggregators and one seed must be Joining before they can be moved to Up. You must also subscribe to the SelfUp cluster domain event to defer the guardian spawning the master.

  If the guardian is created in a director node, two actors are created when SelfUp is received: a group router and a master that uses this router to delegate work to workers at random (the router's default strategy). If the guardian is created in an aggregator node—for example, with runMain example.countwords.App worker 2556—it spawns as many workers as are defined in the configuration value example .countwords.workers-per-node.

Listing 8.9 Guardian setup and registration

```
import akka.cluster.Cluster
import akka.actor.typed.scaladsl.{ Behaviors, Routers }
import akka.actor.typed.{ ActorSystem, Behavior }
import com.typesafe.config.ConfigFactory
```

```
object CountWordsApp {

  def main ...

  def startup(role: String, port: Int): Unit = ...

  private object ClusteredGuardian {

    def apply(): Behavior[SelfUp] =
      Behaviors.setup[SelfUp] { context =>
        val cluster = Cluster(context.system)
        if (cluster.selfMember.hasRole("director")) {
          Cluster(context.system).subscriptions ! Subscribe(
            context.self,
            classOf[SelfUp])
        }
        if (cluster.selfMember.hasRole("aggregator")) {
          val numberOfWorkers =
              context.system.settings
                .config.getInt("example.countwords.workers-per-node")
          for (i <- 0 to numberOfWorkers) {
            context.spawn(Worker(), s"worker-$i")
          }
        }
        Behaviors.receiveMessage {
          case SelfUp(_) =>
            val router = context.spawnAnonymous {
              Routers
                .group(Worker.RegistrationKey)
            }
            context.spawn(Master(router), "master")
            Behaviors.same
        }
      }
  }
}
```

Only spawns a master with its router if this node has a director role

Only spawns workers if the node is started with an aggregator role

Subscribes to be notified when Up after the minimum number of members is reached

The number of workers to create is taken from the word.conf file.

Spawns a router with a random name

Spawns a router. The master under the notification node director is Up.

Next, let's examine the master.

8.4.3   *Work distribution in the master*

This chapter is about communication between different JVMs; therefore, messages sent to another node—here, from the aggregator to the director—must be serialized. For this reason, part of the protocol of the master is defined with CborSerializable. You learn more about serialization later, when you have a complete picture of the master and worker implementation. For now, let's focus on the master's protocol:

```
object Master {

  sealed trait Event
  final case object Tick extends Event
  final case class CountedWords(aggregation: Map[String, Int])
      extends Event
      with CborSerializable
```

To schedule the creation of text to count

To process the words grouped and counted by the worker

```
final case class FailedJob(text: String) extends Event                    ◄─────┐

  ...                                                                            │
}
```

To deal with failed jobs by adding
the text back to the lag queue

At initialization, the master schedules a `Tick` message to itself every second, generating a fake text for processing. After initialization, it changes its state to `working`:

```
import akka.actor.typed.{ ActorRef, Behavior }
import akka.actor.typed.scaladsl.Behaviors

object Master {

    ...        ◄──┤ Protocol

  def apply(workerRouter: ActorRef[Worker.Command]): Behavior[Event] =
    Behaviors.withTimers { timers =>
      timers.startTimerWithFixedDelay(Tick, Tick, 1.second)          ◄───────┐
      working(workerRouter)    ◄──┐
    }                              │   Behavior after              Timer to emulate an
                                   │   initialization              event per second. The
    final def working ...    ◄─────┘                               signature is (key,
                                                                   message, delay).
}
```

Each generated text is added to the lag queue. From there, a batch the size of `example.countwords.delegation-parallelism` is sent to the router, which forwards the messages to the workers. Each request to a worker is executed by an `ask` with a timeout of 3 seconds. With four aggregator nodes, each with five workers, a delegation parallelism of 20 texts would be fully utilized.

When the worker's response comes back, the master sends itself `CountedWords` when the response is `Success` or `FailedJob` when the response is `Failure`.

Listing 8.10 Master's working method implementation, part 1

```
object Master {

  ...
  def working(
      workersRouter: ActorRef[Worker.Command],
      countedWords: Map[String, Int] = Map(),        ◄──┐ State that contains
      lag: Vector[String] = Vector()): Behavior[Event] =    the counted words
    Behaviors.setup[Event] { context =>                  ◄──┐ State that contains
                                                              the lag and total
      implicit val timeout: Timeout = 3.seconds               aggregated words
      val parallelism = ...                   Timeout for asking
      Behaviors.receiveMessage[Event] {
        case Tick =>
          context.log.debug(s"receiving, current lag ${lag.size} ")

          val text = "this simulates a stream, a very simple stream"
          val allTexts = lag :+ text
          val (firstPart, secondPart) = allTexts.splitAt(parallelism)
```

Degree of
parallelism
read from the
configuration

```
            firstPart.map { text =>
              context.ask(workersRouter, Worker.Process(text, _)) {    ⟵
                case Success(CountedWords(map)) =>
                  CountedWords(map)                                    Asks for aggregation
                case Failure(ex) =>                                    to the workers via
                  FailedJob(text)                                           the router
              }
            }
            working(workersRouter, countedWords, secondPart)
        case ...
      }
    ...
}
```

If the message the master sends to itself is `CountWords`, it adds the count to the total
number of `countedWords` using a `merge` function. If the message is `FailedJob`, it
sends the failed text to itself and puts it back into the `lag` queue.

Listing 8.11   Master's working method implementation, part 2

```
object Master {

  ...
  def working(
      workersRouter: ActorRef[Worker.Command],       ⟞ State that contains
      countedWords: Map[String, Int] = Map(),    ⟵     the counted words
      lag: Vector[String] = Vector()): Behavior[Event] =   ⟵
    Behaviors.setup[Event] { context =>                    State that contains
                                                           the lag and total
      ...                                                  aggregated words
      Behaviors.receiveMessage[Event] {
        case Tick =>
          ...                            After a successful
        case CountedWords(map) =>    ⟵   request, aggregation
          val merged = merge(countedWords, map)
          context.log.debug(s"current count ${merged.toString} ")
          working(workersRouter, merged, lag)
        case FailedJob(text) =>
          context.log.debug(
            s"failed, adding text to lag ${lag.size} ")
          working(workersRouter, countedWords, lag :+ text)
      }
    }
                                     Merge function to add the
    private def merge(           ⟵   new count to current
        currentCount: Map[String, Int],
        newCount2Add: Map[String, Int]): Map[String, Int] = ...
}
```

After a failed request, unprocessed text goes back to lag. ⟶ (pointing to `case FailedJob(text) =>`)

Let's take another look at the master business logic; see figure 8.13. The worker has
only one message type in its protocol, with the text to process and the reference to
reply to the master:

```
final case class Process(text: String, replyTo: ActorRef[Master.Event])
    extends Command with CborSerializable
```

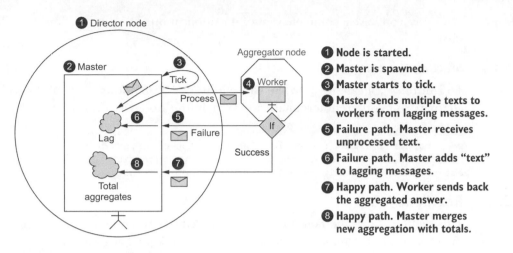

Figure 8.13   Master business flow

During setup, the worker registers itself in the registration key so the master's router can find it later. After setup, each time it receives a Process message, it splits the text into words, counts them, and sends the result back to the master.

Listing 8.12   Worker implementation

```scala
import akka.actor.typed.{ ActorRef, Behavior }
import akka.actor.typed.scaladsl.Behaviors
import akka.actor.typed.receptionist.{ Receptionist, ServiceKey }

object Worker {

  val RegistrationKey = ServiceKey[Worker.Command]("Worker")

  sealed trait Command
  final case class Process(text: String, replyTo: ActorRef[Master.Event])
      extends Command
      with CborSerializable        ◁─┤ Serialization

  def apply() = Behaviors.setup[Command] { context =>
    context.log.debug(
      s"${context.self} subscribing to $RegistrationKey")
    context.system.receptionist ! Receptionist       ◁─┐ Registration at
      .Register(RegistrationKey, context.self)            │ initialization

    Behaviors.receiveMessage {
      case Process(text, replyTo) =>
        context.log.debug(s"processing $text")
        replyTo ! Master.CountedWords(processTask(text))    ◁─┐ Processes the
        Behaviors.same                                          │ message
    }
  }

  private def processTask(text: String): Map[String, Int] = ...
}
```

Protocol *(label for the* sealed trait Command */* Process *block)*

With this, you have a complete view of the application. The next section shows how to start it.

8.4.4   *Starting the cluster*

To run the application, go to the Git repository. Launch four sbt shells by typing sbt chapter08b in different terminals, and launch four nodes as follows:

```
sbt:chapter08b>runMain example.countwords.App seed 2551
sbt:chapter08b>runMain example.countwords.App director 2555
sbt:chapter08b>runMain example.countwords.App aggregator 2556
sbt:chapter08b>runMain example.countwords.App aggregator 2557
```

8.5   *Resilient job*

This section shows the fault tolerance of the cluster when nodes fail. After you start the cluster and the master processes texts, you can kill all aggregator nodes and wait. Before you start a new aggregator, while no workers are available, the master collects every failure as lag, and nothing is lost. As soon as a new aggregator joins the cluster, the master can successfully delegate work again until the lag eventually reaches zero. Here is the output after shutting down all aggregator nodes:

```
[18:45:15,531] [DEBUG] - failed, adding text to lag 59      ◁      Result of a timeout
[18:45:15,540] [DEBUG] - tick, current lag 60          ◁──┐      after the master sends
[18:45:15,540] [DEBUG] - failed, adding text to lag 56         requests to workers
[18:45:15,540] [DEBUG] - failed, adding text to lag 57
[18:45:15,540] [DEBUG] - failed, adding text to lag 58      Result when the master
                                                            creates a new text
```

The lag is not ordered, which illustrates the essence of the indeterminacy of messaging.

When a new aggregator node is added to the cluster and the workers are spawned and registered, they start working, and the master's lag decreases:

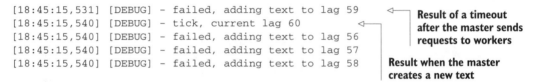

```
                                                      Result when the master
                                                      creates a new text
[18:50:14,499] [DEBUG]—tick, current lag 351      ◁──┘
[18:50:14,505] [DEBUG]—current count HashMap(this -> 16, a -> 32, very ->
➡16, simulates -> 16, simple -> 16, stream -> 32)                        ◁──────────┐
[18:50:14,505] [DEBUG]—current count HashMap(this -> 17, a -> 34, very ->          │
➡17, simulates -> 17, simple -> 17, stream -> 34)                                   │
[18:50:14,505] [DEBUG]—current count HashMap(this -> 18, a -> 36, very ->          │
➡18, simulates -> 18, simple -> 18, stream -> 36)                                   │
[18:50:14,505] [DEBUG]—current count HashMap(this -> 19, a -> 38, very ->          │
➡19, simulates -> 19, simple -> 19, stream -> 38)                                   │
[18:50:14,505] [DEBUG]—current count HashMap(this -> 20, a -> 40, very ->          │
➡20, simulates -> 20, simple -> 20, stream -> 40)                                   │
[18:50:15,510] [DEBUG]—receiving, current lag 347       Result when a text
                                                        comes back aggregated
                                                        from the worker
```

The lag accumulated in the master decreases more quickly than new texts are created. You would see a similar result if you dropped one of the two aggregators—the application would still work. This is the fault tolerance you expect from a cluster.

This simple case shows how Akka provides a powerful abstraction. You can build your business logic without worrying about degradation or failure and deal with it when you design the application entry point and roles. This essential part of Akka, along with supervision, provides the fault tolerance needed to build reliable distributed systems.

8.5.1 Serialization

Up to this point, sending messages between actors has not been a problem because they have run on the same JVM. But when actors run on different JVMs, either on the same host or on different machines, the messages must be converted from objects into bytes and vice versa. Let's look at how to serialize them.

You can add various libraries to help with this or create your own serializer. The most common option, recommended for its good performance and easy setup, is an Akka module that uses Jackson serialization. It comes with two serializers to choose from. To use it, add its dependency in build.sbt:

```
val AkkaVersion = "2.6.20"

libraryDependencies += "com.typesafe.akka" %% "akka-serialization-jackson"
➥% AkkaVersion
```

Then add one of these two serializers to your application configuration:

```
akka {
  actor {
    serializers {                                                    Serializes to JSON
      jackson-json = "akka.serialization.jackson.JacksonJsonSerializer"   ◄─────
      jackson-cbor = "akka.serialization.jackson.JacksonCborSerializer"   ◄───
    }
  }                                                                  Serializes to a
}                                                                  compact binary form
```

These two are included in reference.conf, which is included in the `akka-serialization-jackson` library to provide the default configuration for this library. `JacksonCborSerializer` provides a binary format that is more compact and has slightly better throughput than `JacksonJsonSerializer`, which is text-based. To select either format, set the binding as follows:

```
serialization-bindings {
    "example.countwords.CborSerializable" = jackson-cbor     ◄────
}                                                           Binds the trait
                                                    example.countwords.CborSerializable
                                                       to the jackson-cbor serializer
```

With this configuration, you must ensure that you have such a trait in your application and mix it with the messages you need to serialize. In this chapter's example, that means all messages going from the master to workers or vice versa. The example.countwords.CborSerializable trait is nothing more than a place-holder that points to the serialization of your choice. Here is the implementation:

```
package example.countwords

trait CborSerializable
```

For example, as you saw in the master, you need to use the trait with the message that requires serialization:

```
object Master {
  ...
  final case class CountedWords(aggregation: Map[String, Int])
      extends Event
      with CborSerializable
  ...
}
```

Another serialization library is Google Protocol Buffers. This option has better throughput than Jackson and very flexible schema development. The downside is that it requires more work to set up and maintain. Whichever serialization you choose, it's important to consider schema evolution (but that's a topic in itself and not specific to Akka, as you may know). In most cases, the serialization chosen in this example is sufficient to use in production.

8.5.2   *Testing is no different*

One of Akka's powerful abstractions is that you don't need to add anything additional to test your actors. You can emulate your application without having to start a cluster. The following listing shows how to create a test that proves that the master generates tick after tick and gets the expected number of words each time.

Listing 8.13   Testing the master and worker processing words

```
class WordsSampleSpec ... {

  "The words app" should {
    "send work from the master to the workers and back" in {
      //given
      val numberOfWorkers =
        system.settings.config
          .getInt("example.countwords.workers-per-node")

      for (i <- 0 to numberOfWorkers) {          ◁─┐  Sets five workers, as
        spawn(Worker(), s"worker-$i")              │  per the configuration
      }

      val router = spawn {
        Routers
          .group(Worker.RegistrationKey)         ◁─┐  Creates
      }                                            │  a router
      //when
      val probe = createTestProbe[Master.Event]
```

```
      val masterMonitored =
        Behaviors.monitor(probe.ref, Master(router))
      spawn(masterMonitored, "master0")          ◄─┐ Creates a master with
      //then                                        │ a router and a probe
      probe.expectMessage(Master.Tick)
      probe.expectMessage(
        Master.CountedWords(
          Map(
            "this" -> 1,
            "a" -> 2,
            "very" -> 1,
            "simulates" -> 1,
            "simple" -> 1,
            "stream" -> 2)))
      ...                          ◄─┐ Repeats both
    }}                               │ expectations
}
```

NOTE The Akka test kit provides tools to create automated tests that form clusters in multiple JVMs, but developers rarely use them. The Akka Cluster codebase is full of them, as they are necessary to test the properties of the cluster in an automated way. However, this is a topic beyond the scope of this book. You can find more information at http://mng.bz/wvEa.

Dynamically growing and shrinking a simple application is simple with the Cluster extension. Joining and leaving the cluster is easy, and you can test the functionality in a REPL console, a tool that allows you to experiment and verify how things work. If you've followed along with the REPL sessions, it should be apparent how solid this extension is; crashes in the cluster are properly detected.

Clustering is a notoriously painful chasm to cross, usually requiring many admin and programming changes. In this chapter, you've seen that Akka makes it much easier and doesn't require rewriting code. The word-counting example is about the generic way Akka processes jobs in a cluster in parallel. You used cluster routers and ask to make the actors cooperate and deal with failure, and you got a taste of how easy it would be to test the application. The ability to test the logic of a distributed application without any additional effort is a significant advantage that you quickly get used to with the Akka test kit: you can find problems in your application before you put it into operation on a large scale.

In the next chapter, you learn how to distribute actors evenly in the cluster to avoid having too many actors in one node and too few in another. You also see how to persist the state of an actor in a durable store.

Summary

- Creating a cluster is as simple as setting the actor provider, remote, and seed nodes in the configuration and creating an ActorSystem at the command line.
- The node's lifecycle is a state machine, from Joining the cluster to being Removed, with all the intermediate states: WeaklyUp, Up, Leaving, Down, and Exiting.

- With the cluster configuration, you can use the word-counting application and run actors on different nodes. When you shut down some nodes and create new ones, the application reaches a new level of resilience and scalability. No work is lost, and counting can continue when new nodes are added to the cluster.
- When you test the application logic, you don't have to worry about the cluster. These areas are separated, and you can focus on the business logic without thinking about clustering. Akka takes care of that for you.

Sharding and persistence

This chapter covers

- Distributing actors in a cluster
- Storing each change of the actor's state in a database

This chapter discusses two of the seven tools used to build microservices: Akka Sharding and Akka Persistence. The others are Akka Streams, Persistence Query, Projections, HTTP, and gRPC, which you learn about in chapters 10 and 11.

These Akka tools can be used separately (and are traditionally used that way). However, they are increasingly used as a functional unit: looking at them all together helps us better understand them. We call this functional view *Akka microservices* (to learn more, see appendix B).

> **NOTE** The source code for this chapter is available at www.manning.com/books/akka-in-action-second-edition or https://github.com/franciscolopezsancho/akka-topics/tree/main/chapter09a. You can find the contents of any snippet or listing in the .scala file with the same name as the class, object, or trait.

171

9.1   *Akka sharding and stateful systems*

Akka cluster sharding distributes the locations of actors; they are called *entities* when sharding. With cluster sharding, you can ensure that each entity is unique and that there is at most one in the cluster at any given time.

> **DEFINITION**   *Shards* are logical containers in which entities are grouped.

Entities are automatically relocated when new nodes are added or current nodes leave the cluster. This is primarily useful for two reasons. Perhaps most obvious is the sharing of resources so the memory required by the actors is distributed among the nodes.

> **NOTE**   The node of an entity is selected by the modulus of its ID hashed over the number of shards.

Relocating entities also helps in case of failures. The entities are protected when a node fails by moving them to another healthy member of the cluster. Isolation by node also protects entities that live in healthy nodes from failures of other nodes. However, when an entity is moved, it loses its state because the entity is restarted. To preserve its state, you need a storage mechanism: Akka Persistence, which we discuss later in this chapter.

9.1.1   *The big picture*

A node in a sharded cluster can create shard regions (SRs) that contain shards, which in turn contain distributed entities. Shards are groups of entities: the number of shards is determined by the configuration, and their content is determined by the sharding function mentioned previously. SRs contain shards and are responsible for routing messages to entities. These relationships are shown in figure 9.1.

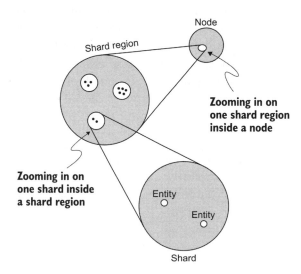

Figure 9.1   Relationships among nodes, shared regions, shards, and entities

Which shards belong to which SR and how to find the entities is ultimately managed by the shard coordinator (SC). Figure 9.2 shows all of these sharding components.

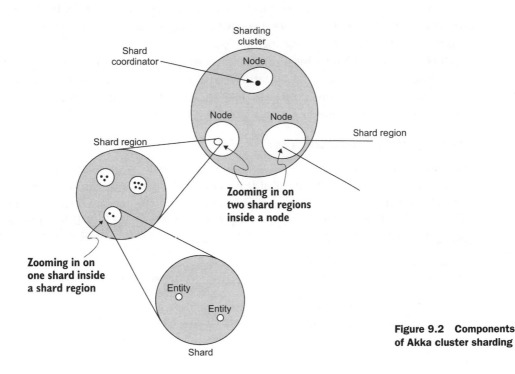

Figure 9.2   Components of Akka cluster sharding

There is only one SC in the entire cluster, and it has two main tasks: monitoring the state of the shards and facilitating access to each entity. SR monitoring is necessary to ensure that shards are moved from a congested or unhealthy region to a healthy one. This means an unreachable node must be removed from the cluster before the shard and its entities can be moved. Otherwise, a previously unreachable node could rejoin the cluster after rebalancing, and there would be duplicates in the cluster. Fortunately, the Split Brain Resolver (SBR) manages unreachable nodes (more on the SBR in chapter 13).

The SC provides the necessary mechanism to communicate with entities. The same function used to assign entities is also used to find them; however, this is done indirectly. When a message is sent to an entity, it must be done through an SR. If this SR does not know where the entity lives, and in which node, it asks the SC. You might think it could lead to a bottleneck if the SC received a query for every message, but this is not the case. Once the SC finds the correct SR to forward the message, it passes this information to all SRs in the cluster and delegates all further forwarding to the entities to the SRs.

Through the API, you can send messages to an entity two ways. The first technique is indirect: send the message to the SR of the same node. If the entity is in a different node—that is, in a different SR—the local SR forwards the message to the SR where the entity is located, and the latter forwards the message to the entity itself. The second technique is to send messages directly by obtaining a reference to the entity and then sending the message with a normal `tell(!)`.

During normal rebalancing—that is, not during a failure—messages are kept in a buffer until the displaced entity is restored. However, if you lose a node, you may lose messages before all regions notice the loss and start buffering: the messages are not buffered until the SR is marked unavailable.

9.1.2 *An example: A shipping container*

Let's say you have a shipping company that needs to move containers. You want to choose the origin and destination of the shipment, the type of cargo—a large bag, a sack, a barrel, and so on—and the type of container for the cargo. You also want to distribute the application load evenly, so you use Akka Sharding. To do so, add the following dependency in build.sbt:

```
val AkkaVersion = "2.6.20"
libraryDependencies += "com.typesafe.akka" %% "akka-cluster-sharding-typed"
⟿% AkkaVersion
```

Let's start by defining the actor's protocol so you can add loads to a container and check its status:

```
object Container {

  final case class Cargo(id: String, kind: String, size: Int)

  sealed trait Command
  final case class AddCargo(cargo: Cargo)
      extends Command
      with CborSerializable
  final case class GetCargos(replyTo: ActorRef[List[Cargo]])
      extends Command
      with CborSerializable


  ...
}
```

To become an entity, an actor needs a key of type `EntityTypeKey` and an ID (a `String`). The combination of the two must be unique in the cluster. The `Entity-TypeKey` refers to the type of the actor. This way, you can have two different types of entities with the same ID without collisions. The following listing shows the entity's ID (`containerId`) in its constructor. The container is initialized with an empty list (no cargo) and set to the `ready` behavior that allows you to `AddCargo` and `GetCargos`.

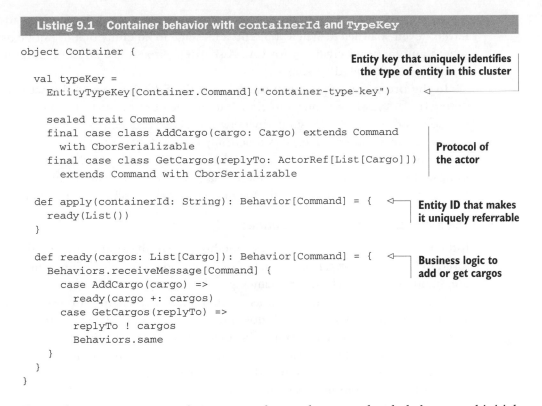

Listing 9.1 Container behavior with `containerId` and `TypeKey`

```
object Container {

  val typeKey =
    EntityTypeKey[Container.Command]("container-type-key")

  sealed trait Command
  final case class AddCargo(cargo: Cargo) extends Command
    with CborSerializable
  final case class GetCargos(replyTo: ActorRef[List[Cargo]])
    extends Command with CborSerializable

  def apply(containerId: String): Behavior[Command] = {
    ready(List())
  }

  def ready(cargos: List[Cargo]): Behavior[Command] = {
    Behaviors.receiveMessage[Command] {
      case AddCargo(cargo) =>
        ready(cargo +: cargos)
      case GetCargos(replyTo) =>
        replyTo ! cargos
        Behaviors.same
    }
  }
}
```

- Entity key that uniquely identifies the type of entity in this cluster
- Protocol of the actor
- Entity ID that makes it uniquely referrable
- Business logic to add or get cargos

To send a message to an entity, you must have at least one sharded cluster and initial-ize an SR from it. You can have one SR in a node and thus have only one type of entity, or more than one SR and different entity types. Once you have an SR, you can send a message to an entity by wrapping it in an envelope along with the entity's ID:

```
class ContainerSpec ... {

  ...

  val sharding = ClusterSharding(system)
  val entityDefinition = Entity(Container.typeKey)(createBehavior =
      entityContext => Container(entityContext.entityId)))

  val shardRegion: ActorRef[ShardingEnvelope[Container.Command]] =
    sharding.init(entityDefinition)

  val containerId = "id-1"
  val cargo = Container.Cargo("id-c","sack",3)

  shardRegion ! ShardingEnvelope(containerId, Container.AddCargo(cargo))

  ...
}
```

- Sharded cluster
- Entity definition
- Sharding region created from the key and containerId
- Sends the message wrapped in an envelope

It may surprise you that you don't have an `ActorRef` to send the message to—you haven't even spawned it. When you send a message to an entity that doesn't exist, the system automatically creates it for you. A sharded actor is not an `ActorRef`; it is an `EntityRef`, but the API is similar.

In the preceding snippet, you can see that the SR is built using the actor's key—`Container.TypeKey`—and a function that sets the `containerId` from the `Entity-Context`'s `entityId`. The similarity between the `EntityContext` and the `Actor-Context`—from an `ActorRef`—is practically nonexistent. `EntityContext` contains little more than the `EntityTypeKey` and the `EntityId: String`. Among other things, this means an `EntityContext` has no `watch` as you would find in an `ActorContext` and no methods for logging, spawning, or scheduling, to name a few.

9.1.3   *The simplicity of the sharded entities*

If the `EntityContext` had `watch` as a method, the entity abstraction could be monitored to be notified on termination, but that contradicts the idea of an entity. The system handles the lifecycle and rebalancing.

The essence of an entity is that its creation and maintenance are overseen by the sharding module, not by you. This does not mean it is impossible to watch the entity; you can still get a reference to its `ActorRef` from `self` and interact with it as you would with a normal actor. However, doing so can have unexpected consequences. For example, if you send messages directly to the `ActorRef`, the passivation mechanism—which adds or removes entities from memory depending on their activity—will not register those messages as activity (more about passivation later in this chapter).

The following listing has the same code as in the previous snippet, but in the context of a test with a probe that checks whether the container has the expected cargo after cargo is added.

Listing 9.2   Creating cluster shading and an SR and sending messages to an entity

```
import akka.cluster.sharding.typed.scaladsl.{        ←┐
  ClusterSharding,
  Entity,                                              Only shows the
  EntityRef,                                           import-related
  EntityTypeKey                                        cluster sharding
}
import akka.cluster.sharding.typed.ShardingEnvelope   ←┘

class ContainerSpec
    extends ScalaTestWithActorTestKit
    with AnyWordSpecLike
    with Matchers
    with LogCapturing {

  "a sharded freight entity" should {
    "be able to add a cargo" in {
```

```
      val sharding = ClusterSharding(system)
      val entityDefinition =
        Entity(Container.TypeKey)(createBehavior = entityContext =>
          Container(entityContext.entityId)))

      val shardRegion: ActorRef[ShardingEnvelope[Container.Command]] =
        sharding.init(entityDefinition)


      val containerId = "id-1"
      val cargo = Container.Cargo("id-c","sack",3)

      shardRegion ! ShardingEnvelope(
        containerId,
        Container.AddCargo(cargo))

      val probe = createTestProbe[List[Container.Cargo]]()                  Gets EntityRef
                                                                            by containerId
      val container: EntityRef[Container.Command] =          ◄───────────┘
        sharding.entityRefFor(Container.TypeKey, containerId)

      container ! Container.GetCargos(probe.ref)      ◄──┐   Sends a message without
      probe.expectMessage(List(cargo))                   │   ShardingEnvelope
    }
  }
}
```

As you can see, working with cluster sharding is simple. But keep in mind that shard-ing is a cluster feature, so you need to provide a configuration for it. The following configuration makes the preceding test work.

Listing 9.3 Container configuration

```
akka {
  actor {
    provider = cluster

    serialization-bindings {
      "example.persistence.CborSerializable" = jackson-cbor      ◄──┐  Maps
    }                                                                │  CborSerializable
  }                                                                  │  to jackson-cbor
                                                                     │  serialization
  remote {
    artery {                          ◄──┐  Sets the hostname
      canonical.hostname = 127.0.0.1     │  and port
      canonical.port = 2552
    }
  }

  cluster {
    seed-nodes = [
      "akka://ContainerSpec@127.0.0.1:2552"]   ◄──┐  Includes the name of the Spec
  }                                               │  as the ActorSystem in the URI
}
```

Because `ScalaTestWithActorTestKit` is used in the test, the name of the `ActorSystem` is the name of the `Spec: ContainerSpec`. Therefore, it is set as such in the seed-nodes URI in the configuration.

9.1.4 *Rebalancing configuration*

To deploy a shard rather than test it, you choose and set the number of shards with `akka.cluster.sharding.number-of-shards`. The optimal value is 10 times the number of nodes, because with 10 shards per node, the shard-to-node ratio remains reasonably balanced when a new node is added. For example, if you planned five nodes with two shards each, adding a new node would result in one node rebalancing only one of the two shards and the other four nodes not rebalancing at all (see figure 9.3).

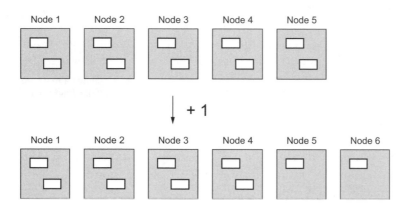

Figure 9.3   Rebalancing shards after adding a new node (shard region)

On the other hand, with 10 shards per node, as shown in figure 9.4, you have at most a 10% difference in load between nodes when you add a new node. Of course, the same is true for the loss of nodes.

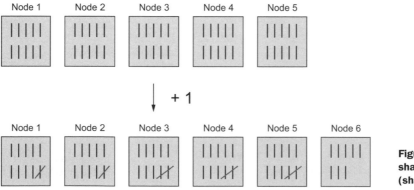

Figure 9.4   Ten shards per node (shard region)

The default algorithm for shuffling shards is implemented by `LeastShard-AllocationStrategy`, which shuffles shards from the regions with the most shards to the regions with the fewest shards. The default setting for rebalance, which you can find in reference.conf, is

```
akka.cluster.sharding.least-shard-allocation-strategy.rebalance-relative-
limit = 0.1
```

which means only 10% of the total shards may be moved per round. In general, this is good enough.

9.1.5 Passivation

Actors are very cheap to create—each is about 300 KB, so you can create thousands in 1 GB. But if you use them to store large objects, the memory requirements are quite different, and memory can be exhausted much faster. In these cases, it makes sense to *passivate* the entities: that is, to store them by specifying how long they should remain in memory after their last received message. The default is the following:

```
akka.cluster.sharding.passivate-idle-entity-after = 120s
```

However, passivation is disabled if `remember-entities` is enabled, which is not the case by default:

```
akka.cluster.sharding.remember-entities = off
```

When a passivated entity starts receiving new messages, the entity's mailbox is not yet active. Instead, the system buffers the messages and stores them until the entity is active again. But the buffer has a limit. Remember that only messages sent through an SR count, not direct messages to the underlying `ActorRef`.

9.1.6 Remembering entities

After a rebalance or entity crash, entities are automatically reloaded into memory if they have a backup. You need to set `akka.cluster.sharding.remember-entities-store` to one of these to create an entity backup: `ddata` or `eventsourced`. Both settings also disable passivation. Akka Distributed Data (`ddata`) is a structure that can handle concurrent updates without coordination and is the default setting, while `eventsourced` keeps the events in a persistent storage.

> **NOTE** Messages are sent with at-most-once semantics by default, and the order is maintained by the SR. All messages sent to the same SR maintain the order of receipt.

But when an entity is reloaded into memory, its state is not restored. In the container example, you get the container back, but it's empty, with no cargo. So, you probably need something more than sharding. You need Akka Persistence.

9.2   *Persistence*

Akka Persistence follows the event sourcing (ES) modeling style. This means events that take place in your actor are attached like a ledger rather than being kept as a single value that is updated and replaced after each event.

> **DEFINITION** An *event* is the output (stored as a ledger entry) that a persistent actor generates when it receives a message.

This ledger is called a *journal* and is a table in a database that only grows (appends). The entire history of a persistent actor is stored in its journal. The journal begins with a message: a command representing the intention to change the actor. But before this transformation can take place, the command must be validated by executing it in the actor to ensure that the new state created by the command is accepted. If it is, an event can be generated and stored, as shown in figure 9.5.

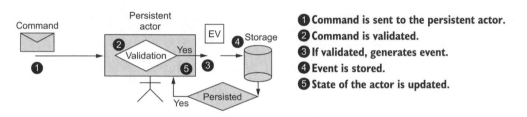

① Command is sent to the persistent actor.
② Command is validated.
③ If validated, generates event.
④ Event is stored.
⑤ State of the actor is updated.

Figure 9.5   From command to a stored event

When the actor needs to be restarted, it reads the journal and replays all the events. Thus, the actor returns to its last known state, as illustrated in figure 9.6. Let's look at this in action.

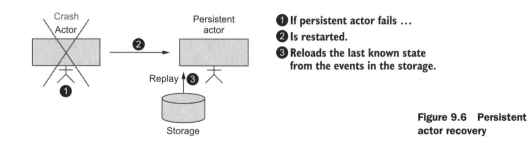

① If persistent actor fails …
② Is restarted.
③ Reloads the last known state from the events in the storage.

Figure 9.6   Persistent actor recovery

9.2.1   *The ingredients*

To add the persistence API to your project, add the following to build.sbt. You will be testing the application, so also add the specific test kit:

```
val AkkaVersion = "2.6.20"
libraryDependencies ++= Seq(
```

```
  "com.typesafe.akka" %% "akka-persistence-typed" % AkkaVersion,
  "com.typesafe.akka" %% "akka-persistence-testkit" % AkkaVersion % Test
)
```

> **NOTE** The source code for this example is available at www.manning.com/
> books/akka-in-action-second-edition or https://github.com/franciscolopez
> sancho/akka-topics/tree/main/chapter09b. You can find the contents of any
> snippet or listing in the .scala file with the same name as the class, object, or
> trait.

To create a persistent actor, you need to create a specific behavior of type `Event-SourcedBehavior`. Its constructor takes four parameters (`persistenceId`, `state`, `commandHandler`, and `eventHandler`) and three types (`Command`, `Event`, and `State`). All of them together make an `EventSourcedBehavior`:

```
import akka.persistence.typed.scaladsl.EventSourcedBehavior
import akka.persistence.typed.PersistenceId

object PersistentActorExample {

  def apply[Command, Event, State](          ←  Generic types with
                                                 descriptive meanings

    persistenceId: PersistenceId,             ←  ID used to keep a reference to the
                                                 actor when the actor is stored

    state: State,           ←┤  Initial state of the persistent actor

    commandHandler: (State, Command) => Effect[Event, State],   ←
                                                                    Function that
                                                                    applies a
    eventHandler: (State, Event) => State)                          command to a
          :EventSourcedBehavior[Command, Event, State]   ←┐         state, producing
                                                                    an event
                                     Function that stores an        and a state
}                                    event with a state
```

The names of the types are just that: names. They are not types that exist outside of this definition, with the exception of the `State` type, which refers to a class within the actor. Nevertheless, it is common to use the same names when creating a behavior. Let's look at the four parameters.

The `persistenceId` must be unique. Note that there are scenarios where collisions can occur. For example, in a cluster, you can create an actor with the same ID in different nodes. Akka Persistence doesn't have a mechanism to check the uniqueness of a single node, but Akka Sharding does. To solve this problem, you can easily create a sharded entity from an `EventSourcedBehavior` just as you would with a simple actor: by adding an `EntityTypeKey`.

Another scenario is two different types of entities with the same ID. Again, Akka Sharding is used to solve this problem. In this case, the type key of the entity is appended to the ID of the persistent actor. This combination guarantees the uniqueness of the entity.

The `state` is the simplest of the four parameters. Its type (`State`) must be defined as a class when writing the persistent actor to provide a placeholder for the current state. In the container, the `State` is a list of cargo:

```
final case class State(cargos: List[Cargo] = Nil)
```

The function `commandHandler (State, Command) => Effect[Event, State]` takes as input any message of type `Command` sent to the actor, as well as its current `State`. From this, it creates an `Event` and a new `State`. Commands create reactions on the actor—called *effects*—such as persist, reply, and stop. Depending on the received message and the actor's state, you can pattern-match on both to achieve the desired effects.

Side effects—which are different from effects—are, for example, a post to an HTTP server or a database insert and should also be executed in the command handler. With the `thenRun` function, the side effect can be added to effects like `persist`:

```
Effect.persist([Event]).thenRun(//**side effect**//).    ◁——  Side effect such as a
                                                               database insertion
```

When the command handler has successfully persisted the event, the `eventHandler` function is executed (you don't want to change the actor's state if the command handler has not validated the event). This has to do with the fact that saved events will be processed again by the event handler when the persistent actor is restarted on recovery. Only what is saved can determine the current state of the actor.

When the event is persisted, the `eventHandler` function receives the event and the state from the command handler, which can now update the actor's state. The `eventHandler` function has the following signature:

```
def eventHandler(state: State, event: Event): State
```

Be careful to avoid side effects in the event handler. When a persistent actor is restarted, each entry is replayed to return to its last state by being passed as input to the `eventHandler` function. Thus, if the event handler has side effects, they will also be replayed.

The flow between the command handler and the event handler is as follows: the command sent to the actor may trigger an event, which can modify the state. The state is passed from the command handler to the event handler—quite different from the simple actors you've seen so far. The state can be persisted by the command handler, and only then can the event handler change the state in the actor. So, when the next message arrives, the command and the current state determine the actor's behavior. You can pattern-match with both the actor's state and the command to define what the actor does. But for now, let's keep it simple and use only the command. You see how to use both state and command to define behavior in chapter 12.

In the container example, when receiving `AddCargo`, the actor tries to store a `CargoAdded` event and, if successful, changes the actor's state by adding that cargo to its list of cargo. Note that `CargoAdded` is also part of the actor's protocol and is of type `Event`.

Listing 9.4 `Container` implemented as event sourcing with Akka Persistence

```scala
import akka.actor.typed.scaladsl.Behaviors
import akka.actor.typed.{ ActorRef, Behavior }

import akka.persistence.typed.scaladsl.{
  Effect,
  EventSourcedBehavior
}
import akka.persistence.typed.PersistenceId

object Container {

  final case class Cargo(id: String, kind: String, size: Int)

  sealed trait Command                            ⟵┐  Messages to interact
  final case class AddCargo(cargo: Cargo)          │  with the actor
      extends Command
      with CborSerializable
  final case class GetCargos(replyTo: ActorRef[List[Cargo]])
      extends Command
      with CborSerializable
                                         ┐  Event that can
  sealed trait Event              ⟵──────┘  be triggered
  final case class CargoAdded(containerId: String, cargo: Cargo)
      extends Event
      with CborSerializable
                                                    ┐  State of
  final case class State(cargos: List[Cargo] = Nil) ⟵┘  the actor

  def apply(containerId: String): Behavior[Command] =   ⟵┐  Initializes the
    EventSourcedBehavior[Command, Event, State](          │  persistence entity
      PersistenceId.ofUniqueId(containerId),
      State(),
      commandHandler = (state, command) =>
        commandHandler(containerId, state, command),
      eventHandler)

  def commandHandler(          ⟵┐  Handles commands
      containerId: String,      │  and triggers events
      state: State,
      command: Command): Effect[Event, State] =
    command match {
      case AddCargo(cargo) =>
        Effect.persist(CargoAdded(containerId, cargo))
      case GetCargos(replyTo) =>
        Effect.none.thenRun(state => replyTo ! state.cargos)
    }
                                                     ┐  Handles events triggered
  def eventHandler(state: State, event: Event): State =  ⟵┘  from commandHandler
    event match {
```

```
      case CargoAdded(containerId, cargo) =>
        state.copy(cargos = cargo +: state.cargos)
  }
}
```

`PersistenceId.ofUniqueId` checks that the value passed is not `null` or empty and re-creates `toString`, `hashCode`, and `equals`.

9.2.2 *Persistence combined with sharding: A persistent entity*

To guarantee the uniqueness of a persistent actor in a cluster, you can combine it with sharding. You need to add an `EntityTypeKey` and use it when setting the persistence ID of the persistent actor. To do so, you can use one of the `PersistenceId` constructors:

```
def apply(entityTypeHint: String, entityId: String)
```

Typically, you combine the `EntityTypeKey` with the actor's ID—here, `typeKey` with `containerId`:

```
object SPContainer {

  val typeKey =
    EntityTypeKey[SPContainer.Command]("spcontainer-type-key")   ◁──┐ Adds the
                                                                    │ EntityTypeKey
    ...                                                             │ of the entity

  def apply(containerId: String): Behavior[Command] =
    EventSourcedBehavior[Command, Event, State](
      PersistenceId(typeKey.name, containerId),   ◁──┐ Combines the containerId
      State(),                                        │ with the typeKey
      commandHandler,
      eventHandler)

  ...
}
```

To instantiate the actor, you need to treat it like an entity. Create a sharded cluster (an SR), and instantiate it from there:

```
object Main {
  ...                                                │ Creates a sharded
  val sharding = ClusterSharding(system)   ◁──┘ cluster
  val entityDefinition = Entity(SPContainer.typeKey)(entityContext =>
        SPContainer(entityContext.entityId)))

  val shardRegion: ActorRef[ShardingEnvelope[SPContainer.Command]] =   ◁──────┐
      sharding.init(entityDefinition)
  ...                                                        Creates the SR
}                                                            holding SPContainer
```

9.2.3 *Available effects*

Let's quickly run down the options regarding command handler effects. `Effect` is a factory of functions available to persistent actors that represents the different reactions to a `Command`. The functions are as follows:

- persist—Persists a single event or multiple events. There are several functions with this name that accept one or more events. This operation is performed atomically: all or none of the events are persisted.
- none—Does not persist the event. Not all commands produce an event, as in the example GetCargos.
- unhandled—Indicates that the command is intentionally not operational to avoid throwing an exception when such a command is received.

These three functions are mutually exclusive. You can add side effects to them with

```
thenRun(callback: State => Unit): EffectBuilder[Event, State]
```

to which you must pass the desired callback. The signature shows that this side effect can access the state and doesn't need to return anything. You can chain several side effects with the guarantee that their callbacks will be executed in order. However, effects appended to persist will not be executed if persist fails.

You can run persist after another effect, but doing so is not recommended. There is an important drawback: persist can always fail, and if that happens, the actor can signal with that other effect something that didn't occur. For example, the persistent entity could send a message to another actor, notifying it about Added-Cargo, and then persist it. In doing so, the notified actor assumes that the cargo was added to the container—but if persistence fails, the assumption is false.

To reply to an actor, you can use the more specific thenReply, which is provided as a convenience method. Add .withEnforceReplies to your persistent entity, and it will throw a compilation error if no thenReply is added.

Finally, you can add thenStop to stop the actor if needed. For example, you may want to stop the container if it has been emptied. To do so, use something like this:

```
case StopIt =>
    Effect.none.thenStop()
```

Buffering in Akka

In some cases, you may want to wait until your application has reached a certain state before processing messages: for example, not processing any message until some initial values have been loaded from the database. For this purpose, you can add the following after thenRun:

- stash—Keeps the commands in a buffer
- unstash all—Flushes the commands from the buffer, which can be done with thenUnstashAll

It is important to note that this buffer only lives in memory and is lost when the actor restarts or stops. This can happen with any exception, but with a persistent failure, it can be handled so that the buffer is not lost. You can handle this scenario by using EventSourcedBehavior.onPersistFailure with a SupervisorStrategy .restartWithBackoff, available in the Akka Persistence API.

(continued)

Stashing and unstashing happen automatically when one or multiple events are persisted. Commands are buffered while persisting; when persistence succeeds, they are unstashed.

9.3   *Customizing the persistent entity*

Now that you know some of the problems you face when managing persistent actors, let's try to solve some of them.

9.3.1   *Failure*

If `persist` fails, you can recover by adding a `restartWithBackoff` supervision strategy, setting it via `.onPersistFailure`:

```
EventSourcedBehavior[Command, Event, State](
  persistenceId = ...,
  emptyState = ...,
  commandHandler = ...,
  eventHandler = ...,
).onPersistFailure(
    SupervisorStrategy.restartWithBackoff(          Adds supervision to
        minBackoff = 10.seconds,                    recover from failure
        maxBackoff = 60.seconds,
        randomFactor = 0.1))
```

This also preserves all buffered commands and makes them available for the next incarnation of the actor. With this configuration, if the actor crashes, it will attempt to restart after 10 seconds with a random accuracy of 10%. If it cannot be restarted within this time, it will attempt to do so with an increasing delay of 20, 30, 40, and 50 seconds, up to a maximum of 60 seconds.

9.3.2   *Recovery*

When an actor starts or is restarted, it always receives a recovery status signal, regardless of whether it has entries to read in the journal. After the actor has finished reading the events available in the journal, it receives the signal. This is useful, for example, if you want to send a message to another actor to let it know that this actor is ready to process data, or if you want to publish this signal so that it can be monitored by application operators.

As with any other signal, add `receiveSignal`, which gets two parameters (the current status and the message):

```
EventSourcedBehavior[Command, Event, State](
  persistenceId = ...,
  emptyState = ...,
  commandHandler = ...,
  eventHandler = ...,
).receiveSignal {
```

```
    case (state, RecoveryCompleted) =>
        ...
    case (state, RecoveryFailed(failure)) =>
        ...
}
```

Possibility to react after state reload is completed

Possibility to react if state reload can't complete

If the entire journal is read without trouble, the signal received is a `Recovery-Completed`. If it fails, a `RecoveryFailed(failure: Throwable)` signal is emitted, the cause is logged, and a `JournalFailureException` is thrown that stops or restarts the actor if a `restartWithBackoff` has been set. Some of the most common reasons for failure are that the event is corrupted or becomes corrupted during the transfer, or a new version of the actor is incompatible with an event.

9.3.3 *Snapshotting*

Restoring the state of the persistent entity by reading each event can take a very long time. The more extensive the actor's history is, the worse its initialization time. To reduce the load time, you can take snapshots when one of two types of conditions is met: an event contains a certain value, or a number of events have been stored in the journal.

Suppose you add a new event called `QuarterReached` to the sharded container to indicate that it has reached a quarter of its capacity. Upon receiving this event, or after a certain number of events, you want to take a snapshot:

Snapshots each time the entity receives QuarterReached

```
EventSourcedBehavior[Command, Event, State](...).snapshotWhen {
    case (state, QuarterReached(_), sequenceNumber) => true
    case (state, event, sequenceNumber)             => false
}
.withRetention(
    RetentionCriteria.snapshotEvery(numberOfEvents = 100,
        keepNSnapshots = 2))
```

Doesn't snapshot otherwise when matching events

Snapshots each 100 events, and keeps the two previous snapshots

A snapshot is created every time the message `QuarterReached` is received by the actor and after every 100 events are processed. In both cases, `keepNSnapshots` indicates that you are deleting previous snapshots. Here only the last two are available. This releases resources while keeping two previous snapshots in case something goes wrong.

By default, the snapshot feature is enabled and configured to read the last snapshot. However, if an error occurs, a `SnapshotFailed` signal is triggered, but the actor does not stop; it just logs the error.

If you know you have a corrupted snapshot or that it is incompatible with your actor—after you have written a new version—you can avoid loading it by setting the recovery to `SnapshotSelectionCriteria.none`:

```
EventSourcedBehavior[Command, Event, State](...)
    .withRecovery(Recovery.withSnapshotSelectionCriteria(SnapshotSelection
        Criteria.none)
```

9.3.4   Tagging

When you save to the journal, you usually mark each event so other processes can read the journal by filtering for those marks. After all, the journal is just a table in a database. The tagging is done as follows:

```
EventSourcedBehavior[Command, Event, State](...)    Adds these two tags
   .withTagger( _ => Set("tag1", "tag2"))           no matter what event
```

Another typical use case for tagging is to parallelize reading by assigning a set of IDs to a tag so each reader can focus on a particular tag, just like a partition. You can use both in the container to tag specific events and parallelize:

```
.withTagger{                                           Adds these two tags
    case event: CargoAdded =>                          when CargoAdded
            Set("container-tag-"+ containerId.toInt % 3, "CargoAdded")
    case _ => Set("container-tag-"+ containerId.toInt % 3)
}
                                                       Adds only this tag
                                                       for the rest of the events
```

These settings allow a maximum parallelism of 3 to read `CargoAdded` events or the rest of the events as a whole.

9.3.5   *A peek at serialization and schema evolution*

Everything stored on disk must be serialized. Serializing the events of a persistent actor is no different than serializing the messages of an actor. The problem arises when the schema of events changes and evolves.

When Akka restores an actor from the journal, it uses the message's serializer/ deserializer (SerDe) to convert the events back into objects. For example, in the container, the SerDe is the binding to `CborSerializable`. The same SerDe can be used for certain schema changes, but for others, you need to find a way to accommodate the changes.

Schema evolution occurs in most mature applications when the events that the application processes evolve and need to coexist with older versions. New features are added, bugs are found, or technical debts are addressed; events can change as new fields are added or others are lost; they can be split into multiple events or merged into one.

Let's look at this with `AddCargo(id, kind, size)`. After a while, the company realizes it wants to record the process by which the cargo is loaded into the container by a human or a robot. So, a `loadedBy` field is added to `AddCargo` and also to `CargoAdded`. Once this is done, you redeploy the new version. But events loaded from the journal have no reference to this new field.

One solution would be to migrate all data from the journal to the new event type and fill it with a third value, such as "no data" in the new `loadedBy` field. However, doing so would sacrifice the advantages of the event-sourcing approach. Events are immutable facts—the past is not there to be changed. Now imagine that instead of adding a new field, you want to get rid of one. If you delete that field in the journal, it will be unrecoverable.

With an event-sourcing approach, you can solve these problems by doing two things: choose a strategy to deserialize multiple versions of events, and decide how to load the old events into the new event type. To find SerDe for different versions of the events, you can rely on the available functions in Jackson or Google Protocol Buffers. If you follow their rules, you can safely add, remove, and update fields. If you decide to use a custom serializer, you need several SerDes; depending on the version of the event, the right one will be selected.

If a new field is added when loading the data into the persistent actor, a default value must be added to the field. This is an alternative to updating all previous events, as mentioned earlier. A third value, such as "no data," could be added to the old event values when the event is loaded—but this would require using the Akka Persistence event adapters, which is beyond the scope of this chapter (see http://mng.bz/7De7).

9.4 Running example

The `Main` application in the book's Git repository in the chapter09b project uses what you saw in the previous section. This application adds tagging, snapshotting, and monitoring to the `SPContainer` as follows:

```
object SPContainer {
    ...

    .withTagger {
      case _ => Set("container-tag-" + containerId.toInt % 3)
    }
    .withRetention(RetentionCriteria
      .snapshotEvery(numberOfEvents = 100, keepNSnapshots = 2))
    .onPersistFailure(
      SupervisorStrategy.restartWithBackoff(
        minBackoff = 10.seconds,
        maxBackoff = 60.seconds,
        randomFactor = 0.1))
    ...
}
```

You should always add these to any application. With the preceding configuration, the application takes a snapshot after every 100 events. If the actor crashes, it tries to restart after 10 seconds with a random accuracy of 10% and with an increasing delay of 20, 30, 40, and 50 seconds, up to a maximum of 60 seconds. With the tags, all events are divided into three categories: `container-tag-0`, `container-tag-1`, and `container-tag-2`. This way, three consumers can use the journal in parallel.

The chapter09b project also has a database that uses three tables—`event _journal`, `event_tags`, and `snapshots`—to store the events in the journal, along with the application's configuration. The code sets up a Postgres database via `docker-compose up` and provides the SQL scripts to create the tables for journal events, tags, and snapshots. All the details are in README.md. Once the database is running and the three tables are created, you can start the application by typing `sbt chapter09b/run` at the command line.

When the application starts, you can interact with the cluster through the sbt shell by writing in it the message you want to send to the container. To send a message, enter values for `containerId`, `cargoId`, `cargoKind`, and `cargoSize`, separated by spaces, and press Enter.

> **NOTE** You haven't learned how to interact with a cluster from the outside. Sending messages through the console is not how you would usually do this. This solution is implemented for you so you can play with it. Chapter 11 covers how to send messages to a cluster through HTTP and gRPC.

When you send a message to the entity, an event is generated and stored in the database. Here's how three messages are sent to the `SPContainer`:

```
$ 9 456 sack 22          Enter these values, pressing
$ 9 459 bigbag 15        Enter after each one.
$ 11 499 barrel 120
```

These messages add cargos 456 and 459 to container 9 and cargo 499 to container 11; table 9.1 shows the resulting journal entries in the database table `journals_events`. (Not all table fields are shown.)

Table 9.1 Journal entries in the database table `public.journal_events`

ordering	persistence_id	sequence _number	deleted	event_ser_id	event _payload	event_ ser_id
1	SPContainer - type-key|9	1	false	33	binary data	33
2	SPContainer - type-key|9	2	false	33	binary data	33
3	SPContainer - type-key|11	3	false	33	binary data	33

The `persistence_id` field consists of the `typeKey` and `containerId`. The `sequence_number` is an ascending number for each entity. The `deleted` field allows you to mark events as deleted because in certain cases, for compliance or security reasons, you need to delete the data. (In the event-sourcing approach, the data is not deleted but only marked as such.) The `event_payload`, the actual `CargoAdded` message, is stored in cbor-jackson, so it is binary. If you choose the `json-jackson` binding, you can read the message directly in the table.

If the `event_ser_id` is between 0 and 40, it means the SerDe used is from an Akka module. For example, 33 is `jackson-cbor` from the module `akka-serialization-jackson`.

> **NOTE** You can find these IDs in the value of `akka.actor.serialization-identifiers` in the reference.conf files of the Akka modules.

If you use a SerDe that is not defined in Akka, the custom SerDe must have an `event_ser_id` value higher than `40`. This is defined by the `identifier` in the SerDe (see http://mng.bz/mVmW).

The tags created in the `tags` database are related to the events (see table 9.2). Because these tags can be joined in a database query with the previous table, such as

```
event_tag.event_id = event_journal.ordering
```

a reader can consume only the events for specific tags, increasing the overall capacity for parallelism. In chapter 10, you learn how to consume the journal to produce different views using queries like selecting containers that hold a specific cargo.

Table 9.2 Events in the `event_tag` table

event_id	tag
1	container-tag-0
2	container-tag-0
3	container-tag-2

Summary

- Akka Sharding allows you to distribute actors evenly in a cluster and address them by ID, leaving the location and relocation to the underlying mechanism.
- Akka Persistence gives you the ability to store the state of an actor in an event-sourcing fashion instead of using the standard approach of storing state by updating the previous state. With an event-sourcing approach, each change is stored as an entry in a ledger, always appending instead of updating. This way, you keep the history of all changes.
- Akka Persistence provides an interface based on commands and events you define with the command handler and the event handler. Each command triggers a function in the actor that can raise an event, which is usually stored in the database and changes the actor's state. This cycle is repeated for each received message.
- It's recommended that you add tags to events to provide parallelism when reading the journal. You can define the retention strategy for snapshotting and a supervision strategy to handle failure on persist.
- Serialization is necessary to store the events. Otherwise, the journal cannot be deserialized and thus cannot be read.

Streams, persistence queries, and projections

This chapter covers

- Creating a simple stream from its basic components: source, flow, and sink
- Reading events from the journal of the persistence entities
- Writing events from the journal into another table

In this chapter, you learn how to read from the journal and create views from it. To do this, Akka uses Akka Streams explicitly to read the journal—with the persistence-query module—and implicitly to create views—with the projections module.

NOTE   The source code for this chapter is available at www.manning.com/ books/akka-in-action-second-edition or https://github.com/franciscolopez sancho/akka-topics/tree/main/chapter10a. You can find the contents of any snippet or listing in the .scala file with the same name as the class, object, or trait.

10.1 Akka Streams

A *stream* is a sequence of data. It can be infinite, but it doesn't have to be. Examples include the messages you send or receive via email, tweets posted each day, clicks on a website, and videos you watch. From the perspective of the application that processes all of these events, they sometimes involve a huge amount of interaction.

There are a few problems when interacting with live events or a constant flow of information. Sometimes the flow is infinite by definition, so you can't wait until the process is finished to process its contents. Other flows, like audio, are not infinite, but you don't want to wait until the whole song or video is transferred to play it.

That's why there are streaming libraries that allow you to interact element by element in a potentially unlimited stream. But once you start consuming the stream, you inevitably run into the next problem. If the stream producer is faster than the consumer, two things can happen: the consumer takes each new item and keeps it in memory until it runs out of memory and crashes, or you can set an upper limit above which the consumer will discard messages and ask for them to be resent (like TCP). The first option is obviously a problem, but the second may not be as clear. A fast producer that is constantly asked to resend messages must keep an ever-growing list of messages to resend. In the end, it has the same problem as the slow consumer: if the producer doesn't drop the messages, it will crash.

The Reactive Streams initiative on which Akka Streams is based was created with this dual problem in mind. The main idea is to enable "live" streaming through asynchronous communication and backpressure. You're probably familiar with the asynchronous part: communication is nonblocking, meaning the producer doesn't have to synchronize with the consumer. Sending or requesting messages happens independently.

Its other essential property, backpressure, is an effect achieved by a combination of pulling and pushing. From this perspective, a producer cannot send a message to a consumer without first receiving confirmation that the consumer wants to receive it. The flow is reversed in this sense. Consumers—also called *downstreams*—set the flow in motion. They have to signal to the producers—called *upstreams*—that they can process data so the producer can send data downstream (see figure 10.1).

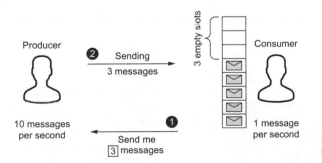

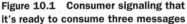

Figure 10.1 **Consumer signaling that it's ready to consume three messages**

10.1.1 Basic semantics

The basic abstractions of Akka Streams are the source, sink, and flow, which can be viewed respectively as a publisher, a consumer, and a combination of the two (see figure 10.2). The data flow goes from upstream to downstream, from source to sink, usually with a conversion in between.

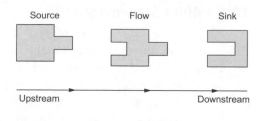

Figure 10.2   Akka Streams abstraction flow

You first need to import the Streams library, whether you're working with finite or infinite streams. Add the following to your build.sbt:

```
val AkkaVersion = "2.6.20"
libraryDependencies += "com.typesafe.akka" %% "akka-stream" % AkkaVersion
```

10.1.2 Finite streams

Let's start with finite data streams, which are easier to understand than infinite ones (the API is the same). Suppose you have a finite data source and you want to filter only the even values and store the result in a database. Let's sketch a scenario with a `List[Int]` of items as the source and a fake database implemented as a simple variable, also a `List[Int]`.

There are three stages available to build Akka Streams: `Sources` as producers, `Flows` as transformations, and `Sinks` as consumers. They are used in both finite and infinite streams; this is a finite example.

10.1.3 Source

In general, a `Source` comes from reading a file, database query, topic, queue, HTTP endpoint, or, as the following example shows, simple collection. The `Source` is lazy: it delays its evaluation until its values are needed. It waits for the consumer to send messages downstream. The combination of the three stages is called a *blueprint* or *graph* and is a pure function. It does nothing until it is asked to `run`, and when it does, it gives back a result. In this chapter, each result has at least a `Future[Done]`. You learn about different results in chapter 16.

The following snippet shows how the `Source` is created with a list of integers and `runForeach` executes the blueprint. This processes each element and stores it in the fake database:

```
class StreamsSpec ... {

  ...

  "a producer of fixed elements 1,2,3 and a function" should {
    "allow when consumed see the side effects | simple test version" in {
      var fakeDB: List[Int] = List()
      def storeDB(value: Int) =
        fakeDB = fakeDB :+ value
```

Stores the function →

Variable representing a side effect ←

```
        val future = Source(List(1, 2, 3))
           .filter(_ % 2 == 0)                    ◄───┤ Filters the function
           .runForeach(i => storeDB(i)))          ◄──┐
                                                      │  RunForeach creates a
        Await.result(future, 1.seconds)              │  consumer for the source and
        assert(fakeDB == List(2))                    │  executes the blueprint.
      }
    }


    ...
}
```

In this simple example, there is already a lot to unpack. You only see a Source in this graph, but it has all the stages. Let's look at it again but without the syntactic sugar of the Akka Streams API. You map each stage to a variable individually and then map all of them at once. Let's start with the producer:

```
val producer: Source[Int, NotUsed] = Source(List(1, 2, 3))
```

Source[Int, NotUsed] expresses that this producer generates integers, while NotUsed takes the position of the materialized value. To understand what *materialized* means, you need more context than the Source alone. You learn about NotUsed in section 10.1.7.

10.1.4 Flow

The transformation function—also called the *processor*—is the filtering part of the previous stream:

```
val processor: Flow[Int, Int, NotUsed] = Flow[Int].filter(_ % 2 == 0)
```

The first Int in Flow[Int, Int, NotUsed] indicates that the flow accepts integers as input and the second produces integers as output. NotUsed, again, refers to the materialization of the flow.

10.1.5 Sink

The third element is the consumer:

```
val consumer: Sink[Int, Future[Done]] = Sink.foreach(i => storeDB(i))
```

Sink[Int, Future[Done]] indicates that it consumes integers and produces a Future[Done]. This byproduct is called a *materialized value* and is produced when the stream is executed. It is the output of the graph. This can be confusing at first because the output of the graph in the future will be Done, while the values it processes are integers.

10.1.6 Blueprint

The blueprint is the product of mixing and matching the different stages. It's an abstraction that gives you composability and testability:

```
val blueprint
    : RunnableGraph[scala.concurrent.Future[akka.Done]] =
  producer.via(processor).toMat(consumer)(Keep.right)
```

Once stages compose a `RunnableGraph`, you have a function that is decoupled from the execution of the stream. You can pass it around and execute it at will:

```
val future: Future[Done] = blueprint.run
```

10.1.7 *Materialization*

Materialization is the execution of a blueprint, and its by-products are called *materialized values*. Materialization is similar to an `ActorRef` in that one behavior spawns multiple `ActorRefs`. With Akka Streams, you have one graph; each time you run it, you get its instance: a tuple with materialized values.

An `ActorSystem` handles the execution. Akka Streams are, after all, nothing more than actors processing data. In fact, by default, a stream is just one actor. To run the blueprint, you need an `implicit ActorSystem`.

> **NOTE**   Don't forget to stop the `ActorSystem` if nothing else needs to run on it. Perhaps you are creating a finite stream in an actor, and the actor should still be running when the stream is finished. This is not the case in the previous example. Nothing else needs to be executed there. If you use the `Scala-TestWithActorTestKit`, it terminates the system for you. If you need to terminate manually in a blueprint that creates a `Future[Done]`, you can use `future.onComplete(_ => system.terminate())`. To run this future, you need an execution context that you can get from the `ActorSystem` with `system.executionContext`.

The materialized values are there so that you can interact with the graph once it has been executed. In this example, the only materialized value is `Future[Done]`. This allows you to wait until the sink completes the future to make the assertion.

Both the source and the flow have materialized values, but they are not used here. There is no interaction with either after the graph is executed. Therefore, they are set to `NotUsed`:

```
val producer: Source[Int, NotUsed] = ...
val processor: Flow[Int, Int, NotUsed] = ...
```

However, in many use cases—especially with infinite streams—you want to interact with a flow or source: for example, to add more values to a stream or cancel it. In either case, if the materialized value is set to something other than `NotUsed`, it can travel through the stream until it reaches the materialization, where you can pull it out of the stream with `.toMat` and assign it to a variable for later use.

The materialization can be on the left or right side of the `.toMat` method. On the left side is `NotUsed`, produced by the previous flow; and on the right side—more precisely, within `.toMat`—is `Future[Done]`, produced by the `Sink.foreach`. The following listing shows the parts of the example: producer, processor, consumer, blueprint, and materialization.

Listing 10.1   Stream components

```
object Main extends App {                              System that provides the
                                                       materialization resources
  implicit val system = ActorSystem(Behaviors.empty,"runner")   ◄─────┘

  var fakeDB: List[Int] = List()
  def storeDB(value: Int) = fakeDB = fakeDB :+ value

                                                                    Source
        val producer: Source[Int, NotUsed] = Source(List(1, 2, 3))  ◄─┘
Flow  ├──►  val processor: Flow[Int, Int, NotUsed] = Flow[Int].filter(_ % 2 == 0)
        val consumer: Sink[Int, Future[Done]] = Sink.foreach(i => storeDB(i))  ◄─┤ Sink

  val blueprint: RunnableGraph[scala.concurrent.Future[akka.Done]] =
      producer.via(processor).toMat(consumer)(Keep.right)          ◄─┤ Blueprint

  val future: Future[Done] = blueprint.run()                       ◄─┤ Execution
  future.onComplete( _ => system.terminate)(system.executionContext)  ◄───────┐
}                                                                   Terminates the
                                                                     ActorSystem
```

10.1.8 Infinite streams

Examples of infinite streams are tweets received through an endpoint, updates read from a database from a table representing new orders on a website, and events from a car's telemetry read from a Kafka topic. Let's look at a scenario similar to the previous one. The only difference is that the data source is infinite, randomly produces integers from 0 to 3 (not including 3), and has a materialized value `Cancellable` that can be used to cancel the stream. This cancellable value traverses the stream until the `Sink`.

The next listing shows all of this in compact stream form in the next listing. Note that each text describing the test is unique; otherwise, the spec wouldn't compile. This is an infinite producer with a consumer that creates a side effect.

Listing 10.2   Cancelling an infinite stream

```
import akka.stream.scaladsl.{
  Keep,
  Sink,
  Source
}

import akka.Done
import akka.actor.Cancellable

import scala.concurrent.{ Await, Future }
import scala.concurrent.duration._

class StreamsSpec ... {

  ...
```

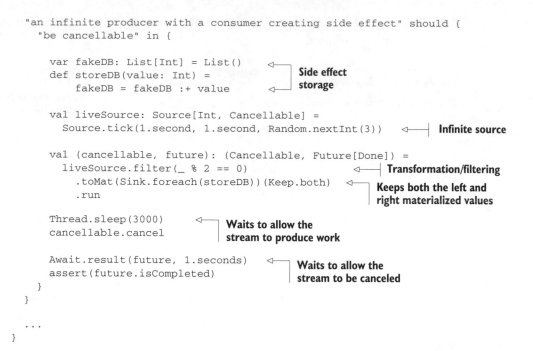

```
"an infinite producer with a consumer creating side effect" should {
  "be cancellable" in {

    var fakeDB: List[Int] = List()
    def storeDB(value: Int) =
        fakeDB = fakeDB :+ value

    val liveSource: Source[Int, Cancellable] =
      Source.tick(1.second, 1.second, Random.nextInt(3))

    val (cancellable, future): (Cancellable, Future[Done]) =
      liveSource.filter(_ % 2 == 0)
        .toMat(Sink.foreach(storeDB))(Keep.both)
        .run

    Thread.sleep(3000)
    cancellable.cancel

    Await.result(future, 1.seconds)
    assert(future.isCompleted)
  }
}

...
}
```

Side effect
storage

Infinite source

Transformation/filtering

Keeps both the left and
right materialized values

Waits to allow the
stream to produce work

Waits to allow the
stream to be canceled

The stream continues to send messages and "store" them in the database for about three seconds, after which it will be `.cancelled`. Then you can prove that the stream is finished when the future is completed.

This section discussed the basic features of Akka Streams that we use in the next two sections. In the next section, we cover a specific case of how to effectively read the journal from the database. This scenario is common when you use the persistence entities covered in chapter 9. The journal is a list of events optimized for writing, not reading. The persistence query is the first step in converting the journal to a readable format. Finally, we cover reading the journal and writing part of it in a new format so you can query the data without having to read the journal each time.

10.2   *Akka Persistence Query*

Akka provides an interface to read the journal written in chapter 9 using the Akka Persistence module. The journal contains the events of the persistent entity that represent a state change: that is, the event-sourcing part of the entity. With this interface, you can read these events and project them into another store that is optimized to be queried.

The journal is read in a stream fashion—more precisely, in an Akka Streams fashion, with the Akka Persistence Query module. The module's API provides queries to run against the journal. These are divided into *standard* and *current* queries. Standard queries—those that don't have `current` in their name—read all events since the beginning of the journal, and current queries read only new events after the query has been executed. All these queries belong to the interface `ReadJournal` (see table

10.1). All queries are infinite streams. Once you connect to the journal database, you can expect events at any time.

Table 10.1 Methods available to consume the journal: inputs and outputs

Interface methods	Input	Output
`eventsByTag` `currentEventsByTag`	`tag: String` `offset: Int`	`List[EventEnvelope]`
`persistenceIds` `currentPersistenceIds`		`List[String]`

`eventsByPersistenceId`
`currentEventsByPersistenceId`
	`id: String`
	`from: Int`
	`to: Int`
		`List[EventEnvelope]`

To retrieve events by tag, whether current or not, you must pass the tag and offset. Events have a `sequence_number` when stored in the journal; the offset is the corresponding number that marks the latest `sequence_number` read. To read from the beginning, you can pass a special object, the `Offset.noOffset`.

To read from the journal, you must first select a plugin that implements the Akka Persistence Query API. Akka provides and maintains three plugins: Cassandra, Couchbase, and JDBC. (You can find others at http://mng.bz/5wN8.)

In chapter 9, we used a database configuration for the connection to write the journal, but this was not explicitly mentioned in the chapter. Listing 10.3 shows that configuration, which can also be used to read the journal. It uses the JDBC plugin to store snapshots and journal events. The underlying storage is PostgreSQL.

> **NOTE** The source code for this example is available at www.manning.com/ books/akka-in-action-second-edition or https://github.com/franciscolopez sancho/akka-topics/tree/main/chapter10b. You can find the contents of any snippet or listing in the .scala file with the same name as the class, object, or trait.

Listing 10.3 JDBC persistence configuration

```
akka.persistence {                                    Journal plugin configuration entry
    journal.plugin = "jdbc-journal"          ◁───┘    used by a persistent actor by default
    auto-start-journals = ["jdbc-journal"]      ◁──   List of journal plugins
                                                      to start automatically
    snapshot-store.plugin = "jdbc-snapshot-store"  ◁──   Snapshot plugin
    auto-start-snapshot-stores = ["jdbc-snapshot-store"] ◁──  configuration entry
}                                                            used by a persistent
                                          List of snapshot stores  actor by default
jdbc-journal {                            to start automatically
  use-shared-db = "default"     ◁──   References the
}                                     database to use
```

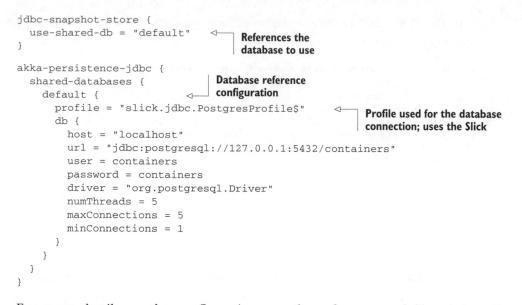

```
jdbc-snapshot-store {
  use-shared-db = "default"        ◁─┐  References the
}                                     └  database to use
akka-persistence-jdbc {
  shared-databases {            ┌─ Database reference
    default {                   └  configuration
      profile = "slick.jdbc.PostgresProfile$"    ◁─┐  Profile used for the database
      db {                                         └  connection; uses the Slick
        host = "localhost"
        url = "jdbc:postgresql://127.0.0.1:5432/containers"
        user = containers
        password = containers
        driver = "org.postgresql.Driver"
        numThreads = 5
        maxConnections = 5
        minConnections = 1
      }
    }
  }
}
```

For more details on the configuration, see the reference.conf file of the akka-persistence and akka-persistence-jdbc projects.

Let's continue the example from chapter 9: you have containers to which you can add cargo of different types and sizes. In this example, three pieces of cargo are added: two to one container and the third to another. The events in table 10.2 show the entries in the journal.

Table 10.2   Events from the table `journal_events`

ordering	persistence_id	sequence _number	deleted	event _ser_id	event_ser_manifest	event _payload
1	spcontainer-type-key|9	1	FALSE	33	example.persistence .SPContainer$Cargo Added	Binary data
2	spcontainer-type-key|9	2	FALSE	33	example.persistence .SPContainer$Cargo Added	Binary data
3	spcontainer-type-key|11	1	FALSE	33	example.persistence .SPContainer$Cargo Added	Binary data

To get all the IDs of the persistent entities of this journal, you can create a stream by calling the API method `persistenceIds`. It outputs the following:

```
spcontainer-type-key|9
spcontainer-type-key|11
```

To do this, you need a `ReadJournal` implementation such as `JdbcReadJournal`. The `ReadJournal` is the API for reading the entities' stored persistent events, and the `JdbcReadJournal` is the Akka implementation for JDBC-compliant databases to interact with Postgres, MySQL, Oracle, H2, and SQL Server. You can get one instance of `JdbcReadJournal` via the `PersistenceQuery`, which requires an `ActorSystem` and the ID of your implementation of choice of the `ReadJournal`. Once you have the instance, you can query the journal IDs.

Listing 10.4 Test to print a list of IDs

```
import akka.stream.scaladsl.Source
import akka.persistence.query.PersistenceQuery
import akka.persistence.jdbc.query.scaladsl.JdbcReadJournal
import akka.NotUsed

object Main extends App {

  implicit val system = ActorSystem(Behaviors.ignore, "runner")

  val readJournal: JdbcReadJournal = PersistenceQuery(system)
    .readJournalFor[JdbcReadJournal](JdbcReadJournal.Identifier)

  val source: Source[String, NotUsed] = readJournal.persistenceIds

  source.runForeach(println)
}
```

Obtains a JDBC Implementation of ReadJournal

Creates a Producer

Executes the stream

As useful as `.persistenceIds` may be for understanding how the API works, it is not the most commonly used method. That's `.eventByTag`. It allows you to filter events, which is usually done for two reasons. The most obvious is that you're only interested in a certain type of event, such as `CargoAdded`. This is the only event currently implemented, but if you extended the example, you would probably add `CargoRemoved` or `ContainerShipped`. The less obvious reason to filter events is to tag events for scaling out. So far there are only two tags, `container-tag-0` and `container-tag-2`, as shown in table 10.3.

Table 10.3 Tags from table `event_tag`

event_id	tag
1	container-tag-0
2	container-tag-0
3	container-tag-2

`container-tag-0` points to the events from the journal with `ordering` values 1 and 2 that have the `persistence_id` value `spcontainer-type-key|9`, while tag `container-tag-2` points to ordering 3 and `persistence_id` value `spcontainer-type-key|11`. Thanks to these tags, when using `.eventsByTag`, you can create two different streams to read the two tags in parallel, maybe on different machines.

To read events by tag, specify the tag you are looking for and the offset. As you know, using `Offset.noOffset` sets the offset to zero, which reads from the beginning of the journal. The output is a `Source[EventEnvelope]`:

```
class PersistenceQuerySpec ... {
  ...
  "a persistence query" should {
    "retrieve the events from db and printing them" in {
      ...
      val source: Source[EventEnvelope, NotUsed] =
        readJournal.eventsByTag("container-tag-0", Offset.noOffset)
      ...
  }}
  ...
}
```

Passes the tag and offset

This query returns the following `EventEnvelope` from the journal:

```
EventEnvelope(
    akka.persistence.query.Sequence(1),         Offset
    "spcontainer-type-key|9",                   Persistence_id
    1L,                                          Sequence_number
    SPContainer.CargoAdded("9",SPContainer.Cargo("456","sack",22)),    Event
    1622299422183L)                             Timestamp
```

10.2.1 Where the rubber meets the road

In most cases, you read the journal to create a side effect, such as creating a table, pushing a topic, or calling an external service. For example, suppose the container company tells you that it needs to know the weight of each container including its load. This data should be passed to the dock operators so they can stack the containers better. To do this, you can read the `eventsByTag` stream to create and update a database table containing the total weight per container. You might imagine it would be better to add a variable to your `SPContainer` for this purpose.

One solution could be to add the `totalWeight` variable to the `SPContainer`. That would work for this particular requirement, but it's hopeless to try to think in advance about all future requirements that might interest the company. You might be able to anticipate some of them, but the company will probably request new insights into the data that you didn't account for.

The better solution is to use the data implicit in the journal. Doing so is better for maintainability. You can read the journal and create the `totalWeight` by aggregating `AddCargo` events by container. And for scalability reasons, it's better to extract the data and store the aggregation in a different location. This way, you decouple reading from writing.

Figure 10.3 shows the components of this approach. Here, an Akka cluster with three nodes reads from the journal and stores the data in another store after aggregation.

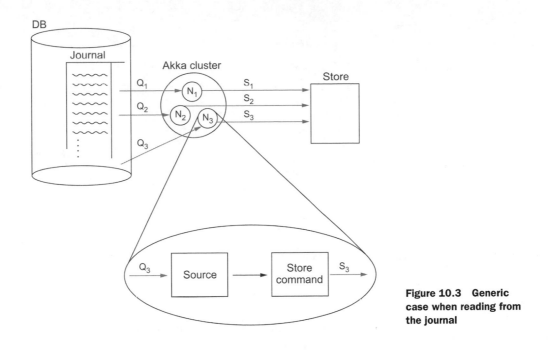

Figure 10.3 Generic case when reading from the journal

Clustering is not mandatory for persistence queries, but the cluster gives you fault tolerance and scalability, which you probably need anyway. The store in the upper-right corner can be a database or a topic. The `store` command is the connector: the producer responsible for writing to the store, upserting in the database, or committing to the topic.

> **DEFINITION** An *upsert* behaves like an insert if there is no previous data to update or like an update if there is data already.

An addition to figure 10.3 would be to enrich the events with an external service after reading them. For example, you are only interested in cargo that contains certain materials. Depending on the contents, you may want to classify cargo as hazardous and treat it differently. With this information, the operator can make appropriate decisions at the docks—for example, to transfer hazardous cargo from one container to another or to prohibit it altogether.

An implementation using Akka Persistence Query first reads the journal, then filters the hazardous cargos, then calls an external service that adds some extra information about the related hazard, and finally writes them to a topic or database (see figure 10.4).

These streams are often seen in ETL (extract, transform, load) processes. In Akka, you can create similar processes with a *projection* that is a higher abstraction than a stream.

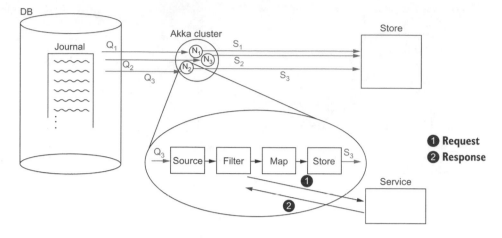

Figure 10.4   Pipes and filters with transformations

10.3   *Projections*

The epitome of a projection is mapping a sphere's points into a plane. It is a transformation from one form to another. A map, the end product of a mapping, is a projection, also called the *action* of its systematic representation. The same name is used for the product and the process.

An Akka projection can convert the events from the journal and move them to another type of storage, such as a database, a B-tree, or a list of logs like Kafka. One way or another, the data is transferred from the journal to another type of storage. You can read from Kafka and a database as source and write not only to Kafka or a database but also to a gRPC service.

Akka projections take care of reading the journal and offset for you. If the projection crashes, you don't have to worry about whether you've read an event when you restart. Projections can take care of that by setting offset semantics as effectively-once delivery—commonly called *exactly-once*. The other big advantage is scalability: projections have a built-in configuration that lets you set the level of parallelism you want. However, this is limited by the persistence entity tags.

There is a limitation with Akka projections using the Persistence Query module: the only method they implement from `ReadJournal` is `eventsByTag`. This is the only query you can ask for, but usually this is the query you are most interested in. This chapter covers the case of reading from the journal and writing to a database table.

> **NOTE**   The source code for this section is available at www.manning.com/ books/akka-in-action-second-edition   or   https://github.com/franciscolopez sancho/akka-topics/tree/main/chapter10c. You can find the contents of any snippet or listing in the .scala file with the same name as the class, object, or trait.

To create a projection, you need two kinds of things:

- *Read side*—The selection of the source
- *Write side*—The implementation of a handler to convert the data to the new storage (for example, an upsert) and a connection pool (such as a database session)

These are shown in the following listing.

Listing 10.5 Akka projection ingredients

```
import akka.projection.eventsourced.scaladsl.EventSourcedProvider
import akka.persistence.jdbc.query.scaladsl.JdbcReadJournal
import example.repository.scalike.ScalikeJdbcSession
import example.persistence.SPContainer

object CargosPerContainerProjection {

  ...

  val sourceProvider =
    EventSourcedProvider.eventsByTag[SPContainer.Event](          ⟵  Reads from the
      system = system,                                               event journal;
      readJournalPluginId = JdbcReadJournal.Identifier,              read side
      tag = tag)

  JdbcProjection.exactlyOnce(
    projectionId =
      ProjectionId("CargosPerContainerProjection", tag),
    sourceProvider = sourceProvider,                            Handler to upsert
    handler =                                                   into the database;
      () => new CPCProjectionHandler(tag, system, repository),  write side
    sessionFactory = () => new ScalikeJdbcSession())   ⟵         ⟵
  (system)                                             Pool of connections
}                                                      to provide to the
                                                       handler; write side
```

Let's look at these three building blocks

10.3.1 Reading

To read from the database, you need the `EventSourcedProvider` specifying that it reads `eventsByTag` from the `SPContainer`. That is `SPContainer.Event`.

The projection runs on the `ActorSystem`. The `readJournalPluginId` selects the plugin to read the event. If the events were stored in Cassandra, you would select `CassandraReadJournal.Identifier` instead.

Finally, the tag must match the tags from the journal, so you need to be aware of the tags the application is generating—in this example, `container-tag-[0|1|2]`.

10.3.2 Writing

To write to the RDBMS, you need a handler that extends `JdbcHandler[Event-Envelope[SPContainer.Event], ScalikeJdbcSession]` and a repository to define the SQL statement. This handler must override the `process` method from the `JdbcHandler`

```
def process(session: S, envelope: Envelope): Unit
```

where `Envelope` is a wrapper containing the event retrieved from the journal, like `EventEnvelope[SPContainer.Event]`, and `S` is a subtype of `JdbcSession`, like `ScalikeJdbcSession`.

Listing 10.6   Extension of `JdbcHandler`

```
import example.repository.scalike.{
  CargosPerContainerRepository,
  ScalikeJdbcSession
}
import akka.projection.jdbc.scaladsl.JdbcHandler
import akka.projection.eventsourced.EventEnvelope

import example.persistence.SPContainer

class CPCProjectionHandler(                            Passes through
    repository: CargosPerContainerRepository)   ◁──   the repository
    extends JdbcHandler[
      EventEnvelope[SPContainer.Event],
      ScalikeJdbcSession] {

  val logger = LoggerFactory.getLogger(classOf[CPCProjectionHandler])

  override def process(              ◁──   Overrides the JdbcHandler
    session: ScalikeJdbcSession,             process  method
    envelope: EventEnvelope[SPContainer.Event]): Unit = {
    envelope.event match {
      case SPContainer.CargoAdded(containerId, cargo) =>
        repository.addCargo(containerId, session)      ◁──     Updates the database
      case x =>                                                when processing
        logger.debug("ignoring event {} in projection",x)      CargoAdded events
    }
  }
}
```

This cargo-per-container projection handler stores the events by grouping the sum of `CargoAdded` by container. This is accomplished by a repository implementation that converts the `CargoAdded` envelope to an upsert in the database. This database statement creates the tuple (`[containerId], 1`) the first time; otherwise, it adds one to the existing tuple.

Listing 10.7   Repository Implementation

```
trait CargosPerContainerRepository {      ◁──   Interface to abstract any
                                                repository implementation
  def addCargo(containerId: String, session: ScalikeJdbcSession): Unit
}
```

```
class CargosPerContainerRepositoryImpl extends CargosPerContainerRepository {

    override def addCargo(
        containerId: String,
        session: ScalikeJdbcSession): Unit = {
        session.db.withinTx { implicit dbSession =>
            sql"""INSERT INTO cargos_per_container (containerId, carg
                    VALUES ($containerId, 1)
                    ON CONFLICT (containerId) DO
                    UPDATE SET cargos = cargos_per_container.cargos + 1
                    """.executeUpdate().apply()
        }
    }
}
```

Transaction ◁— (points to `session.db.withinTx { implicit dbSession =>`)

Postgres upsert statement —▷ (points to the `sql"""INSERT INTO ...` block)

You could forgo creating the interface in this example, but the code is short and it is always best practice to add this level of indirection. This way, you can test the projection without needing a database up and running. (You could simulate it by creating a `Map[String,Int]` inside the class and updating it instead of the SQL statement.) Most of this code is implementation details that are secondary to the fact that you need to add an implementation to the repository. You can use any means to store the event you are processing. In this case, you use `ScalalikeJDBC` as the database access library. Although the details of using this library are beyond the scope of this book, let's clarify a few details.

`session.db.withinTx` executes the statement as a transaction and initiates a beginning with two possible outcomes: commit or rollback. `implicit dbSession =>` states that this transaction needs a variable of type `scalikejdbc.DBSession` on the scope, which means you have to define such an `implicit` variable before you can call this repository. You learn how to implement this with the `ScalikeJdbcSetup` later in this chapter.

10.3.3 *Putting everything together*

To create the projection, assemble the following:

- The `EventSourcedProvider` is the read side.
- The `JdbcProjection` with `CPCProjectionHandler` and `Cargos-PerContainerRepository` compose the write side.

Typically, you create a method like the following in your projection class:

```
object CargosPerContainerProjection {

    def createProjectionFor(
        system: ActorSystem[_],
        repository: CargosPerContainerRepository,
        indexTag: Int):
            ExactlyOnceProjection[Offset, EventEnvelope[SPContainer.Event]]

    ...
}
```

Instantiates the projection ◁— (points to `def createProjectionFor(`)

This is used in an application with an `ActorSystem`, so you have the `system`. Then `indexTag` creates the tags for querying the journal, as mentioned earlier.

The `createProjectionFor` method is coded in the `CargosPerContainer-Projection` class. Here is the complete implementation previously shown partially in listing 10.5.

> **Listing 10.8 `CargosPerContainerProjection` implementation**

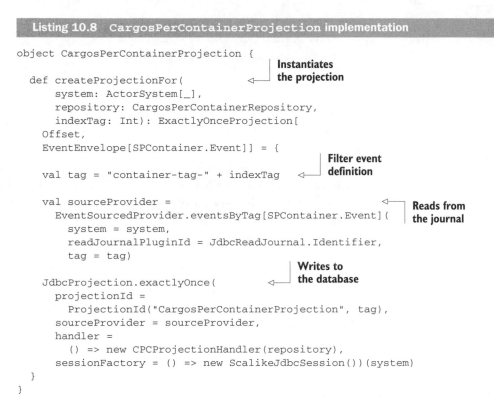

```
object CargosPerContainerProjection {

  def createProjectionFor(          ⟵┘ Instantiates
      system: ActorSystem[_],             the projection
      repository: CargosPerContainerRepository,
      indexTag: Int): ExactlyOnceProjection[
    Offset,
    EventEnvelope[SPContainer.Event]] = {
                                          Filter event
    val tag = "container-tag-" + indexTag  ⟵┘ definition

    val sourceProvider =                             ⟵┐ Reads from
      EventSourcedProvider.eventsByTag[SPContainer.Event](  │ the journal
        system = system,
        readJournalPluginId = JdbcReadJournal.Identifier,
        tag = tag)
                                      Writes to
    JdbcProjection.exactlyOnce(  ⟵┘ the database
      projectionId =
        ProjectionId("CargosPerContainerProjection", tag),
      sourceProvider = sourceProvider,
      handler =
        () => new CPCProjectionHandler(repository),
      sessionFactory = () => new ScalikeJdbcSession())(system)
  }
}
```

Depending on the index you pass to this method, a projection is created for different events. If you specify index 1, a projection is created that reads only events with the tag `container-tag-1`. An interesting question is how to create multiple projections, one per tag, running on different nodes to scale out and isolate possible failures.

To do this, you can reuse an idea you know about: sharding—spawning behaviors evenly in a cluster. Instead of Akka Sharding, you can use `ShardedDaemonProcess`, which is similar to Akka Sharding on the spawning side but significantly different in terms of communication.

As far as spawning is concerned, they are similar in that they distribute the entities. However, `ShardedDaemonProcess` has limitations. It needs to know in advance, when it is created, how many instances of the behavior you want to create. This is not the case with Akka Sharding; you can create as many sharded actors as you need.

On the communication side, Akka Sharding has the sharded region (SR), which you use as a proxy to send messages to actors. However, the `ShardedDaemonProcess` does not provide this capability. You cannot send messages directly to these behaviors; they are processes implemented in Akka Streams. With a `ShardedDaemonProcess`, you use the receptionist you saw in chapter 6, but that's secondary now.

10.3.4 The ShardedDaemonProcess

To understand the `ShardedDaemonProcess` more quickly without the added complexity of the `SPContainer`, let's look at a minimal example with only one behavior spawned by the `ShardedDaemonProcess` in an Akka cluster. Starting this cluster triggers the `ShardedDaemonProcess`, which creates three `LoggerBehaviors` in a node. To keep things simple, this behavior logs `tag-1`, `tag-2`, or `tag-3` when created, depending on the order of creation. (You can read how this is executed in the README.md.)

As soon as the first node starts, it generates the following output:

```
[INFO] [example.shardeddeamon.LoggerBehavior$] [] [LoggerSharded-
➥akka.actor.default-dispatcher-3] - spawned LoggerBehavior tag-2
[INFO] [example.shardeddeamon.LoggerBehavior$] [] [LoggerSharded-
➥akka.actor.default-dispatcher-25] - spawned LoggerBehavior tag-1
[INFO] [example.shardeddeamon.LoggerBehavior$] [] [LoggerSharded-
➥akka.actor.default-dispatcher-5] - spawned LoggerBehavior tag-3
```

Then you can add another node to the cluster to trigger a rebalance and get the following output from the original node:

```
[INFO] [akka.cluster.sharding.DDataShardCoordinator] [] [LoggerSharded-
➥akka.actor.default-dispatcher-25] - sharded-daemon-process-tagger:
➥Starting rebalance for shards [0]. Current shards rebalancing: []
```

In the logging of the new node, you eventually read that the `LoggerBehavior tag-1` is rebalanced to this new node:

```
[INFO] [example.shardeddeamon.LoggerBehavior$] [] [LoggerSharded-
➥akka.actor.default-dispatcher-5] - spawned LoggerBehavior tag-1
```

The idea is that with three nodes, you have one `ShardedDaemonProcess` in each with one `LoggerBehavior`. The following configuration from the file sharded-deamon.conf suffices. It is similar to what you've seen so far.

Listing 10.9 ShardedDaemon cluster configuration

```
akka {
  actor {
    provider = cluster     ◁—┤ Provider
  }
  remote {
    artery {
      canonical.hostname = "127.0.0.1"     ◁—┤ Hostname
    }
  }
  cluster {
```

```
    seed-nodes = [                                        ◁─┤ Seed-nodes
      "akka://MiniCluster@127.0.0.1:25251",
      "akka://MiniCluster@127.0.0.1:25252"]
  }
}
```

LoggerBehavior does only one thing. It logs the `tag` you pass to it when initializing
and then ignores any message:

```
import akka.actor.typed.Behavior
import akka.actor.typed.scaladsl.Behaviors

object LoggerBehavior {
  def apply(tag: String): Behavior[Unit] = {
    Behaviors.setup { context =>
      context.log.info("spawned LoggerBehavior {}",tag)      ◁─┤ Logs the tag
      Behaviors.ignore
    }
  }
}
```

Finally, you can create a `ShardedDaemonProcess` with an `ActorSystem`, the
`LoggerBehavior`, and the `tags`. Here is a simple approach to create such a
`ShardedDaemonProcess` in a cluster. The tags are a fixed variable, whereas normally
they would be read from the configuration.

Listing 10.10   Using a `ShardedDaemonProcess`

```
import akka.cluster.sharding.typed.scaladsl.ShardedDaemonProcess

object MiniCluster {

  def main(args: Array[String]): Unit = {
      startup(args(0).toInt)
  }

  def startup(port: Int): Unit = {
    val config = ConfigFactory
      .parseString(s"""                            Loads the configuration from
      akka.remote.artery.canonical.port=$port      the shardeddeamon.conf file
      """)
      .withFallback(ConfigFactory.load("shardeddeamon"))     ◁─

    val system = ActorSystem[Nothing](Behaviors.empty, "MiniCluster", config)

    val tags = Vector("container-tag-1",
                "container-tag-2",
                "container-tag-3")        ◁─┐  Fixed tags, thus
                                             │  parallelism
    ShardedDaemonProcess(system)
          .init(
              "loggers",
              tags.size,
```

```
        index => LoggerBehavior(tags(index)))
    }
}
```
◁─┐ **Initialization of
    the behavior**

Tags are used to determine the number of instances of `LoggerBehaviors`, and they can be used to select a specific tag to read events from the journal. This was exactly what the `SPContainer` example needed to do. With this knowledge about the `ShardedDaemonProcess`, you can understand how to use it with the projection of `SPContainer`.

10.3.5 *Back to the SPContainer projection*

Let's recap. To create a projection, pass an `ActorSystem`, a `CargosPerContainer-Repository`, and an `indexTag` to the `createProjectionFor` method, which creates the read and write sides. To shard the projections, use the `ShardedDaemon-Process`.

The main idea is to use the `ShardedDaemonProcess` to spawn the `Cargos-PerContainerProjection`. But note that you can't spawn a projection inside the `ShardedDaemonProcess`; only a behavior can be spawned. So you have to wrap the projection in a `ProjectionBehavior`.

Listing 10.11 Initializing projections through a `ShardedDaemonProcess`

```
import akka.actor.typed.ActorSystem

import akka.cluster.sharding.typed.ShardingEnvelope

import akka.cluster.sharding.typed.ShardedDaemonProcessSettings
import akka.cluster.sharding.typed.scaladsl.ShardedDaemonProcess

import example.repository.scalike.CargosPerContainerRepositoryImpl

object Main {

  def main(args: Array[String]): Unit = ...

  def initActorSystem(port: Int):ActorSystem[_] = ...

  def initProjection(system: ActorSystem[_])
      : Unit  = {
    ShardedDaemonProcess(system).init(
      name = "cargos-per-container-projection",
      3,                                             ◁─┐  Number of instances of
                                                        the ProjectionBehavior
      index =>
        ProjectionBehavior(                ◁──────────┐ Behavior
          CargosPerContainerProjection.createProjectionFor(  factory
            system,
            new CargosPerContainerRepositoryImpl(),
            index)),
      ShardedDaemonProcessSettings(system),   ◁─┤ Settings
      Some(ProjectionBehavior.Stop))    ◁───┐ Stops when rebalanced or passivated and
  }                                          closes the connection to the database
}
```

This `ShardedDaemonProcess` is essentially the same one you saw earlier. It has a name, the number of behaviors to spawn, and the behavior, along with two other attributes you haven't seen before:

- `settings`—`ShardedDaemonProcessSettings`
- `stopMessage`—`Optional[T]`

`ShardedDaemonProcessSettings(system)` exists so you can read from your configuration if you want to configure `akka.cluster.sharded-daemon-process` `.keep-alive-interval`. By default, the cluster pings each `ProjectionBehavior` every 10 seconds to make sure it is running. When rebalancing occurs, those behaviors are stopped. With this keep-alive interval, you make sure those behaviors are started afterward.

`ProjectionBehavior.Stop` is the message sent to the actor when the behavior is rebalanced or the cluster shuts down. This can be useful if you want to perform actions before a projection stops, like closing the connection to the database.

10.3.6 *All the main parts*

To complete the application, you need to create three things in the `main` method:

- The `ActorSystem`
- The projection
- The database connection

These are shown in listing 10.12. By now, you are probably familiar with instantiating the `ActorSystem`. Here you create it with a default configuration and add a `port` variable so you can run multiple nodes locally if necessary to avoid port conflicts. The only thing we haven't covered is the database connection—the `ScalikeJdbc-Setup.init(system)`—but that has little to do with Akka, and explaining it here would complicate the discussion. The code is available in the Git repository if you want to take a closer look.

Listing 10.12   Complete entry point of the application

```
import scala.util.control.NonFatal
import org.slf4j.LoggerFactory
import akka.actor.typed.ActorSystem
import example.repository.scalike.ScalikeJdbcSetup

object Main {

  val logger = LoggerFactory.getLogger(Main + "")

  def main(args: Array[String]): Unit = {
    logger.info("initializing system")
    val system = if (args.isEmpty) {
      initActorSystem(0)              ⟵── Sets a
    } else {                              random port
      initActorSystem(args(0).toInt) ⟵── Sets a port passed
    }                                     as a parameter
```

```
          try {
            ScalikeJdbcSetup.init(system)          ◁──────        Initializes the connection
            initProjection(system)     ◁──┐ Initializes the projection with  to the database
          } catch {                        └──  ShardedDaemonProcess
          case NonFatal(ex) =>      #E
            logger.error(s"terminating by NonFatal Exception", ex)
            system.terminate()
        }
      }
```

Graceful shutdown → (points to `case NonFatal(ex) =>`)

```
      def initActorSystem(port: Int):ActorSystem[_] = {   ◁──┐ Creates an ActorSystem with
        val config = ConfigFactory                            a port and default config
          .parseString(s"""
          akka.remote.artery.canonical.port=$port
          """)
          .withFallback(ConfigFactory.load())
          ActorSystem[Nothing](Behaviors.empty,"containersprojection",config)
      }

      def initProjection (system: ActorSystem[_]): Unit  = ...
    }
```

10.4   Projections in action

You can create the journal with the chapter09b project and the projection with chapter10c. First you create persistence entity entries. To do this, create the database and the necessary persistence entity tables to store the journal, tags, and snapshots. Then start the cluster and create persistence entities using the console. Here are the steps to follow:

1 Start the Postgres database with the script in the project persistence docker-compose.yml by running the following from the command line in the root directory of the chapter09b project:

```
$ docker compose up
```

2 Create the event_journal, event_tag, and snapshot tables with the projections/persistence_create_tables.sql script by executing the following from the command line in the root directory of the chapter09b project:

```
$ psql -h 127.0.0.1 -d containers -U containers \
      -f persistence_create_tables.sql          ◁──┐ Enter
$ Password for user containers:                     containers
```

3 Launch one node of the persistence entity application from chapter 9 in the sbt console by running the following from the command line in the root of the Git repository:

```
$ sbt chapter09b/run
```

4 In this console, add three entries of the type [containerId, cargoId, cargoKind, cargoSize] by pressing Enter before and after the following values:

```
9 456 sack 22
9 456 sack 22
11 499 barrel 120
```

This will give you the data listed in table 10.4 in the journal.

Table 10.4   Events from table `event_journal`

ordering	persistence_id	sequence _number	event_ser_manifest	event_payload
3	pcontainer-type-key|11	1	example.persistence.SP Container$CargoAdded	Binary data
1	pcontainer-type-key|9	1	example.persistence.SP Container$CargoAdded	Binary data
2	pcontainer-type-key|9	2	example.persistence.SP Container$CargoAdded	Binary data

You've written the journal. Now comes the second part, the projection:

1 Create the tables `akka_projection_offset_store` and `cargos_per _container` using the scripts with the same names in the folder projections by executing the following from the command line in the root directory of the chapter10c project:

```
$ psql -h 127.0.0.1 -d containers -U containers \
    -f projection_offset_store.sql
$ psql -h 127.0.0.1 -d containers -U containers \
    -f projection_cargos_per_container.sql
```

2 Start the projection with only one node by running the following from the command line in the root of the Git repository:

```
$ sbt "chapter10c/runMain example.projection.Main 25525"
```

– This will create three projections, one per tag. You can see the following output in the projection node:

```
[INFO] [akka.projection.ProjectionBehavior$] [] [containersprojection-
➥akka.actor.default-dispatcher-22] - Starting projection
➥[ProjectionId(CargosPerContainerProjection, container-tag-0)]
[INFO] [akka.projection.ProjectionBehavior$] [] [containersprojection-
➥akka.actor.default-dispatcher-3] - Starting projection
➥[ProjectionId(CargosPerContainerProjection, container-tag-1)]
[INFO] [akka.projection.ProjectionBehavior$] [] [containersprojection-
➥akka.actor.default-dispatcher-5] - Starting projection
➥[ProjectionId(CargosPerContainerProjection, container-tag-2)]
```

Each projection immediately fetches the events from the journal corresponding to its tag and finds that it has no offset stored in `akka_projection_offset_store`. Since there is no offset yet, the projection reads the journal from the beginning until the `akka_projection_offset_store.offset` is equal to the `event_journal` `.sequence_number`. Again, this is different for each tag.

For each of these events, the application executes the SQL statement from the CargosPerContainerRepositoryImpl, shown again here:

```
INSERT INTO cargos_per_container (containerId, cargos) VALUES ($containerId, 1)
    ON CONFLICT (containerId) DO
        UPDATE SET cargos = cargos_per_container.cargos + 1
```

This produces the data in table 10.5. The akka_projection_offset_store table is updated to match the sequence_number of the event on the journal per container, as shown in table 10.6.

Table 10.5 `cargos_per_container` **for projections**

containerId	cargo
11	1
9	2

Table 10.6 `akka_projection_offset_store` **for projections**

projection_name	projection_key	current_offset	manifest	mergeable	last_updated
CargosPerContainer Projection	container-tag-0	1	SEQ	FALSE	1622299533384
CargosPerContainer Projection	container-tag-2	2	SEQ	FALSE	1622299533296

From now on, any new event added to the journal of the SPContainer will be picked up for the projection, and the tables cargos_per_container and current _offset will be updated accordingly.

This example doesn't take full advantage of the ShardedDaemonProcess running multiple processes on different nodes. You can easily start another node by opening another sbt console in the root of the Git repository and running main with a different port:

```
$ sbt "chapter10c/runMain example.projection.Main 25526"
```

You will quickly find that this new node takes over one of the three tags of the other node, balancing a shard and its projection onto this new node. In the log of the new node is an entry like the following:

```
[INFO] [akka.projection.ProjectionBehavior$] [] [containersprojection-
⮡akka.actor.default-dispatcher-5] - Starting projection
⮡[ProjectionId(CargosPerContainerProjection, container-tag-0)]
```

The next chapter is about ports. So far, you've connected to an Akka application through the console, but that is just for convenience. In the real world, you usually connect to an Akka application through endpoints like HTTP and gRPC. Chapter 11 examines how to create a server with these endpoints.

Summary

- Akka Streams abstract from producers, transformations, and consumers as data streams, creating pure functions that are composable.
- Akka Streams are useful in their own right, but they also form the basis for other modules such as Akka Persistence Query and Akka Projections.
- Akka Persistence Query gives you an infinite stream of persistence IDs, events by tag, or events by persistence ID. But normally, you don't use the persistence query on its own. To consume the journal, you typically use Akka projections.
- Akka Projections are Akka Streams that can consume from Kafka or a database transformed and written to Kafka, a database, or a gRPC service.
- With an Akka Projection, you can read the journal and create a view from it. This way, you can group the events of the journal in a view optimized for consumption and meet different business needs with each view, independent of the writing of the journal.
- The main components of a projection from database to database are the `EventSourceProvider` to read the journal and the handler to write the view that implements a `JdbcProjection`.
- The `ShardedDaemonProcess` allows you to distribute behaviors in a cluster, similar to sharding. And it is what you use to scale a projection.

Akka ports

This chapter covers

- Creating an HTTP server with Akka HTTP
- Connecting through HTTP with actors from outside the cluster
- Creating a gRPC server with Akka gRPC
- Connecting through gRPC with actors from outside the cluster

In this chapter, you learn how to connect to an `ActorSystem` to send messages from the outside. This is done so that any application can interact with actors. You see how to create servers in Akka that provide endpoints that can be used by HTTP or gRPC clients.

11.1 Akka HTTP

This module builds on Akka Streams and shares its semantics. Its components are internally defined in terms of `Sources`, `Flows`, and `Sinks`. However, these are hidden, and your interaction with this API is through an expressive DSL that lets you create URL paths, manage requests and responses, and more.

Akka HTTP is a comprehensive module that covers HTTP clients, HTTP servers, JSON and XML encoding, caching, and anything else you can think of to serve or use HTTP endpoints. However, this chapter focuses on the HTTP server you need to expose your `ActorSystem`.

> **NOTE** The source code for this chapter is available at www.manning.com/ books/akka-in-action-second-edition or https://github.com/franciscolopez sancho/akka-topics/tree/main/chapter11a. You can find the contents of any snippet or listing in the .scala file with the same name as the class, object, or trait.

11.1.1 Akka HTTP servers

An Akka HTTP server is nothing more than a process that listens for HTTP requests on a port and generates responses. An `ActorSystem` maintains this process. Let's cover the basic primitives of Akka HTTP:

- Path
- Routes
- Directives
- Marshalling/unmarshalling

In the first simple scenario, you have a server that accepts requests on the path /ping and responds with "pong":

```
$ curl localhost:8080/ping
pong
```

11.1.2 The path

The server path, the endpoint, is defined by a `Route`. To create it, use `path("ping")` and listen for HTTP GET methods to respond—`complete`—with "pong":

```
import akka.http.scaladsl.server.Route
import akka.http.scaladsl.server.Directives._

object HttpServer {

    ...

      val route: Route =          Server
        path("ping") {      ⟵─┘   route path
  HTTP ┌─▷  get {
method │       complete("pong")    ◁─  Returns a value
       │    }                          to the client
        }

    ...

}
```

`path` is a directive available through `Directives`, as you can see in the imports, but let's not get into directives yet. If you bind this route to a specific host and port, you have an Akka HTTP server:

```scala
import akka.http.scaladsl.Http
import akka.http.scaladsl.Http.ServerBinding

object HttpServer {
  ...

    val bindingFuture: Future[ServerBinding] =
      Http().newServerAt("localhost", 8080).bind(route)
  ...
}
```

This starts the server, although the HTTP constructor requires an implicit `Actor-System`. The server is started with `newServerAt` on the host and port of your choice, and then you can `bind` a `Route` to that server. Note that the binding to the server is wrapped in a future, which means it will be created eventually. That takes time—only a little, but time is part of the equation.

It is recommended to provide a way to shut down the server gracefully. To do this, you can include a listener that registers each new line in the sbt shell so that when Enter is pressed, the shutdown is triggered by unbinding the server and exiting the `ActorSystem`:

```scala
object HttpServer {
  ...

    StdIn.readLine()            ◁── Listens to the input
    bindingFuture                   in the sbt console
      .flatMap(_.unbind())      ◁── Unbinds
      .onComplete(_ => system.terminate())   the server
  ...                           ◁── When unbinding is complete,
}                                   terminates the system
```

Just as the HTTP server requires an implicit `ActorSystem`, `bindingFuture` requires an execution context to run. This is available in the `ActorSystem`, and you can use it for now, although you'll learn better options:

```scala
implicit val executionContext = system.executionContext
```

All of this is put together in the following listing.

Listing 11.1 Basic server with a `GET` method

```scala
import akka.actor.typed.ActorSystem
import akka.actor.typed.scaladsl.Behaviors
import akka.http.scaladsl.Http
import akka.http.scaladsl.model._
import akka.http.scaladsl.server.Directives._
import scala.io.StdIn

object HttpServer {

  def main(args: Array[String]): Unit = {            ActorSystem to
                                                     run the server
    implicit val system = ActorSystem(Behaviors.empty, "simple-api")   ◁──
```

```
    implicit val executionContext = system.executionContext          ◁──────┐

    val route: Route =           │ Server                                Thread pool of the
      path("ping") {      ◁──────┘ route path                            ActorSystem to run
        get {                                                            bindingFuture
          complete("pong")   ◁──────┐ Returns the value
        }                           │ to the client
      }

    val bindingFuture: Future[ServerBinding] =                         Starts the server
      Http().newServerAt("localhost", 8080).bind(route)   ◁──────┘     with a route

    println(s"server at localhost:8080 \nPress RETURN to stop")
    StdIn.readLine()
    bindingFuture                                          Listens to Enter at the
      .flatMap(_.unbind())                                 command line to trigger
      .onComplete(_ => system.terminate())                 a system shutdown
  }
}
```

HTTP method and *get {* are labeled to the left.

You can run this example from the command line by entering the following in the root of the Git repository:

```
$ sbt "chapter11a/runMain example.http.HttpServer"
```

Once the server is running, you can call it with a `curl` command:

```
$ curl localhost:8080/ping
pong
```

11.1.3 Directives

You can use directives to create paths and routes, extract data from the request, create exceptions, and more. Directives provide a DSL that offers a variety of ways to create all kinds of routes with very concise expressions. The generic usage of a directive is as follows:

```
directiveName(arguments) { extractions =>      ◁───┐ Extraction
  ... // inner route                                │ is optional.
}
```

In general, directives can do the following:

- Transform the request and pass it to the inner route.
- Filter the request to exclude some of the inner routes.
- Extract values from the request with, for example, `parameters` or `extractUri`.
- Intercept an intermediate result and modify it with `handle`, `failWith`, and `reject`.
- Create the final result using `complete`, or `redirect` a request.

This chapter gives examples of the last three.

11.1.4 *Route directives*

Routes are like the branches of a tree. You use them to define how each request is processed. Depending on the request, the route traverses one branch or another until the request completes—or fails—and returns a response to the caller.

THE COMPLETE METHOD

The previous example returned "pong" inside an HTTP response with 200 OK. You don't have to stick to 200 OK (that's the default value); complete has many constructors to create the HttpResponse. You can use different media types, status codes, and headers to create the HttpResponse along with the object you want to send back—the entity (HttpEntity):

```
complete(HttpResponse(entity = "pong"))          ◁──── Creates an
                                                        HttpResponse

complete(HttpResponse(        ◁──── Specifies a more elaborate
         201,                       entity with HttpEntity
         entity = HttpEntity(ContentTypes.`application/json`, "created"))

complete(StatusCodes.OK,
         headers = List(`Content-Type`(`text/plain(UTF-8)`)),       ◁──┐
         entity =  "pong")
                                              Creates an HttpResponse
                                              via the complete method
```

The last entry in this example is similar to the first, where there is no explicit Http-Response. You can rely on Akka HTTP to do this with the default values 200 OK and content type text/plain; charset=UTF-8.

TRAVERSING THE ROUTE

To traverse the directives of a path—when processing a request—Akka HTTP can *reject* a directive if it doesn't match the request and try with the remaining directives. So far, you've only seen one directive, so there wasn't much choice; let's add another.

To add a directive, you can use the tilde (~) operator, which adds a post to the previous path:

```
val route: Route =
  path("ping") {
    get {
      complete("pong")       │ Concatenates
    } ~                    ◁  │ the two routes
    post {                    ◁──────── Second directive to try
      println("fake storing op")        if the first is rejected
      complete("ping stored")
    }
  }
```

If you call a service with such a route with curl localhost:8080/ping -XPOST, the first directive (get) is tried and rejected because it does not match the call. Then post follows, which matches the request and processes the call.

You will see a tilde in many Akka HTTP applications, but it is not recommended as an operand. You can achieve the same with the operand `concat` and avoid the drawbacks. The problem with a tilde is that there is no compilation guarantee. You can use it, but if you forget to add it, the code will still compile but will interpret only the last `route` statement.

To avoid this pitfall, you can use `concat` with a comma to separate the route directives. If you forget the comma, the compiler will alert you:

```
object HttpServerConcat {
  ...

    val route: Route =
      path("ping") {                    Concatenates the
        concat(              ◁─┘        route directives
          get {
            complete("pong")
          },                ▷─┐
          post {
            println("fake storing op")
            complete("ping stored")
          })
      }
  ...
}
```

Route directives separator points to the comma after `},`

Concatenates the route directives points to the `concat(` line.

`concat` lets you create routes by nesting paths and directives like this:

```
val route =
  path("a") {
    concat(
      path("b") {
        concat(
          get {complete("I'm path(a/b) -XGET")},
          post {complete("I'm path(a/b) -XPOST")}
        )
      },
      path("e"){
        get {complete("I'm path(a/e) -XGET")}
      }
    )
  }
```

You can try this by executing from the root of the repository:

```
$ sbt chapter11a/run
```

Pick option [2], `example.http.HttpServerConcat`, and send a GET command to /ping with the command line

```
$ curl localhost:8080/ping
```

Or send a POST:

```
$ curl  localhost:8080/ping -XPOST
```

FAILING

Routes can fail when processing requests, and you can catch their exceptions with an `ExceptionHandler`. Exceptions rise from the inner paths to the outer paths until an `ExceptionHandler` catches them. If an exception reaches the top path without being explicitly handled, a default `ExceptionHandler` catches it, and the client gets the usual cryptic message "There was an internal server error at 500 HTTP." Not ideal. At any point in the processing of the request, you can also throw an exception with the directive `failWith(error: Throwable)` and have the `ExceptionHandler` handle it.

Whether exceptions are thrown by you intentionally or by an unexpected circumstance, the sooner you can catch them, the better. Exceptions have significant performance penalties every time they are handled. This is a JVM feature, not an Akka one. A significant cost is associated with creating a stack trace for each nested `try/catch` and unwinding all the levels when a new exception is thrown.

Let's look at an example of adding an exception handler to prevent an `ArithmeticException` from bubbling up to the default exception handler. This route fails quite often because it randomly divides a random number by 0 or 1. Half the time, it ends up dividing by zero and issuing a message that something went wrong with the URI. To extract the URI, the directive `extractUri` is used. Other directives like this—for example, `extractEntity`—are often used in exception handlers to extract information from the request.

Listing 11.2   Adding an `ExceptionHandler` to a route

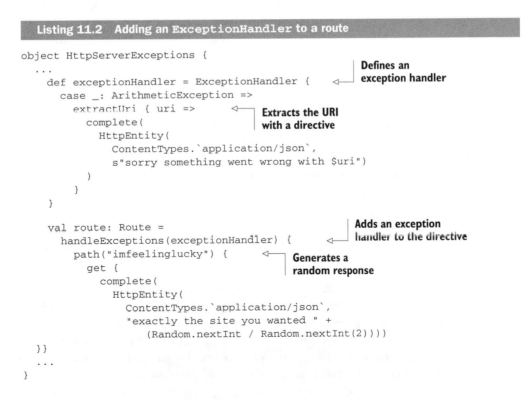

```scala
object HttpServerExceptions {
  ...
    def exceptionHandler = ExceptionHandler {          ←┘ Defines an
      case _: ArithmeticException =>                         exception handler
        extractUri { uri =>          ←┐ Extracts the URI
          complete(                    │ with a directive
            HttpEntity(
              ContentTypes.`application/json`,
              s"sorry something went wrong with $uri")
          )
        }
    }

    val route: Route =                          ┌ Adds an exception
      handleExceptions(exceptionHandler) {    ←┘ handler to the directive
        path("imfeelinglucky") {      ←┐ Generates a
          get {                          │ random response
            complete(
              HttpEntity(
                ContentTypes.`application/json`,
                "exactly the site you wanted " +
                  (Random.nextInt / Random.nextInt(2))))
  }}
  ...
}
```

You can try this by executing from the root of the repositor:

```
$ sbt chapter11a/run
```

Choose option [3], `example.http.HttpServerExceptions`, and send a GET command to `/imfeelinglucky` from the command line:

```
$ curl localhost:8080/imfeelinglucky
```

If you keep trying your luck, you will get an exception sooner rather than later.

11.1.5 *Marshalling and unmarshalling*

Marshalling is a loose synonym for serialization. It is commonly used in the context of remote procedure calls (RPCs). Typically, marshalling is part of a whole where there is communication between a client and a server.

In general terms, *serialization* means converting a high-level representation such as a Java `Object`—like a `String`—into a sequence of bytes. In an HTTP call, the default sequence of bytes today is JSON, which is, by default, UTF-8 encoded. In Akka HTTP, this is achieved using the library `akka-http-spray-json`, which uses the library `spray-json`.

Akka HTTP marshallers are tricky to understand but easy to use. We focus on how to use them, and to do that, you need to understand that they work by implicit resolution. *Implicit* means marshallers must be defined with the `implicit` keyword and available to the class that uses them through its imports, variables, or methods. To transform from class A to class B, you need a `Marshaller[A,B]` in the scope.

For example, to serialize a `String` into a JSON format, import `SprayJson-Support._` and `DefaultJsonProtocol._` as follows:

```
import akka.http.scaladsl.marshallers.sprayjson.SprayJsonSupport._
import spray.json.DefaultJsonProtocol._
```

`spray-json` provides such a marshaller through `akka-http-spray-json` and can directly convert *basic* classes such as `String`, `Int`, `Byte`, `Option`, `List`, and others (see https://github.com/spray/spray-json#jsonprotocol). If the class is not a basic class, you must provide a formatter in the implicit resolution:

```
import spray.json.RootJsonFormat

final case class Cargo(kind: String, size: Int)

implicit val bFormat: RootJsonFormat[Cargo] =
          jsonFormat2(Cargo("bigBag",1))
```

[Cargo] is composed of two serializable basic classes: String and Int.

`jsonFormat2` is an `akka-http-spray-json` method that signals with its name that the B constructor has two parameters. However, they don't have to be basic parameters as long as they have their own formatters. You can see that B has two parameters, a `String` and an `Int`. There are `jsonFormat3`, `jsonFormat4`, and so forth.

Once `spray` knows how many parameters the constructor has, it can create the necessary formatter. There are two types: `JsonFormat` and `RootJsonFormat`. Since formatters can be composed just like the classes they format, a class B(f1: C, f2: D) needs one formatter for B, another for C, and another for D. Here, B is the root formatter and must be a RootJsonFormat. The other two can be JsonFormatters.

In practice, this distinction is not very important, and it may be better if you use RootJsonFormat everywhere and forget which object is the root. This way, you avoid compilation errors when you need a JsonFormat formatter that acts as root. This is what spray-json does by default to give you flexibility: it sets every formatter to RootJsonFormat. A counterargument is that you want to align the formatting with the hierarchy in your domain to ensure that the business modeling is followed.

Now that you know about routes, directives, and marshallers, you can learn how to use them to connect to an actor from outside the ActorSystem.

11.1.6 Akka HTTP communicating with actors

Let's continue with the example from chapter 10 but without persistence, only sharding. You can add cargo to the following container and query how much cargo it has.

Listing 11.3 Domain object

```
object Container {

  val typeKey = EntityTypeKey[Command]("container")       ◁⎤ Sharding
                                                             ⎦ key

  final case class Cargo(kind: String, size: Int)          │ Business objects of the actor
  final case class Cargos(cargos: List[Cargo])             │

  sealed trait Command                                                    Protocol of
  final case class AddCargo(cargo: Cargo)                                 the actor
      extends Command
  final case class GetCargos(replyTo: ActorRef[Cargos]) extends Command   ⎦

  def apply(                                              ⎤ Initializes the
      entityId: String,                                  ⎥ container with an
      cargos: List[Cargo] = Nil): Behavior[Command] = {  ◁⎦ empty list of cargo
    Behaviors.receive { (context, message) =>
      message match {
        case AddCargo(cargo, replyTo) =>       ◁⎤ Adds
          println(s"adding cargo $cargo")        ⎦ cargo
          apply(cargo +: cargos)
        case GetCargos(replyTo) =>           ◁⎤ Gets
          replyTo ! Cargos(cargos)             ⎦ cargos
          Behaviors.same
      }
    }
  }
}
```

First, let's look at the expected behavior. The following snippet shows how to send two items of cargo to a container and retrieve their status:

```
$ curl -XPOST "localhost:8080/cargo?entityId=1&kind=sack&size=12"
Adding Cargo requested

$ curl -XPOST "localhost:8080/cargo?entityId=1&kind=bigbag&size=4"
Adding Cargo requested

curl localhost:8080/cargo?entityId=1
{"cargos":[{"kind":"bigbag","size":4},{"kind":"sack","size":12}]}
```

**Adds cargo
to the
container**

**Retrieves cargos
from the container**

To make the container accessible from outside the `ActorSystem`, you have to create
an endpoint by doing two things:

1. Transform the request into a case class using the directive `.parameters`.
2. Transform the response into a JSON format using `akka-http-spray-json`.
   You do so with marshalling/unmarshalling.

TRANSFORMING THE REQUEST

To handle the request, you can use the directive `parameters`. Pass a list of names and
types to get the `parameter` extraction:

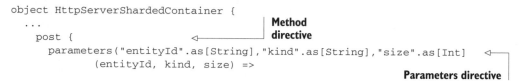

```
object HttpServerShardedContainer {
  ...
    post {
      parameters("entityId".as[String],"kind".as[String],"size".as[Int]
             (entityId, kind, size) =>
```

**Method
directive**

Parameters directive

With the extraction (`entityId, kind, size`), you can create the `Cargo` and then
send it to the container. You can `tell` and reply to the user immediately or `ask` and wait
for the container to reply. The choice depends on the business case. In this scenario, let's
prioritize performance and opt for `tell` rather than informing the user only after
ensuring that the cargo has been added by using `ask`. This looks like the following:

```
                (entityId, kind, size) =>

            val cargo = Container.Cargo(kind, size)
            shardingRegion ! ShardingEnvelope(
              entityId,
              Container.AddCargo(cargo))
      ...
}
```

**Creates
the cargo**

**Adds the cargo
to the container**

TRANSFORMING THE RESPONSE

The creation of the response uses `SprayJsonSupport._` and `DefaultJson-`
`Protocol._`as before and then two JSON formatters, `jsonFormat1` and `jsonFormat2`:

```
import akka.http.scaladsl.marshallers.sprayjson.SprayJsonSupport._
import spray.json.DefaultJsonProtocol._

object HttpServerShardedContainer {
  ...

  implicit val cargoFormat: JsonFormat[Container.Cargo] =
      jsonFormat2(Container.Cargo)
```

```
        implicit val cargosFormat: RootJsonFormat[Container.Cargos] =
            jsonFormat1(Container.Cargos)
    ...
}
```

To serialize `Container.Cargos`, `jsonFormat1` handles its basic `List` type. But since it is a `List[Cargo]`, you also need to provide the formatter for `Cargo`: `json-Format2`, which has the two basic fields `String` and `Int`.

Unmarshalling the request

In this example, you use these formatters only for marshalling. You can also use them for unmarshalling when reading the request instead of using the parameters directive:

```
post { entity(as[Container.Cargo]) { cargo => ... }
```

This wouldn't work in the current example because you need the entity's ID to send the message to the entity, and the `Cargo` class doesn't have such a field. Nevertheless, the `entity` directive is very handy and often used.

With these formatters, you can create the following `get` to create a route at URL cargo?entityId=[myId], as follows:

```
object HttpServerShardedContainer {
  ...|
                              ┌─ This get is inside a
    get {              ⟵──┘   path("cargo").
      parameters("entityId".as[String]) { entityId =>
        val container = sharding.entityRefFor(Container.TypeKey, entityId)

        val response: Future[Container.Cargos] =
            container
              .ask(Container.GetCargos)
              .mapTo[Container.Cargos]

        complete(response)
      }
    })
  ...
}
```

With this last part, you have everything you need to create the Akka application with an Akka HTTP server as the port.

Listing 11.4 Akka application with ports to `Container`

```
object HttpServerShardedContainer {

  def main(args: Array[String]): Unit = {
    implicit val system = ActorSystem(Behaviors.empty, "simple-api")
```

```
          implicit val executionContext = system.executionContext     ◁──┐  To run the future
                                                                          │  when binding
To run ┌─ ▷ implicit val timeout: Timeout = 3.seconds                     │  the route
the .ask│
in the get│  implicit val cargoFormat: JsonFormat[Container.Cargo] = ...
          implicit val cargosFormat: RootJsonFormat[Container.Cargos] = ...  ──┐

          val sharding = ClusterSharding(system)                             Deals with
                                                                             serialization
          val shardingRegion =
            sharding.init(Entity(Container.TypeKey)(entityContext =>
              Container(entityContext.entityId)))

          val route: Route =                   ◁──┐  Definition
            path("cargo") {                        │  of routes
              concat(
                post { ...
                },
                get { ...
                })
            }

          val bindingFuture: Future[ServerBinding] =                    ┐  Starts the server
            Http().newServerAt("localhost", 8080).bind(route)      ◁──  │  and sets the route

          println(s"server at localhost:8080 \nPress RETURN to stop")
          StdIn.readLine()
          bindingFuture
            .flatMap(_.unbind())
            .onComplete(_ => system.terminate())
      }
}
```

Now that you know how to create an Akka HTTP port, it's time to look at the other types of ports you can create.

11.2   Akka gRPC

Akka gRPC is another option that allows you to create ports to communicate with your ActorSystem. As with Akka HTTP, you can create both the server and the clients. In this section, you learn about the server side. The client side is discussed in chapter 16.

The advantages of this module are numerous. You can use HTTP/2, and it creates all the necessary classes once you have defined the interface you want. This is done in a so-called *.proto file.* Let's start with some basics to understand these advantages and the underlying mechanism. gRPC consists of two components: Protocol Buffers and the classic remote procedure call (RPC).

> **NOTE**   The source code for this section is available at www.manning.com/
> books/akka-in-action-second-edition   or   https://github.com/franciscolopez
> sancho/akka-topics/tree/main/chapter11b. You can find the contents of any
> snippet or listing in the .scala file with the same name as the class, object, or
> trait.

11.2.1 *The Protocol Buffers side*

Protocol Buffers is an interface definition language (IDL) that lets you define data structures without being tied to a specific language implementation like Scala, Go, Java, or Python. You define your data structures in a .proto file. The protobuf compiler libraries read this file and create the corresponding data structures in the implementation language of your choice. In Java, for example, these are classes with getters and builders instead of setters.

Serializers/deserializers are generated for you. Protocol Buffers has an efficient format compression rate and high serialization/deserialization performance. Last but not least, its schema development is flexible and robust, which is a crucial aspect for the long-term development of an application.

11.2.2 *The RPC side*

The RPC part enables HTTP/2 communication with multiplexing. This means you can have data belonging to multiple client/server connections within one HTTP/2 connection, which makes each connection more efficient. With HTTP/1, there is no multiplexing, which is similar to how walkie-talkies work: while one is talking, the other can only listen, and vice versa. HTTP/2, on the other hand, is like WhatsApp, where you can chat with someone while both can write and read independently.

gPRC allows different communication patterns:

- *Unary RPC*—A single request from the client generates a single response from the server.
- *Server streaming*—The server issues multiple responses to a single request from the client.
- *Client streaming*—Multiple messages sent by the client generate a single request from the server.
- *Bidirectional*—The client and server can send multiple requests and responses during the lifetime of the connection. The way requests and responses are handled is application-specific. In a logical sense, there are two different streams, one from the client and one from the server, which are managed separately at the application level.

You can find more on this at https://grpc.io/docs/what-is-grpc/core-concepts.

11.2.3 *The plugin and the .proto file*

Akka gRPC is a plugin you can add to the project/plugins.sbt file:

```
addSbtPlugin( "com.lightbend.akka.grpc" % "sbt-akka-grpc" % "2.1.6")
```

This plugin uses Akka HTTP, Akka Streams, `akka-discovery`, and `akka-http2-support`. Add the first three to your build.sbt to avoid conflicts with transitive dependencies and the last one to enable HTTP/2:

```
val AkkaVersion = "2.6.20"
val AkkaHttpVersion = "10.2.9"
```

```
libraryDependencies ++= Seq(
    "com.typesafe.akka" %% "akka-http" % AkkaHttpVersion,
    "com.typesafe.akka" %% "akka-stream" % AkkaVersion,
    "com.typesafe.akka" %% "akka-discovery" % AkkaVersion,
    "com.typesafe.akka" %% "akka-http2-support" % AkkaHttpVersion)
```

You enable the plugin in the build.sbt. In the Git repository in the project, gRPC is set as follows:

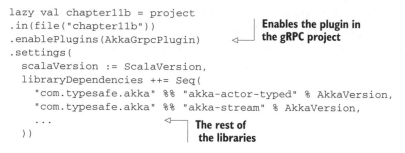

```
lazy val chapter11b = project
.in(file("chapter11b"))
.enablePlugins(AkkaGrpcPlugin)          Enables the plugin in
.settings(                              the gRPC project
  scalaVersion := ScalaVersion,
  libraryDependencies ++= Seq(
    "com.typesafe.akka" %% "akka-actor-typed" % AkkaVersion,
    "com.typesafe.akka" %% "akka-stream" % AkkaVersion,
    ...                         The rest of
  ))                            the libraries
```

After all this preparation, you can create the .proto file to generate a service like the one in section 11.1.6, where you can add cargo to the container and query the list. But first, let's create a dummy service that responds to adding cargo.

You can use an RPC called `AddCargo` to create a .proto file that defines the request message `Cargo`, the response message `AddedCargo`, and the gRPC service called `ContainerService`. This .proto file must be in the proto folder inside the src folder (for example, src/main/proto/container.proto).

Listing 11.5   .proto file

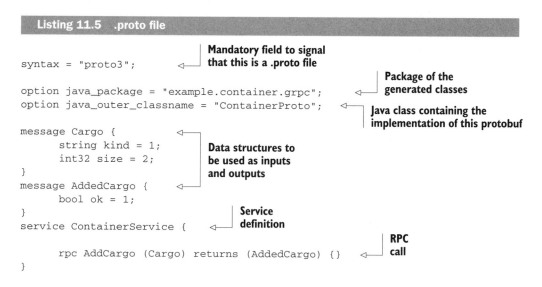

```
syntax = "proto3";                                  Mandatory field to signal
                                                    that this is a .proto file

option java_package = "example.container.grpc";     Package of the
option java_outer_classname = "ContainerProto";     generated classes

                                                    Java class containing the
                                                    implementation of this protobuf
message Cargo {
      string kind = 1;              Data structures to
      int32 size = 2;               be used as inputs
}                                   and outputs
message AddedCargo {
      bool ok = 1;
}                                   Service
service ContainerService {          definition

                                                    RPC
      rpc AddCargo (Cargo) returns (AddedCargo) {}   call
}
```

The string fields are converted to `String`, int32 to `Int`, and bool to `Boolean`. The `java_package` option sets the package in each of the generated classes, and `java_outer_classname` forces the `messages` to be implemented under this class.

Note that there is no trace of Akka in the definition of this file. This is the abstraction that gRPC provides. Once this file is present and the project is compiled—for example, with sbt compile—the `AkkaGrpcPlugin` creates all the classes representing these messages and RPC calls.

From each message in the file, the plugin creates the Scala classes `Cargo`, `AddCargo`, and `AddedCargo` using the third-party Scala library `scalapb`, which is included in the `AkkaGrpcPlugin`. The part of the plugin specific to Akka creates a `ContainerClient` and a `ContainerService`. You can find all the created classes in the chapter11b/target/scala-2.13/akka-grpc folder after you compile the code.

In that folder, the `ContainerClient` is a prebuilt client that you can use to call the service programmatically. The `ContainerService` is a prebuilt server that you need to extend to implement your own server that you can later bind like a route in Akka HTTP.

The following listing shows part of the prebuilt implementation of this service. The trait defines the gRPC call `addCargo` from the .proto file, and a descriptor indicates that it is a unary call, a one-to-one request response.

Listing 11.6   gRPC unary definition of the call

```
// Generated by Akka gRPC. DO NOT EDIT.
...

trait ContainerService {

  def addCargo(in: example.container.grpc.Cargo):
     scala.concurrent.Future[example.container.grpc.AddedCargo]
}

object ContainerService extends akka.grpc.ServiceDescription {
  val name = "ContainerService"
...
  val addCargoDescriptor: MethodDescriptor[
     example.akka.grpc.Cargo, example.akka.grpc.AddedCargo] =
       MethodDescriptor.newBuilder()
       .setType(MethodDescriptor.MethodType.UNARY)          <──┐ Unary call: one
       .setFullMethodName(                                     │ request, one response
         MethodDescriptor
         .generateFullMethodName("ContainerService","AddCargo"))
       .setRequestMarshaller(new Marshaller(CargoSerializer))
       .setResponseMarshaller(new Marshaller(AddedCargoSerializer   <──┐
```

Marshalling/ unmarshalling request ──> (points to `.setRequestMarshaller`)

Marshalling/unmarshalling response (points to `.setResponseMarshaller`)

Thanks to the autogenerated marshallers, you have direct access to Scala objects like cargo in `addCargo(in: Cargo)`.

11.2.4   Akka gRPC in action

You need to implement the `addCargo` method from the previous trait. To implement this dummy service, you can return a completed `Future[AddedCargo]`. To do so, implement the `ContainerService`; and for the execution of the future, you need an implicit `executionContext` that you can add in the constructor of the implementation of the service. To return the completed future, use `Future.successful ([response])`:

```
import example.container.grpc.{ AddedCargo, Cargo, ContainerService }
import scala.concurrent.{Future, ExecutionContext}

class ContainerServiceImpl(implicit executionContex: ExecutionContext)     ◄──
    extends ContainerService {                                  Execution context
                                                             with a thread pool to
  override def addCargo(in: Cargo): Future[AddedCargo] = {        run the future
    Future.successful(AddedCargo(true))    ◄──┐ Future is precomputed;
  }                                           returns immediately
}
```

Once this is implemented, you can create an instance of it. To pass the execution context, use the one from the `ActorSystem`. You can also add bidirectionality—reflection—to this service so you can call it from the command line and receive a response:

```
object ContainerServer {
  ...                                                     Adds reflection with
  val service: HttpRequest => Future[HttpResponse] =      ContainerServiceHandler,
      ContainerServiceHandler                             which is created
        .withServerReflection(new ContainerServiceImpl())  ◄── by akka-gRPC
  ...
}
```

Adding reflection means a consumer can send a text to the server and have it automatically converted to the protobuf format the server understands. This also works with the response being converted to text, which is what humans understand. Otherwise, the consumer must send the proto definitions for the request and the response along with the message.

Once you have the service instance, you can bind it to `Http().newServerAt()`, as you've seen before. The entire application with the gRPC server is shown next.

Listing 11.7 gRPC server

```
import akka.actor.typed.ActorSystem
import akka.actor.typed.scaladsl.Behaviors
import scala.concurrent.{ ExecutionContext, Future }
import akka.http.scaladsl.{ Http, HttpConnectionContext }
import akka.http.scaladsl.model.{ HttpRequest, HttpResponse }

import scala.io.StdIn

object ContainerServer {

  def main(args: Array[String]): Unit = {

    implicit val system =
      ActorSystem(Behaviors.empty, "ContainerServer")

    implicit val ec: ExecutionContext = system.executionContext
```

```
                    val service: HttpRequest => Future[HttpResponse] =       ◁─┐ Creates a service
ContainerService ┐    ContainerServiceHandler.withServerReflection(          ◁─┤ to handle request
implementation   ├─▷    new ContainerServiceImpl())              Adds reflection │ => response
                 ┘                                               to the handler ┘

                    val bindingFuture: Future[Http.ServerBinding] =  ◁─┐ Starts
                      Http().newServerAt(                                │ the server
                        "localhost",
                        8080).bind(service)

                    println(s"server at localhost:8080 \nPress RETURN to stop")   ◁────┐
                    StdIn.readLine()                                                    │
                    bindingFuture                                       Stops the server │
                      .flatMap(_.unbind())                                at Return     │
                      .onComplete(_ => system.terminate())
                  }
                }
```

Note that there is no reference to serialization here, nor to formatters as in Akka HTTP. This makes things easier.

11.2.5 Running the service

You can run this server by executing in the command line at the root of the Git repository: sbt "chapter11b/run". Then use the command line to send a message as follows:

```
$ grpcurl -plaintext -d '{"kind": "bigbag", "size": 2}' localhost:8080 \
    ContainerService/AddCargo
{
    "ok": true      ◁──┤ Result
}
```

Here, grpcurl uses -plaintext to signal that it is not using Transport Layer Security (TLS). With -d, you can add the input data. Then comes the URL localhost:8080, and finally, the RPC service name and /rpc name from the .proto file.

11.2.6 Akka gRPC with an actor

Let's add the container actor to back up the state, just like in the Akka HTTP example. To do this, you need to modify the .proto file accordingly, adding the entity ID when adding the cargo so it can be created and retrieved.

> **NOTE** The source code for this example is available at www.manning.com/
> books/akka-in-action-second-edition or https://github.com/franciscolopezsan
> cho/akka-topics/tree/main/chapter11c. You can find the contents of any snippet or listing in the .scala file with the same name as the class, object, or trait.

Listing 11.8 .proto file with a new getter RPC call

```
message CargoEntity {          ◁──┐ This is like the previous Cargo,
      string entityId = 1;         │ but it has an entityId property.
      string kind = 2;
      int32 size = 3;
}
```

```
message AddedCargo {
      bool ok = 1;
}
message EntityId {
      string entityId = 1;
}
message Cargo {                    ◁──   Now only used as a returning object,
      string kind = 1;                    not as an input to AddCargo
      int32 size = 2;
}
message Cargos {
      repeated Cargo = 1;         ◁──   Cargos have a collection of Cargo. The
}                                        key "repeated" implements a collection.         Previous RPC call
service ContainerService {                                                               with a new input
      rpc AddCargo(CargoEntity) returns (AddedCargo) {         ◁──                        CargoEntity

      rpc GetCargos(EntityId) returns (Cargos) {}         ◁──   New RPC call for getting
}                                                               cargo by entity ID
```

The previous `Cargo` is now only used by the new RPC call `GetCargos`. In the current
.proto file, you could optimize `CargoEntity` and reuse `Cargo` inside it, but that
would make it difficult to manipulate on the Scala side. If `CargoEntity` had a `Cargo`
type field, you would have to deal with an `Option[Cargo]` when manipulating it.
That's not bad, but for simplicity, let's leave it out.

Finally, the `Cargos` message contains a list of `Cargo` achieved by the `repeated`
notation. Internally, this is implemented by a `Seq[Cargo]` within a `Cargos` case class.

With this new .proto definition, you need a different implementation of the
`ContainerServiceImpl`. This implementation needs not only the execution context to run futures but also a `ClusterSharding` reference to find the entities.

To add a cargo by sending it to the `Container` actor, you now have direct access to
the `CargoEntity`; and with it, you can create a `Cargo` to send to the container:

```
class ContainerServiceImplSharding(
    sharding: ClusterSharding)(
    implicit val executionContext: ExecutionContext)
    extends ContainerService {                              Has direct access to
                                                            a CargoEntity Object

  override def addCargo(in: CargoEntity): Future[AddedCargo] = {         ◁──
    val container =                               ◁──
      sharding.entityRefFor(Container.TypeKey, in.entityId)             Searches for
                                                                        the entity

    container ! Container.AddCargo(Container.Cargo(in.kind, in.size))    ◁──
    Future.successful(AddedCargo(true))          ◁──
  }                                                    Always responds          Converts the input of the
                                                       AddedCargo(true)         service into the protocol
  override def getCargos ...                                                    of the actor and sends it
}
```

Finally, let's implement the second RPC call whose signature is implemented as
follows:

```
def getCargos(in: EntityId): Future[Cargos]
```

It is almost the same as the previous Akka HTTP example, except that there are inconsistencies between the objects in the response. You get an actor message type, but you need a .proto message type. You need to convert the actor `Cargos` to .proto `Cargos`. You can do this by mapping the response from `ask` to `Cargos` with `.mapTo[Container.Cargos]` and then map over the cargos to convert them to an `example.container.grpc.Cargo`.

Listing 11.9 `getCargos` implementation

```
class ContainerServiceImplSharding(sharding: ClusterSharding)(
  ...

  implicit val timeout: Timeout = 3.seconds        ⟵ Timeout
                                                       for .ask

  override def getCargos(in: EntityId): Future[Cargos] = {
    val container =
      sharding.entityRefFor(Container.TypeKey, in.entityId)

    container
      .ask(Container.GetCargos)
      .mapTo[Container.Cargos]
      .map { containerCargos =>
        val c = containerCargos.cargos.map { each =>     Each Container.Cargo is
          Cargo(each.kind, each.size)                    transformed to a grpc.Cargo.
        }
        Cargos(c)        ⟵  All the grpc.Cargos are
      }                      used to build a grpc.Cargos.
  }
}
```

Converting actor `Cargos` to .proto `Cargos` is intuitive, but it may not be obvious how it returns a `Future` after the `map`. If you look at the signature of `mapTo`, it becomes clear (probably not how it works, but at least that a `Future` is produced):

```
def mapTo[S](...): Future[S]
```

With the latest implementation of the service, you can bind it and create the application just as before (shown again for completeness in the following listing).

Listing 11.10 Application with an actor and gRPC port

```
object ContainerServerSharding {

  def main(args: Array[String]): Unit = {

    implicit val system =
      ActorSystem(Behaviors.empty, "ContainerServer")

    implicit val ec: ExecutionContext = system.executionContext
    val sharding: ClusterSharding = ClusterSharding(system)

    val shardingRegion =
      sharding.init(Entity(Container.TypeKey)(entityContext =>
        Container(entityContext.entityId)))
```

```
val service: HttpRequest => Future[HttpResponse] =
  ContainerServiceHandler.withServerReflection(
    new ContainerServiceImplSharding(sharding))

val bindingFuture: Future[Http.ServerBinding] =
  Http().newServerAt("localhost", 8080).bind(service)

println(s"server at localhost:8080 \nPress RETURN to stop")
StdIn.readLine()
bindingFuture        ()
  .flatMap(_.unbind())()
  .onComplete(_ => system.terminate())()
}
}
```

- **Adds reflection to the handler**
- **Creates a service to handle request => response**
- **Uses the ContainerService implementation**
- **Starts the server**
- **Stops the server at Return**

11.2.7 *Running the example*

You can run this example by executing the following at the root of the Git repository:

```
$ sbt chapter11c/run
```

To use it, run the following commands at the command line:

```
$ grpcurl -plaintext -d '{"entityId": "id1", "kind": "bigbag", "size": 2}' \
      localhost:8080 ContainerService/AddCargo
{
  "ok": true
}
```

- **Adds one cargo**

```
$ grpcurl -plaintext -d '{"entityId": "id1", "kind": "sack", "size": 4}' \
      localhost:8080 ContainerService/AddCargo
{
  "ok": true
}
```

- **Adds another cargo**

```
$ grpcurl -plaintext -d '{"entityId": "id1"}' localhost:8080 \
      ContainerService/GetCargos
{
  "cargo": [
    {
      "kind": "sack",
      "size": 4
    },
    {
      "kind": "bigbag",
      "size": 2
    }
  ]
}
```

- **Retrieves the total cargo**

You now have a complete picture of how to use Akka gRPC as a port for your `ActorSystem`. This chapter covered how to create servers with Akka so clients can connect through HTTP/1 and with gRPC through HTTP/2. In the next chapter, you put most of what you have learned so far into practice to implement a betting house.

Summary

- Akka HTTP lets you create servers—also called ports in Akka—by defining their paths, the parameters they accept, and other directives to create the routes bound to an Akka HTTP server.
- Akka HTTP provides serialization for the actor's messages via JSON formatters. You can assemble the specific serializer you need—also called a marshaller—from the basic `jsonFormats`.
- With Akka gRPC, you can also create servers, but using protobuf files. When compiling the code, these files automatically generate Scala code that implements the messages and interfaces of the service. The implementation creates the marshallers out of the box.
- If you have an Akka server—HTTP or gRPC—you can forward its input to an actor using `ask` or `tell`. Conversely, you can send the actor's response to the output of the service. This way, you enable communication with an actor from outside the `ActorSystem`.

Real-world example:
An Akka betting house

This chapter covers

- Creating an elaborate use case
- Creating the entities and ports for them

This chapter presents a real-world example. The functionality is only part of a large business use case: sports betting. The idea is to create three actors at the business's core:

- The *market* is a sporting event with specific odds that can be bet against. For example, the Liverpool vs. Real Madrid soccer match has a market where bets can be placed on a home win, an away win, or a draw.
- The *wallet* represents a user's account with their balance.
- The *bet* is the amount of money invested in a market and secured by a wallet.

These entities reside in a cluster, so they can communicate directly. To communicate with them from the outside, the application has ports: two gRPC services and one Akka HTTP service. Figure 12.1 shows the big picture of how everything is related.

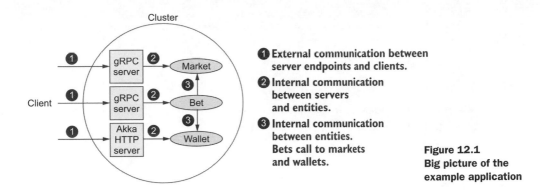

Cluster

1 External communication between server endpoints and clients.

2 Internal communication between servers and entities.

3 Internal communication between entities. Bets call to markets and wallets.

Figure 12.1
Big picture of the example application

This example is just the first step to give you insight into the process of beginning a professional project, including how to get started and what to focus on. Like any project, it will evolve later, further splitting some boundaries and blending others. So, the actors will also evolve. Let's look at the definition of the actors and their protocols.

> **NOTE** The source code for this chapter is available at www.manning.com/ books/akka-in-action-second-edition or https://github.com/franciscolopez sancho/akka-topics/tree/main/betting-house.

12.1 The actors

We begin with the wallet, the simplest of the three actors.

12.1.1 The wallet

This actor allows you to `ReserveFunds` for a bet. When a bet is created, it is necessary to check if the required funds are available. Like all others in the actor model, this message is processed individually and provides the consistency you need. You know there are no race conditions when funds are requested. Funds are granted only if they are available when the message is processed. If that is the case, a `FundsReserved` event is generated; otherwise, a `FundsReservationDenied` event is generated. You can also use `AddFunds`, which generates a `FundsAdded` event. And there's `CheckFunds`, which does exactly what it says. These events are shown in the following snippet:

```
object Wallet {

    ...

  sealed trait Command extends CborSerializable
  case class ReserveFunds(
      amount: Int,
      replyTo: ActorRef[UpdatedResponse])
      extends Command
  case class AddFunds(amount: Int, replyTo: ActorRef[UpdatedResponse])
      extends Command
  case class CheckFunds(replyTo: ActorRef[Response]) extends Command
```

Commands

```
sealed trait Event extends CborSerializable
case class FundsReserved(amount: Int) extends Event          Events
case class FundsAdded(amount: Int) extends Event
case class FundsReservationDenied(amount: Int) extends Event
...
}
```

There is a `Response` and an `UpdatedResponse` in its protocol. A command can be accepted or rejected or get back the current balance:

```
object Wallet {
  ...

  sealed trait Response extends CborSerializable
  trait UpdatedResponse extends Response
  case object Accepted extends UpdatedResponse
  case object Rejected extends UpdatedResponse
  case class CurrentBalance(amount: Int) extends Response
 ...
}
```

`Accepted` and `Rejected` extend from `UpdatedResponse`. This is useful because it simplifies pattern matching when requesting or adding funds. Only these two cases need to be considered.

Finally, the `State` is where the current balance is. It simply contains an integer:

```
object Wallet {
  ...

  case class State(balance: Int) extends CborSerializable
  ...
}
```

Depending on the business requirements, the application may need to access millions of wallets when a major event occurs. To distribute the load, you use Akka Sharding, distributing the actors into multiple nodes according to ID. You can always add more nodes if needed by adding an `EntityTypeKey` to the wallet:

```
object Wallet {
  ...

  val typeKey = EntityTypeKey[Command]("wallet")
  ...
}
```

The following listing shows the code so far.

Listing 12.1   Wallet protocol, state, and sharding type key

```
object Wallet {

  val typeKey = EntityTypeKey[Command]("wallet")     ◁─┐ Key to be used as
                                                         a sharding entity
```

```
sealed trait Command extends CborSerializable
final case class ReserveFunds(
    amount: Int,                                              Commands
    replyTo: ActorRef[UpdatedResponse])
    extends Command
final case class AddFunds(amount: Int, replyTo: ActorRef[UpdatedResponse])
    extends Command
final case class CheckFunds(replyTo: ActorRef[Response]) extends Command

sealed trait Event extends CborSerializable
final case class FundsReserved(amount: Int) extends Event
final case class FundsAdded(amount: Int) extends Event          Events
final case class FundsReservationDenied(amount: Int) extends Event

sealed trait Response extends CborSerializable
trait UpdatedResponse extends Response
final case object Accepted extends UpdatedResponse
final case object Rejected extends UpdatedResponse              Responses
final case class CurrentBalance(amount: Int) extends Response

final case class State(balance: Int) extends CborSerializable   State
...
}
```

You need to make sure the state is durable so it can survive processes crashing or racks catching fire. To do that, you use Akka Persistence, adding the usual snapshotting and persistence failure.

Listing 12.2 Entity constructor

```
object Wallet {

  val typeKey = EntityTypeKey[Command]("wallet")      Adds a key to make
                                                       the actor sharded
  ...      Protocol
  def apply(walletId: String): Behavior[Command] =
    EventSourcedBehavior[Command, Event, State](      Adds EventSourcedBehavior
      PersistenceId(typeKey.name, walletId),          to make the actor persistent
      State(0),
      commandHandler = handleCommands,
      eventHandler = handleEvents)
      ...
      .withRetention(RetentionCriteria
        .snapshotEvery(numberOfEvents = 100, keepNSnapshots = 2))
      .onPersistFailure(
        SupervisorStrategy.restartWithBackoff(
          minBackoff = 10.seconds,
          maxBackoff = 60.seconds,
          randomFactor = 0.1))
  ...
}
```

Note that the initial balance in the constructor is set to zero with `State(0)`. You also add snapshot retention and restart with back-off. Depending on the specifics of the betting office, these parameters may vary, but that's an optimization problem. The settings are good enough for now.

In the construction of this actor, in the `apply` method, you start with a balance of zero and then redirect the processing of commands and events to their respectively named methods, `handleCommands` and `handleEvents`. The tagging, snapshotting, and restarting strategies are like those you saw in chapter 9.

The actor's business logic is minimal. A funds reservation is accepted if the balance is sufficient or denied otherwise, persisting `FundsReserved` or `FundsReservation-Denied`, respectively. Adding funds is always accepted, and the `FundsAdded` event is persisted.

Listing 12.3   Command handler

```
object Wallet {
  ...

  def handleCommands(
      state: State,
      command: Command): ReplyEffect[Event, State] = {
    command match {
      case ReserveFunds(amount, replyTo) =>          Reserves funds if the amount
        if (amount <= state.balance)          ◁─┘   is less than the balance
          Effect
            .persist(FundsReserved(amount))
            .thenReply(replyTo)(state => Accepted)
        else
          Effect
            .persist(FundsReservationDenied(amount))
            .thenReply(replyTo)(state => Rejected)
      case AddFunds(amount, replyTo) =>
        Effect
          .persist(FundsAdded(amount))
          .thenReply(replyTo)(state => Accepted)
      case CheckFunds(replyTo) =>
        Effect.reply(replyTo)(CurrentBalance(state.balance))   ◁─┐ Checking funds
    }                                                              has nothing
  }                                                                to persist.
  ...
}
```

Finally, the event handler updates the balance when you add or reserve funds; otherwise the state remains unchanged:

```
object Wallet {
  ...

  def handleEvents(state: State, event: Event): State = event match {
    case FundsReserved(amount) =>
      State(state.balance - amount)          ◁─┐ Reduces
    case FundsAdded(amount) =>                     the balance
      State(state.balance + amount)
```

Increases
the balance ──▷

```
    case FundsReservationDenied(_) =>
      state         ◁─┐ Balance
  }}                   │ unchanged
  ...
}
```

This is the most basic implementation of a wallet. You could extend the use case by, for example, verifying with third parties that the request is allowed under gambling laws. Or you could link this wallet to a customer entity that contains more information about the user. But we'll leave it at this.

12.1.2 *The market*

This actor is responsible for holding the odds on a sporting event for a given bet. The winner of a soccer game, a player scoring a certain number of goals, and a horse finishing last in a race are all examples of markets, but this example betting house only models soccer games where the outcome can be a home win, an away win, or a draw. This sports event is modeled as a `Fixture` and the possible outcomes with `Odds`:

```
object Market {
  ...

  final case class Fixture(id: String, homeTeam: String, awayTeam: String)
      extends CborSerializable
  final case class Odds(winHome: Double, winAway: Double, draw: Double)
      extends CborSerializable
  ...
}
```

A market can be requested to be opened, updated, closed, or canceled. And, of course, you can check its status.

Listing 12.4   Market commands

```
object Market {
  ...

  sealed trait Command extends CborSerializable {
    def replyTo: ActorRef[Response]
  }
  final case class Open(
      fixture: Fixture,
      odds: Odds,
      opensAt: OffsetDateTime,
      replyTo: ActorRef[Response])
      extends Command

  final case class Update(
      odds: Option[Odds],
      opensAt: Option[OffsetDateTime],
      result: Option[Int], //1 =  winHome, 2 = winAway, 0 = draw
      replyTo: ActorRef[Response])
      extends Command
```

```
final case class Close(replyTo: ActorRef[Response]) extends Command

final case class Cancel(reason: String, replyTo: ActorRef[Response])
    extends Command
final case class GetState(replyTo: ActorRef[Response]) extends Command
...
}
```

Cancel stops the market and makes it unavailable for betting. Close registers the
normal end of the event, whereas Cancel does not; therefore Cancel has a reason
field.

The market can respond to a command by accepting the changes or not. It can
also respond with its current status when asked:

```
object Market {
  ...

  sealed trait Response extends CborSerializable
  final case object Accepted extends Response
  final case class CurrentState(status: Status) extends Response
  final case class RequestUnaccepted(reason: String) extends Response
  ...
}
```

Now the state. The market starts with UninitializedState. The state can then be
updated, canceled, or closed. This State and the rest have a Status that holds all
the market variables. These are the different states:

```
object Market {
  ...

  sealed trait State extends CborSerializable {      Must be implemented in any
    def status: Status;                          ◁─┘ class extending this trait
  }
  final case class UninitializedState (status: Status) extends State
  final case class OpenState(status: Status) extends State
  final case class ClosedState(status: Status) extends State
  final case class CancelledState(status: Status) extends State
  ...
}
```

Status has the market ID, the fixture, and the odds. And for convenience, there is a
constructor to create an empty market:

```
object Market {
  ...

  final case class Status(marketId: String, fixture: Fixture, odds: Odds)
      extends CborSerializable
  object Status {
    def empty(marketId: String) =
      Status(marketId, Fixture("", "", ""), Odds(-1, -1, -1), 0)
  }
  ...
}
```

The `apply` method of the market is in essence the same as the wallet, with a slightly different initial state:

```
object Market {
  ...

  def apply(marketId: String): Behavior[Command] =
    EventSourcedBehavior[Command, Event, State](
      PersistenceId(typeKey.name, marketId),
      UninitializedState(Status.empty(marketId)),       ⊲─┤ Initial state
      commandHandler = handleCommands,
      eventHandler = handleEvents)
    ...

  ...
}
```

The market is a finite state machine. For example, in an `UninitializedState`, the actor responds only to `Open` messages that cause it to switch to an `OpenState`. When it is in the `OpenState` state, receiving `Open` again is not defined as a valid entry and as such is interpreted as an invalid command. The `handleCommands` method expresses the entity's business requirements.

To express how the market reacts to each command depending on its state, there is no more concise way than the following code:

```
object Market {
  ...

  def handleCommands(
      state: State,
      command: Command): ReplyEffect[Event, State] =
    (state, command) match {
      case (state: UninitializedState, command: Open) =>
                                              open(state, command)
      case (state: OpenState, command: Update) =>
                                              update(state, command)
      case (state: OpenState, command: Close) => close(state, command)
      case (_, command: Cancel)               => cancel(state, command)
      case (_, command: GetState)             => tell(state, command)
      case _                                  => invalid(state, command)
    }
  ...
}
```

The method `open(state, command)` and the rest trigger events that can change the actor's state and thus its behavior (see figure 12.2).

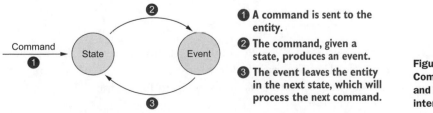

① A command is sent to the entity.

② The command, given a state, produces an event.

③ The event leaves the entity in the next state, which will process the next command.

Figure 12.2
Command, state, and event interactions

The open method generates an Opened event, persists it, and then replies with Accepted:

```
object Market {
  ...

  private def open(
      state: State,
      command: Open): ReplyEffect[Opened, State] = {
    val opened =
      Opened(state.status.marketId, command.fixture, command.odds)   ◁── Event
    Effect                                                                creation
      .persist(opened)
      .thenReply(command.replyTo)(_ => Accepted)   ◁── Reply to
  }                                                     the sender
  ...
}
```

Event persisting in the journal (annotation pointing to `.persist(opened)`)

Each of the command handler methods includes a variation of this structure. The command creates an event, persists it, and finally responds to the caller. Not every command handler methods has persistence or a response, but their structure is basically the same.

The list of events is the effect of a command with the same root name. The command Open creates an event Opened, and so on. The following snippet shows the list of events:

```
object Market {
  ...

  sealed trait Event extends CborSerializable {
    def marketId: String
  }
  final case class Opened(marketId: String, fixture: Fixture, odds: Odds)
      extends Event
  final case class Updated(
              marketId: String,
              odds: Option[Odds],
              result: Option[Int]) extends Event
  final case class Closed(
              marketId: String,
              result: Int,
              at: OffsetDateTime) extends Event
  final case class Cancelled(
              marketId: String,
              reason: String) extends Event
  ...
}
```

When an event is persisted, the event handler (shown in the next listing) adds the last piece of the puzzle. The actor reacts differently depending on its current state and the processing event, often updating its own state in different ways.

Listing 12.5 Event handler and event

```
object Market {
  ...

  private def handleEvents(state: State, event: Event): State = {
    (state, event) match {
      case (_, Opened(marketId, fixture, odds)) =>
        OpenState(Status(marketId, fixture, odds, 0))
      case (state: OpenState, Updated(_, odds, result)) =>
        state.copy(status = Status(
          state.status.marketId,
          state.status.fixture,
          odds.getOrElse(state.status.odds),
          result.getOrElse(state.status.result)))
      case (state: OpenState, Closed(_, result, _)) =>
        ClosedState(state.status.copy(result = result))
      case (_, Cancelled(_, _)) =>
        CancelledState(state.status)
    }
  ...
}
```

> Each time events are processed, different states are produced.

This brings us full circle: the actor receives a command that can trigger an event that can change the state, and this happens over and over again for each message.

With these three parts—the protocol, the command handler that connects states and commands, and the event handler that connects events and states—you have a complete picture of the actor's behavior. But since the devil is in the details, let's look at the rest of the command handler methods of the market actor.

Listing 12.6 Remaining command handler methods

```
object Market{
  ...

  def open(
      state: State,
      command: Open): ReplyEffect[Opened, State] = {
    Effect
      .persist(Opened(state.status.marketId))
      .thenReply(command.replyTo)(_ => Accepted)
  }

  def update(
      state: State,
      command: Update): ReplyEffect[Updated, State] = {
    val updated = Updated(state.status.marketId, command.odds)
    Effect
      .persist(updated)
      .thenReply(command.replyTo)(_ => Accepted)
  }

  def close(
      state: State,
```

> Creates an event, persists it, and replies to the caller

```
              command: Close): ReplyEffect[Closed, State] = {
      val closed = Closed(
        state.status.marketId,
        OffsetDateTime.now(ZoneId.of("UTC")))
      Effect
        .persist(closed)
        .thenReply(command.replyTo)(_ => Accepted)
    }

    def cancel(
        state: State,
        command: Cancel): ReplyEffect[Cancelled, State] = {
      val cancelled = Cancelled(state.status.marketId, command.reason)
      Effect
        .persist(cancelled)
        .thenReply(command.replyTo)(_ => Accepted)
    }

    def tell(
        state: State,
        command: GetState): ReplyEffect[Event, State] = {
      Effect.none.thenReply(command.replyTo)(_ => CurrentState(state))
    }

    def invalid(
        state: State,
        command: Command): ReplyEffect[Event, State] = {
      Effect.none.thenReply(command.replyTo)(
        _ =>  RequestUnaccepted(
              s"[$command] is not allowed upon state [$state]"))
    }
}
```

Creates an event,
persists it, and
replies to the caller

Does not
persist; only
replies to
the caller

There is nothing surprising in these methods. They persist an event and then respond, except `tell` and `invalid`: `tell` correspond to the `GetState` command, so there is nothing to persist when the actor is queried; and `invalid` is used to channel any command that does not match the actor's state, so again, there is nothing to persist. These two commands do not change the actor's state in content or in type.

12.1.3 *The bet*

The `bet` actor coordinates with the other two. When a client initializes a bet, the actor must verify that the market odds are still available (as they can change quickly) and that the wallet has enough money to cover the bet. If both verifications are successful, the bet is considered valid and remains open until settlement when the market closes.

Once a bet is opened, these two validations must occur in less than a few seconds. The actor schedules a check that, if not passed, rejects the bet. You'll see two different approaches to perform these checks.

On the one hand, you ask the market if the odds are still available or if the market has moved. You want to process this request in less than a certain amount of time. If the answer comes later, you can't be sure if it reflects the market, and it is therefore considered a failed answer.

On the other hand, you tell the wallet to verify that it has the requested money. The bet instructs the wallet to reserve funds and eventually (at most once) gets an answer. (If you chose to ask instead of tell in this situation, you would be chaining questions together, which is not advisable. Figuring out what timeout is needed for the total length of nested requests is usually a losing battle.)

Let's get to the details of the bet. Be aware that this is by far the most complicated of the three actors.

The protocol has two kinds of commands—those that expect a reply and those that don't:

```
object Bet {
  ...

  sealed trait Command
  trait ReplyCommand extends Command with CborSerializable {
    def replyTo: ActorRef[Response]
  }
  ...
}
```

The instances with `replyTo` are for external communication, and the others are for internal communication. That is why the external messages are public and the others are private, as you can see in the next two snippets.

PUBLIC PROTOCOL

Let's start with the public messages that allow you to open a bet, settle it, cancel it, and check its status. `Settle` matches the final result of the market with the bet. If the market result is in favor of the bet, the stake multiplied by the odds is added to the wallet:

```
object Bet {
  ...

  final case class Open(
      walletId: String,          ← The wallet to get funds
                                    from or add to
      marketId: String,          ← The market to
      odds: Double,                check for availability
      stake: Int,
      result: Int,               ← 0 represents winHome,
      replyTo: ActorRef[Response])  1 winAway, and 2 draw.
      extends ReplyCommand
  final case class Settle(result: Int, replyTo: ActorRef[Response])
      extends ReplyCommand
  final case class Cancel(reason: String, replyTo: ActorRef[Response])
      extends ReplyCommand
  final case class GetState(replyTo: ActorRef[Response]) extends ReplyCommand
  ...
}
```

These messages can respond as follows

```
object Bet {
  ...
```

```
sealed trait Response
final case object Accepted extends Response
final case class RequestUnaccepted(reason: String) extends Response
final case class CurrentState(state: State) extends Response
...
}
```

depending on whether the bet is accepted or not when it is requested, or only the current state of the bet.

PRIVATE PROTOCOL

The private messages have to do with various validations. They check whether the market is still available or the wallet has the money. The actor sets a time limit for itself for checking both validations when opening. If it does not receive a confirmation within this time, it sends itself a `ValidationsTimedOut`. This is private because it belongs to the internal logic of the actor.

There are also `Fail` and `Close`, which are the two sides of the bet's final state. `Close` is the happy path: the final state when all the checks—and settlements, in case of a bet win—have been successfully completed. `Fail` is the unhappy ending that occurs when the checks or settlements are not completed successfully:

```
object Bet {
  ...

  private final case class MarketOddsAvailable(
      available: Boolean,
      marketOdds: Option[Double])
      extends Command
  private final case class RequestWalletFunds(
      response: Wallet.UpdatedResponse)
      extends Command
  private final case class ValidationsTimedOut(seconds: Int)
      extends Command
  private final case class Fail(reason: String) extends Command
  private final case class Close(reason: String) extends Command
  ...
}
```

These private classes conform to the internal logic of the actor.

Before using the command handler to link commands and states together, let's look at the actor's different states.

STATES

The `State` and the `Status` work the same as in the market actor. One is the type, and the other represents the moving parts (the variables):

```
object Bet {
  ...

  final case class Status(
      betId: String,
      walletId: String,
      marketId: String,
      odds: Double,
```

Variables that represent the state of the bet

```
        stake: Int,
        result: Int)
        extends CborSerializable
    object Status {
      def empty(marketId: String) =        ◁── To be used in
        Status(marketId, "uninitialized", "uninitialized", -1, -1, 0)   creating the market
    }
    sealed trait State extends CborSerializable {   ◁── Placeholder for the Status, which
      def status: Status                                can represent any market state
    }
    ...
}
```

From an uninitialized state, the bet can open, settle, and close if successful. Otherwise, it fails. In either case, it can be canceled. This is reflected in the following states:

```
object Bet {
  ...

  sealed trait State extends CborSerializable {
    def status: Status
  }
  final case class UninitializedState(status: Status) extends State
  final case class OpenState(
      status: Status,
      marketConfirmed: Option[Boolean] = None,     ◁── Registers if the
      fundsConfirmed: Option[Boolean] = None)          market is available
      extends State                                ◁── Registers if funds
  final case class SettledState(status: Status) extends State   were reserved
  final case class CancelledState(status: Status) extends State
  final case class FailedState(status: Status, reason: String) extends State
  final case class ClosedState(status: Status) extends State
  ...
}
```

It is worth noting that `marketConfirmed` and `fundsConfirmed` are relevant only for `OpenState`. No other state keeps track of them; whether the bet is closed, canceled, or failed is recorded in other ways. `Fail` keeps it explicitly in the `reason` and `Close` and `Cancelled` keep it implicitly.

INITIALIZATION

Now let's look at the constructor, mainly to see how it initializes sharding and the timer and passes them along with the context to the command handler:

```
object Bet {
  ...

  def apply(betId: String): Behavior[Command] = {   │ Timer scheduler used later
    Behaviors.withTimers { timer =>                  ◁── to start the countdown
      Behaviors.setup { context =>                   ◁── Sets up the
        val sharding = ClusterSharding(context.system)   initial state
        EventSourcedBehavior[Command, Event, State](
          PersistenceId(TypeKey.name, betId),
          UninitializedState(Status.empty(betId)),
```

```
commandHandler = (state, command) =>
    handleCommands(state, command, sharding, context, timer),    <──┐
eventHandler = handleEvents)                                         Command handler
    ...          <──┐  Taggers, snapshot strategy,                   using sharding, the
}}}                 │  and restarting strategy                      context, and the timer
...
}
```

Let's see how these commands and states work together.

HANDLING COMMANDS: OPEN

In the uninitialized state, the only valid action is to open. Once you are in the `Open-State`, all commands are accepted, such as confirming funds or the market, settling, or closing. Regardless of the state, you can request to cancel the bet. However, a request can also be rejected. For example, if you try to validate or settle a bet after it has been closed, it will be rejected. Finally, there is an `invalid` option that handles all other combinations of commands that are not explicitly handled; it's like saying you can't select something if it's not on the menu.

Listing 12.7   Entity constructor and handling commands

```
object Bet {
  ...

  def handleCommands(
      state: State,
      command: Command,
      sharding: ClusterSharding,
      context: ActorContext[Command],
      timer: TimerScheduler[Command]): Effect[Event, State] = {
    (state, command) match {
      case (state: UninitializedState, command: Open) =>
        open(state, command, sharding, context, timer)
      case (state: OpenState, command: CheckMarketOdds) =>
        validateMarket(state, command)
      case (state: OpenState, command: RequestWalletFunds) =>
        validateFunds(state, command)
      case (state: OpenState, command: ValidationsTimedOut) =>
        checkValidations(state, command)
      case (state: OpenState, command: Settle) =>
        settle(state, command, sharding, context)
      case (state: OpenState, command: Close) =>
        finish(state, command)
      case (_, command: Cancel) => cancel(state, command)
      case (_, command: ReplyCommand)   => reject(state, command)
      case (_, command: Fail)           => fail(state, command)
      case _                            => invalid(state, command, context)
      }
    }
  }
  ...
}
```

Let's take a closer look at the open method. With the Open command in an UninitializedState, the bet starts a timer that schedules sending a message to the bet itself. Once this message arrives, all validations must be completed. The bet checks whether the market is available and the funds are reserved. After the timer is started, the open method generates and persists an Opened event. Then it initiates the two required validations: market and funds. Finally, it responds to the caller with Accepted.

Listing 12.8 Opening the bet

```
object Bet {
  ...

  private def open(
      state: UninitializedState,
      command: Open,
      sharding: ClusterSharding,
      context: ActorContext[Command],
      timers: TimerScheduler[Command]): ReplyEffect[Opened, State] = {
    timers.startSingleTimer(              ←─┐ Starts a timer to
      "lifespan",                            │ validate the bet state
      ValidationsTimedOut(10),
      10.seconds)
    val open = Opened(            ←─┐ Creates the
      state.status.betId,            │ Opened event
      command.walletId,
      command.marketId,
      command.odds,
      command.stake,
      command.result)
    Effect                      ┐ Persists
      .persist(open)     ←──────┘ the event                    ┐ Request to verify
      .thenRun((_: State) =>                                    │ that the odds are
        requestMarketStatus(command, sharding, context)  ←──────┘ still available
      .thenRun((_: State) =>
        requestFundsReservation(command, sharding, context))  ◁──┐ Request to
      .thenReply(command.replyTo)(_ => Accepted)  ◁────          │ reserve the funds
  }                                          ┐ Responds to       │ to the wallet
  ...                                        │ the caller
}                                            ┘
```

Remember that saving the Opened event does not mean the entity has executed any of the requests or even the response: that is, thenRun or thenReply. The JVM may fail immediately after persisting.

> **NOTE** If that is the case, the timer will no longer be present when the entity respawns. Fortunately, this is not a problem. If the validations are not triggered, the initial value for marketConfirmed and fundsReserved is None, which can be interpreted as "not true" when the bet is settled.

Events and the event handler

`Opened` and the remaining events are shown in the following listing. Like all events, they correspond to a command with the same root name.

Listing 12.9 Events

```scala
object Bet {

  ...

  sealed trait Event extends CborSerializable
  final case class MarketConfirmed(state: OpenState) extends Event
  final case class FundsGranted(state: OpenState) extends Event
  final case class ValidationsPassed(state: OpenState) extends Event
  final case class Opened(
      betId: String,
      walletId: String,
      marketId: String,
      odds: Double,
      stake: Int,
      result: Int)
    extends Event
  final case class Settled(betId: String) extends Event
  final case class Cancelled(betId: String, reason: String) extends Event
  final case class Failed(betId: String, reason: String) extends Event
  final case object Closed extends Event
  ...
}
```

Again, it is generally easier to understand the events and their relationship to the state than the relationships between states and commands. The event handler is generally easier to understand than the command handler. Each event comes from a command with the same root name. And the event's name pretty much tells you what state the entity will transition to.

Listing 12.10 Event handler

```scala
object Bet {

  ...

  def handleEvents(state: State, event: Event): State = event match {
    case Opened(betId, walletId, marketId, odds, stake, result) =>
      OpenState(
        Status(betId, walletId, marketId, odds, stake, result),
        None,
        None)
    case MarketConfirmed(state) =>
      state.copy(marketConfirmed = Some(true))
    case FundsGranted(state) =>
      state.copy(fundsConfirmed = Some(true))
    case ValidationsPassed(state) =>
      state
    case Closed =>
```

```
        ClosedState(state.status)
    case Settled(_) =>
        SettledState(state.status)
    case Cancelled(betId, reason) =>
        CancelledState(state.status)
    case Failed(_, reason) =>
        FailedState(state.status, reason)
  ...
}
```

Note that `MarketConfirmed` and `FundsGranted` update the `Status` but do not change the `State`. `ValidationsPassed` refers to the fact that the timeout has expired. When all validations have passed, this event is generated.

HANDLING COMMANDS: VALIDATING THE MARKET AND THE FUNDS

Let's finish with the rest of the command handler methods. When the bet queries the market status (`requestMarketStatus`), it must get a quick answer from the market. Let's say that according to business requirements, you cannot use market information more than three seconds old. There is a financial risk, and business experts have requested this feature.

If the actor receives a positive response from the market, it sends itself `MarketOddsAvailable(true,[odds])` to indicate that the validation has passed, along with the odds; otherwise, it sends `MarketOddsAvailable(false, [odds])`. Sending the odds helps operators understand the system's behavior by registering what odds were requested for the bet.

Listing 12.11 Market validation request

```
object Bet {
  ...

  private def requestMarketStatus(
      command: Open,
      sharding: ClusterSharding,
      context: ActorContext[Command]): Unit = {
    val marketRef =
      sharding.entityRefFor(Market.typeKey, command.marketId)
```
Finds an ActorRef for the market

```
    implicit val timeout: Timeout = Timeout(3, SECONDS)
    context.ask(marketRef, Market.GetState) {
      case Success(Market.CurrentState(marketState)) =>
        val matched = oddsDoMatch(marketState, command)
        MarketOddsAvailable(
          matched.doMatch,
          Option(matched.marketOdds))
      case Failure(ex) =>
        context.log.error(ex.getMessage())
        MarketOddsAvailable(false, None)
    }
  }
  ...
}
```
Asks the market its state

Sets the timeout for .ask to 3 seconds

Verifies that the market's odds match the bet's odds

A failure marks the odds as unavailable.

If the market responds in time, the bet takes the odds from the response and matches them with the odds requested by the user. If they match, it creates a `Market-OddsAvailable`. No event is recorded; the actor sends this message to itself and processes it accordingly. Let's look at the command handler again to see how the actor processes this message:

```
object Bet {
  ...
  def handleCommands(...){
      ...
      case (state: OpenState, command: MarketOddsAvailable) =>
        validateMarket(state, command)
      ...
  }
  ...
}
```

The next stop is `validateMarket`, which is like all the other persists you've seen so far:

```
object Bet {
  ...

  private def validateMarket(
      state: OpenState,
      command: MarketOddsAvailable): Effect[Event, State] = {
    if (command.available) {
      Effect.persist(MarketConfirmed(state))        If the market is available, the bet
    } else {                                        state is updated accordingly.
      Effect.persist(                               If the market is not available, the
        Failed(                                     bet gets into a FailedState.
          state.status.betId,
          s"market odds [${command.marketOdds}] not available"))
    }
  }
  ...
}
```

If the bet receives a `MarketConfirmed` event, it persists the event and keeps in memory the information in the `OpenState` by setting `marketConfirmed` to `Some(true)`; otherwise, it goes to the `FailedState`.

Let's look at the second validation when opening the bet: `requestFunds-Reservation`. To check whether the wallet can reserve the necessary funds, there is no business requirement like in the market. In general, it is cleaner to `tell` than to `ask`. The wallet may also have to make calls to other services: for example, to check that the customer is not overspending or breaking a law. If you expect a chain of calls, `tell` is usually the best option. Here's the code:

```
object Bet {
  ...
```

```
private def requestFundsReservation(
    command: Open,
    sharding: ClusterSharding,
    context: ActorContext[Command]): Unit = {
  val walletRef =
    sharding.entityRefFor(Wallet.typeKey, command.walletId)
  val walletResponseMapper: ActorRef[Wallet.UpdatedResponse] =
    context.messageAdapter(rsp => RequestWalletFunds(rsp))

  walletRef ! Wallet.ReserveFunds(
    command.stake,
    walletResponseMapper)
}
...
}
```

Retrieves the wallet's ActorRef

Creates a method to adapt the wallet's response to the Bet's protocol

Tells the wallet to reserve funds

The wallet's response is a `Wallet.Response` wrapped in a `RequestWalletFunds` command, which is subsequently processed by the command handler. It is processed by `validateFunds`, which persist the event or fails:

```
object Bet {
  ...

  private def validateFunds(
      state: OpenState,
      command: RequestWalletFunds): Effect[Event, State] = {
    command.response match {
      case Wallet.Accepted =>
        Effect.persist(FundsGranted(state))
      case Wallet.Rejected =>
        Effect.persist(
          Failed(state.status.betId, "funds not available"))
    }
  }
  ...
}
```

Now let's move on to the settlement.

HANDLING COMMANDS: SETTLE

When a sporting event is over, the application must settle all bets to determine which bets won. What you see here is from the bet's point of view when it receives the Settle with the market information, uses it to check the result of the sporting event, and, if it has won, returns the profit to its wallet.

> **NOTE** You could argue that it would be better and more reliable to have a blank Settle message that forces the bet to request the result from the market to get the information directly from the source. On the other hand, each bet would have to contact the market, which would mean another call for each bet. For a game like the Champions League final, that could be millions of additional calls. Whether one approach is better cannot be determined without more context.

The settlement is partially implemented here with a projection that reads from the market journal. When such a projection generates an event that corresponds to `Market.Closed`, a listener can query the bets of that market and send the `Settle` message to each bet. Remember that the projection is implemented, but the listener is not. Since this listener has some information about the market, it can query the market's odds and embed that information in the `Settle` message.

> **NOTE**   You may wonder how the listener knows all the bets on a market. This information can be found in another projection, this time of bets. Each time a bet is opened, its identifier can be stored in a database table together with the market's identifier. Both projections are implemented in this book but are not discussed until chapter 15.

Listing 12.12 shows how the `bet` actor processes the `Settle` message. It uses a helper method that lets you `ask` with more parameters than `replyTo`. The bet must pass its stake to the wallet, and for this, you have `auxCreateRequest(stake: Int)` `(replyTo: ...)`. If the market responds in time, the request is considered successful, and the bet is closed. If, on the other hand, the market does not respond, the bet is ended with a `FailedState`. An `ask` is used here instead of a `tell` to leave a trail as to why the money was not paid. This information can be queried later with a projection: for example, to give the operator of the betting house the necessary information to solve the problem.

Listing 12.12   Processing the `Settle` message

```
object Bet {
  ...

  private def settle(
      state: State,
      command: Settle,
      sharding: ClusterSharding,                                    Ask timeout
      context: ActorContext[Command]): Effect[Event, State] = {
    implicit val timeout = Timeout(10, SECONDS)

    def auxCreateRequest(stake: Int)(                               Auxiliary method
        replyTo: ActorRef[Wallet.Response]): Wallet.AddFunds =      to produce an ask
      Wallet.AddFunds(stake, replyTo)                               message with
                                                                    parameters, apart
    if (isWinner(state, command.result)) {                         from replyTo
      val walletRef =
        sharding.entityRefFor(Wallet.typeKey, state.status.walletId)
      context.ask(walletRef, auxCreateRequest(state.status.stake)) {
        case Success(_) =>
          Close(s"stake reimbursed to wallet [$walletRef]")        Asks the wallet
        case Failure(ex) => //I rather retry                       to add the winnings
          val message =
            s"state NOT reimbursed to wallet [$walletRef]. Reason
            ➥[${ex.getMessage}]"
```

Annotations:
- Checks whether the bet chose the winning result → `if (isWinner(state, command.result)) {`
- Finds the wallet ActorRef → `sharding.entityRefFor(Wallet.typeKey, state.status.walletId)`

```
            context.log.error(message)
            Fail(message)
        }
      }
    Effect.none          ◁─┐  Doesn't persist
  }                        │  any event
  ...
}
```

12.2 The ports

Let's create some ports that act as entry points to these actors. You can use Akka gRPC to provide an order guarantee when you update the market and the bet, which happens frequently. Creating a stream with gRPC gives you these features as opposed to a unary call or a normal HTTP call to Akka HTTP. gRPC also allows you to query the service via reflection to see the list of available calls, which is convenient.

Akka HTTP is easy to implement, and you can do that for the wallet for simplicity. You know how to handle ports, so this section is more about the business logic than anything else. The market port is shown here, and the rest are in the repository.

12.2.1 The market

The gRPC .proto for the market actor includes the equivalent of each `ReplyCommand` of the market: `Open`, `Update`, `CloseMarket`, `Cancel`, and `GetState`.

Listing 12.13 Protobuf file for the market

```
message FixtureData {        ◁─┐
      string id = 1;
      string homeTeam = 2;
      string awayTeam = 3;
}

message OddsData {           ◁─  API messages
      double winHome = 1;        types
      double winAway = 2;
      double tie = 3;
}

message MarketData {         ◁─┘
      string marketId = 1;
      FixtureData fixture = 2;
      OddsData odds = 3;
      enum Result {
            HOME_WINS = 0;
            HOME_LOSES = 1;
            TIE = 2;
      }
      Result result = 4;
      uint64 opensAt = 5;
}
```

```
message MarketId {
      string marketId = 1;
}

message Response {
      string message = 1;
}

message CancelMarket {
      string marketId = 1;
      string reason = 2;
}

service MarketService {

      rpc Open(MarketData) returns (Response) {}

      rpc Update(stream MarketData) returns (stream Response) {}

      rpc CloseMarket(MarketId) returns (Response) {}

      rpc Cancel(CancelMarket) returns (Response) {}

      rpc GetState(MarketId) returns (MarketData){}
}
```

API messages types

Service with calls proxying the market commands and responses

NOTE CloseMarket has the suffix *market* in its name to avoid conflicts with the close() method generated by Akka gRPC in the MarketService-Client class. gRPC uses this method to close the channel with the server.

Let's look at one of these methods in the implementation of the service: GetState in MarketServiceImplSharding. This listing shows how the shard region is created and how the gRPC message is converted to the market protocol in the request and vice versa in the response.

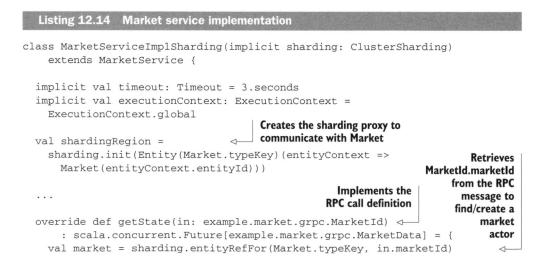

Listing 12.14   Market service implementation

```
class MarketServiceImplSharding(implicit sharding: ClusterSharding)
    extends MarketService {

  implicit val timeout: Timeout = 3.seconds
  implicit val executionContext: ExecutionContext =
    ExecutionContext.global

  val shardingRegion =
    sharding.init(Entity(Market.typeKey)(entityContext =>
      Market(entityContext.entityId)))

      ...

  override def getState(in: example.market.grpc.MarketId)
      : scala.concurrent.Future[example.market.grpc.MarketData] = {
    val market = sharding.entityRefFor(Market.typeKey, in.marketId)
```

Creates the sharding proxy to communicate with Market

Implements the RPC call definition

Retrieves MarketId.marketId from the RPC message to find/create a market actor

```
market.ask(Market.GetState).mapTo[Market.CurrentState].map {
  state =>
    val (
      marketId,
      Market.Fixture(id, homeTeam, awayTeam),
      Market.Odds(winHome, winAway, draw)) = (
      state.status.marketId,
      state.status.fixture,
      state.status.odds)

    MarketData(
      marketId,
      Some(FixtureData(id, homeTeam, awayTeam)),
      Some(OddsData(winHome, winAway, draw)))
  }
}
...
}
```

← **Asks Market and transforms the response to an RPC message**

← **Remainder of the RPC call implementations**

To communicate with the market, you need access to the sharding regions. Through this proxy, you request the market entity by its ID. If the entity does not exist yet, one is created.

It is important to note that this request differs from the request within entities. There you call `context.ask`, while here you use `[entityRef].ask`. The former uses the context to pass the `ActorRef` to `replyTo` so the callback stays in the context of the actor. Otherwise, the actor's context could be accessed from another thread, breaking the consistency of the actor's state provided by Akka. On the other hand, `market.ask` is not called inside any actor context. `MarketServiceImplSharding` is not an actor. The callback executed upon the response can't break anything here.

The server with this implementation is shown in the next listing.

Listing 12.15 Market server

```
import example.market.grpc.{ MarketServiceHandler, MarketServiceImplSharding
  }

object MarketServiceServer {

  def init(
      implicit system: ActorSystem[_],
      sharding: ClusterSharding,
      ec: ExecutionContext): Future[Http.ServerBinding] = {
    val marketService: HttpRequest => Future[HttpResponse] =
      MarketServiceHandler.withServerReflection(
        new MarketServiceImplSharding())
    val port =
      system.settings.config.getInt("services.market.port")
    val host = system.settings.config.getString("services.host")
```

← **Selects MarketServiceImplSharding**

```
        Http().newServerAt(host, port).bind(marketService)    ◄──┐  Starts the server
    }                                                             │  and binds the service
}
```

All the inputs in the `init` method of this server are implicit. And thanks to that, the sharding is also passed implicitly to the service implementation constructor:

```
class MarketServiceImplSharding(implicit sharding: ClusterSharding)
```

> **NOTE** Using `implicit` allows you to avoid passing the same input to chained functions repeatedly. This is less work and less noise—although you could argue that this is less explicit and therefore more complex.

The market server is added to the entry point of the application, and with it, the market service.

Listing 12.16   Entry point of the betting-house application

```
object Main {

  val log = LoggerFactory.getLogger(Main + "")

  def main(args: Array[String]): Unit = {
    implicit val system =
      ActorSystem[Nothing](Behaviors.empty, "betting-house")
    try {
      implicit val sharding = ClusterSharding(system)           ◄──
      implicit val ec: ExecutionContext = system.executionContext

      AkkaManagement(system).start()        ◄──┐  HTTP server to provide endpoints
      ClusterBootstrap(system).start()         │  for cluster bootstrapping
      ...
      BetServiceServer.init(system, sharding, ec)       Starts the HTTP servers, allowing
      MarketServiceServer.init(system, sharding, ec)    communication with the Bet,
      WalletServiceServer.init(system, sharding, ec)    Market, and Wallet entities
      ...
    } catch {
      case NonFatal(ex) =>
        log.error(
          s"Terminating Betting App. Reason [${ex.getMessage}]")
        system.terminate
      }
    }
}
```

Sharding extension to be passed around, allowing entities such as Bet, Market, and Wallet and the Bet and Market projections to register with it

Projection-related functionality (ignored for now)

You can see on the repository how the server endpoints can be started: bet, market, and wallet. All of them follow the same structure. The ports for each service are as follows:

```
services {
  bet.port = 9000
  wallet.port = 9001
  market.port = 9002
}
```

You can run this locally by executing the betting-house project with the local configuration, following the instructions in betting-house/README.md.

If the cluster is running, you can query the market service with `grpcurl local-host:9002 -list` to get the list of available RPC calls. Or you can query the status of a market as follows:

```
grpcurl -d '{"marketId": "1243"}' -plaintext localhost:9002 \
 MarketService/GetState
```

With this, you have seen in this chapter how to create the first part of a microservice in Akka, creating entities and their business logic and adding endpoints. Chapter 13 takes an in-depth look at clustering so you can deploy an Akka application in Kubernetes.

Summary

- You create a betting house by implementing the following:
  - The bet, market, and wallet as persistent sharded actors
  - Command handlers and event handlers for each actor, using the behavior primitives to define the business logic as a finite state machine
  - Akka endpoints to allow access to the actors from outside the `ActorSystem`

Creating complex actors often requires writing a set of commands that are only used internally by the actors to meet specific business needs, such as the validation in the bet that `asks` the market and `tells` the wallet.

Clustering, part 2 13

This chapter covers

- Bootstrapping a cluster in Kubernetes
- Using Split Brain Resolver to automate shutting down nodes
- Creating a singleton actor

In chapter 8, you learned how to create a cluster with seed nodes defined in the configuration. These are fixed IPs. Creating a cluster this way is practical, but it isn't a setup you'll use to go into production. This chapter starts with the same idea of fixed IPs to local deployment but uses the Akka Cluster Bootstrap module. You learn how to use this module to create an Akka cluster in Kubernetes using the Kubernetes API.

> **NOTE** The source code for this example is available at www.manning .com/books/akka-in-action-second-edition or https://github.com/francis colopezsancho/akka-topics/tree/main/chapter13a. You can find the contents of any snippet or listing in the .scala file with the same name as the class, object, or trait.

264

13.1   *Akka Cluster Bootstrap*

To create a cluster with Akka Cluster Bootstrap, you need the following dependencies:

```
val AkkaVersion = "2.6.20"
val AkkaManagementVersion = "1.1.4"

libraryDependencies ++= Seq(
  "com.lightbend.akka.management" %% "akka-management-cluster-bootstrap" %
[CA]AkkaManagementVersion,
  "com.typesafe.akka" %% "akka-discovery" % AkkaVersion
)
```

`akka-discovery` may not be needed because `akka-management-cluster-bootstrap` transitively depends on and retrieves it along with many other modules like `akka-cluster` and `akka-management`. However, explicitly adding `akka-discovery`—and some of the other modules—is safer because it saves you from having different versions loaded from the various modules that transitively depend on it. If you let each module import its `akka-discovery` version—or any other, for that matter—you may end up with different versions and get a warning or even an exception when loading the classes.

13.1.1   *Clustering in local*

Now you can set the following to create a local cluster:

- Set `akka.actor.provider` to `cluster`.
- Set the `discovery` method to find the services—the nodes—by specifying the `ActorSystem` name and the IPs and ports of the nodes.
- Set Akka Management to expose the nodes so that the `discovery` method can find them.

In chapter 8, the configuration referenced a specific host and port, but here you reference the `discovery` method. You have only two initial nodes that match the default `contact-point-discovery.required-contact-point-nr = 2` specified in the `akka-management-cluster-bootstrap` module's reference.conf. It is recommended that you set this number to the number of nodes intended to form the initial cluster.

Listing 13.1   Configuration with fixed IPs

```
akka {
     actor.provider = cluster          ◁─┐  Cluster
                                          │  mode
     discovery {
            config.services = {
                testing-bootstrap = {          ┌┐  IPs and
 Reference    ┌─▷                          ◁─┘│  ports
to the service │            endpoints = [
               │               {
                                   host = "127.0.0.1"
```

```
                                    port = 8558
                                    },
                        {
                                    host = "127.0.0.2"
                                    port = 8558
                        }
                        ]
                }
            }
        }

        management {
                cluster.bootstrap {
                    contact-point-discovery {
                        service-name = "testing-bootstrap"        ◁──┐ Names
                        discovery-method = config   ◁──┐              the service
                    }                                  Discovery
                }                                      by fixed IPs
        }
}
```

Now you can create the application and start both modules: `ClusterBootstrap` and `AkkaManagement`. This way, the application exposes the nodes, and the bootstrap can create the cluster. The following listing shows a minimal application.

Listing 13.2   App to form the cluster

```scala
import akka.management.scaladsl.AkkaManagement
import akka.management.cluster.bootstrap.ClusterBootstrap
import akka.actor.typed.ActorSystem
import akka.actor.typed.scaladsl.Behaviors
import com.typesafe.config.ConfigFactory

object App {

  def main(args: Array[String]): Unit = {          Parameter to fix the IP of
    val i = args(0)                    ◁──┐         the node's configuration

    val config = ConfigFactory              Fixes the IP of the
      .parseString(s"""        ◁──┐        node's configuration
        akka.remote.artery.canonical.hostname = "127.0.0.$i"
        akka.management.http.hostname = "127.0.0.$i"
        """)
      .withFallback(ConfigFactory.load())    ◁──┐ Loads the default: that
    val system =              ◁──┐               is, application.conf
      ActorSystem[Nothing](      Starts the system with
        Behaviors.empty,         no functionality but
        "testing-bootstrap",     the basic cluster
        config)
                                     To expose HTTP nodes'
    AkkaManagement(system).start()   ◁──┐ liveliness endpoints
    ClusterBootstrap(system).start()  ◁──┐
  }                                       To find
}                                         the nodes
```

This application starts an Akka cluster with a `Behavior.empty`. You don't need to add a function to this behavior to see how the cluster is formed; the business logic and the formation of a cluster are independent. In this example, `akka.remote.artery .canonical.hostname` and `akka.management.http.hostname` must be set to avoid conflicting IPs because the cluster is running locally. Bear in mind that this is for demo purposes only.

13.1.2 Cluster in action

To start the first node, enter the following command in the root of the Git repository:

```
$ sbt "chapter13a/runMain example.clustering2.App 1"
```

The result is the following output. It is a rich and understandable and is worth some attention:

In the first line, the node looks for the list of seed nodes (`akka.cluster.seed-nodes`), and they are not present. Since the node doesn't find them, it switches to Cluster Bootstrap. `akka.cluster.seed-nodes` takes precedence over bootstrap configuration. You must be careful not to mix the two and to use only one method in your configuration.

Then the node starts the Akka Management Service and loads the `discovery` method specified in application.conf. By default, the service looks for the member with the lowest address to set it as the starting node. Eventually, the service finds the IPs of the members in the configuration, but it can't retrieve them all. It only finds the node you just started, and since it doesn't reach the minimum number of contact points, the cluster can't be formed; therefore, this node can't be set as the seed node. Hence the "empty list of seed nodes" message in the output. From this point on, the output is in a loop with the last two messages: empty seed nodes and fewer contact points than required.

Now you can start node 2 with this command:

```
sbt "chapter13a/runMain example.clustering2.App 2"
```

Look at the output of node 1, which shows the following:

Sets itself as leader

Gets to the Joining state

```
Node [akka://testing-bootstrap@127.0.0.1:25520] is JOINING itself (with
➥roles [dc-default], version [0.0.0]) and forming new cluster
Node [akka://testing-bootstrap@127.0.0.1:25520] is the new leader among
➥reachable nodes (more leaders may exist)
Leader is moving node [akka://testing-bootstrap@127.0.0.1:25520] to [Up]
Bootstrap request from 127.0.0.1:50504: Contact Point returning 1 seed-
➥nodes [akka://testing-bootstrap@127.0.0.1:25520]
```

Returns itself as the only seed node

Gets to the Up state

Once the number of contact points matches the required number, the node with the lowest IP address (172.0.0.1) starts the cluster. It switches from `Joining` to `Up` and makes itself available as a seed node for all other nodes via Akka Management. Node 1 then receives the request from node 2 to join the cluster, as you can see in its logs:

```
Received InitJoin message from [Actor[akka://testing-
➥bootstrap@127.0.0.2:25520/system/...]] to [akka://testing-
➥bootstrap@127.0.0.1:25520]
Sending InitJoinAck message from node [akka://testing-
➥bootstrap@127.0.0.1:25520] to [Actor[akka://testing-
➥bootstrap@127.0.0.2:25520/system/...] (version [2.6.20])
Node [akka://testing-bootstrap@127.0.0.2:25520] is JOINING, roles [dc-
➥default], version [0.0.0]
Node added [UniqueAddress(akka://testing-
➥bootstrap@127.0.0.2:25520,8717661260050472844)]
Leader is moving node [akka://testing-bootstrap@127.0.0.2:25520] to [Up]
```

Initial request to join

Sends back ack

Node 2 advertises its Joining state

Node 1 accepts node 2

Node 2 advertises its Up state

The output of node 2 is very similar to that of node 1, except that from the moment it is discovered by node 1 until the time node 1 forms the seed node, it loops only over empty seed nodes and fewer contact points than required. Node 2 is informed by the configuration that it does not have the lowest IP, so it doesn't try to discover whether the number of contact points is sufficient. It waits until it finds a seed node via the Akka Management HTTP endpoint, and it also uses the endpoint to send an `Init-Join`. The following output of node 2 shows the final cluster greeting by node 1, indicating that it is considered `Up`:

```
Cluster Node [akka://testing-bootstrap@127.0.0.2:25520] - Welcome from
➥[akka://testing-bootstrap@127.0.0.1:25520]
ClusterReceptionist [akka://testing-bootstrap@127.0.0.2:25520] - Node added
➥[UniqueAddress(akka://testing-bootstrap@127.0.0.1:25520,-
➥2336789632363653010)]
```

You've seen how to start a two-node cluster using Akka Bootstrap. Now let's look at how to bootstrap the cluster in Kubernetes.

13.2   Clustering with the Kubernetes API

Instead of using fixed IPs, you can use the most common solution: the Kubernetes API. To begin, you need to pack the application into a container. Usually, you create a Docker container using `sbt-native-packager`. To do this, import its plugin by adding it to the plugins.sbt file:

```
addSbtPlugin("com.typesafe.sbt" % "sbt-native-packager" % "1.9.11")
```

Before you create the Docker image, you need more dependencies in addition to the previous `akka-management-cluster-bootstrap`. To use the Kubernetes API server to find the nodes, it needs the `akka-discovery-kubernetes-api` module and `akka-management-cluster-http` to publish the `/health` and `/ready` endpoints. Kubernetes needs these to verify that the service is alive and ready to take work:

```
val AkkaManagementVersion = "1.1.4"

  "com.lightbend.akka.management" %% "akka-management-cluster-http" %
  ➥AkkaManagementVersion,
  "com.lightbend.akka.discovery" %% "akka-discovery-kubernetes-api" %
  ➥AkkaManagementVersion
```

With the plugin and these two libraries in place, you can create the Docker image and deploy it as a cluster.

> **NOTE**   The source code for this example is available at www.manning.com/
> books/akka-in-action-second-edition   or   https://github.com/franciscolopez
> sancho/akka-topics/tree/main/chapter13b. You can find the contents of any
> snippet or listing in the .scala file with the same name as the class, object, or trait.

13.2.1   Creating the Docker image

To create the container, add the following to the build.sbt file:

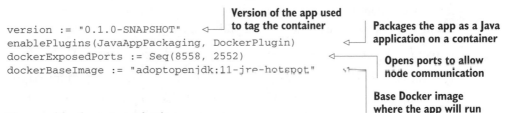

```
version := "0.1.0-SNAPSHOT"        ◁── Version of the app used to tag the container
enablePlugins(JavaAppPackaging, DockerPlugin)   ◁── Packages the app as a Java application on a container
dockerExposedPorts := Seq(8558, 2552)   ◁── Opens ports to allow node communication
dockerBaseImage := "adoptopenjdk:11-jre-hotspot"   ◁── Base Docker image where the app will run
```

You enable these two plugins:

- `JavaAppPackaging`—An archetype
- `DockerPlugin`—A format plugin in the `sbt-native-packager` sense

The archetype is responsible for what is packaged, the type of content, and its internal structure (hence the name). The format plugin determines how the content is packaged, the form it takes, and its external structure—the image.

`JavaAppPackaging` packages the project into a Java application that places all the JAR dependencies on the classpath. This project must have a class with a `main` executable method to create the entry point. You could use `JavaServerAppPackaging` instead, which provides additional features such as the ability to select the user (called a *daemon*) that runs the application, but we'll keep things as simple as possible here.

Before creating the image, make sure the project contains the necessary configuration:

```
akka.management {
    cluster.bootstrap {
        contact-point-discovery {
            discovery-method = kubernetes-api      ◁─┐ Sets the Kubernetes API
        }                                             as the discovery method
    }

    http{                    ┌─ Binds to
        port = 8558     ◁───┘  this port
        bind-hostname = "0.0.0.0"      ◁──┐ Binds to all IP
    }                                       addresses of this host
}
```

With this configuration, you offload node discovery to the Kubernetes API instead of configuring it for fixed IPs. You must also set Akka Management to port 8558 and host 0.0.0.0 to enable the readiness and liveness probe endpoints.

> **NOTE** 0.0.0.0 means the service listens on every available interface. For example, if the host has two IP addresses, 192.168.1.1 and 10.1.2.1, a server running on the host and listening on 0.0.0.0 is reachable on both IPs.

Now you can build the JAR file and put it into a Docker container. To do so, you use the `DockerPlugin`. This format plugin defines the outer structure as a Docker image and lets you set parameters like `dockerExposedPorts` and `dockerBaseImage`. There are quite a few of these parameters, but these two are enough to create the Docker image you need. You can do this from the chapter13b folder of the Git repository: at the command line, enter `sbt docker:publishLocal`. The output of this command displays the name of the build image:

```
[info] Built image chapter13b with tags [0.1.0-SNAPSHOT]
```

Version `0.1.0-SNAPSHOT` is the project version specified in the build.sbt file. Once it's created, this Docker image is in the local Docker repository on your computer.

Normally, you need to push this image to an external repository that Kubernetes can reach and create the pods from it. To push the image, you must first tag it with the name of the registry you want to upload it to. If nothing is specified, the default is https://hub.docker.com/. To use the default, log in to this registry from the command line by entering

```
docker login
```

Once you have specified the user and password, you can push the image after tagging it with the repository as follows:

```
$ docker tag chapter13b:0.1.0-SNAPSHOT \
yourrepositoryhere/chapter13b:0.1.0-SNAPSHOT
```
← **Tags the image to the yourrepositoryhere repository**

```
$ docker push yourrepositoryhere/chapter13b:0.1.0-SNAPSHOT
```
← **Pushes to docker.io hub (that is, hub.docker.com)**

To deploy to Kubernetes, you need the following:

- A Kubernetes `Deployment`
- A Kubernetes `Role` and a `RoleBinding`
- A Kubernetes `ServiceAccount`
- A Kubernetes server

13.2.2 Kubernetes deployment

To create the `Deployment`, you need to do a few things you can break down into parts:

1 Set the Docker image.
2 Set the node discovery.
3 Set the liveness/readiness.

You can set the Docker image, the number of replicas, the name of the deployment, and the policy for pulling images as follows:

```
apiVersion: apps/v1
kind: Deployment
...
spec:
  replicas: 3            ←⎤ Number
...                         ⎦ of pods
    template:
      ...
      spec:
        containers:                               ⎤ Base name of
        - name: testing-bootstrap13b    ←⎦ each pod
          image: my-docker-registry/chapter13b:0.1.0-SNAPSHOT
          imagePullPolicy: IfNotPresent
```
Route to the image → (pointing to `image:` line)

Pulls the image only if it is not present → (pointing to `imagePullPolicy` line)

This deployment creates three pods, each of which has the setting defined in the `template`. These three pods are named `testing-boostrap21-[deployment-id] [[0-9a-z]{5}]` and contain the Docker image, which Kubernetes can obtain from Docker Hub if it is not present yet in its local repository.

Next, set node discovery on the deployment.

Listing 13.3 Setting the labels to discover the nodes belonging to the Akka cluster

```
apiVersion: apps/v1
kind: Deployment
...
spec:
...
```

```
selector:
  matchLabels:
    app: testing-bootstrap13babc        ◁
...

  template:
    metadata:
      labels:
        app: testing-bootstrap13babc    ◁
        actorSystemName: testing-bootstrap13b
    spec:
...
        env:
        - name: AKKA_CLUSTER_BOOTSTRAP_SERVICE_NAME    ◁
          valueFrom:
            fieldRef:
              apiVersion: v1
              fieldPath: "metadata.labels['app']"
```

Must be the same for Kubernetes to recognize them as belonging to the cluster

Environment variable that Akka reads to find the labels that are part of the cluster

Filtering by label

The `template.metadata.label` property belongs to the pod and can be used like any other label to group pods so you can perform bulk actions on them. For example, you can filter using the `get` action: `kubectl get pod -l app=testing-boot-strap13babc`. If you can filter with `template.metadata.label`, why is `selector.matchLabels.app` needed? This has little to do with Akka; it is purely a Kubernetes requirement used to relate the deployment to the pods, and they need to have the same value.

With this background, let's go back to Akka discovery, where you have three options. You can add them in Akka Bootstrap's reference.conf file:

```
akka.management {
    cluster.bootstrap {
              contact-point-discovery {

  # Define this name to be looked up in service discovery for
➥ "neighboring" nodes
  # If undefined the name will be taken from the
➥ AKKA_CLUSTER_BOOTSTRAP_SERVICE_NAME
  # environment variable or extracted from the ActorSystem name
    service-name = "<service-name>"
    service-name = ${?AKKA_CLUSTER_BOOTSTRAP_SERVICE_NAME}

    ...
}
```

Order of reading: service-name environment variable, ActorSystem name

In order of precedence, you can specify what the Kubernetes API looks for such that it matches `template.metadata.label` with one of the following:

- *The* `service-name`—That is, `akka.management.cluster.bootstrap.contact-point-discovery.service-name`, which you need to define in your Akka configuration file.

- *The* `AKKA_CLUSTER_BOOTSTRAP_SERVICE_NAME` *environment variable*—You can define this in the Kubernetes deployment.
- *The name of your* `ActorSystem`—You can define this in the source code of your application when creating the guardian.

Whichever option you choose becomes the value of `%s` in the following Akka Bootstrap default configuration:

```
discovery {
    kubernetes-api {
            pod-label-selector = "app=%s"    ⊲⎯⎤  %s is set based
    }                                            ⎦  on your choice.
}
```

The previously shown deployment file uses the option `AKKA_CLUSTER_BOOTSTRAP _SERVICE_NAME` to avoid being bound to the project source code. You don't have to worry about setting the service name in application.conf or using the `ActorSystem` name. This way, the source code remains independent of the deployment. If you need to change the deployment name in the Kubernetes cluster later, you don't need to rename the `ActorSystem` or change the configuration and then rebuild the image.

> **NOTE** You set `AKKA_CLUSTER_BOOTSTRAP_SERVICE_NAME` by referencing the deployment itself. This variable gets its value from `template.metadata .labels`, which is `testing-bootstrap13babc`.

Finally, readiness and liveness are set via the deployment by specifying the endpoints where Kubernetes checks if the pod is ready and alive. Readiness can be used to check whether the pod is accepting traffic, while liveness checks whether it is responding in a timely manner. Here you use the same endpoint for both checks. (For more information about readiness and liveness, see http://mng.bz/Q81Q.)

Listing 13.4 Setting probes for readiness and liveness

```
spec:
...
  template:
    metadata:
...
    spec:
      containers:
      - name: testing-bootstrap13b
...
        livenessProbe:
          httpGet:                   ⎤  Akka Management path
            path: /alive       ⊲⎯⎯⎦  for checking liveness
            port: management
        readinessProbe:
          httpGet:                   ⎤  Akka Management path
            path: /ready       ⊲⎯⎯⎦  for checking readiness
            port: management
```

```
        ports:
        - name: management        ◁──┤ Names the port used
          containerPort: 8558      ◁──┐ Akka Management port defined
          protocol: TCP                in the application.conf file
```

In this part of the deployment, you reference the paths of the two probes—`alive` and `ready`—available through the Akka Management module configured via the `akka.manangement.http` settings in application.conf and started with `Akka-Management(system).start()`. This is enough to set the deployment, but you may want a few extras.

13.2.3 *Optional: Setting Java options*

It is often necessary to pass Java options to your application: for example, to set the memory. To do so, you can use the `JavaAppPlugin` from `sbt-native-packager`. Among other parameters, it accepts `JAVA_OPTS`, which you can set in the deployment.yml file as follows:

```
apiVersion: apps/v1
kind: Deployment
...
spec:
...
  template:
...
    spec:
      containers:
      - name: testing-bootstrap13b
...
        env:
        - name: JAVA_OPTS        ┌─ Sets the maximum size of the
          value: "-Xmx1024m"  ◁──┘ memory allocation pool in bytes
```

The analysis of the deployment is divided into many parts. Let's look at the entire file to get a good overview of what you have seen so far in this section.

Listing 13.5   Deployment in the deployment.yml file

```
apiVersion: apps/v1
kind: Deployment
metadata:
  labels:
    app: testing-bootstrap13bxyz
  name: testing-bootstrap13b
spec:
  replicas: 3
  selector:
    matchLabels:
      app: testing-bootstrap13b-env   ◁──┐ To allow discovery
  strategy:                                of nodes
    rollingUpdate:
      maxSurge: 1
```

```
          maxUnavailable: 0
        type: RollingUpdate

    template:
      metadata:
        labels:
          app: testing-bootstrap13b-env
          actorSystemName: testing-bootstrap13b
      spec:
        serviceAccountName: my-cluster
        containers:
        - name: testing-bootstrap13b
          image: my-docker-registry/chapter13b:0.1.0-SNAPSHOT
          imagePullPolicy: Always
          livenessProbe:
            httpGet:
              path: /alive
              port: management
          readinessProbe:
            httpGet:
              path: /ready
              port: management
          ports:
          - name: management
            containerPort: 8558
            protocol: TCP
          env:
          - name: AKKA_CLUSTER_BOOTSTRAP_SERVICE_NAME
            valueFrom:
              fieldRef:
                apiVersion: v1
                fieldPath: "metadata.labels['app']"
          - name: JAVA_OPTS
            value: "-Xmx1024m"
```

To bind to the service account, which is bound to the role that can get, watch, and list pods

Docker image you created and pushed to a repository

To allow probing readiness and liveness

To allow discovery of nodes

13.2.4 *Kubernetes role and role binding*

You need to create a `Role` with the appropriate permission and bind it to a Kubernetes service account (SA). Every time you run `kubectl` to access the cluster—the Kubernetes API server—you do so through a user account. However, when a process in a pod calls the Kubernetes API server, such as your app, it does so via the default SA, which is called `default`.

Adding a role and binding it to a SA allows the Akka cluster to fetch, watch, and list the pods. The `Role` and `RoleBinding` you need are shown in the following listing.

Listing 13.6 `Role` and `RoleBinding` to allow the cluster to get, watch, and list pods

```
kind: Role
apiVersion: rbac.authorization.k8s.io/v1
metadata:
  name: pod-reader
rules:
- apiGroups: [""] # "" indicates the core API group
  resources: ["pods"]
```

Role permissions refer to pods.

```
    verbs: ["get", "watch", "list"]                Queries available
---                                                on the resources
kind: RoleBinding
apiVersion: rbac.authorization.k8s.io/v1
metadata:
  name: read-pods
subjects:
- kind: ServiceAccount        Binds to the default
  name: default               service account
roleRef:
  kind: Role                  Binds it to
  name: pod-reader            the role
  apiGroup: rbac.authorization.k8s.io
```

13.2.5 *Service account*

You can use the default SA to create the `RoleBinding`. However, it is recommended to create a different SA to bind the `Role` and the `Deployment`. To do this, you only need to create the SA by entering its name as follows:

```
kubectl create serviceaccount my-cluster
```

Then add the following reference to the `Deployment`:

```
apiVersion: apps/v1
kind: Deployment
metadata: ...
spec:
  template:
    metadata: ...
    spec:
      serviceAccountName: my-cluster
      containers: ...
```

Finally, you have everything you need to deploy the application to a Kubernetes cluster. You can do this in Minikube, which you installed earlier (see appendix A), by running the following commands from the root of folder chapter13b:

```
$ minikube start
...
Done! kubectl is now configured to use "minikube" cluster and "default"
➥namespace by default

$ kubectl create ns akka-cluster            Creates the namespace
namespace/akka-cluster created              akka-cluster
                                                                    Creates the SA
                                                                    in the namespace
                                                                    akka-cluster
$ kubectl -n akka-cluster create serviceaccount my-cluster
serviceaccount/my-cluster created

$ kubectl -n akka-cluster apply -f roles.yml           Creates the role binding to
role.rbac.authorization.k8s.io/pod-reader created      the SA akka-cluster in the
rolebinding.rbac.authorization.k8s.io/read-pods created    namespace akka-cluster

$ kubectl -n akka-cluster apply -f deployment.yml      Deploys the app as a cluster in
deployment.apps/testing-bootstrap13b created           the namespace akka-cluster
```

Once this is done, your Akka cluster is in place. You can check by typing `kubectl -n akka-cluster get po` like this:

```
$ kubectl -n akka-cluster get po
```

**All nodes are alive and
ready after 47 seconds.**

```
NAME                                   READY   STATUS    RESTARTS   AGE
testing-bootstrap13b-565d68bd5b-ggljg  1/1     Running   0          47s
testing-bootstrap13b-565d68bd5b-s5vz2  1/1     Running   0          47s
testing-bootstrap13b-565d68bd5b-wls2d  1/1     Running   0          47s
```

In the logs of the `testing-bootstrap13b-565d68bd5b-ggljg` node shown in the following snippet, the cluster is formed:

```
$ kubectl -n akka-cluster logs testing-bootstrap13b-565d68bd5b-ggljg
```

**Moves itself
to the Up state**

```
Cluster Node [akka://testing-bootstrap13b@172.17.0.3:25520] - is the new
➥leader among reachable nodes (more leaders may exist)
...
Leader is moving node [akka://testing-bootstrap13b@172.17.0.3:25520] to [Up]
...
Leader is moving node [akka://testing-bootstrap13b@172.17.0.4:25520] to [Up]
...
Leader is moving node [akka://testing-bootstrap13b@172.17.0.5:25520] to [Up]
```

**Moves the other
nodes to the Up state**

13.3 Split Brain Resolver

The problem that the Split Brain Resolver (SBR) solves is how to automatically shut down nodes that become unreachable under certain rules. To set it up, add the following to your configuration:

```
akka.cluster.downinig-provider-class = "akka.cluster.sbr.SplitBrainResolver"
```

Becoming *unreachable* is a relative term that expresses what a node experiences relative to another node. The formation and maintenance of a cluster are done by communication between the nodes using a protocol called *gossip*. Each node sends messages to all the others to check whether they are reachable and responsive. When you combine unreachability with Akka sharding—which distributes actors evenly across the cluster—you can run into the following problem.

13.3.1 An unreachable problem

Imagine that one node becomes unreachable from the other nodes of the cluster. All sharded entities located on that node are replicated to the healthy nodes. But in that case, the entities are duplicated.

To understand this problem better, let's look at what happens when the cluster splits. By now you may be familiar with the states of a node, which are shown again in figure 13.1.

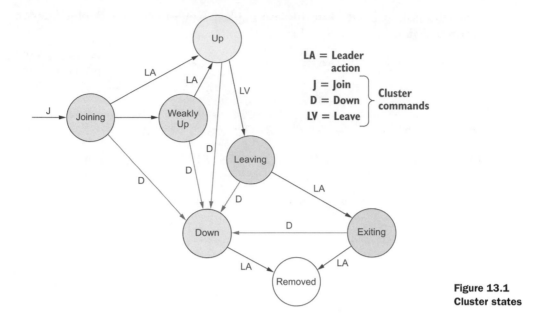

LA = Leader action
J = Join
D = Down } **Cluster commands**
LV = Leave

Figure 13.1
Cluster states

As you can see, there is no unreachable state. On the one hand, there is an unreachable event: `Cluster.MemberUnreachable`, which is of the same type as `ClusterEvent.MemberJoined` or `ClusterEvent.MemberUp`. On the other hand, there is an `unreachable` tag. When a node receives this event, it updates its view of the cluster and adds this tag. Let's take an example where a cluster consisting of three nodes is divided into two parts by a network partition, as shown in figure 13.2.

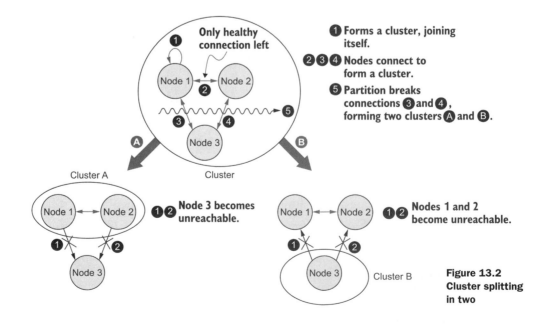

Figure 13.2
Cluster splitting in two

Because `akka-management-cluster-http` is enabled in this example, you can query the status of the cluster in node 1—the one using port 2551—to check its view of the cluster. To do so, follow the README.md instructions. The result is shown in the following listing.

Listing 13.7 Viewpoint of the cluster from node 1

```
{
  "leader": "akka://cluster@127.0.0.1:2551",        Three
  "members": [                                  ◄── members
    {
      "node": "akka://cluster@127.0.0.1:2551",...
      "status": "Up"
    },
    {
      "node": "akka://cluster@127.0.0.1:2552",...
      "status": "Up"
    },
    {
      "node": "akka://cluster@127.0.0.2:2553",...
      "status": "Up"
    }
  ],
  "oldest": "akka://cluster@127.0.0.1:2551",...      Name of
  "selfNode": "akka://cluster@127.0.0.1:2551",  ◄── this node
  "unreachable": [
    {
      "node": "akka://cluster@127.0.0.2:2553",  ◄──  Node 3 is unreachable
      "observedBy": [                                by the other two nodes.
        "akka://cluster@127.0.0.1:2551",
        "akka://cluster@127.0.0.1:2552"
      ]
    }
  ]
}
```

This node belongs to a cluster with three members, one of which is marked unreachable—but note that all three are in the Up state. From the point of view of node 3 (with port 2553), you can see the other side of the coin in the next listing.

Listing 13.8 Point of view from node 3

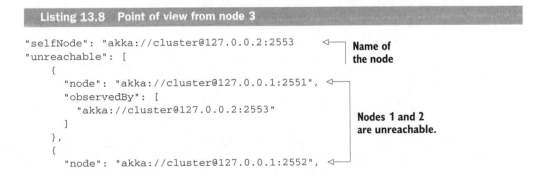

```
"selfNode": "akka://cluster@127.0.0.2:2553       ◄──  Name of
"unreachable": [                                      the node
    {
      "node": "akka://cluster@127.0.0.1:2551",  ◄──
      "observedBy": [
        "akka://cluster@127.0.0.2:2553"                   Nodes 1 and 2
      ]                                                    are unreachable.
    },
    {
      "node": "akka://cluster@127.0.0.1:2552",  ◄──
```

```
      "observedBy": [
        "akka://cluster@127.0.0.2:2553"
      ]
    }
  ]
```

Here you can see the problem better. *Unreachability* is a relative term. When this cluster splits, its members remain in the Up state. So, if you have sharding entities, they are replicated on both sides of the cluster. Entities are missing on both sides, and the underlying mechanism restores them.

You have two clusters of actors that are no longer unique, at least when you consider the two clusters together. You can use a port connected to one side and change the value of one actor, and then, in the next call, use another port pointing to the other side and change a value in its duplicate. For example, suppose that wallet A is duplicated after a cluster split. If you deposit $100 on one side of the cluster and another $100 on the other, neither of the two wallets has received $200.

If your sharding entities are persisted, the problem gets worse. You can have two entities writing a different story in the same journal. Replaying those events would most likely be problematic.

To solve this problem, you need a strategy to shut down the nodes if one of them splits from the cluster. The only question is on which side. This is a hard problem, and the SBR helps you solve it, but it is not a panacea. There are corner cases where no solution is possible and the SBR shuts down all the nodes to end the cluster.

Before a node considers another node unreachable, a certain amount of time must pass during which the cluster view is stable: by default, `akka.cluster.split-brain-resolver.stable-after=20s`. During this time, at least one group of members must see the same thing before a decision can be made.

The network may be unstable, and perhaps no group can agree on a view of the cluster. When this happens, `akka.cluster.split-brain-resolver.down-all-when-unstable` comes into play. By default, the timeout is 15 seconds. If no decision can be made in `stable-after + down-all-when-unstable`, the network is considered unreliable, and all nodes are shut down.

13.3.2 *SBR strategies*

The strategies available in SBR are the following:

- `Keep-majority`—The default value. The cluster with the smaller number of nodes DOWNs all its nodes and stops:
  - *Recommended for*—Resizing the cluster with minimal operating costs.
  - *Options*—You can filter the number by role.
  - *Corner case*—If each split cluster contains the same number of nodes, all clusters are terminated.
- `Lease-majority`—Combines `keep-majority` with distributed locking. In partitioning, each cluster attempts to obtain the lock, and the cluster with fewer

nodes is penalized with a delay. Only the cluster that acquires the lock stays alive. There is only one implementation in Akka (http://mng.bz/eJWZ), and it is built on a Kubernetes lease (http://mng.bz/pdA0):

- *Recommended for*—This is the safest option but incurs higher operational costs as various Kubernetes resources need to be created.
- *Options*—You can filter the number by role, set the delay for the cluster with fewer nodes, and set the duration of the lease after which the lock is released.
- *Corner case*—If the node acquiring the lease crashes before notifying its cluster, the lease cannot be reached by any other node, and all clusters are terminated. In either case, it depends on the Kubernetes lease working properly. If the lease cannot be acquired, all clusters are terminated.

- `Static-quorum`—Any cluster with fewer nodes than specified in the configuration is terminated:

  - *Recommended*—If there is a fixed number of nodes in the cluster.
  - *Options*—You can filter the number by role.
  - *Corner cases*—If the cluster splits into three instead of two and no cluster meets the quorum, all stop. If the cluster splits into two and no node is added to the one that stays alive, any further splits will stop all clusters.

- `Keep-oldest`—Keeps the cluster containing the node with the lowest IP, which is the oldest:

  - *Recommended*—To avoid restarting singletons because they are on the oldest node.
  - *Options*—You can filter the number by role. The default is `down-if-alone=on`, which downs the oldest if it remains as a cluster of one.
  - *Corner case*—If communication breaks down while the oldest node is `Leaving` the cluster before this information is gossiped, the SBR shuts down all nodes: the cluster with the second-oldest node because it did not get the memo, and the one with the oldest node because it expects the other side to continue.

13.4 Cluster singletons

Similar to a singleton in any programming model, a cluster singleton in Akka refers to an actor that has only one instance in the entire cluster. This instance is assigned to the oldest node—that is, the node with the lower IP address—and is automatically moved when its node is removed from the cluster.

Singletons are used in applications for many reasons, but the underlying function is always to provide a single point of access. This can be done to provide a single consistent value, such as a global variable, a cache, or a dictionary. It can be used as a proxy for tunnel communication, such as to provide authentication; as a logger or coordinator, such as a scheduler; and also as a manager, such as a job manager or file system manager.

On the other hand, a singleton can be considered an anti-pattern because it can become a single point of failure or a bottleneck in the application. This is because if the singleton has a critical responsibility for the system, the application breaks when it fails. Whether you use it or not, every decision is a tradeoff.

When an Akka singleton is respawned in another node, there is downtime in the relocation. Another problem is that singletons live in the oldest node. So if an application has multiple singletons, this node may be overloaded.

To create a singleton, you need a singleton factory: the behavior you want to use as a singleton and a singleton wrapper that wraps that behavior. Your behavior may look something like this:

```
object MyBehavior {
  def apply(): Behavior[String] = Behaviors.Ignore
}
```

If you have an `ActorSystem`, you can create the singleton factory as follows:

```
val singletonFactory = ClusterSingleton(system)
```

Then wrap the behavior in a `SingletonActor` and set up the supervision strategy to restart:

```
Val wrappedBehavior = SingletonActor(
                    Behaviors
                .supervise(MyBehavior())
                .onFailure(SupervisorStrategy.restart),
                    "myShardingCoordinator"))
```

Now you can create the singleton:

```
val mySingletonActor = singletonFactory.init(wrappedBehavior)
```

It doesn't matter how often you run this line of code in your application; there will only ever be one instance available in the cluster. Remember, this actor is not persistent; it loses its state every time it is moved from one node to another. You need to add a persistence mechanism yourself to make its state durable.

Summary

- Akka Cluster Bootstrap allows you to eliminate seed-node configuration and make cluster creation dynamic. You can still use fixed IPs with `.cluster` `.bootstrap.discovery-method = config`, or you can use dynamic Kubernetes configuration with `.discovery-method = kubernetes-api`.
- Package the application in a Docker image using the plugins `JavaApp-Packaging` and `DockerPlugin`.
- Use Akka Kubernetes Deployment to set the `AKKA_CLUSTER_BOOTSTRAP` `_SERVICE_NAME` environment variable to find the pods belonging to the cluster in combination with `.cluster.bootstrap.contact-point-discovery` `.service-name`.

- Use Akka Management HTTP endpoints to set the readiness and liveness probes to check if the pods in the deployment are ready to accept traffic and are alive (that is, ready to respond in a timely manner).
- Add a Kubernetes role, a service account, and a role binding so the deployment has the required permissions to find the pods in the Kubernetes cluster.
- Avoid shutting down the nodes during network partitioning, but rely on the Split Brain Resolver to help the cluster to maintain a consistent state.
- You can configure the SBR to `keep-majority`, `lease-majority`, `static-quorum`, or `keep-oldest`.
- You can create an actor and make sure there is only one instance in the entire cluster with Akka Singleton.

14 *Connecting to systems with Alpakka*

This chapter covers

- Reading from and writing to Kafka
- Reading from and writing to CSV

Alpakka is a project that implements multiple connectors that allow you to interact with different technologies in a reactive streaming way according to the principles of the Reactive Streams project (www.reactive-streams.org). For example, you can read from a Kafka topic with an asynchronous stream with no blocking backpressure.

This chapter covers two of the most commonly used connectors, Kafka and CSV. The CSV Alpakka connector can be classified as *finite streams* because it ends after the file is read. The Kafka Alpakka connector, on the other hand, is an example of an *infinite stream* where there is an open connection to a topic that can produce records at any time.

Alpakka Kafka has an extensive API; most of this chapter is dedicated to it. The rest of the chapter is dedicated to CSV, which has a relatively simple API.

NOTE The source code for this chapter is available at www.manning.com/books/akka-in-action-second-edition or https://github.com/franciscolopezsancho/akka-topics/tree/main/chapter14. You can find the contents of

284

any snippet or listing in the .scala file with the same name as the class, object, or trait.

14.1   Alpakka Kafka

Alpakka Kafka is built on Kafka Streams (https://kafka.apache.org/27/javadoc/index.html). The next question might be this: Why not use Kafka Streams instead? You can, but Alpakka allows you to interact with Akka Streams and connect with actors out of the box.

In this chapter, you use the Jackson library—a JSON parser—for serialization, so the data in these examples is stored as JSON in Kafka. To get started, import the following dependencies:

```
val AkkaStreamKafka = "3.0.1"
val AkkaVersion = "2.6.20"
val JacksonVersion = "2.11.4"

libraryDependencies ++= Seq(                                        Used for
  "com.typesafe.akka" %% "akka-stream-kafka" % AkkaStreamKafka,   serialization
  "com.typesafe.akka" %% "akka-stream" % AkkaVersion,
  "com.fasterxml.jackson.core" % "jackson-databind" % JacksonVersion    <──
)
```

With all these dependencies, let's look at a simple example of consuming from a topic. The main component of this example is the Kafka consumer source and its settings. Before you can create the consumer, you need to select the settings. These are the deserializers for reading the messages, containing the key and value, the group ID, and the URL of the bootstrap server (consisting of the host and port):

```
import akka.kafka.ConsumerSettings

object ConsumerPlainSource {
  ...
  val consumerSettings: ConsumerSettings =
      ConsumerSettings(
        config,
        new StringDeserializer(),
        new StringDeserializer())
        .withBootstrapServers("127.0.0.1:9092")
        .withGroupId("group01")
  ...
}
```

By default, along with each value, a Kafka topic stores a key that refers to its partition. This is the default strategy when a Kafka producer commits to Kafka, and it can be changed. And you need to pick a deserializer for both the key and the value. Of course, this depends on which serialization has been previously used when pushing data into the topic. Here we assume the producer has pushed it with UTF-8 encoding. (The default setting for Jackson is UTF-8.)

The `groupId` is used to track consumption of the topic. Consumption is stored in what is called the *offset*, and each `groupId` has its own offset. As soon as a batch of elements from the topic is consumed, a new offset is stored. This marks the last read position in the topic for that `groupId`. This action is called *committing the offset*. By default, the Alpakka plain consumer—`plainSource`—does not commit this offset. When the application restarts, it does not pick up where it left off.

The `config` points to the default Kafka Streams configuration (http://mng.bz/Op5O), and you need the `ActorSystem` to retrieve it:

```
object ConsumerPlainSource {                                    Implicit system to
  ...                                                        provide the materializer
                                                                   to the stream

  implicit val system = ActorSystem(Behaviors.empty, "consumerOne")   ◁──────

  val config = system.settings.config.getConfig("akka.kafka.consumer")
  ...
}
```

The `ActorSystem` allows you to load the configuration, and making it implicit lets you use it to run the Akka Streams application, as you see at the end of the example. Using the `system` to load the default configuration for the Akka Kafka consumer gives you all the settings, such as `poll-interval`, `commit-timeout`, `enable.auto.commit`, and a few more. The default values are reasonable to start with.

When you set properties in `akka.kafka.ConsumerSettings`, you have access to the underlying Apache Kafka object `org.apache.kafka.clients.consumer.ConsumerConfig`. Therefore, you can configure all the settings of an Apache Kafka consumer.

NOTE   For more information, see http://mng.bz/6Djp.

With these settings, you can create a plain Alpakka source and add the topic you want to read from:

```
import akka.kafka.Subscriptions

object ConsumerPlainSource {
  ...
                                                          Gets consumer records from
    Consumer                                                the source and prints them
      .plainSource(consumerSettings, Subscriptions.topics("test"))
      .map { msg: ConsumerRecord[String, String] =>         ◁──────
        println(s"key = ${msg.key},
                   value = ${msg.value},
                   offset = ${msg.offset}")
      }
      .runWith(Sink.ignore)      ◁──┐  Consumes and discards the
  ...                                │  elements
}
```

You can put all this together to make the application shown in the following listing.

Listing 14.1 Basic example of a Alpakka Kafka consumer

```
import akka.actor.typed.ActorSystem
import akka.actor.typed.scaladsl.Behaviors
import akka.kafka.{ ConsumerSettings, Subscriptions }
import akka.kafka.scaladsl.Consumer
import akka.stream.scaladsl.Sink
import org.apache.kafka.clients.consumer.ConsumerConfig
import org.apache.kafka.common.serialization.StringDeserializer
import scala.io.StdIn

object ConsumerPlainSource {

  def main(args: Array[String]) = {

    implicit val system = ActorSystem(Behaviors.empty, "consumerOne")

    val config =
      system.settings.config.getConfig("akka.kafka.consumer")

    val consumerSettings: ConsumerSettings =
      ConsumerSettings(
        config,
        new StringDeserializer(),
        new StringDeserializer())
        .withBootstrapServers("127.0.0.1:9092")
        .withGroupId("group01")

    Consumer
      .plainSource(consumerSettings, Subscriptions.topics("test"))
      .map { msg: ConsumerRecord[String, String] =>
        println(
          s"key = ${msg.key},
          value = ${msg.value},
          offset = ${msg.offset}")
      }
      .runWith(Sink.ignore)

    StdIn.readLine("Consumer started \n Press Enter to stop")
    system.terminate()
  }
}
```

Implicit ActorSystem to provide a materializer to run the stream

Loads the Kafka default configuration from the Alpakka reference.conf file

Alpakka consumer settings

Consumes and discards the elements

14.1.1 Consuming from Kafka in action

You can run the example from your Git repository using the docker-compose.yml on the base of the Alpakka project to start a Kafka server. You need to run `docker compose up` from the base of the chapter 14 folder in the command line. After a few seconds, Kafka should be running. By default, this Docker compose file creates six topics: `test`, `test2`, ..., `test6`.

On another command line, start the `ConsumerPlainSource` application by typing `sbt chapter14/run` and selecting option 1. When this application starts, it outputs information about the Kafka consumer's configuration, Kafka version, and more:

```
[INFO] [...] - [Consumer clientId=consumer-group01-1, groupId=group01]
Subscribed to topic(s): test

[INFO] [...] - [Consumer clientId=consumer-group01-1, groupId=group01]
Finished assignment for group at generation 1: {consumer-group01-1-
a37940c9-2767-4983-b2b7-005340617066=Assignment(partitions=[test-0])}

[INFO] [...] - [Consumer clientId=consumer-group01-1, groupId=group01]
Found no committed offset for partition test-0

[INFO] [...] - [Consumer clientId=consumer-group01-1, groupId=group01]
Resetting offset for partition test-0 to position
FetchPosition{offset=0, ...}
```

Subscription to the topic test

Assigns one partition to your group's consumer

No offset found for this group

Resets the offset to position 0 for this group

Once the application is running, you can send messages with `kcat` by starting a producer with the following command on another command line:

```
$ kcat -P -b localhost:9092 -t test
```

`-P` stands for *producer*. Now, each line you type sends a message to the test topic. If you enter `hello` and `hi`, you see the following in the `ConsumerPlainSource` output (partially formatted to make it easier to read):

```
key = null, value = hello, offset = 0
key = null, value = hi, offset = 1
```

The two lines sent through `kcat` are converted into records—more precisely, into two `org.apache.kafka.clients.consumer.ConsumerRecord` objects with all their fields available to you. Other than the value, the most important fields are the offset and the key.

You have a first example of consuming from a Kafka topic. Now let's go a little further. Start with the following test:

1 Exit the application.
2 Push two more elements into the Kafka topic.
3 Restart the application.
4 Push another element into the Kafka topic.

The consumer only outputs this last element. The other two are missing because the `plainSource` does not keep the offset by default. It starts with the last element.

> ### Key Kafka concepts
>
> To better understand the rest of the chapter, you should be familiar with the following Kafka concepts. As mentioned earlier, Alpakka consumers are built on top of the Apache Kafka API, specifically `KafkaConsumer`.

KAFKA CONSUMERS

A Kafka consumer takes care of the failures of Kafka brokers and the migration of topics between brokers. If a broker goes down while you're consuming from it, or the topic you're reading gets moved to another broker, it's not your problem. The consumer takes care of that for you. However, a TCP connection to the brokers is established; if you don't close the connection, it will remain open on the broker's side, causing a leak on the server.

OFFSETS AND CONSUMER POSITIONS

The offset is an index that indicates the position of a record in a partition and is stored with the record, as you saw in the previous example. Each consumer—defined by its `groupId`—can store the offset of the last element read in Kafka or elsewhere.

Each time a consumer starts reading a topic, you can specify the offset from which the consumer begins reading records. Some of those choices are to start reading from the first or the last item.

The *committed position* refers to the offset relative to the consumer, which is stored in permanent memory so it can be retrieved in the event of a failure. In this way, a consumer can resume reading if communication is interrupted, whether the customer gives up or the broker fails.

CONSUMER GROUPS AND TOPIC SUBSCRIPTIONS

A consumer group is a single logical subscriber that can contain multiple consumers that share the consumption of one or more topics. The pairing between the partitions of the topic and the consumers can dynamically adjust to the increase or decrease of the consumers. This is called rebalancing. Depending on the ratio of partitions and consumers, the partitions are assigned to consumers, as shown in the following figure.

If there are fewer consumers than partitions, each consumer is assigned more than one partition. If the number of consumers is greater than the number of partitions, the additional consumers become inactive.

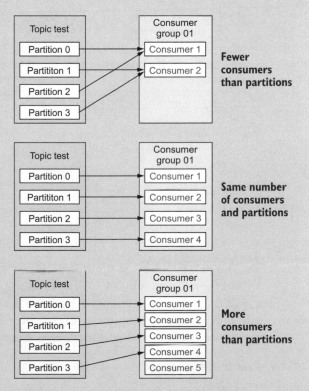

Pairing of topic partitions and consumer groups

14.1.2 Detecting consumer failures

Consumers maintain their assignment to their partitions through regular polling. If the consumer does not reach the broker within a certain period of time, its partition is assigned to another consumer in the same group. This duration can be set with `akka.kafka.consumer.poll-timeout`.

The consumer may fail because the connection to the bootstrap servers is not working. To work around this, you can connect to a single bootstrap server that acts as a proxy for multiple brokers. However, it is recommended to specify a list of bootstrap servers to connect to instead of relying on a single proxy. This way, you avoid the single point of failure.

In the previous example, you didn't commit the offset. If you don't, your stream will start at the very end every time you start the application. This probably is not what you want. You usually need to continue reading where you left off. Let's look at one way to do this.

14.1.3 Auto-commit

If auto-commit is set to `true`—the default is `false`—the consumer is committed at regular intervals. This interval is set with `auto.commit.interval.ms`.

> **NOTE** This option can be changed by setting the property `Consumer-Config.AUTO_COMMIT_INTERVAL_MS_CONFIG` like this: `.withProperty (ConsumerConfig.AUTO_COMMIT_INTERVAL_MS_CONFIG, [millis here])`. For more information, see http://mng.bz/91x0.

To set auto-commit to `true`, use `ConsumerConfig.ENABLE_AUTO_COMMIT_CONFIG` in the consumer's settings as follows:

```
val consumerSettings: ConsumerSettings[String, String] =
    ConsumerSettings(
      config,
      new StringDeserializer(),
      new StringDeserializer())
      .withBootstrapServers("127.0.0.1:9092")
      .withGroupId("group01")
      .withProperty(
          ConsumerConfig.ENABLE_AUTO_COMMIT_CONFIG, "true")
```

Kafka keeps the committed position every 5 seconds (the default).

But here's a problem. Suppose your application reads a message and starts processing it, and then auto-commit kicks in before you're done processing the message. If your application crashes and comes back up, it won't process the last message again. It is considered to be committed. Thus, you can lose messages. Fortunately, you have another option besides `plainSource` with auto-commit: a committable source.

14.1.4 Committable sources

This option allows you to set the delivery guarantees of the commit, giving you at-least-once semantics. You can be sure each message is processed before the offset is committed.

The messages you get from this consumer are of type `CommittableMessage`; they are still a `ConsumerRecords` but with a `CommittableOffset`. In the following snippet, you use the `ConsumerRecord` only to print and then pass the `Committable-Offset` to the next stage of the stream:

```scala
object ConsumerCommittableSource {
  ...
  Consumer
    .committableSource(consumerSettings, Subscriptions.topics("test2"))
    .map { msg: CommittableMessage[String, String] =>
        println(
          s"${msg.record.key} => ${msg.record.value.toUpperCase}")
        msg.committableOffset}
  ...
}
```

> **Committable source that produces records of CommittableMessages**

> **Retrieves the offset from the record to pass to the next stage**

For simplicity, this example has only one transformation.

Now imagine that you have many messages to process. You probably want to commit in batches; otherwise, the stream will be very slow. To do this, you can use the following `flow`:

```scala
object ConsumerCommittableSource {
  ...

  Consumer
    ...
    .via(Committer.flow(committerSettings.withMaxBatch(100)))
    ...
}
```

This sets the commit every 100 records or after 10 seconds if fewer than 100 have been processed in that time. You can get the `committerSettings` directly from the `system` as follows:

```scala
import akka.kafka.CommitterSettings

object ConsumerCommittableSource {
  ...

  val committerSettings = CommitterSettings(system)
  ...
}
```

You can use the offset from the `CommittableMessage` in the `Committer.flow`, as you can see in its signature:

```scala
package akka.kafka.scaladsl

object Committer {
  ...

  def flow(settings: CommitterSettings): Flow[Committable, Done, NotUsed]
  ...

}
```

Since this is a `flow[Committable, Done, NotUsed]`, you need input elements of type `Committable`, like `CommittableOffset`. The output is of type `Done`, and it doesn't have a materialized value and thus is `NotUsed`. To the `flow`, you can pass the following settings:

- `maxBatch`—Maximum number of messages in a single commit. Default: 1000.
- `maxInterval`—Maximum interval between commits. Default: 10 seconds.
- `maxParallelism`—Parallelism for async committing. Default: 100.

Two things can happen when processing messages: you process more than the maximum batch per max interval, or you don't. For example, by default, if it takes 20 seconds to receive 100 messages, the flow commits after the first 10 seconds. Or if the flow receives 2,000 messages per second, two batches of 1,000 messages per second are committed in parallel.

After the flow, you can use the drain control materialization to drain the stream before shutting it down:

```
object ConsumerCommittableSource {
  ...

  Consumer
    ...
    .toMat(Sink.seq)(DrainingControl.apply)
    ...
}
```

With this feature, you can shut down the stream while waiting for all the messages in flight to be consumed. This way, you avoid reprocessing messages that have already been consumed by the source but not fully processed and committed.

Putting all of the preceding information together, it looks like this:

```
import akka.kafka.scaladsl.Committer
import akka.kafka.scaladsl.Consumer.DrainingControl
import akka.kafka.CommitterSettings
import akka.kafka.ConsumerMessage.CommittableMessage

object ConsumerCommittableSource {
  ...
  val drainingControl: DrainingControl[_] =
    Consumer
      .committableSource(
        consumerSettings,
        Subscriptions.topics("test2"))
      .map { msg: CommittableMessage[String, String] =>
        println(
          s"${msg.record.key} => ${msg.record.value.toUpperCase}")
        msg.committableOffset
      }
      .via(Committer.flow(committerSettings.withMaxBatch(100)))
      .toMat(Sink.seq)(DrainingControl.apply)
      .run()
  ...
}
```

Annotations:
- **CommittableSource that produces records of CommittableMessages. Reads from topic "test2".** (points to `.committableSource(...)`)
- **Retrieves the offset from the record to pass it to Committer.flow** (points to `msg.committableOffset`)
- **Sets the commit every 100 records or 10 seconds** (points to `.via(Committer.flow(committerSettings.withMaxBatch(100)))`)
- **Drains the current messages on the stream before shutdown** (points to `.toMat(Sink.seq)(DrainingControl.apply)`)

You can use `Committer.sink(settings: CommitterSettings)` instead of `Committer.flow`, as follows:

```
Consumer.committableSource(...)
  .map( ... )
  .toMat(Committer.sink(committerSettings)(DrainingControl.apply))
  .run()
```

If the commit is the last thing you want to do, this is the best option. But part of the flow may be nice to have but not a must in your application, such as telemetry. In that case, you can include telemetry after the `committer.flow`.

14.2   Pushing to Kafka

In most streaming applications, you need to read from Kafka, but you also need to write to it. The classic case is ETL (extract, transform, load).

14.2.1   At-most-once delivery guarantee

You can push to Kafka with a `ProducerRecord` and a `plainSink`. The `Producer-Record` needs the element to push along with the topic name, and the `plainSink` needs the properties of the Kafka configuration. This is similar to the consumer settings, as you can see:

```
class KafkaSpec ... {

  ...

  Source(1 to 10)
    .map(_.toString)
    .map(elem => new ProducerRecord[String, String]("test", elem))
    .runWith(Producer.plainSink(producerSettings))
  ...
}
```

The producer settings set the serializers instead of the deserializers you saw in the consumer. That's not a surprise now that you're writing. The producer settings also set the bootstrap server URL. Here is one for simplicity:

```
class KafkaSpec ... {
  ...

  val producerSettings =
      ProducerSettings(
        config,
        new StringSerializer(),
        new StringSerializer())
      .withBootstrapServers("127.0.0.1:9092")
```

The remaining producer settings from reference.conf in `akka-stream-kafka` are sufficient for now.

Having a look at the `plainSink`'s signature may be helpful:

```
package akka.kafka.scaladsl

object Consumer {
  ...

  def plainSink[K, V](settings: ProducerSettings[K, V])      ⟵  K and V are the types
      : Sink[ProducerRecord[K, V], Future[Done]]                 of Key and Value.
  ...
}
```

Once you pass in `producerSettings`, the function returns a `Sink` that expects elements of type `ProducerRecord` and returns a `Future` that is `Done` when the stream is finished.

When you wrap the elements in `ProducerRecord`, you can specify the target topic. So, you can specify different topics for different messages if you want to fan them out. For example, elements that pass validation are routed to one topic, while elements that don't are routed to another. Another option is to write each item to more than one topic. You can put all this together in the following test.

Listing 14.2   `plainSink` producing to Kafka from the `KafkaSpec` test

```
import org.apache.kafka.common.serialization.StringSerializer
import org.apache.kafka.clients.producer.ProducerRecord

class KafkaSpec ... {
  ...

  "a producer" should "write to Kafka" in {              Loads defaults from
                                                          reference.conf from
    val config =                                           Alpakka Kafka
      system.settings.config.getConfig("akka.kafka.producer")   ⟵

    val topicDest =                                       Reads the destination
      system.settings.config.getString("kafka.test.topic") ⟵  topic from the
                                                              project's configuration
    val producerSettings = ProducerSettings(
      config,                                             Sets the
      new StringSerializer(),                             connection
      new StringSerializer()).withBootstrapServers("127.0.0.1:9092")

    val done: Future[Done] = Source(1 to 10)              Creates a record to
      .map(_.toString)                                     push to Kafka
      .map(elem => new ProducerRecord[String, String](topicDest, elem))  ⟵
      .runWith(Producer.plainSink(producerSettings))   ⟵
                                                          Executes the
    Await.ready(done, 3.second)                           producer to Kafka
  }
  ...
}
```

You can see this in action by listening to the `test` topic. Enter the following at the command line:

```
kcat -C -b localhost:9092 -t test
```

-C sets up `kcat` as a consumer. Then you can run `KafkaSpec` to push records to the topic by entering the following in the root of the Git repository:

```
sbt -Dkafka.test.topic="test" "chapter14/testOnly *KafkaSpec"
```

Here's the output:

```
hello        | Previous message from other runs
hi           |
1      ◁
2
3
4
5            Messages from
6            KafkaSpec
7
8
9
10     ◁
% Reached end of topic test [0] at offset 12
```

Because you're using the same topic as in the consumer example, you also see "hello" and "hi" and possibly more if you've tested further.

14.2.2 At-least-once delivery guarantee

To read from and write to Kafka, you can combine the `CommittableSource` with a `CommittableSink`. Let's look at the latter, together with its `Envelope` and `pass-Through`.

To fully understand a `CommittableSink`, you need to take a step back and understand `plainSink` a little better, among other things. This builds on a stage called `flexiFlow`, which, as the name suggests, is not a sink. Let's look at the implementation of `plainSink`:

```
package akka.kafka.scaladsl

object Producer {
  ...

  def plainSink[K, V](settings: ProducerSettings[K, V]):
      Sink[ProducerRecord[K, V], Future[Done]] =
    Flow[ProducerRecord[K, V]]
      .map(Message(_, NotUsed))          ◁──────── Wraps into
      .via(flexiFlow(settings))                    ProducerMessage.Message
      .toMat(Sink.ignore)(Keep.right)    ◁──┐ Ignores the result of the flexiFlow and
  ...                                        │ keeps the materialization of the
}                                            │ Sink.ignore. That is, Future[Done].
```

Uses flexiFlow

This is interesting for a couple of reasons. First, the implementation starts with a `map` that wraps each element that reaches the `plainSink` into a `ProducerMessage.Message`. The type of this message is a `ProducerMessage.Envelope`:

```
package akka.kafka

object ProducerMessage {
  ...
```

```
final case class Message[K, V, +PassThrough](
    record: ProducerRecord[K, V],
    passThrough: PassThrough
) extends Envelope[K, V, PassThrough]
...
}
```

With this constructor, each `ProducerRecord` is converted into a `Message` and thus into an `Envelope`. The envelope has a `passThrough`, but in `plainSink` this is not used, as you've seen in `.map(Message(_, NotUsed))`.

With this in mind, let's return to `committableSink` and look at its signature:

```
package akka.kafka.scaladsl

object Producer {
  ...

  def committableSink[K, V](
      producerSettings: ProducerSettings[K, V],
      committerSettings: CommitterSettings
  ): Sink[Envelope[K, V, ConsumerMessage.Committable], Future[Done]]
  ...
}
```

It needs as input the producer settings, which specify, among other things, the serialization and the location of the bootstrap servers, just as with the `plainSink`.

However, the most revealing part is the signature of the output—more precisely, the type of elements that the `Sink` must consume: `Envelope[K, V, Consumer-Message.Committable]`. You are again dealing with an `Envelope`, as you saw in `plainSink`, but now you use the `passThrough`. Here the `passThrough` is a `ConsumerMessage.Committable` instead of `NotUsed` as in the `plainSink`.

The easiest way to understand the `passThrough` is along with `flexiFlow`. You use a `flexiFlow` when you need to process something after you commit it to Kafka. The `passThrough` is what you keep after the commit—what passes to the next stage.

The `plainSink` does nothing after the `flexiFlow`. Let's take another look at it:

```
package akka.kafka.scaladsl

object Producer {
  ...

  def plainSink[K, V](settings: ProducerSettings[K, V]):
          Sink[ProducerRecord[K, V], Future[Done]] =
    Flow[ProducerRecord[K, V]]
      .map(Message(_, NotUsed))
      .via(flexiFlow(settings))
      .toMat(Sink.ignore)(Keep.right)
  ...
}
```

It ignores the `passThrough` by setting `Sink.ignore` and `Keep.right`. It keeps the `Future[Done]` to return when the stream is finished.

With that understanding, let's look at the following example that reads from a topic, wraps each message in an `Envelope`, and commits it with a `committableSink`:

```
object ConsumerProducerAtLeastOnce {
  ...

    Consumer
    .committableSource(consumerSettings, Subscriptions.topics("test3"))
    .map { msg: CommittableMessage[String, String] =>
      ProducerMessage.single(                         <─┐  ProducerMessage.Envelope
        new ProducerRecord[String, String](
          "test4", msg.record.key, msg.record.value),
       msg.committableOffset)
    }
    .toMat(Producer.committableSink(producerSettings, committerSettings))(
      Consumer.DrainingControl.apply)
    .run()
  ...
}
```

PassThrough as an input for committableSink

`ProducerMessage.single` creates the `Envelope` and sets the `passThrough` with the `committableOffset` you get from `committableSource`. This way, you provide the necessary `Envelope[K,V,ConsumerMessage.Committable]` for the `committableSink`.

Other ProducerMessage methods

For completeness, it's useful to know that `ProducerMessage.single` is not your only option. You can use two other envelopes with a `committableSink`:

- `ProducerMessage.multi`—Produces a sequence of `ProducerRecord`s instead of only one as `ProducerMessage.single`.
- `ProducerMessage.passThrough`—Only holds the `passThrough` and does not add any record to Kafka. Its only function is to commit the offset from the read records of a `committableSource`. This is like the `Committer.flow` you saw in the previous section or the `Committer.sink`.

Before we finish this section, let's review by seeing a complete example that consumes and produces from and to Kafka using at-least-once semantics.

Listing 14.3 Reading from and writing to Kafka

```
object ConsumerProducerAtLeastOnceConsumerProducerAtleastOnce {

  implicit val system = ActorSystem(Behaviors.empty, "producerOne")

  implicit val ec = ExecutionContext.Implicits.global

  def main(args: Array[String]) = {

    val bootstrapServers = "127.0.0.1:9092"
```

```
val consumerConfig =
  system.settings.config.getConfig("akka.kafka.consumer")

val consumerSettings: = ConsumerSettings(
    consumerConfig,
    new StringDeserializer(),
    new StringDeserializer())
  .withBootstrapServers(bootstrapServers)
  .withGroupId("group01")
  .withProperty(
    ConsumerConfig.AUTO_OFFSET_RESET_CONFIG,
    "earliest")

val producerConfig =
  system.settings.config.getConfig("akka.kafka.producer")

val producerSettings = ProducerSettings(
  producerConfig, new StringSerializer(),new StringSerializer())
  .withBootstrapServers(bootstrapServers)

val drainingControl: Consumer.DrainingControl[_] = Consumer
  .committableSource(consumerSettings, Subscriptions.topics("test3"))
  .map { msg: CommittableMessage[String, String] =>
    ProducerMessage.single(
      new ProducerRecord[String, String](
        "test4",msg.record.key, msg.record.value),
        msg.committableOffset)
  }
  .toMat(Producer.committableSink(producerSettings))(
    Consumer.DrainingControl.apply)
  .run()

StdIn.readLine("Consumer started \n Press Enter to stop")
val future = drainingControl.drainAndShutdown
future.onComplete(_ => system.terminate)

  }
}
```

Group to which to assign each consumer; each instance of this class

Default parameters and deserializers

Earliest means to consume from the first element at the start

Default parameters and serializers

ProducerMessage. Envelope writes to the topic test4 key and value from the Source.

Reads from test3 the key, value, and reference to the offset included

ProducerMessage.Envelope passes through the offset from the Source to the Sink.

Commits the passThrough and materializes the stream into a DrainingControl

You can run the `ConsumerProducerAtleastOnce` with the following:

```
sbt "chapter14/runMain ConsumerProducerAtleastOnce"
```

Now let's move on to what is commonly referred to as exactly-once delivery.

14.3   *Effectively-once delivery*

Alpakka Kafka uses underlying Kafka transactions or so-called *exactly-once* delivery. However, to be accurate and to clarify part of the underlying mechanism, it is worth noting that there is no such thing as exactly-once delivery, in Kafka or anywhere else. A better term is effectively-once. This means you get at-least-once semantics, and when duplicates appear, they are deduplicated.

Let's say you have a process that moves items from A to B to C. It starts by moving 10 items in a batch from A to B, and if it processes only 5, the process fails. Now you have 5 items in B that can also go to C; but A didn't finish the batch, and when it restarts, it does so from the first element of the 10. After the restart, B gets the 10 elements, and so does C. If that is the case, you have at-least-once semantics. However, if B keeps track of what it has received and sent to C, it can verify that the first 5 elements have been sent to C. If that is the case, you have effectively-once semantics.

Akka Transactional has effectively-once semantics, and its API is very similar to what you learned in the previous section. You use the following:

- `Transactional.source` instead of `Consumer.commitableSource`
- `TransactionalMessage` instead of `CommittableMessage`
- `Transactional.sink` instead of `Producer.commitableSink`

You can use these just like the committable versions, with one exception: the transactional ID. This ID must be unique at runtime, and two applications *cannot* use it simultaneously. Attempting to do so throws a fatal `ProducerFencedException` when Kafka detects a running process using that transactional ID. So, if you are using multiple instances of the same application, you must assign a unique ID to each.

Listing 14.4 Transactional source and sink

```
object ConsumerProducerEffectivelyOnce {

  val transactionalId = args(0)

  ...

  val drainingControl: Consumer.DrainingControl[_] =
      Transactional                      ⟵── Transactional.source instead of
        .source(                              Consumer.committableSource
          consumerSettings,
          Subscriptions.topics("test5")
        )
        .map { msg: TransactionalMessage[String, String] =>   ⟵── TransactionalMessage
          ProducerMessage.single(                                  instead of
            new ProducerRecord[String, String](                    CommittableMessage
              "test6",
              msg.record.key,              partitionOffset from
              msg.record.value),           TransactionalMessage instead
            msg.partitionOffset)     ⟵──   of committableOffset
        }
        .toMat(Transactional.sink(producerSettings, transactionalId))(   ⟵──
          Consumer.DrainingControl.apply)
        .run()                           Sink with a transactionalId that
}                                        committableSink doesn't have
```

NOTE The property `isolation.level` must be `read-committed`. So, you need to add this property and value to the `producerSettings`.

The `commit` settings are like auto-commit, which you saw in the `ConsumerSettings` with the `plainSink`. However, instead of `auto.commit.interval.ms`, for transactions, this is set in `akka.kafka.producer` via the `eos-commit-interval` property. The default value is 100 milliseconds.

The tradeoff between at-least-once and effectively-once is performance, as you may have guessed. This is because the stream stops processing records every time the transaction is committed. Committing the offset of the processed records locks the stream from further processing.

You can run `ConsumerProducerEffectivelyOnce` as follows:

```
sbt "chapter14/runMain ConsumerProducerEffectivelyOnce 12345"    ◁─┐  12345 is the
                                                                    transactional ID.
```

If you don't want to face the drawbacks of a transactional Kafka approach but still need the effectively-once semantics, you can defer the effectively-once semantics in your processing chain. You can defer deduplication to the last component in your infrastructure.

Alpakka Kafka is used again in chapter 15, but the following two connectors—CSV and S3—do not appear in the rest of the book. However, these two connectors are among the most used.

14.4 *Alpakka CSV*

To read a CSV file, it must contain a delimiter that you can set when parsing the lines, and it deserializes/serializes only UTF-8, ISO-8859-1, and ASCII. You need the following dependencies in your build.sbt file:

```
val AkkaStreamAlpakka = "4.0.0"
val AkkaVersion = "2.6.20"

libraryDependencies ++= Seq(
  "com.lightbend.akka" %% "akka-stream-alpakka-csv" % AkkaStreamAlpakka,
  "com.typesafe.akka" %% "akka-stream" % AkkaVersion
)
```

Before reading an actual CSV file, let's begin with a `Source` containing some data and a `Flow` in charge of parsing each line. For a CSV connector—and most other connectors—Alpakka produces a `Source[ByteString]`. A `ByteString` is a binary tree of bytes representing strings. It is immutable, provides more performance than a `String`, and is thread-safe. In the following listing, these bytes are extracted from a single `ByteString` passed as input, which is serialized as UTF-8 by default.

> **Listing 14.5   Simple source and parsing**

```
import akka.stream.alpakka.csv.scaladsl.CsvParsing
import akka.util.ByteString
...                           ◁─┐  Remaining
                                 imports
class CSVSpec
    extends AnyFlatSpec
    with Matchers {
```

```
implicit val system =
  ActorSystem(Behaviors.empty, "alpakkaExamples")          ←  Required ActorSystem
                                                              to run the Stream
"A CSV Source" should "be readable" in {
                                                                  Source of one
  val result: Future[Seq[List[ByteString]]] =                       ByteString
    Source
      .single(ByteString("Alice,Pleasence,19\nBob,Marley,30\n"))  ←
      .via(CsvParsing.lineScanner())       ←  Flow to
      .runWith(Sink.seq)                      scan lines

    ...
  }
}
```

This source contains a single `ByteString`, which is then parsed. The `CsvParsing`
`.lineScanner()` is a `Flow[ByteString,List[ByteString],NotUsed]`. A list of
words is created for each line break in the `ByteString`. Since it's a flow, you apply it
as a `.via`.

The next listing shows the rest of the previous test. To check the result, wait until
the `Future` is complete.

Listing 14.6   Scanning a CSV source

```
class CSVSpec
    extends AnyFlatSpec
    with Matchers
    with BeforeAndAfterAll {              Required ActorSystem to        Thread pool used
                                          run your Stream, shown        to run the callback
                                          in the previous listing       attached to the
  implicit val system = ...    ←┘                                       Future

  implicit val ec: ExecutionContext = ExecutionContext.Implicits.global  ←

  "A CSV Source" should "be readable" in {
                                                        Result of parsing, shown
    val result: Future[Seq[List[ByteString]]] = ...  ←  in the previous listing

    result.onComplete {              Callback to execute when the
      case Success(lines) =>         Future completes with Success
        lines.head should be(        to assert your expectations
          List(
            ByteString("Alice"),
            ByteString("Pleasence ")))

        lines(1) should be(
          List(
            ByteString("Bob"),
            ByteString("Marley"),
            ByteString("Jung")))
    }
  }
```

To execute the future, you need the usual `ExecutionContext`. Then you can
pattern-match on the `Future` callback `Success`.

To save work when testing futures, you can use `ScalaFutures` from the Scala-Test library to extend the `*Spec`. This way, you can skip the verbose `onComplete` pattern-matching with `Success` and the `ExecutionContext`.

Listing 14.7   Shorter assert

```
import org.scalatest.concurrent.ScalaFutures

class CSVSpec
    extends AnyFlatSpec
    with Matchers
    with ScalaFutures          Adds
    with BeforeAndAfterAll {    ScalaFutures

  implicit val system =
    ActorSystem(Behaviors.empty, "alpakkaExamples")

  "A CSV" should "be readable in shorter test" in {

    val result: Future[Seq[List[ByteString]]] = ...

    val lines = result.futureValue       Waits for the future to complete
    lines.head should be(                and extracts a value from Success
      List(
        ByteString("Alice"),
        ByteString("Pleasence"),
        ByteString("19")))

  }
}
```

NOTE `ScalaFutures` works by being in scope and implicitly wrapping each future in an `org.scalatest.concurrent.FutureConcept`. This wrapper has the `futureValue` method, which gives you direct access to the completed successful `Future` in this example.

14.4.1 *Mapping by column*

To be able to refer to the individual columns of a CSV file, you need headers. Depending on whether the CSV file has them, you can use `CsvToMap.toMap()` or `CsvTo-Map.withHeaders()`. Both methods create a `Map[String, ByteString]` for each line, so the final result is `Seq[Map[String, ByteString]]`. The following listing shows an example of a CSV file that initially has no headers and how to add them manually.

Listing 14.8   CSV to a seq of maps

```
import akka.stream.alpakka.csv.scaladsl.CsvToMap

class CSVSpec {
  ...
```

```
"A CSV with NO headers" should "be able to get into a Map" in {
  val result: Future[Seq[Map[String, ByteString]]] =
    Source
      .single(ByteString("Alice,Pleasence,19\nBob,Marley,30\n"))
      .via(CsvParsing.lineScanner())
      .via(CsvToMap.withHeaders("name", "surname", "age"))      ◁─────┐
      .runWith(Sink.seq)
```

Converts to Seq[Map[String, ByteString]] with headers

```
  val lines = result.futureValue
  lines.head should be(
    Map(
      "name" -> ByteString("Alice"),
      "surname" -> ByteString("Pleasence"),
      "age" -> ByteString("19")))
  }
  ...
}
```

The method `.withHeaders` not only adds the headers but also returns a map that you can use later.

Strings as values instead of ByteString

A method similar to `.withHeaders` is `CsvToMap.toMapAsStrings()`, which returns a `Seq[Map[String,String]]` as a result instead of a `Seq[Map[String, ByteString]]`. With `String` values as results, you have a much richer API thanks to `StringsOps`.

In Scala, any `String` gets wrapped in a `StringOps` through `Predef` by `.augmentString` (see http://mng.bz/jmMV). Both `.toMap` and `.withHeaders` have `asString` flavors, which are `.toMapAsString` and `.withHeaders-AsString`, respectively.

14.4.2 Reading and writing with FileIO

To read a CSV file or any other file, you can use `FileIO`. First, import the following dependencies in your build.sbt file:

```
val AkkaStreamAlpakka = "4.0.0"
val AkkaVersion = "2.6.20"

libraryDependencies ++= Seq(
  "com.lightbend.akka" %% "akka-stream-alpakka-file" % AkkaStreamAlpakka,
  "com.typesafe.akka" %% "akka-stream" % AkkaVersion
)
```

Let's combine it with what we have covered so far. The goal of this example is to read a file with the following content

```
name,surname,age
Alice,Pleasence,19
Bob,Marley,30
Benjamin,Button,2
```

and filter out people younger than 18, resulting in the following:

```
Alice,Pleasence,19
Bob,Marley,30
```

To write the result to a file, you must format the filtered rows back into a single `ByteString`. You can do this with the `CsvFormatting.format()` method. With this command and `FileIO` to read from and write to, you have everything you need.

When reading a file with `FileIO.fromPath(f: Path): ByteString`, you get the contents as a single `ByteString`. You also need a single `ByteString` to write to a file with `.toPath`, but in between, you have to convert the `ByteString` into something you can filter and convert it back to a `ByteString` with `CsvFormatting.format()`.

Listing 14.9   Reading and writing a file

```
import akka.stream.scaladsl.FileIO
import java.nio.file.{ FileSystems, Paths }

object CSVSpec {

  ...

  "A CSV file" should "be able to be read and write another CSV file" in {

    val fs = FileSystems.getDefault                                          Reads a
    val source: Source[ByteString, Future[akka.stream.IOResult]] =           CSV file
      FileIO.fromPath(
        fs.getPath("./chapter14/src/test/resources/characters.csv"))    ◁

    val filterAndGetValues:
        Flow[Map[String, String], Seq[String], NotUsed] =    ◁┐  Filters the data
    Flow[Map[String, String]]                                 │  and gets values
      .filter(eachMap => eachMap("age").toInt > 18)
      .map(eachMap => eachMap.values.toSeq)    ◁    toSeq is needed to transform
    source                                          collection.Iterable to
      .via(CsvParsing.lineScanner())                collection.immutable.Iterable.
      .via(CsvToMap.toMapAsStrings())
      .via(filterAndGetValues)              ┌ Formats the lines into
      .via(CsvFormatting.format())    ◁─────┘ a single ByteString
      .runWith(FileIO.toPath(
        fs.getPath("./chapter14/src/test/resources/result.csv")))
  }
  ...
}
```
Writes to / a CSV file ⟶

Here you parse the initial `ByteString` as in the previous example with `Csv-Parsing.lineScanner()` and create a map from `CsvToMap.toMapAsStrings()`. Then you apply the `filterAndGetValues` function and get back the needed `ByteString` with `CsvFormatting.format()`.

With `CsvFormatting.format()`, you can convert the `Seq[String]` you got from `.filterAndGetValues` into a `ByteString`. This is necessary to write

.toPath, but it also has some nice extras. You can choose the separator between the columns, the quote character, the end of line, and more.

FileSystems.getDefault is tangential to Akka. You can use it to access the file system in Java and to create a file, a path, and other containers for data, as well as other structures and mechanisms to support buffers.

It is important not to confuse FileIO (http://mng.bz/WAJd) with the Alpakka File Connector (https://doc.akka.io/docs/alpakka/current/file.html). The former creates a finite stream when reading, while the latter opens an infinite stream and gives you more options. As an infinite stream, it is meant to keep an open connection to an opened file and tail it.

Summary

- You can read from a Kafka topic using Consumer.plainSource and passing basic ConsumerSettings. The disadvantage of the basic consumer settings is that they don't preserve the offset. Therefore, when you restart the stream, you begin reading at the beginning or end of the topic.
- Adding ConsumerConfig.ENABLE_AUTO_COMMIT_CONFIG to Consumer-Settings keeps the offset as long as your application doesn't crash in the middle of a transaction.
- Consumer.commitableSource gives you at-least-once semantics, so you can ensure that no message is lost. Each message will be processed at least once.
- You can write to Kafka with Producer.plainSink with at-most-once semantics, with Producer.committableSink with at-least-once semantics, and with Transactional.sink with effectively-once semantics.
- FileIO.fromPath and FileIO.toPath allow you to read and write files.
- You can convert the contents of a CSV file by first parsing it into lines with CsvParsing.lineScanner(). Then you convert it to a map with headings and values with CsvToMap.toMapAsStrings(), so you can filter and transform the values by columns, and finally convert back to CSV format with Csv-Formatting.format().

Akka betting house, part 2

This chapter covers

- Creating projections and endpoints for them
- Running an app locally and in Kubernetes

We began the betting-house example in chapter 12. There we had the three main actors representing the business: the bet, the market, and the wallet. The market is a specific sports event with odds to bet against. The wallet represents the account of a user with its balance. The bet is the amount of money invested in a market and backed by a wallet.

In this chapter, you add two projections: one for the markets and one for the bets. These projections transform some of the events they receive from the entities and push them—those from the markets into a Kafka topic, and those from the bets into a database (see figure 15.1).

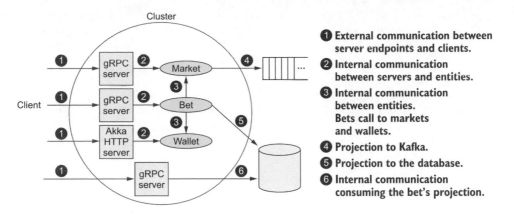

① External communication between server endpoints and clients.

② Internal communication between servers and entities.

③ Internal communication between entities. Bets call to markets and wallets.

④ Projection to Kafka.

⑤ Projection to the database.

⑥ Internal communication consuming the bet's projection.

Figure 15.1   Big picture of the example

15.1   Projections

This chapter shows how to add a database projection and a Kafka projection to the example project. Both read from the journal, but they differ on the writing side: the first writes to a database, and the second writes to Kafka. Now that you know Alpakka and Kafka (covered in chapter 14), this discussion should be easy for you.

> **NOTE**   The source code for this chapter is available at www.manning.com/ books/akka-in-action-second-edition or https://github.com/franciscolopez sancho/akka-topics/tree/main/betting-house. You can find the contents of any snippet or listing in the .scala file with the same name as the class, object, or trait.

15.1.1 Database projection

The database projection does two things. On the one hand, it creates a row in a table that links the bet, market, and wallet. Each time the journal receives a `BetOpened`, a record is upserted with the following fields:

```
betId, walletId, marketId, odds, stake, result
```

On the other hand, a query is created to this table, which retrieves how much money the betting company has to return to the users for a market, depending on the result. For example, the market for the Liverpool vs. Real Madrid soccer match may look like this:

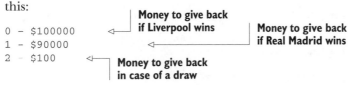

```
0 - $100000
1 - $90000
2 - $100
```

Money to give back if Liverpool wins

Money to give back if Real Madrid wins

Money to give back in case of a draw

This query is provided as a gRPC service and helps with risk management. An operator can retrieve this information via HTTP and set a cap for a particular market if the return becomes too risky for the house.

The following listing shows these two actions in the repository implementation.

Listing 15.1   Repository actions in the database projection

```
class BetRepositoryImpl extends BetRepository {

  override def addBet(
      betId: String,
      walletId: String,
      marketId: String,
      odds: Double,
      stake: Int,
      result: Int,
      session: ScalikeJdbcSession): Unit = {
    session.db.withinTx { implicit dbSession =>
      sql"""                                          Creates entries on
          INSERT INTO                          ◄──┘   bet_wallet_market
            bet_wallet_market (betId, walletId, marketId, odds, stake, result)
            VALUES ($betId, $walletId, $marketId, $odds, $stake, $result)
          ON CONFLICT (betId) DO NOTHING""".executeUpdate().apply()
    }

  }


  override def getBetPerMarketTotalStake(
      marketId: String,                              Queries the total per
      session: ScalikeJdbcSession): List[StakePerResult] = {   market per result
    session.db.readOnly { implicit dbSession =>
      sql"""SELECT sum(stake * odds), result FROM bet_wallet_market   ◄──
                WHERE marketId = $marketId GROUP BY marketId, result"""
        .map(rs => StakePerResult(rs.double("sum"), rs.int("result")))
        .list
        .apply()
    }
  }
}
```

This repository implementation is then used by the handler of the projection, which links the events from the journal to the upsert.

Listing 15.2   `BetProjectionHandler`

```
class BetProjectionHandler(repository: BetRepository)
    extends JdbcHandler[EventEnvelope[Bet.Event], ScalikeJdbcSession] {   ◄──┐

  val logger = LoggerFactory.getLogger(classOf[BetProjectionHandler])

  override def process(                              Extends from JdbcHandler
                                                        to write in the DB
```

```
          session: ScalikeJdbcSession,
          envelope: EventEnvelope[Bet.Event]): Unit = {        ◁── Events from Bet
      envelope.event match {
        case Bet.Opened(betId,walletId,marketId,odds,stake,result) =>    ◁───┐
          repository.addBet(betId,walletId,marketId,odds,stake,result,session)│
        case x =>                                              ◁──           │
          logger.debug("ignoring event {} in projection", x)               Passes Bet.Opened
                                                                            to the repository
      }                                           Ignores any other         implementation
    }                                             event from Bet
  }
}
```

This session is loaded when JdbcProjection.exactlyOnce is created. More about this in the next listing.

Now you need to specify the source of the events: what kinds of events to feed into the projection. Here the source is an `EventSourcedProvider.eventsByTag[Bet .Event]`. This means it only picks up `Bet.Event` entries from the journal. You need `jdbc-connection-settings` in your configuration with the database connection details; you can reuse those connection details for writing, but you also need a database session, which here is a `ScalikeJdbcSession`. Finally, set the tags to provide parallelization. To review these ideas, see chapter 10, sections 10.2 and 10.3.

With the source provider, the handler, the repository implementation, and the JDBC connection, you can create the projection.

Listing 15.3 Basic components of the projection

```
object BetProjection {
  ...

  def createProjection(
      system: ActorSystem[_],
      repository: BetRepository,
      index: Int)
      : ExactlyOnceProjection[Offset, EventEnvelope[Bet.Event]] = {

    val tag = Bet.tags(index)

    val sourceProvider =                                       ◁──┐
      EventSourcedProvider.eventsByTag[Bet.Event](                 │
        system = system,                                           │
        readJournalPluginId = JdbcReadJournal.Identifier,          │
        tag = tag)                                              Source of events
                                                                from the journal
    JdbcProjection.exactlyOnce(
      projectionId = ProjectionId("BetProjection", tag),         │
      sourceProvider = sourceProvider,                        ◁──┘
      handler = () => new BetProjectionHandler(repository),       ◁──┐
      sessionFactory = () => new ScalikeJdbcSession())(system)       │
  }                                                                  │
}                                               Handles events, filters them,
                                                and upserts to the database
```

Database session used to write ⌐─▷ `sessionFactory = () => new ScalikeJdbcSession())(system)`

All these components are combined in a `JdbcProjection` with effectively-once semantics.

The handler takes each event and passes the `Opened` ones to the repository to save them. It is worth noting that you pass only the repository to the handler in its constructor. The `ScalikeJdbcSession` is not passed directly to this method; it must be included in the scope, and that is done by creating a connection pool in `Main`. So when you initialize the projection, the database connection pool is already available. You see this later in section 15.1.3.

To expose the HTTP endpoint so operators can consume it, you can wrap the `BetRepositoryImpl` in a gRPC. To do so, you need the following:

- The .proto definition of the service
- An implementation of the service
- An HTTP server to expose the service

With this service, you can send a market ID to get a response with the total for each result. The bet.proto definition is as follows:

```
message MarketIdsBet {
    string marketId = 1;
}
message SumStakes {
    repeated SumStake sumstakes = 1;
}
message SumStake {
    double total = 1;
    int32 result = 2;
}

service BetProjectionService {
    rpc GetBetByMarket(MarketIdsBet) returns (SumStakes) {}
}
```

Service to retrieve the list of totals per result per market ← (points to `rpc GetBetByMarket(MarketIdsBet) returns (SumStakes) {}`)

`SumStakes` can display a table with *n* rows, each one a `SumStake`. For the example, the Liverpool vs. Real Madrid table has three rows.

This .proto file generates the service interface for you, and then you need to implement it. In its implementation, you can use the `ScalaJdbcSession`—added to the scope in `Main`—to access the database and the repository implementation to call the `SELECT` query. This service needs to implement the method `getBetByMarket`:

```
class BetProjectionServiceImpl ... {
  ...

  def getBetByMarket(
      in: MarketIdsBet): scala.concurrent.Future[SumStakes] = {
    Future {
      ScalikeJdbcSession.withSession { session =>
        val sumStakes = betRepository
          .getBetPerMarketTotalStake(in.marketId, session)
          .map { each =>
            SumStake(each.sum, each.result)
```

Input from the RPC call ← (points to `in: MarketIdsBet`)

Calls to the repository to retrieve the data ← (points to `.getBetPerMarketTotalStake(in.marketId, session)`)

```
        }
      SumStakes(sumStakes)
    }
 }}
...
}
```

NOTE The future in the output indicates that the result will come back at some point, and when that happens, a thread will be used. You could use the same thread pool from the `ActorSystem`, but since the connection to the database is a blocking call, you should use a different thread pool. Otherwise, you can block the `ActorSystem` so that it can no longer run actors, send messages, and function as expected.

The following snippet shows how to use `akka.projection.jdbc.blocking-jdbc-dispatcher` from the `akka-projection-jdbc` module along with the rest of the service implementation:

```
class BetProjectionServiceImpl(
    system: ActorSystem[_],
    betRepository: BetRepository)
    extends BetProjectionService {

  implicit private val jdbcExecutor: ExecutionContext =         Separate executor
    system.dispatchers.lookup(                                  to provide the future
      DispatcherSelector.fromConfig(                            computation for
        "akka.projection.jdbc.blocking-jdbc-dispatcher"))  ◁── getBetByMarket

  def getBetByMarket(
      in: MarketIdsBet): Future[SumStakes] = ...
  ...
}
```

Once the .proto that uses the `BetRepository` SELECT query is implemented, you just need to expose it. Choose a port and a host, and bind it to an Akka HTTP server.

Listing 15.4 Bet projection server

```
object BetProjectionServer {

  def init(repository: BetRepository)(          Execution context for the
    implicit ec: ExecutionContext,          ◁── bind that returns a future
      system: ActorSystem[_]): Unit = {
    val service: HttpRequest => Future[HttpResponse] =
      BetProjectionServiceHandler.withServerReflection(        Uses the .proto service
        new BetProjectionServiceImpl(system, repository))  ◁── implementation

    val port =
      system.settings.config.getInt("services.bet-projection.port")   Starts the
    val host = system.settings.config.getString("services.host")      server and
                                                                       binds the
    Http().newServerAt(host, port).bind(service)          ◁───────────  service
}}
```

The `BetProjectionServiceHandler` wraps the implementation of the service into a function of `HttpRequest => Future[HttpResponse]`, as specified in the signature of the service value. To start the server, as mentioned earlier, make sure you have a `ScalikeJdbcSession` in scope with `ScalikeJdbcSetup.init(system)`. You see this in the `Main` of the application, but before that, let's create the final projection.

15.1.2 *Kafka projection*

This projection is used to publish the market events in a Kafka topic. It can be used to react to the `Market.Close` event to settle all bets related to that market and pay the winners or, for example, notify multiple clients that a market has opened or closed so they can react accordingly. For example, a notification can be sent to app users that a new market is available to bet.

Essentially, this projection is like the previous one, except that the handler writes to Kafka instead of a database. This difference is divided into two parts: processing the message in the handler, and the settings for the Kafka producer.

The Kafka producer has producer settings like any other producer you learned about in chapter 14. It uses a string serializer for the key and a byte array serializer for the value. The rest of the configuration is read from the betting-house project's application.conf file.

However, you are not in an Akka Stream here, so you can't just use a producer like `Producer.committableSink`. But you can use something you haven't seen before—a `SendProducer` that requires producer settings and an `ActorSystem`, as shown here:

```
package akka.kafka.scaladsl

final class SendProducer[K, V] private (
                val settings: ProducerSettings[K, V],
                system: ActorSystem)
}

object SendProducer {
  def apply[K, V](settings: ProducerSettings[K, V])
      (implicit system: ClassicActorSystemProvider):      Curried factory
    SendProducer[K, V] = new SendProducer(settings, system.classicSystem)
  ...
}
```

You can use it like this in its curried form.

```
val sendProducer = SendProducer(producerSettings)(system)
```

Now that you have the producer, you need a coordinated termination for it. You must close the producer before you exit the `ActorSystem` so the producer registry is freed. Otherwise, the attempt to restart the application will fail due to a conflicting registry. Kafka does not allow the same producer to be registered multiple times once it is open.

You can do this with `CoordinatedShutdown`, an extension that registers tasks—internal to the `ActorSystem` or from the user—to be executed when the system is shut down. There are several phases, but only three are intended to be used by Akka users:

- `Before-service-unbind`—The tasks set here run at the very beginning. This is the initial phase of the shutdown. You saw several examples of unbinding HTTP services in chapter 11.
- `Before-cluster-shutdown`—The tasks set here run after the service shutdown and before the cluster initiates the shutdown.
- `Before-actor-system-terminate`—The tasks set here are executed after the cluster is shut down but before the system is shut down.

In this projection, the producer releases its registration before the `ActorSystem` terminates. This is shown in the following listing along with the rest of the producer's build.

Listing 15.5 Kafka producer creation

```
object MarketProjection {

  def init(system: ActorSystem[_]): Unit = {...}          Initialization of the
                                                          projection (ignored here)
  def createProducer(
      system: ActorSystem[_]): SendProducer[String, Array[Byte]] = {

    val producerSettings =       Loads parameters from the
      ProducerSettings(          akka.kafka.producer configuration
        system,
        new StringSerializer,        Configures the producer settings for
        new ByteArraySerializer)     serialization for the key and value
    val sendProducer = SendProducer(producerSettings)(system)
    CoordinatedShutdown(system).addTask(                    Closes the connection,
      CoordinatedShutdown.PhaseBeforeActorSystemTerminate,  coordinated with
      "closing send producer") { () =>                      ActorSystem termination
      sendProducer.close()
    }
    sendProducer
  }

  private def createProjection(
      system: ActorSystem[_],
      topic: String,                                              Creates a
      producer: SendProducer[String, Array[Byte]],                projection
      index: Int)
      : AtLeastOnceProjection[Offset, EventEnvelope[Market.Event]] = {...}
}
```

To complete the Kafka projection, let's now look at the handler. This handler does not connect to a database and therefore does not need to extend a `JdbcHandler` to process the message.

To process the event, create a `ProducerRecord`—the Kafka class you learned about in chapter 14. You instantiate this class with a subject, a key, and a value for each market event and send it using the `sendProducer` from the `MarketProjection`:

```
class MarketProjectionHandler ... {
  ...

  override def process(
      envelope: EventEnvelope[Market.Event]): Future[Done] = {
    log.debug(
      s"processing market event [$envelope] to topic [$topic]}")

    val event = envelope.event
    val serializedEvent = serialize(event)        ◁─┐ Creates a record
    if (!serializedEvent.isEmpty) {                  │ to push to Kafka
      val record =
        new ProducerRecord(topic, event.marketId, serializedEvent)
      producer.send(record).map { _ =>
        log.debug(s"published event [$event] to topic [$topic]}")
        Done                                    ◁─┐
      }                                           │ Returns Done whether it
    } else {                                      │ pushes to Kafka or not
      Future.successful(Done)                   ◁─┘
    }
  ...
}
```

The event is serialized according to the producer settings. The key is `String`, and the value is an `Array[Byte]`. To serialize the value, you can use Google's `protobuf` library—which is included in `akka-projection-eventsourced` as a dependency—as follows:

```
import com.google.protobuf.any.{ Any => PbAny }

class MarketProjectionHandler ... {

  def serialize(event: Market.Event): Array[Byte] = {
    val proto = ...
    PbAny.pack(proto, "market-projection").toByteArray
  }
}
```

To use this, you need a `proto` object that you can create with the values from the `Market.Event`. The definition of the `proto` objects corresponds to the events `MarketClosed`, `MarketOpened`, and `MarketCancelled`:

```
syntax = "proto3";

option java_package = "betting.house.projection.proto";

message MarketClosed {
    string marketId = 1;
    int32 result = 2;
}
```

```
message MarketOpened {
      string marketId = 1;
}
message MarketCancelled {
      string marketId = 1;
      string reason = 2;
}
```

With these definitions and the automatically generated `proto` objects, you can pack the market events into an `Array[Byte]` like this:

```
class MarketProjectionHandler ... {

 def serialize(event: Market.Event): Array[Byte] = {        Filters events and
    val proto = event match {                                creates the proto
      case Market.Closed(marketId, result, _) =>
        projection.proto.MarketClosed(marketId, result)
      case Market.Opened(marketId, _, _) =>
        projection.proto.MarketOpened(marketId)
      case Market.Cancelled(marketId, reason) =>
        projection.proto.MarketCancelled(marketId, reason)
      case x =>
        log.info(s"ignoring event $x in projection")
        Empty.defaultInstance    }
    PbAny.pack(proto, "market-projection").toByteArray        Transforms the proto
 }                                                            to a byte array
}
```

With all the parts that make up the process and serialization, you can create the handler, as shown in the next listing.

Listing 15.6 Market Kafka projection

```
class MarketProjectionHandler(
    system: ActorSystem[_],
    topic: String,
    producer: SendProducer[String, Array[Byte]])        Extends from Handler, not
    extends Handler[EventEnvelope[Market.Event]] {       JdbcHandler as in BetProjection

  val log = LoggerFactory.getLogger(classOf[MarketProjectionHandler])
  implicit val ec = ExecutionContext.global        This executor uses a pool with
                                                   as many threads as the number
  override def process(                            of available processors.
      envelope: EventEnvelope[Market.Event]): Future[Done] = ...

  def serialize(event: Market.Event): Array[Byte] = ...        Serializes each event
  ...                                                          and pushes it to Kafka
}
```

When the cluster starts, you need to initialize both projections: `BetProjection` and `MarketProjection`. This is done with an `init` method that uses the `Sharded-DaemonProcess` to spawn as many actors/projections as tags in the entities, bet and market. Each projection is wrapped in a `Behavior` distributed in a sharded fashion across the cluster. Here is the `MarketProjection`:

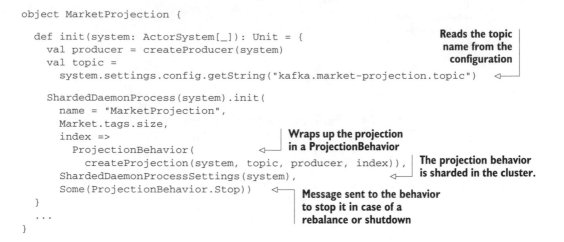

```
object MarketProjection {

  def init(system: ActorSystem[_]): Unit = {
    val producer = createProducer(system)
    val topic =
      system.settings.config.getString("kafka.market-projection.topic")

    ShardedDaemonProcess(system).init(
      name = "MarketProjection",
      Market.tags.size,
      index =>
        ProjectionBehavior(
          createProjection(system, topic, producer, index)),
      ShardedDaemonProcessSettings(system),
      Some(ProjectionBehavior.Stop))
  }
  ...
}
```

Annotations:
Reads the topic name from the configuration
Wraps up the projection in a ProjectionBehavior
The projection behavior is sharded in the cluster.
Message sent to the behavior to stop it in case of a rebalance or shutdown

The initialization of both projections is almost identical, as you can see in the bet projection:

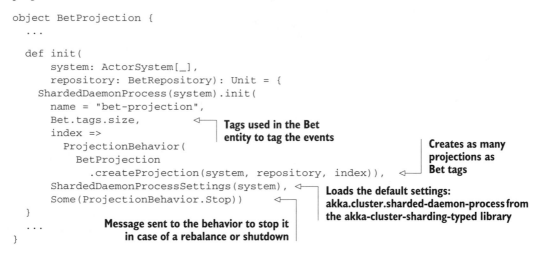

```
object BetProjection {
  ...

  def init(
      system: ActorSystem[_],
      repository: BetRepository): Unit = {
    ShardedDaemonProcess(system).init(
      name = "bet-projection",
      Bet.tags.size,
      index =>
        ProjectionBehavior(
          BetProjection
            .createProjection(system, repository, index)),
      ShardedDaemonProcessSettings(system),
      Some(ProjectionBehavior.Stop))
  }
  ...
}
```

Annotations:
Tags used in the Bet entity to tag the events
Creates as many projections as Bet tags
Loads the default settings: akka.cluster.sharded-daemon-process from the akka-cluster-sharding-typed library
Message sent to the behavior to stop it in case of a rebalance or shutdown

15.1.3 *The betting-house entry point*

Finally, we have reached the entry point of the betting-house application: `Main`, with everything you've learned since chapter 12. It includes sharding, the cluster bootstrap, management, adding the JDBC session in scope, the services as ports to the actors, and the projections.

Listing 15.7   Entry point of the betting-house application

```
object Main {

  val log = LoggerFactory.getLogger(Main + "")

  def main(args: Array[String]): Unit = {
    implicit val system =
```

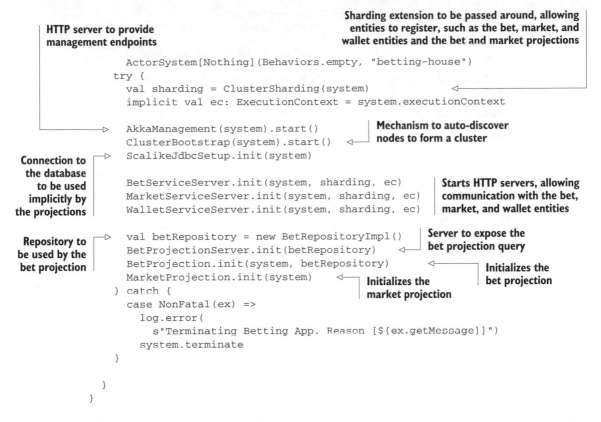

With this, you have an application you can deploy and for which you need the configuration.

15.2 Configuration

You need to configure the application. You can create a configuration to run it locally or in Kubernetes. The betting-house project includes local.conf and application.conf files for these two environments.

15.2.1 Persistence

The configurations are almost identical when it comes to persistence. Here you need to specify the persistence plugins—journal and snapshot store—for the entities to be persisted. To do this, specify which database you want them to read from and write to.

Listing 15.8 `akka.persistence` local configuration

```
akka {
  ...
  persistence {            Links Akka persistent entities
                           with the JDBC configuration
    journal.plugin = "jdbc-journal"
    auto-start-journals = ["jdbc-journal"]
```

```
      snapshot-store.plugin = "jdbc-snapshot-store"
      auto-start-snapshot-stores = ["jdbc-snapshot-store"]
  }
}
...
jdbc-connection-settings {        ◁────┐
  driver = "org.postgresql.Driver"
  url = "jdbc:postgresql://127.0.0.1:5432/betting"
  user = betting
  password = betting


  ...
}
```

> JDBC configuration for the persistent entities and projections for the akka-persistence-jdbc plugin and ScalikeJdbc

```
akka-persistence-jdbc {      │ Database
  shared-databases {         │ connection
    default {          ◁─────┘ details
      profile = "slick.jdbc.PostgresProfile$"
      db {
        host = "localhost"
        url = ${jdbc-connection-settings.url}
        user = ${jdbc-connection-settings.user}
        password = ${jdbc-connection-settings.password}
        driver = ${jdbc-connection-settings.driver}
        numThreads = 5
        maxConnections = 5
        minConnections = 1
      }
    }
  }
}
```

> Links the event_journal table for writes to the default connection details

```
jdbc-journal {      ◁─────┘
  use-shared-db = "default"
}
```

```
jdbc-snapshot-store {       ◁────┐ Links the snapshot table to
  use-shared-db = "default"      │ the default connection details
}
```

```
jdbc-read-journal {       ◁────┐ Links the event_journal table for
  use-shared-db = "default"    │ reads to the default connection details
}
```

You may have noticed that the URL contains 127.0.0.1. This is local.conf. In application.conf, you have `postgres-betting-db` instead. You'll see why in section 15.3.2.

To write the events, create the corresponding tables: `event_journal`, `snapshots`, and `event_tags`. The latter correlates tags and entity IDs so that entities can be grouped when queried. Regardless of whether you are working locally or in Kubernetes, you must run the SQL from the akka-persistence.sql file to create the three tables. For detailed instructions, see sections 15.3.1 and 15.3.2.

15.2.2 Cluster local

On local, specify the settings for `remote` and `cluster`. You need to ensure that the port in the seed nodes matches the `canonical.port` in the configuration, at least in one node. Otherwise, no cluster can be formed.

Local and Kubernetes deployments have common configurations: `serialization-bindings`, `SplitBrainResolverProvider`, and `enable-http2`. As usual, you add the SBR as the `downing-provide-class`.

Listing 15.9   Cluster local configuration

```
akka {
  actor {          ⊲──┐ Common to local and
    provider = cluster    Kubernetes configurations

    serialization-bindings {
      "example.betting.CborSerializable" = jackson-cbor
    }
  }

  remote {                                    ⊲──┐
    artery {
      canonical.hostname = "127.0.0.1"
      canonical.port = 25525                     This only appears
    }                                            in local.conf.
  }
  cluster {
    seed-nodes = [                           ⊲──┘
      "akka://betting-house@127.0.0.1:25525]
    downing-provider-class = "akka.cluster.sbr.SplitBrainResolverProvider"  ⊲──┐
  }                                              Common to local and
                                                 Kubernetes configurations
  http.server.preview.enable-http2 = on    ⊲────────────────────

  persistence {...}    ⊲──┐ Shown in the previous
}                          section (ignored here)
```

Remember that `Commands`, `Events`, and `State` must be `CborSerializable`; otherwise, the events can't be stored in the journal. And if you spin multiple nodes, the commands must be serialized so the entities can communicate. That's why `serialization-bindings` is in the configuration. Setting HTTP/2 to on allows you to use reflection, query the list of calls of the gRPC services, and help clients build requests and responses at runtime, as with `grpcurl`.

15.2.3 Cluster Kubernetes

The following configuration has neither `remote.artery` nor `cluster.seed-nodes`. You leave Akka Cluster Bootstrap responsible for resolving the cluster consensus via the Kubernetes API.

Listing 15.10   Cluster configuration for Kubernetes

```
akka {

  actor {...}              ◁─┐ Same as local.conf
                             │ (ignored here)
  discovery {
    kubernetes-api {
        pod-label-selector = "app=%s"   ◁──┐ %s is replaced with the configured
    }                                       │ effective name, which defaults to
  }                                         │ the ActorSystem name.
  management {
    cluster.bootstrap {
      contact-point-discovery {
        discovery-method = kubernetes-api   ◁──┐ Sets the Kubernetes API
      }                                        │ as the discovery method
    }

    http{                    ┌ Binds to
       port = 8558    ◁──────┘ this port
       bind-hostname = "0.0.0.0"   ◁──┐ Binds to all IP
    }                                  │ addresses of this host
  }
  persistence {...}    ◁──┐ Same as local.conf
}                          │ (ignored here)
```

15.2.4 Services, sharding, and projections

This code is the same for both configurations, except for Kafka bootstrap-servers.

Listing 15.11   Services, sharding, and projections configuration

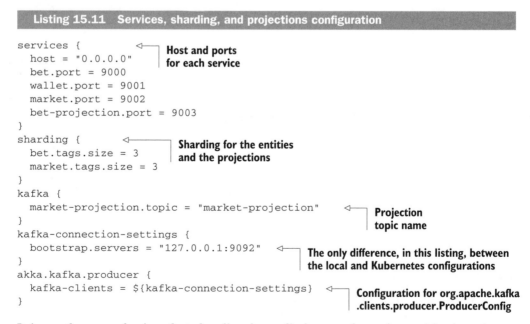

```
services {               ◁──┐ Host and ports
  host = "0.0.0.0"          │ for each service
  bet.port = 9000
  wallet.port = 9001
  market.port = 9002
  bet-projection.port = 9003
}
sharding {               ◁──┐ Sharding for the entities
  bet.tags.size = 3          │ and the projections
  market.tags.size = 3
}
kafka {
  market-projection.topic = "market-projection"   ◁──┐ Projection
}                                                      │ topic name
kafka-connection-settings {
  bootstrap.servers = "127.0.0.1:9092"   ◁──┐ The only difference, in this listing, between
}                                            │ the local and Kubernetes configurations
akka.kafka.producer {
  kafka-clients = ${kafka-connection-settings}   ◁──┐ Configuration for org.apache.kafka
}                                                     │ .clients.producer.ProducerConfig
```

It is worth remembering that sharding is applied not only to the entities but also to the projections that use `ShardedDaemonProcess` with the tags as partition keys. On the Kubernetes configuration, `bootstrap.servers` has `my-cluster-kafka-bootstrap` instead of the fixed host. This name resolves to a service in Kubernetes that proxies the connection to the brokers. For more information, see section 15.3.2.

Note that `akka.kafka.producer` refers to the previously defined `kafka-connection-settings`. You can add any additional configuration that you want to apply to `org.apache.kafka.clients.producer.ProducerConfig`. The producer settings use this in the market projection, shown again in the following snippet:

```
object MarketProjection {
  ...

  def createProducer(
      system: ActorSystem[_]): SendProducer[String, Array[Byte]] = {

    val producerSettings =
      ProducerSettings(
        system,
        new StringSerializer,
        new ByteArraySerializer)

    val sendProducer = SendProducer(producerSettings)(system)
    ...
}
```

> These settings read the rest of their properties from **akka.kafka.producer** in the .conf.

Any property added to `akka.kafka.producer` in the configuration is passed to the producer settings.

15.3 Deployment

Once the code and configuration are ready, you can deploy locally or to Kubernetes. Let's see how.

15.3.1 Running local

To start the Postgres database and Kafka, execute the following at the command line from the betting-house/local-deployment folder:

```
docker compose up
```

Then apply all the SQL files in the betting-house/common-deployment folder: akka-persistence.sql, akka-projection.sql, and bet-projection.sql. When you are asked for the password, enter betting, which is set in local-deployment/docker-compose.yml:

```
psql -h 127.0.0.1 -d betting  -U betting -f bet-projection.sql
psql -h 127.0.0.1 -d betting  -U betting -f akka-persistence.sql
psql -h 127.0.0.1 -d betting  -U betting -f akka-projection.sql
```

To start a node, start sbt in the root of the Git repository and set local.conf as the configuration resource:

```
sbt "-Dconfig.resource=local.conf"
```

Once the sbt server is up, enter

```
sbt:code> betting-house/run
```

To play around with the different calls, you can find examples in the README.md file of the betting-house project.

15.3.2 Running in Kubernetes

This section assumes a basic understanding of Kubernetes and databases. To deploy the application to Kubernetes, you need to do the following:

- Have a Kubernetes cluster available.
- Create a service account that your deployment should use. You can do this with the role.yml file in the root directory of the betting-house project.
- Create a Kubernetes deployment. You can do this with the deployment.yml file.
- Create a Docker image for the betting-house JAR.

To make a Kubernetes cluster available, run `minikube start`. (Follow the instructions in appendix A if you haven't already.)

The contents of role.yml and deployment.yml are nothing you haven't seen in chapter 13. Therefore, they are not repeated here. The only relevant information for what follows is the deployment name, since the pods use it: `my-deployment-name`. The other essential piece of information is the image used in deployment.yml, which is the name of the Docker image that wraps the application JAR. Let's look at how you create and name the image.

CREATING THE IMAGE WITH THE JAR

You need to enable the plugins in build.sbt—`JavaAppPackaging` and `Docker-Plugin`—to package the application into a JAR and that into a Docker image. Then set the Docker base image and open the ports for Akka Management, Akka Remote, the services, and the bet projection. Finally, assign a version to the image:

```
lazy val `betting-house` = project
  .in(file("betting-house"))
  .enablePlugins(AkkaGrpcPlugin, JavaAppPackaging, DockerPlugin)
  .settings(
    version := "0.1.1-SNAPSHOT",        ◁──┤ Version of the image

                                                      Entry point of
                                                      the application
    Compile / mainClass := Some("example.betting.Main"),   ◁──┘

    dockerExposedPorts := Seq(8558, 2552, 9000, 9001,9002,9003),

    dockerBaseImage := "adoptopenjdk:11-jre-hotspot",   ◁──  Sets the
                                                             base image

    dockerUsername := "yourusername",   ◁──┐ Registry inside the
                                             repository docker.io
    libraryDependencies ++= Seq(
      ...            ◁──┐ Dependencies
    ))                    go here.
```

Opens the ports — points to `dockerExposedPorts`

The open ports correspond to the following order:

1 Akka Management to expose the state of the nodes
2 Akka Remote to connect node actors with one another
3 The bet entity service
4 The market entity service
5 The wallet entity service
6 The bet projection query

Now you can publish the image by entering the following at the command line in the root directory of the Git repository:

```
sbt betting-house/docker:publish
```

You use deployment.yml and role.yml later.

STARTING THE APPLICATION

Create the Kubernetes namespace where you want the database—and later, the application—to run:

```
$ cd betting-house/k8s-deployment          ⟵——————  From the root folder
                                                      of the Git repository
$ kubectl create ns akka-cluster   ⟵—  Creates the cluster
$ kubectl apply -f postgres-containers-db-deployment.yml -n akka-cluster
$ kubectl apply -f postgres-containers-db-service.yml -n akka-cluster   ⟵——

Creates                                                     Creates a service
the database                                                to act as a proxy
```

The application.conf file you saw earlier had the following value for the JDBC connection:

```
url = "jdbc:postgresql://postgres-betting-db:5432/betting"
```

`postgres-betting-db` is the database's host name and is set in the two .yml files from the previous snippet so that when the application is deployed, it knows where to look.

Once the database is running, create the necessary tables in the database to store journal, tags, and events. You can connect to the database with a Kubernetes port-forward (http://mng.bz/81VW) and then run the SQL scripts as shown in the following snippets. Port forwarding redirects all requests from your local port 5432 to the same port in the Postgres pod:

```
$ kubectl get pod -n akka-cluster
NAME                                          READY   STATUS    RESTARTS   AGE
postgres-containers-db-85b9cf78b6-rw95h       1/1     Running   0          47s

$ kubectl port-forward \                                      Port-forwards
      pods/postgres-containers-db-85b9cf78b6-rw95h 5432:5432 \   directly to the
      -n akka-cluster                                          database pod

Finds the
database pod
```

Once port forwarding is set up, you can open another terminal and apply the SQL in the scripts from betting-house/common-deployment as follows:

```
$ psql -h 127.0.0.1 -d betting  -U betting -f bet-projection.sql          Prompts for the
$ psql -h 127.0.0.1 -d betting  -U betting -f akka-persistence.sql        password, which
$ psql -h 127.0.0.1 -d betting  -U betting -f akka-projection.sql         is "betting"
```

Now you can deploy the Kafka needed for the market projection using Strimzi, (https://strimzi.io/quickstarts), which provides a way to run an Apache Kafka cluster on Kubernetes with two lines of code:

```
kubectl create -f 'https://strimzi.io/install/latest?namespace=akka-
➥cluster' -n akka-cluster                                                         ◄────┐
kubectl apply -f https://raw.githubusercontent.com/strimzi/strimzi-kafka-
➥operator/main/examples/kafka/kafka-persistent-single.yaml -n akka-
➥cluster          ◄───┐  Creates an instance            Installs Strimzi in the
                        of Kafka                         Kubernetes cluster
```

Once the Kafka cluster is in place, you can create the topic for the market projection to write in. Going back to folder betting-house/k8s-deployment, enter the following:

```
kubectl apply -f topic.yml -n akka-cluster
```

With the database set up and Kafka running with the required topic for the market, you can deploy the application. Apply role.yml and then deployment.yml:

```
$ kubectl apply -f role.yml -n akka-cluster
$ kubectl apply -f deployment.yml -n akka-cluster
```

In a couple of minutes, you should have a running application:

```
$ kubectl get deploy -n akka-cluster

NAME                                    READY  STATUS    RESTARTS  AGE
my-deployment-name-849577696c-gtxv7     1/1    Running   0         49s
my-deployment-name-849577696c-mckqg     1/1    Running   0         49s
my-deployment-name-849577696c-zfqw4     1/1    Running   0         49s
```

Now you can create wallets, markets, and bets and check how the projections in the database and Kafka are populated. There are examples to follow in the README.md to interact with the application.

Summary

- The betting database projection was made accessible via an HTTP server by creating a query to access the result of the projection, using the same repository of the betting projection, and providing access to this query via the HTTP server.
- The events of the market were written into Kafka by creating a Kafka projection so they can be consumed by any process—for example, to settle the bets when a market is closed.
- You can run the betting house locally and in Kubernetes with almost the same configuration. The only major differences are the use of seed nodes in local and the use of Akka Cluster Bootstrap and Akka Management in Kubernetes.
- To deploy the application in Kubernetes, package it into a JAR and then into a Docker image. In the Kubernetes cluster, set the Role, RoleBinding, namespace, database, Kafka cluster, and Deployment.

Akka Streams, part 2

This chapter covers

- Processing elements efficiently
- Connecting from a stream to a database, a gRPC service, or an actor
- Dealing with exceptions
- Adding elements to a running stream after it starts

A book dealing only with Akka Streams would be no smaller than this entire book. It's an important topic, but it's too extensive to cover fully here. In this chapter, you learn the basics and the cases you will encounter most often in practice.

Akka Streams has three layers:

1. *The Flow API*—Creates simple linear flows that are taken from a source, transformed, and passed to a sink. A typical example is a source that reads Kafka, enriches the event by calling an external service, and publishes it back to Kafka with a sink.

2. *The GraphDSL*—At this level, you can combine multiple streams to create something more complex than a linear stream, namely a graph. An example

would be a flow that is fanned out into multiple streams so that in each of these streams, a different service enriches the event; later, all these streams are combined into one flow.

3   *The GraphStage API*—This is the lowest-level API, which the Akka Streams library uses to create GraphDSL and the Flow API. It is very unlikely that you will ever need such a low-level composition.

In this chapter, you learn about the Flow API, which you used in chapter 10. It has three types of stages: the `Source` is the producer, a `Sink` is the consumer, and, in the middle, the `Flow` is where the transformations take place.

> **NOTE** The source code for this chapter is available at www.manning.com/ books/akka-in-action-second-edition or https://github.com/franciscolopez sancho/akka-topics/tree/main/chapter16.

16.1 *Processing elements through services*

When you call external services, you may find yourself in either of two situations:

- You call a service that is local and CPU-bounded, which means its execution consumes the resources of the computer.
- You call an external service whose computation is independent of your running application: that is, the resources consumed by this service are independent of those of the running stream.

16.1.1 *CPU-bounded services*

In the following example, you call a computationally intensive method `def parsing-Doc(doc: String): String`, which takes 1–3 seconds to execute. This method is a fake parsing; all it does is calculate the factorial of a relatively large number and output how long it took:

```
class CPUBoundedSpec ... {
  ...

  "calling to a local function sync" should {
    "eventually return" in {

      val result: Future[Done] =
        Source(1 to 10)
          .map(each => parsingDoc(each.toString))    <—⌐ Expensive
          .run()                                        ⌐ operation

      Await.result(result, 30.seconds)
    }
  }
  ...
}
```

The source creates 10 elements and calls `parsingDoc(doc: String)` for each of them. It's worth noting that you must wait for the result as an Akka stream runs in a separate thread from the test. If you don't wait for the result, the test will finish before the stream finishes. Whether you wait or not, the stream does not stop until it has processed all the elements, you cancel it with a `Cancellable`, it throws an exception, or the JVM stops.

You can run this test and all the others shown later with the different `Spec`s in the chapter16 project. Each section has a specific `Spec` with a similar name. The tests are marked `ignore`; to run a test, change `ignore` to `in`, and then execute the following from the command line:

```
$ sbt
sbt:code> chapter16/testOnly *CPUBoundedSpec
```

Here's the output of processing the 10 elements:

```
1.914s
1.765s
1.726s
1.793s
1.758s
1.743s
1.767s
1.841s
1.735s
1.751s

[info] Run completed in 18 seconds, 373 milliseconds.
```

The outputs appear on the screen one by one, almost reluctantly. Execution took 18 seconds for 10 elements. That is too slow. You can easily improve it with a small change.

MAPASYNC

Instead of using `map`, which executes each element in sequence, you can parallelize the execution by using `mapAsync` and setting the degree of parallelism. It is important to know that this operator guarantees the order of results. The result of the first element, even if it takes longer than the second, keeps its order, and it is always handled to the next stage before the second. `mapAsync` has the signature `f: Out => Future[T]`; therefore, you need to wrap the call in a future, which needs an execution context:

```
class CPUBoundedSpec ... {
  ...
                                                          Number of
                                                       available threads
  implicit val ec =
    ExecutionContext.fromExecutor(Executors.newFixedThreadPool(12))   ◁─────┘

  "calling to a local function async" should {
    "eventually return 3 times faster" in {

      val result: Future[Done] =
        Source(1 to 10)
```

```
        .mapAsync(10)(each => Future(parsingDoc(each.toString)))    ⟵───────┐
        .run()
                                                          Sets parallelism and
    Await.result(result, 10.seconds)                      wraps it in a future
  }
}
...
}
```

We ran this on a laptop with 6 cores and 12 processes available for multithreading; hence the setting `Executors.newFixedThreadPool(12)`. This way, the function can run in a different thread than the caller (that is, the stream).

To run this test, set the previous test back to `ignore` and this last one to `in`, and then enter the following:

```
sbt:code> chapter16/testOnly *CPUBoundedSpec
```

This test has much better performance:

```
6.012s
6.064s
6.085s
6.093s
6.095s
6.1s
6.107s
6.12s
6.12s
6.127s

[info] Run completed in 7 seconds, 187 milliseconds.
```

Each line of output is printed almost simultaneously. The total duration of each call, about 6 seconds, is much longer than before. But all the calls started almost simultaneously, which makes a big difference. On the other hand, they took more time to compute because each call has only one thread to run `parseDoc`. However, overall performance is much better now that they run in parallel.

Since this laptop has hyperthreading, calculations can run up to 12 processes in parallel. *Hyperthreading* here means the computer can use each of its six real cores like two virtual cores. That results in 12 effective cores. But what if you have 100 elements instead of 10? Can you increase the number of threads to 100? You can, but you won't get anywhere near a linear increase in performance. You can effectively run only 12 processes in parallel, and if you have more threads, you pay the price of context switching.

16.1.2 *Non-CPU bounded services*

If the function you are calling is running on another machine, you can increase the parallelism much more because you are essentially waiting for the result. To simulate this scenario, the call to the external process is implemented by a scheduler that waits 1 second before returning the result. The machine on which you run the test is idle in the meantime. To ensure that the stream has the expected performance, you can specify a few seconds for the result in `onComplete`. If the stream is not `completed` by then, the test fails.

Listing 16.1   External filter

```
class CPUNonBoundedSpec ... {
  ...

  implicit val ec =
    ExecutionContext.fromExecutor(Executors.newFixedThreadPool(1000))     ⊲──┐
                                                                              Max number of
  "calling to a fake external service" should {                             futures in flight
    "be much faster" in {

      val init = System.currentTimeMillis

      val result: Future[Done] =
        Source(1 to 5000)                                          ┌─ Calls to the
          .mapAsync(1000)(each => externalFilter(each))    ⊲───────┘  external service
          .map(each => print1000th(each, init))     ⊲──┐  Prints each
          .run()                                       │  thousandth element

      Await.result(result, 6.seconds)
      Assert(result.isCompleted)
    }
  }
  ...
}
```

With this setup, which calls a CPU-unbounded service, you can increase parallelism as much as the JVM has memory. Each thread consumes about 512 KB. The other constraints are the service you call and how many requests it can handle. In this example, the scheduler has little work scheduling 5,000 items. All 5,000 requests can be executed in less than 6 seconds.

MAPASYNCUNORDERED

If the events you are processing do not require an order and can have different processing times, you will benefit from this operator. For example, suppose you call the database, and the query has different response times depending on the processing element. With `mapAsyncUnordered`, the queries that take longer will not block the pipe. The stream processes the faster queries first, and once they are done, it can send the result to the next stage and pick a new element.

The greater the difference in processing time, the greater the performance difference with `mapAsyncUnordered`. Figure 16.1 shows how `mapAsyncUnordered` removes faster elements from the stage and makes room for new elements.

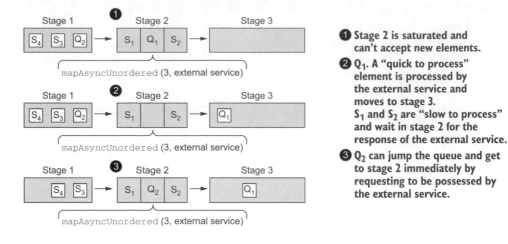

Figure 16.1   `mapAsyncUnordered` allowing new elements to be processed

CONNECTING TO EXTERNAL SERVICES

When you work with streams, you almost always need to call an external service: an HTTP service, a gRPC service, a database call, an FTP server, and many more. Let's look at some of these services.

In most streams, there is a moment when you need to enrich or validate the data through an HTTP call. To test this, you can use an Akka HTTP server where you check whether the quantity you pass it is greater than a number. You can find such a server in `HttpServer.scala`. The endpoint you have available is `/validate?quantity=[x]`, which responds with a validation class `Validated(accepted: Boolean)`. To start this server, enter this:

```
sbt "chapter16/runMain example.validation.HttpServer"
```

Once the server is running, you need the following:

- `RootJsonFormat`—So it can unmarshal the incoming result from the server.
- `Unmarshal`—To wrap the request and turn it into `Validated`.
- `Throttle`—The HTTP server has a maximum number of allowed connections. The default setting is HTTP `max-open-requests = 32`, from the reference .conf file of the `akka-http-core` library.

To call the external HTTP service, use an `Http().singleRequest` and an `HttpRequest`. To build the request, use `RequestBuilding.Get`, as follows:

```
class CPUNonBoundedSpec ... {
  ...
    ...
    Http().singleRequest(
      Get("http://localhost:8080/validate?quantity=" + each)))
  ...
}
```

All this belongs to the Akka HTTP client side. You can deserialize the response using `Unmarshal`, for which you need an implicit `jsonFormatX`. The service response is the `Validated(accepted: Boolean)` class, so you need a `jsonFormat1`:

```
import akka.http.scaladsl.marshallers.sprayjson.SprayJsonSupport._
import spray.json.DefaultJsonProtocol._

class CPUNonBoundedSpec ... {
  ...

  implicit val validatedFormat
      : RootJsonFormat[HttpServer.Validated] =
    jsonFormat1(HttpServer.Validated)
  ...
   Unmarshal(each).to[HttpServer.Validated])
  ...
}
```

You can see this tested in the following listing.

Listing 16.2 Calling an HTTP service from an Akka stream

```
import akka.http.scaladsl.client.RequestBuilding.Get
import akka.http.scaladsl.Http
import akka.http.scaladsl.unmarshalling.Unmarshal
import akka.http.scaladsl.marshallers.sprayjson.SprayJsonSupport._
import spray.json.DefaultJsonProtocol._

import example.streams.two.HttpServer

class CPUNonBoundedSpec ... {
  ...

  "calling to a real service" should {
    "be handle with throttle and mapAsync" in {

      implicit val validatedFormat
          : RootJsonFormat[HttpServer.Validated] =     ◁── RootJsonFormat used
        jsonFormat1(HttpServer.Validated)                   later to unmarshal

      val result: Future[Done] =
        Source(1 to 100)                              Throttles to the default max-open-
          .throttle(32, 1.second)   ◁── requests in Akka HTTP (that is, 32)
          .mapAsync(100)(each =>
            Http().singleRequest(
              Get("http://localhost:8080/validate?quantity=" + each)))
          .mapAsync(100)(each =>
            Unmarshal(each).to[HttpServer.Validated])  ◁── Asynchronously
          .run()                                           transforms each
                                                           response into
      Await.result(result, 5.seconds)                     Validated
    }
  }
  ...
}
```

Asynchronously calls the HTTP service

To run this test, enter the following:

```
sbt "chapter16/testOnly *SamplesSpec -- -z \"calling to a real service\""
```

CONNECTING TO AN EXTERNAL DATABASE

Normally you need to enrich the data you are processing. However, calling a service that, in turn, calls a database may cause too much latency. Let's see how to call the database directly.

You can use `mapAsync` or `mapUnorderedAsync`, as you have seen already. This example shows how to use `mapAsync` with the connection to the database so you get to know a complete use case. Let's look for the IDs of the containers you created in chapter 9.

Each time you added cargo, you created an entry in the journal. Now, in each entry, you can look for the ID of the container. In principle, this is simple—you have to wrap the database call in a future:

```
class CPUNonBoundedSpec ... {
  ...
                                                   Looks up the first 100
    val result = Source(1 to 100)    ⟵┘           entries of the journal
      .mapAsync(10)(each => Future(myGetPersistenceId(each)))
      .run()

  ...
}
```

This example uses the same database as in section 9.4, where you created a journal. To access it, start the database by opening the chapter09b folder at the command line and running `docker-compose up`. The name of the database is `containers`, and the username and password are the same. The data is listed in table 16.1. The contents may differ because they depend on the inputs you used.

Table 16.1   Data in the `containers` database in the `event_journal` table

ordering	persistence_id	sequence_number
3	scontainer-type-key|11	1
2	scontainer-type-key|9	2
5	scontainer-type-key|9	3
6	scontainer-type-key|11	4
7	scontainer-type-key|9	5
8	scontainer-type-key|9	6
9	scontainer-type-key|9	7

For the connection to the database, you can use `ScalikeJdbc` as you did for the projections in chapter 10. In that chapter, the specific implementation of the connection pool was `HikariCP`. This works analogously to SLF4J, where you must choose the logging implementation. `HikariCP` is to `ScalikeJdbc` what `logback-classic` is to SLF4J. In this example, use the `commons-dbcp2` included in the `ScalikeJdbc` library (http://mng.bz/o1Ny). To do so, set the JDBC and connection pool settings in your application.properties file:

```
# JDBC settings
db.containers.driver="org.postgresql.Driver"
db.containers.url="jdbc:postgresql://localhost:5432/containers"
db.containers.user="containers"
db.containers.password="containers"
# Connection Pool settings
db.containers.poolFactoryName="commons-dbcp2"
db.containers.poolInitialSize=5
db.containers.poolMaxSize=100          ◁——— To avoid overloading the
                                             database with connections
```

This `poolMaxSize` value should be chosen depending on the database type and settings. In a Postgres database, the default value is 100 (https://brandur.org/postgres-connections). `db.containers` makes it possible to refer to this database in the code with `Symbol("containers")` alone.

With these settings in place, you can read from the `containers` database using a basic database accessor in read-only mode:

```
import scalikejdbc.NamedDB

class CPUNonBoundedSpec ... {
  ...

  NamedDB(Symbol("containers")).readOnly
```

Add the query to retrieve the ID of each entry by searching for the sequence number:

```
      sql"select persistence_id from event_journal where sequence_number
➡ = ${seqNum}"
        .map(rs => rs.string("persistence_id"))
        .first
        .apply()
  ...
}
```

You select only the `persistence_id` field and, if present, the first result, because you are making a query for a `sequence_number` that occurs only once. The result can be only one row or none.

You can wrap all this in a method to use it from the stream:

```
class CPUNonBoundedSpec ... {
  ...

  def myGetPersistenceId(seqNum: Int): Option[String] = {
    val name: Option[String] = NamedDB(Symbol("containers")).readOnly {
      implicit session =>
        sql"select persistence_id from event_journal where sequence_number
➡ = ${seqNum}"
```

```
              .map(rs => rs.string("persistence_id"))
              .first
              .apply()
       }
     name
   }
   ...
}
```

Now you can test this by establishing the connection and using the method described earlier for the stream. As usual, you should close the connection afterward:

```
class CPUNonBoundedSpec ... {
  ...

  "connecting to a db" should {
    "work" in {

      DBs.setup(Symbol("containers"))          ⟵─┐ Creates the connection pool
                                                  └ out of the configuration

      def myGetPersistenceId...                         Calls the
                                                        database
      val result = Source(1 to 100)
        .mapAsync(100)(each => Future(myGetPersistenceId(each % 10)))  ⟵─┘
        .map(println)
        .run()

      Await.result(result, 5.seconds)
      DBs.close('containers)       ⟵─┐ Closes the
                                     └ connections
  }}

  ...
}
```

Now you can run the test. Depending on the elements in your database, the output looks something like this:

```
Some(scontainer-type-key|11)
Some(scontainer-type-key|9)
Some(scontainer-type-key|9)
Some(scontainer-type-key|11)
...
None
None
...
```

Next you learn how to connect to an actor from within an Akka stream. Actors are useful for maintaining state in a concurrent application. There are no race conditions, so you can focus on the business logic.

16.2 *Connecting to an actor*

You can use an actor for windowing in a stream. This is when you want to process a certain number of elements in groups defined by certain constraints. Usually the constraint is time—elements processed in a certain amount of time—but it can also be domain-oriented, opening and closing the window when specific elements are processed.

An example of these two possible constraints, time and domain, is a user session. You can open the window with the first interaction you receive from a user, indicating the session's beginning. Later, each additional item from that user is added to the window. Finally, when you get an item indicating that the user session is over, you can close the window and examine its contents to analyze it (for example, to check the length of the session). You may never get an event to close the session, but you can also use a time limit to close the window. You can build this logic into the actor that a stream uses.

To learn how streams and actors work together, let's look at a much simpler case, stripped down to the basics: an actor implementing a counter that responds to the stream with the counter value. This counter has a limit (it is capped). It could be used to limit calling an external service, as a kind of throttle. This actor is shown in the following listing.

Listing 16.3 Counter with a `max` value

```
object Cap {

    case class Increment(increment: Int, replyTo: ActorRef[Int])      <──┤ Protocol

    def apply(current: Int, max: Int): Behavior[Increment] = {        <──────────┐
      Behaviors.receiveMessage { message =>                            Initialization and
        message match {                                                state of the actor
          case Increment(increment, replyTo) =>
            if (current + increment > max) {      <──┐ Logic to avoid
              replyTo ! current                       │ surpassing the cap
              Behaviors.same
            } else {
              replyTo ! current + increment
              apply(current + increment, max)
            }
    }}}
}
```

This actor responds with the `current` value, increment included, on each `Increment` requested message. The value of `max` is set to `10`; if the current value is `8`, sending an `Increment(1)` responds with `9`.

To call an actor from a stream, `ask` via the `ActorFlow` class, which expects an actor referenced and a message:

```
import akka.stream.typed.scaladsl.ActorFlow

class ActorSpec ... {

    ...
```

```
ActorFlow.ask(ref)((elem: Int, replyTo: ActorRef[Int]) =>
  Cap.Increment(elem, replyTo))
...
}
```

The first part, `ask(ref)`, is simple: pass a reference to the actor you want to ask. The second part is not so simple. The signature is a function that converts a tuple into an actor's message: here, `(Int, ActorRef[Int]) => Increment`. The tuple is formed from an element of the stream—here, integers—and an `ActorRef`. This `ActorRef` is not the actor you are asking, but a proxy between the stream and that actor. It's a proxy that Akka creates for you. You may recall that this is also the case with a simple ask from one actor to another. Following is a test that creates a `Cap` actor and a flow with a source of integers that call this actor.

Listing 16.4   Connecting to an actor

```
class ActorSpec ... {
  ...

  "connecting to an actor from a stream" should {
    "send each element, wait and get back the answer from the actor" in {

      val ref = spawn(Cap(0, 3))       ◁──┤ Actor to ask
                                               ┌──┤ Flow that
      val askFlow: Flow[Int, Int, NotUsed] =   ◁──┘ represents asking
        ActorFlow.ask(ref)((elem: Int, replyTo: ActorRef[Int]) =>
          Cap.Increment(elem, replyTo))

      val result: Future[Done] = Source(1 to 10)
        .via(askFlow)                    ◁──┤ Flow usage
        .map(println)
        .run()

      Await.result(result, 1.seconds)
    }
  }
  ...
}
```

After you spawn the `Cap` actor, you can use its reference to `ask` with the `ActorFlow`.

> **TIP**   There is a shortened version of `ask` (syntactic sugar) that you should use. We used the previous notation for didactic reasons to show you the element and the proxy actor. But you can forget the tuple and pass the asking message to the constructor: `ActorFlow.ask(ref)(Cap.Increment)`. The compiler can derive the rest based on the message constructor.

It is worth noting that `ActorFlow.ask` has a parallelism of 2. If you send a message with a relatively high payload, you should consider greater parallelism, like this:

```
ActorFlow.ask(10)(ref)(Cap.Increment)
```

16.3 Dealing with exceptions

The supervision model in Akka Streams is the same as you learned about in previous chapters for basic behaviors, but its notation is a bit different. When you deal with an exception in a stream, you can use `recover` to set the supervision strategy. However, with `recover`, you only get the last element before the stream stops. This is similar to an actor that stops by default once it gets an exception.

But before you add recovery, you should `log` all risky operations in your stream. If you don't add logging, you won't know whether an exception was thrown. Without logging, the stream will be stopped, but you won't get any information about it. The following listing adds a log to a source that fails often.

Listing 16.5 Exception caused by an element

```
class ExceptionsSpec ... {
  ...
  "an Exception" should {
    "stop the stream and log 'tried riskyHandle'" in {

      def riskyHandler(elem: Int): Int =        ◁─┐ Handler that fails
        100 / elem                                │ at elem = 0

      val result =
        Source(-1 to 1)
          .map(riskyHandler)
          .log("tried riskyHandler")       ◁─┤ Adds a log
          .map(println)
          .run()

      Await.result(result, 1.seconds)
    }
  }
  ...
}
```

This code outputs `-100` once and then stops the stream, logging the exception caused by dividing by zero:

```
-100
[...][ERROR][...] - [tried riskyHandler] Upstream failed.
java.lang.ArithmeticException: / by zero
    at examples.streams.two.SampleSpec.riskyHandler$1(SampleSpec.scala:247)
    ...
```

In this case, you can use `recover` to replace the exception with a default value that is generated instead:

```
class ExceptionsSpec ... {
  ...
        Source(-1 to 1)
          .map(riskyHandler)
          .log("tried riskyHandler")
```

```
        .recover {
          case e: ArithmeticException => 0        ◁──┐ Final element
        }                                             │ of the stream
        .run()
    ...
}
```

This results in `0` when the `ArithmeticException` is thrown, giving the following output:

```
-100
0
[...][ERROR][...] - [tried riskyHandler] Upstream failed.
java.lang.ArithmeticException: / by zero
      at examples.streams.two.SampleSpec.riskyHandler$2(SampleSpec.scala:264)
        ...
```

But that's probably not what you want, and you have alternatives.

16.3.1 *Alternative 1: Deciders*

You can add a decider to restart or resume the stream. This way, you can keep the stream running while dropping the messages that led to the exceptions:

```
import akka.stream.Supervision
class ExceptionsSpec ... {
  ...

  val decider: Supervision.Decider = {
    case _: ArithmeticException => Supervision.Resume
    case _                      => Supervision.Stop
  }
  ...
}
```

These unprocessable messages are dropped without further notice. To add the decider to the stream, add it as an attribute of the stream:

```
import akka.stream.ActorAttributes

class ExceptionsSpec ... {
  ...

  Source...
  ...
  .withAttributes(ActorAttributes.supervisionStrategy(decider))

  ...
}
```

To test both options of the `decider`, you can raise two different exceptions with the risky handler as follows:

```
class ExceptionsSpec ... {
  ...
```

```
def riskyHandler(elem: Int): Int = {
    if (elem > 2)
      throw new IllegalArgumentException(
        "no higher than 2 please")
      100 / elem
    }
  ...
}
```

And you can test this in a stream as shown in the next listing.

Listing 16.6   Adding supervision to a stream

```
class ExceptionsSpec ... {
  ...

  "an Exception" should {
    "be possible to overcome ArithmeticException" in {

      val result =
        Source(-1 to 3
          .map(riskyHandler)
          .log("tried riskyHandler")
          .map(println)
          .withAttributes(
            ActorAttributes.supervisionStrategy(decider))     ⟵─┐ Ad hoc supervision
          .run()                                                 │ using the decider

      Await.result(result, 1.seconds)
    }
  }
  ...
}
```

The results are as follows:

```
-100
100
50
[2022-07-04 19:25:50,848] [ERROR] [akka.stream.Materializer] []
➥[SampleSpec-akka.actor.default-dispatcher-3] - [riskyHandler] Upstream
➥failed.
java.lang.IllegalArgumentException: no higher than 2 please
```

16.3.2   *Alternative 2: Modeling exceptions as data*

You can model the exception as a class instead of handling it directly in the stream. This is the recommended approach for streams and programming in general. Create a class that wraps the `ArithmeticException` and a method that handles it:

```
class ExceptionsSpec ... {                                    Business class to
  ...                                                          wrap exceptions

  case class Result(value: Int, isValid: Boolean, message: String = "")   ⟵─┘
```

```
def properHandler(elem: Int): Result =        Method modeling
  try {                                        ArithmeticException as data
    Result(100 / elem, true)
  } catch {
    case ex: ArithmeticException =>
      Result(elem, false, s"failed processing [$elem] with $ex.")
  }
...
}
```

If you convert the result you had before (an `Int` or an `ArithmeticException`) into a `Result`, you are in a much better situation. If a method can throw exceptions, that is a problem that the risky method should solve, not the stream or another client.

When you work with streams, they are often sent to one sink or another depending on the content of an element. For example, if the element contains an exception, you may want to divert it to another sink.

16.3.3   *divertTo*

A common scenario is that depending on an element's content, whether it is valid or not, you send the element to a different Kafka topic. In one of these topics, you keep the successfully processed elements, and in the other, the invalid ones. This can be achieved in several ways, one of which is `divertTo`.

The following is a simplification of the original signature:

```
def divertTo(that: Sink[Out], when: Out => Boolean): Flow[Out].
```

Using the previous example's code, `Out` corresponds to the `Result`. In the following listing, the `Result` is diverted if it is invalid—that is, `.isValid` is false.

Listing 16.7   `divertTo` over `Result`

```
class ExceptionsSpec ... {
  ...
                                                   Sink for invalid
    val sink1 = Sink.foreach { each: Result =>     Result elements
      println(
        s"${each.value} has been diverted. Caused by: ${each.message}")
    }
                                                   Sink for valid
    val sink2 = Sink.foreach { each: Result =>     Result elements
      println(s"${each.value} has been successfully processed")
    }

    Source(-1 to 1)
      .map(properHandler)
      .divertTo(sink1, !_.isValid)
      ...                             More processing
      .to(sink2)                      (ignored here)
      .run()
  ...
}
```

One of the advantages of `divertTo` is that once you know you can divert to another sink, you don't have to perform any further operations on that element. The stream becomes more efficient if you send it to its final destination as quickly as possible. The sinks in the example only print, but with everything you know by now, you can easily perform an upsert against a database, send to an HTTP service, or write to a Kafka topic.

Exceptions sometimes occur not within a stream but rather at its source. That is another problem.

16.3.4 *Restarting the source*

One of the most common scenarios when working with streams is creating the source from an external service, an HTTP service, or a Kafka topic. But if this external source is unavailable for some time, your stream will fail.

So far, you haven't seen a way to automatically restart a source. Let's lay the groundwork. The plan is to use a gRPC service from a source so that even if the service shuts down or crashes, the stream can continue once the service comes back online. The following service is in the chapter16 project in the locator.proto file.

Listing 16.8 `LocatorService` locator.proto file

```
import "google/protobuf/empty.proto";        ◁─┐  Input type
                                                │  import
message Location {          ◁─┤ Output type
    double lat = 1;
    double lon = 2;
}
                                                       Service returning
                                                       a stream per call
service LocatorService {
    rpc Follow(google.protobuf.Empty) returns (stream Location) {}   ◁─┘
}
```

This service, named `Follow`, provides a stream of `Location` elements. Don't pay much attention to the implementation of this service because it is mainly a dummy. The idea is that a car has this `LocatorServer` built in and passes its latitude and longitude to the service when the car is started. From there, the service changes its latitude and longitude depending on the car's movement.

For simplicity, you pass only the latitude to the service at startup, and the car's movement is simulated to increase linearly over time. It follows the same longitude as if driving in a straight line.

Start the server from the repository root directory by entering the following at the command line:

```
sbt "chapter16/runMain example.locator.grpc.LocatorServer 1"
```

The value 1 at the end of the command is the initial latitude of the `Location`.

The purpose of this dummy service is to show you two things in practice: `RestartSource` and a gRPC service with a stream as output, also called *server streaming* gRPC. You may remember the example of a unary call in chapter 11, where one request generated one response. Now one request generates a stream of responses—an infinite stream.

Here's how the service works, with a call to the service and its responses. You can find the implementation in the `LocatorServiceImpl` in the Git repository:

```
$ grpcurl -plaintext localhost:8080 LocatorService/Follow          ◁─┐ Call to the
                                                                      │ service
{                              ◁─┐ Infinite stream of responses,
  "lat": 1,                       │ one element per second
  "lon": -3.701101
}
{
  "lat": 2,
  "lon": -3.701101
}
{
  "lat": 3,
  "lon": -3.701101
}                             ┌ More responses
...                        ◁──┘ not printed here
```

This output shows how a call to the service produces an infinite stream of responses. You get a stream that produces one element per second.

Now let's see how a source that can be restarted behaves when you stop the service. The test consumes this service for 90 seconds, giving you time to stop and restart the gRPC service before the test is finished. The test has a client for the locator service and a `RestartSource` that uses that service and can cope with the service being down.

To create the client, you need the settings and the client itself. With the protobuf file and Akka gRPC, you get a client when the code is compiled. A `LocatorService-Client` and the settings are available via the Akka gRPC module `GrpcClient-Settings`:

```
import example.locator.grpc.LocatorServiceClient
import akka.grpc.GrpcClientSettings

class LocatorServiceSpec ... {
  ...

  "A Source" should {
    "be able to keep consuming from a failed and restored service" ...

      val clientSettings =                          ◁─┐ Settings to connect
        GrpcClientSettings                             │ to the locator service
          .connectToServiceAt("127.0.0.1", 8080)
          .withTls(false)

      val client: LocatorService =         ◁─┐ Creates a client for
        LocatorServiceClient(clientSettings)  │ the locator service
    ...
}
```

The source is similar for the restart. You need the restart settings and the client. This time, the client calls the `follow` method from the protobuf definition. As you have seen, external calls are wrapped in futures; in this case, the future needs to be wrapped in a `futureSource`:

```
import akka.stream.scaladsl.RestartSource
import akka.stream.RestartSettings
import example.locator.grpc.{IoT, Location}
...

class LocatorServiceSpec ... {
  ...

      val restartSettings = RestartSettings(        ◁ Restart settings
        minBackoff = 1.seconds,
        maxBackoff = 3.seconds,
        randomFactor = 0.2).withMaxRestarts(30, 3.minutes)

      val restartSource = RestartSource.withBackoff(restartSettings) { () =>
        Source.futureSource {
          val responseStream: Source[Location, NotUsed] =
            client.follow()        ◁ RPC client creates a source
          Future(responseStream)
        }
      }
  ...
}
```

The `minBackoff` is the initial time before the source tries again. If it fails, another second is added each time until the `maxBackoff` is reached. The `.withMaxRestarts` option sets two values, where the first of the two values reached becomes the end of the attempts. The first number is the absolute number of retries, and the second is the duration since the first fail. The `randomFactor` prevents multiple possible clients of the service from bouncing back at the same time. Here you have a deviation of 20% over the time of each retry.

The RPC call doesn't have input, and the response is a `Location`:

```
rpc  Follow(google.protobuf.Empty) returns (stream Location) {}
```

The complete test is shown in the next listing.

Listing 16.9 `RestartSource` consuming a gRPC service for 90 seconds

```
class LocatorServiceSpec ... {
  ...

  "A Source" should {
    "be able to keep consuming from a failed and restored service" in {

      val clientSettings =      ...
                                            Creates an instance
      val client: LocatorService =      ◁  of the gRPC service
```

```
        LocatorServiceClient(clientSettings)

    val restartSettings = RestartSettings(
      minBackoff = 1.seconds,
      maxBackoff = 3.seconds,
      randomFactor = 0.2).withMaxRestarts(30, 3.minutes)
    val restartSource = RestartSource.withBackoff(restartSettings) {
            ...
                client.follow()        ⟵─┐  Creates a RestartSource
            ...                           │  consuming from the gRPC service
    }

    val result =                    ⟵─┐
      restartSource                    │
        .map(println)                  │  Runs and prints
        .run()                         │  responses from the
                                       │  service for 90 seconds
    Await.result(result, 90.seconds) ⟵─┘
  }
 }
 ...
}
```

After you start the test, you can let the service run for a few seconds and then turn it off. The output of the test starts with a location with latitude 1 that is passed as input when the service is started. Once the service is stopped, the consumer finds the service UNAVAILABLE:

```
Location(1.0,-3.701101)
Location(2.0,-3.701101)
Location(3.0,-3.701101)
Location(4.0,-3.701101)
[11:09:22,525] [WARN] [akka.stream.scaladsl.RestartWithBackoffSource] []
➥[SampleSpec-akka.actor.default-dispatcher-3] - Restarting stream due
➥to failure [1]: io.grpc.StatusRuntimeException: UNAVAILABLE: io exception
    ...
[11:09:23,679] [WARN] [akka.stream.scaladsl.RestartWithBackoffSource] []
➥[SampleSpec-akka.actor.default-dispatcher-3] - Restarting stream due
➥to failure [2]: io.grpc.StatusRuntimeException: UNAVAILABLE: io exception
    ...
```

You can see the first four elements of the stream being consumed and then the RestartSource—unable to continue consuming from the gRPC service—attempting to restart the stream but failing due to an error [1], where [1] stands for the first restart attempt (the listing shows two). There will be more of these in the log, each a second later than the previous one, with a maximum of 3 seconds difference: 1 second between [1] and [2], 2 seconds between [2] and [3], and 3 seconds from then on, as specified in the restart settings:

```
class LocatorServiceSpec ... {
  ...
```

```
      val restartSettings = RestartSettings(
        minBackoff = 1.seconds,
        maxBackoff = 3.seconds,
        randomFactor = 0.2).withMaxRestarts(30, 3.minutes)
  ...
}
```

> **NOTE** You may have noticed that the time difference between two consecutive retries is not exactly 1 or 2 seconds. This is because of the `random-Factor`.

After a few seconds, you can restart the service with the following command:

```
sbt "chapter16/runMain example.locator.grpc.LocatorServer 10"
```

Once the gRPC service continues serving `Locations`, the result in `RestartSource` is as expected. It picks the initial element of the service, and in the following seconds, the test continues printing the locations consumed:

```
[11:09:23,679] [WARN] [akka.stream.scaladsl.RestartWithBackoffSource] []
➥[SampleSpec-akka.actor.default-dispatcher-3] - Restarting stream due
➥to failure ...
...                                             ⊲——┤ More failing retries
Location(10.0,-3.701101,UnknownFieldSet(Map()))  ⊲—┐ Consumes one
Location(11.0,-3.701101,UnknownFieldSet(Map()))    │ element per second
Location(12.0,-3.701101,UnknownFieldSet(Map()))
...               ⊲——┐ More consecutive
                     │ Location elements
```

Let's go into a little more detail about how the `RestartSource` is used in combination with the gRPC service:

```
class LocatorServiceSpec ... {
  ...

      val restartSource = RestartSource.withBackoff(settings) { () =>
        Source.futureSource {
          val responseStream: Source[Location, NotUsed] =
            client.follow()
          Future(responseStream)
      }}
  ...
}
```

Once you pass the settings to the `RestartSource`, you need a source that deals with futures—hence the name `Source.futureSource`. After all, you are calling a service that responds asynchronously. Inside the `Source.futureSource`, you call the client's `follow` method, which is generated by Akka gRPC and returns a `Source[Location, NotUsed]`. Finally, you wrap this call in a future (an asynchronous call), and with it, you build the `Source.futureSource`.

Let's close this chapter with another common use case: adding elements to the source of a stream after the stream has been started.

16.4   *Adding elements dynamically to a stream*

Some streams do not have a source completely defined at the beginning. Instead, elements can be added dynamically. You can get a reference to the stream and pass it around so different parts of your program add new elements.

For example, suppose you have an initial set of elements that you want to process to create an inventory (a list of products). These initial items are fixed when the program starts, but you want to be able to add more later. To do so, you can use a `Source.queue`.

The API consists of two basic elements: the queue itself, `Source.queue`, which creates the `SourceQueue` that you can then pass around; and the materialization, `toMat`, to extract the `SourceQueue` object from the `Source.queue` method. Once you have the queue, you can add elements to it using `queue.offer(elem: T)`. This is shown in a test in the following listing.

Listing 16.10   Creating a `Source.queue`

```
class QueueSpec ... {
  ...

  "Source queue" should {
    "allow adding elements to a stream" in {          Max elements to hold
                                                      before they are
                                                      processed downstream
      val bufferSize = 10            ◄──────────────

      val queue: BoundedSourceQueue[Int] =
        Source.queue[Int](          ◄──   Creates the BoundedSourceQueue
          bufferSize                      that drops messages when
        )                                 overflowing
        .map(x => 2 * x)
        .toMat(Sink.foreach(x => println(s"processed $x")))(Keep.left)   ◄──
        .run()
                                                              Materialization
        (1 to 10).map(x => queue.offer(x))
    }
  }
  ...
}
```

You need to pass a `bufferSize` to the `Source.queue`. After all, it is a queue, and it has limits. When the buffer is full, elements are dropped, depending on your strategy. You can drop the new elements added to the stream or existing elements from the buffer.

The signature is this:

```
Source.queue[T](bufferSize: Int): Source[T, BoundedSourceQueue[T]]
```

You need to use its materialized value to get the `BoundedSourceQueue`. You may recall that `Source[T, NotUsed]` is a common form of many sources. But here—similar to `Source.tick` creating `Source[T, Cancellable]`—you get a `Source[T, BoundedSourceQueue[T]]`, so you need the materialization value coming from the

Source.queue. If you picture all the stages one after the other in a single line, the Source is to the left of the Sink.

The output of the previous test is as follows. Note that the buffer never fills up:

```
processed 2
processed 4
processed 6
processed 8
processed 10
processed 12
processed 14
processed 16
processed 18
processed 20
```

If you reduce the buffer to 2, only the first two elements of the previous output are printed. Before the stream starts processing the first element, the buffer becomes full and drops the subsequent elements. Only 1 and 2 are processed.

To be more specific about the strategy for dropping elements, you can pass OverflowStrategy to a SourceQueue instead of using a BoundedSourceQueue. The OverflowStrategy.dropNew is the implicit strategy of the BoundedSource-Queue. To pass OverflowStrategy.dropHead, you can use a SourceQueue. There are many other strategies, including dropNew and dropTail.

To overflow the buffer with just 10 elements, add .throttle(elements: Int, per: java.time.Duration) to the stream. Creating a SourceQueue by setting the OverflowStrategy and throttling the streams looks like this:

```
class QueueSpec ... {
  ...

  val bufferSize = 4
                                            │ SourceQueue instead of
  val queue: SourceQueue[Int] = Source  ◁──┘ BoundedSourceQueue
      .queue[Int](
        bufferSize,                         │ Strategy when the buffer gets full:
        OverflowStrategy.dropHead  ◁────────┘ drops head elements (oldest)
      )
      .throttle(1, 100.millis)
      .map(x => 2 * x)
      .toMat(Sink.foreach(x => println(s"processed $x")))(Keep.left)
      .run()

  (1 to 10).map(x => queue.offer(x))   ◁──┐ Adds elements
  ...                                      │ to the queue
}
```

Added throttle to show the buffer getting full (annotation pointing to `.throttle(1, 100.millis)`)

The output of is as follows:

```
processed 2
processed 4
processed 14
processed 16
```

```
processed 18
processed 20
```

It is important to note that the output is not deterministic. It will behave the same for a few elements, but race conditions apply. The larger the set, the more room to see the not-deterministic behavior of the overflow strategy. In this example, with this output, the first two elements are processed and then the buffer fills up, dropping the older elements until only the last ones remain.

The `queue.offer` method returns a value that you might be interested in. The following example shows two of the possible return values:

```
class QueueSpec ... {
  ...

  (1 to 10)                                                    If offer returns
    .map(x => {                                             Enqueued, prints
      queue.offer(x).map {                                       "enqueued"
        case QueueOfferResult.Enqueued => println(s"enqueued $x")     ◀
        case QueueOfferResult.Dropped  => println(s"dropped $x")}})   ◀
  ...
}                                                      If offer returns Dropped,
                                                            prints "dropped"
```

If you change in the previous example to `OverflowStrategy.dropNew` and add the `queue.offer`, you get this:

```
enqueued 1
processed 2
enqueued 2
enqueued 3
enqueued 4
enqueued 5
enqueued 6
dropped 7
dropped 8
dropped 9
dropped 10
processed 4
processed 6
processed 8
processed 10
processed 12
```

Here you can see which items are queued and which are dropped. For a client pushing data into a stream, it can be important to check whether an item was dropped so it can try to offer the item again.

Summary

- Elements can be efficiently transformed depending on whether the service is CPU-bounded. `mapAsync` provides more parallelism when the service is not CPU-bounded, and `mapAsyncUnordered` provides more performance when the processing time per element has a high variance.

- You can call a database or HTTP endpoint within the stage of a stream with any `*Async` operator. You can use the previous stage as input for the call and the following stage for processing the response.

- Stream from an actor using `ActorFlow.ask` to ask the actor and process the response in the next stage.

- Add elements to an already-running stream using `Source.queue`. With this operator, you can keep a reference to the source to add elements anytime and anywhere in your application.

- Handling exceptions with `recover` only processes one last message before shutting down the stream. You should model exceptions as data to avoid this scenario and later use `divertTo` to change the final output of the elements. That way, the properly processed elements go to one sink and the others to another sink.

- Create sources that are restarted after a failure so the stream continues to consume items from the source after recovery. Depending on your strategy, you can drop the offending messages or treat the exceptions as data, modifying them to become like any other message in the stream.

appendix A
Setting up

This appendix walks you through installing the tools used to follow some of the examples in this book.

A.1 Installing the JDK

You need a JDK. I recommend installing SDKMAN! and, with it, the JDK. SDK-MAN! also facilitates your sbt installation.

A.1.1 Installing SDKMAN!

Go to https://sdkman.io/install, and follow the instructions. If you have Windows, you may prefer to skip this step.

A.1.2 Installing Java

Once SDKMAN! is installed, you can install Java with the following command:

```
$ sdk install java 11.0.2-open
```

You don't necessarily have to install this particular version. To install another, find the SDK you want to install with `sdk list java` and `sdk install java x.y.z-version`. If you have Windows, you can install the Oracle standard JDK (https://www.oracle.com/java/technologies) or the OpenJDK (https://openjdk.org).

A.2 Installing sbt

With SDKMAN!, you can install sbt with `sdk install sbt`. If you have Windows, follow the instructions at https://www.scala-sbt.org/download.html.

A.3 Installing Docker

You need Docker to create the images to run the Akka clusters in Kubernetes and spin up the databases for the Akka persistence examples. Go to https://docs.docker.com/get-docker and follow the instructions.

A.4 Installing curl

You can use curl to interact with the Akka HTTP port. Go to https://curl.se/download .html, and follow the instructions.

A.5 Installing grpcurl

You can use `grpcurl` to interact with Akka gRPC ports. Go to https://github.com/ fullstorydev/grpcurl#installation, and follow the instructions.

A.6 Installing kcat

You can use kcat to interact with Kafka when dealing with Alpakka connectors or Akka projection. Go to https://github.com/edenhill/kcat#install, and follow the instructions.

A.7 Installing the AWS CLI

You can use the AWS command-line interface (CLI) to get credentials to upload files to Amazon when testing the Alpakka S3 connection. Go to https://docs.aws.amazon .com/cli/latest/userguide/getting-started-install.html and follow the instructions.

A.8 Installing Minikube

You can use Minikube to deploy an Akka cluster in a Kubernetes cluster. Go to https://k8s-docs.netlify.app/en/docs/tasks/tools/install-minikube and follow the instructions.

appendix B
Microservices and architectural principles

Microservices, as actors, are autonomous entities that come in systems. In this sense, they can also be considered a model or architectural design. Microservice architectures can be considered a subset of service-oriented architecture (SOA)—another buzzword. This appendix describes some valuable features of this architecture and additional functionality you can use when designing distributed systems.

B.1 Do microservices exist?

One way to understand a thing is to follow its name to see when and how it is used. Figure B.1 shows the usage of the word *microservices* in Google Trends: the term has been widely used since late 2014, declined some in 2020, and now (2023) seems to be on the rise again. There could be several reasons.

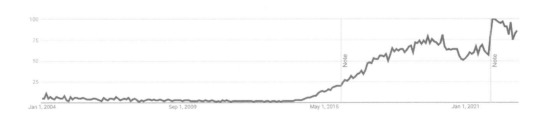

Figure B.1 Microservices topic worldwide since 2004 (Source: Google Trends)

I tend to think that a microservice is just a good, well-designed service. We increasingly say *microservice* when referring to what used to be called a *service*. That could be why the term is on the rise again; but whatever the reason, the question remains: What do we mean when we say *microservice*?

You could look for the answer in a wiki or a blog, but even writing a definition has been tried so many times that each new attempt destroys the credibility of the answer, if not the question itself. So let's try this: let's forget about microservices for a while and look for the characteristics that are important in developing distributed systems. You probably won't be surprised that some of these characteristics are often included in the definition of microservices.

To find these ideas, let's start from the beginning and consider the characteristics of past distributed systems that we still consider important in the development of systems today. I am not a historian, but I believe the exercise will be fruitful.

B.1.1 Let's bound a context

The term *middleware* was first used in a 1968 NATO Science Committee report (Peter Naur and Brian Randell, eds.) to describe "the software we put in the middle to serve as cogs in a system." Figure B.2 shows the diagram from that report.

It was not until the 1980s that middleware became mainstream. In the early 1980s, the telecommunications company AT&T developed Tuxedo, a platform based on the recently created middleware specification with messaging at its core. This architecture was called message-

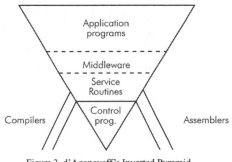

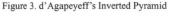

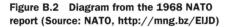

Figure 3. d'Agapeyeff's Inverted Pyramid

Figure B.2   Diagram from the 1968 NATO report (Source: NATO, http://mng.bz/EIJD)

oriented middleware (MOM). The problem of integrating different applications or systems was already pervasive. During this decade, a group of universities in the United States built their own Computer Science Network (CSNET) because the recently created ARPANET was only accessible to the U.S. Department of Defense. These were some of the first steps toward greater integration. With the introduction of protocols such as DNS and TCP/IP on an international level, the internet was born, and numerous internet service providers (ISPs) soon added their resources to the network. At the end of the decade, Tim Berners-Lee, working at CERN, invented nothing less than the World Wide Web.

During this prolific decade, the luxurious problem of distributed computing emerged in the enterprise. Companies of all types were faced with the possibility of connecting multiple applications across the network to create larger applications. To stay competitive, they decided to multiply the value of their data.

In the early 1990s, more middleware ideas emerged. Common Object Request Broker Architecture (CORBA) and its commercial counterpart, the Distributed

Component Object Model (DCOM), became representatives of middleware for remote procedure calls (RPCs), both specifications that define how objects can interact between programs on different computers.

In the early 2000s, the idea behind middleware became known as enterprise application integration (EAI). As David S. Linthicum put it, "It is, at its foundation, a response to decades of creating distributed monolithic, single-purpose applications" (*Enterprise Application Integration*, Addison-Wesley Professional, 2003). Different applications ran on different systems—mainframes, UNIX servers, NT servers—and they needed each other. They benefited from cross-pollination

In the same spirit, the Web Services specification was launched in 2002. The RPC solutions of that time were inadequate because, among other things, communication was mostly only allowed via HTTP, and CORBA communicates via TCP/IP. Even more fundamental, however, is the fallible nature of network communications. In their abstraction, RPC interfaces did not contain the necessary ideas to deal with latency, concurrency, and partial failures (see Jim Waldo et al., "A Note on Distributed Computing," Sun Microsystems Laboratories, 1994, http://mng.bz/NmJx). Gregor Hohpe pointed out that when treating remote calls as local calls, "RPC is not an abstraction, it is an illusion" (YOW! Singapore 2017, http://mng.bz/DZJg). And recently he told me that nowadays, he would even rephrase and say "RPCs in their attempt at abstraction" to underline that the abstraction failed.

But all the work was not in vain. Some of the CORBA ideas were combined with the new XML standard in the form of an interface definition language (IDL) to define messages and their possible operations. As a result, the W3C and some other organizations joined forces to create the Web Services specification (https://www.w3.org/2002/ws/history.html).

Another common term in the software industry around 2000 was *enterprise service bus* (ESB). In the same year as the Web Services specification, Roy Schulte, the most senior analyst at Gartner at the time, coined the term ESB. If it can't send and receive SOAP/HTTP messages or support Web Service Definition Language (WSDL), it's not an ESB (see Jason Stamper, blog, 2005, https://techmonitor.ai/techonology/esb_inventor_ri). However, this does not complete the description of an ESB. Another important feature is the message bus (also called a *broker*), which is used for data transmission on the platform. The ESB design thus includes two types of communication: peer-to-peer via web services and message passing via the message bus.

It would be incomplete to define ESBs without mentioning the features of service discovery, routing, security, and monitoring. In 2003, Gartner coined the term *service-oriented architecture* (SOA); this architecture "produces interoperable, modular systems that are easier to use and maintain" (http://mng.bz/lJgR), while in the background, Simple Object Access Protocol (SOAP) became its de facto implementation.

To shed light on the characteristics of this architecture, SOA attempts to solve three problem dimensions: complexity, which increases as a system reaches the top of an organization, while usability for end users decreases; stability, because a platform must be flexible to create what different users need, but it must be stable as a whole and provide the glue for its parts; and last, but definitely not least, data sharing. Data must be able to be consumed but also secured. Not everyone should have access to everything. And this problem of data discovery and use is exacerbated not only by data within the organization but also by data sent to and from outside the organization. Thanks to the invention of the World Wide Web in recent decades, this door to the outside world has been opened wider than ever.

The idea of interoperability is almost ubiquitous in SOA, where abstractions in departmental applications enable the flow of valuable information. There are echoes here of EAI and, of course, middleware. Figure B.3 shows an SOA representation from this era.

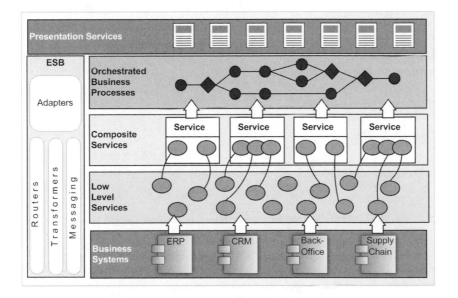

Figure B.3   SOA architecture circa 2005 (Source: Open Source SOA by Jeff Davis, Manning, 2009, http://mng.bz/Blwl)

As you can see on the left, it is no coincidence that an ESB is interwoven with an SOA. It comes full circle, like a car, which is a mix of many inventions. An ESB has the idea of EAI as middleware for the enterprise, with the SOA implemented in SOAP and connected to MOM. From the SOA perspective, it would be too limiting to build a services-based system without a message broker. You can look at the interoperability problem through the old lens of EAI, SOA, or ESB. Nowadays, we have moved from SOAP to REST or the shiny gRPC. Queues are everywhere. Maybe Kafka is the new kid on the block. But the problems are still there, and most of the new solutions are not radically new.

But who could have known? In 2009, "SOA is dead: long live services" (Anne Thomas Manes, blog, http://mng.bz/dJn1) was groundbreaking news. Manes rightly stated in her blog that EAIs are not flexible enough—that as a monolith, they hinder development, and that the culprits are IT systems. They are the basis of the monolith and must be radically changed. But even if the word *SOA* is dead (see figure B.4), the call for service-oriented architecture is stronger than ever. Manes saw this clearly.

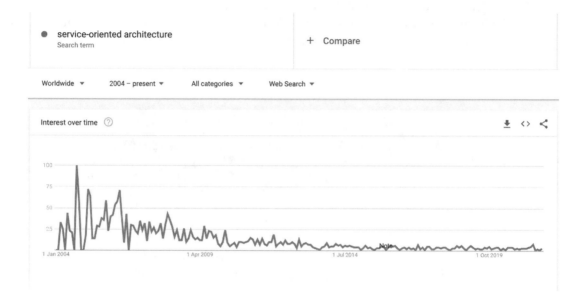

Figure B.4   Usage of the term *service-oriented architecture* (Source: Google Trends)

SOA was dying, but services are here to stay. When we talk about microservices today, we refer to the key features of a service-oriented architecture. These have not disappeared. All the features that came out of early middleware are still there; we need integration in general, interoperability, and governance.

B.1.2   *Characteristics of better services: What were we missing?*

The big idea that paved the way for an entire dimension of solutions was waiting to be discovered. It is often said that the UNIX philosophy is "do one thing and do it well," and in some ways, microservices follow this idea of coherence in their design. But this is not unique to the microservices architecture; SOA had this mentality from the beginning. The key was the same idea, but in a different dimension: the infrastructure.

The fundamental trigger is containerization. Containers arise from the idea of jailing an operative system in a prison by dividing it into folders that become cells in which each user can act like a root. They are not root, but within the confines of their "prison," they behave as such. The idea was first implemented in 1979 in version 7 of

UNIX with the chroot command. It was integrated into BSD with some extensions in 1982 and matured into FreeBSD in 2000. Only then did it have a reliable degree of isolation.

In 2006, a company called Joyent created the infrastructure to provide containers to its users but received little attention, although it continued to innovate in this space. That same year, AWS introduced EC2. In 2013, dotCloud, which was working in this area and failing as a company, opened its code and partnered with Red Hat. The company's new name was Docker, Inc. The industry responded positively and embraced containers as a whole, which changed everything. Containers became the "new black."

The jail had room for the essentials that EAIs, ESBs, and different SOAs craved: infrastructure composition in two dimensions and adding horizontal growth to the old vertical scaling. EAIs were installed as a whole, as were the business applications installed within them. If the application was a monolith, the servers running it were even bigger monoliths. For example, applications such as Java Enterprise Application aRchives (EARs) that contained Web Application ARchives (WARs) and Java ARchives (JARs) had to be deployed entirely on a single server, such as WebLogic. These servers contained multiple services that had different hardware requirements. Some were very compute-intensive and needed high CPU power, while others needed mostly memory. Scaling was vertical—a larger machine for the single server. Thanks to containers, it was now possible to modularize services not logically, as usual, but relative to the infrastructure—and thus deploy them independently of each other.

In addition to all this containerization, the server side was decomposed. The various EAI implementations that ran the applications and orchestration were also broken into pieces. Project Borg, launched by Google in 2003, spawned many key ideas. Some of its developers led the way to Kubernetes, which was announced as an open source project in mid-2014 and became mainstream in just two years. With it, we have the routing, networking, scheduling, and security functions at the heart of any EAI. They not only orchestrate containers but also are built on top of them. Since then, instead of skyscrapers, software engineers have opted for a more down-to-earth architecture on all fronts. Scaling out is the order of the day.

B.1.3 Jailed services and other isolations

With containers, you can increase the isolation of your components. This creates freedom in multiple dimensions, and it's what revived the SOA architecture. If it was dead, we can say SOA was reborn in the microservices architecture.

These are the freedoms you gain when isolating services in different dimensions:

- Deployment
- Language
- Location
- Failure
- Time
- State

Now you can *deploy* your services in isolated containers. You can deploy as many replicas as you need, decoupling the various scaling requirements without disrupting other teams as you add new features or fix bugs. Deployment frequency is much greater and is decentralized, and releases can be customized to each team's schedule.

You have more leeway to use different languages and frameworks. In principle, each team could choose its own, but this needs to match the organization's needs to plan for the maintenance and evolution of these services in the longer term. In any case, the organization has a choice it didn't have before.

The idea of *location transparency or mobility* was present in the earlier SOA implementations. Today, using the container orchestration of your choice or another add-on like service mesh, you have an address that you can rely on, so any service can hide behind it. And the services that are accessible through that address can be relocated without us having to notify their clients. However, this raises the question of a session. What happens to the information that the old service had about the client? If this information is necessary, it must be kept somehow. We discuss this problem in more detail in the next section.

The fact that a *service can fail* without affecting its caller is an essential characteristic of a distributed, reliable system. This feature is the twin of mobility: while a service is temporarily restarted, location transparency provides users with a consistent facade. Thus, the client can be redirected to another healthy service with the same address, just like any load balancer. Another example you know well by now is an actor's address. The fact that you only use its reference serves the same purpose.

Two other concepts are not directly related to containerization but to the virtues of isolation. The *state* of a service is its most valuable asset and should therefore be passed on with extreme care. This idea was present in the original SOA, and the basic idea was to allow access to a service's data only via the service's API. This way, a user can interact with the service without worrying about how it is handled internally. On the other hand, the data owner can ensure that their data is handled as stated in the specification.

At this point, it's helpful to remember how domain-driven design (DDD) can help you define these boundaries. Keep in mind that it's better if each service has its own database. Isolating each service in its own database prevents the database from being overloaded by another service. The obvious downside is that each database must be managed, which drives up operating costs and often leads to abandoning the idea and sharing databases. A middle ground can be found by separating the data from one service to another within the database, sometimes using namespaces.

Our last decoupling feature is *time*. This feature is not new, of course. In any ESB, message brokers provide pub/sub communication to decouple the time of publication from the time of consumption. Queues or topics provide us with time decoupling by design and some leeway to control flow if the producer is faster than the consumer. The disadvantage of pub/sub is traceability. For the same reason that there is no direct contact between publisher and subscriber, it is harder to determine the impact of a message on all possible subscribers. That's why it's important with this architecture to get the observability and monitoring right.

The other way to decouple in time is—no surprise—an asynchronous peer-to-peer call. In this case, the client must provide a callback in the request that is executed when the response is sent or an error occurs. This feature is also related to isolating errors, because in a synchronous call, an error would propagate from the server to the client. A well-known example of these risks is a synchronous call over HTTP, which can be aborted while waiting for a response. If the server crashes, this raises an exception on the client that must be handled, and it waits in the meantime. Table B.1 shows the beneficial properties of isolation.

Table B.1   The benefits of isolation

Isolation on ...	Benefits
Deployment	Adjust deployment frequency, avoid deploying unrelated code, and scale horizontally.
Language	Different languages can be used.
Failure	Contains failures to avoid their propagation.
Space	The mobility, or location transparency, of services enables reinstantiation and horizontal scalability.
State	Strong consistency within the service.
Time	Avoids blocking and avoids propagation of failures.

B.1.4   *Some challenges from isolation*

As with most architectural decisions, some benefits come at a cost. A few examples are location transparency, which makes it difficult to maintain sessions between replicas, and transactions, which are difficult to implement and generally not recommended. Another drawback is data consistency. So, let's go into a little more detail about these difficulties.

SESSIONS

Sessions can be lost due to location transparency if one service fails and another takes over. But this can happen without there being a fault. A proxy that randomly or rotationally selects from a pool of services would have the same effect. Mobility gives resilience and scalability, but state—held in a service's memory—is lost when the proxy selects another instance of the service. To solve this problem, you first need an identifier that provides the possibility of some persistence. Then you can store the data on disk as a stateless service would. Another option is to add another layer so that the service behind the load balancer can communicate with yet another service that maintains state, perhaps in memory, perhaps on disk. For example, a Redis service could be the second service that manages state.

The problem with a stateless service that stores data directly in the database is that it is not scalable. Each instance of the service needs a connection to the database to execute its logic. This makes the database a bottleneck or single point of failure. Each instance of the service competes for this resource, and if you try to scale your services tenfold, your database may not be able to scale as much, for example, in terms of the number of connections. If you decide to partition the database, finding the right sharding is anything but trivial. Stateless services only exchange some problems for others.

ATOMICITY

In distributed systems, *transactions* pose the problem of atomicity (the *A* of ACID). It can also be thought of as the possibility of aborting so either the transaction succeeds completely or nothing changes. Let's focus here on what happens when a transaction involves multiple databases. For example, service T coordinates the booking of a trip and calls service C, which rents a car, and service F, which buys a flight. The services for the car and the flight can fail independently, so you may end up renting the car but not buying the flight. You can see this service dependency in figure B.5.

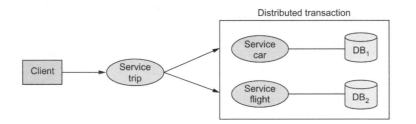

Figure B.5   Distributed transaction

In these scenarios, you can use a database pattern called Saga, although it would be better to avoid the transaction in the first place. Unlike a two-step commit, a Saga is not a blocking protocol. The key concept is to create a counteraction or compensation for each action required for the transaction. Thus, if an action fails, the transaction can be aborted by performing a counteraction for each successful action, and the final state is the same as the initial state before any change was committed.

CONSISTENCY

Now let's talk about consistency. It won't surprise you that replication of data leads to discrepancies between its copies. Whether the data is replicated in a database or a group of services, the fact that there are multiple instances of the same data presents the problem of consistency—or linearizability, to be precise (https://jepsen.io/consistency). Attempting to update the state of each instance of a piece of data takes time for all replicas to receive the message if they receive it.

Suppose you have an account with an identifier that multiple users want to update. Alice and Bob want to withdraw money from the account. If you try to synchronize each operation to make sure the account has enough funds for each requested operation, that means only one user can make changes at a time, and the others have to wait until the blocking user is done. This is not very practical and does not correspond to how banks work. This problem was solved a few centuries ago with general ledgers so that changes could be made to an account in different offices by making a new entry in the respective local ledger. At the end of the day, week, or other period, all general ledgers are combined to total the deposits and withdrawals and calculate the total balance. Of course, this approach or pattern isn't limited to accounting. Database logs are another well-known example and can be used as a recovery mechanism. For example, SQL Server transaction logs store all changes to the database, so they can be restored if you find that a user has deleted important data. It is possible to revert to a previous state. However, this is an administrator mechanism, and it is not used by normal users.

In the example of Alice and Bob, there are two ways to store the state. You can replace the value of a database row while blocking, or you can append the change to the transaction logs without blocking, like an old general ledger. These are the options: replace in place versus append-only. Thinking in terms of "replace in place" is generally a poor choice. As Pat Helland put it brilliantly, "The database is a cache of a subset of the log" (*Queue* 13 (9), 2016, https://queue.acm.org/detail.cfm?id= 2884038). When you query a store, you typically don't want to read a bunch of logs and aggregate them. That takes time. A deformalized table in a database is quicker to read, although this table—this view—is the product of its history. To twist the adage, "Those who cannot remember the past are unable to repeat it."

B.2   *Architectural principles*

Event sourcing, command query responsibility segregation (CQRS), and domain-driven design are ideas you can add to your toolbelt that will bring you great benefits as a developer or architect. Let's take a quick look at them.

B.2.1   *Event-driven systems*

If you capture state changes in an incremental, append-only way, you can build event-driven architectures. In these systems, components communicate via events. From this perspective, an event can be defined as data that refers to a fact, and it is used to communicate with another process.

Events are related to messages, but they have subtle differences. An event is a message sent to a destination whose consumers are unknown. A message, on the other hand, identifies the target with its consumer. All events are messages, but not all messages are events; a message, for example, can also be used as a command or a response.

The fact that events are messages gives event-driven systems the properties of reactive systems, and as such, they are isolated in time, space, and failure. But there are differences here as well. In message-driven systems, a component can send messages to multiple addresses, whereas in an event-driven system, messages are sent to a unique location. In both cases, the messages must be immutable for the systems to work. This is because if a message can be changed before it is consumed, it distorts its intent, just as would happen if someone changed your vote in an election. In the case of events, changing them would make the history unreliable, as they represent facts.

Event- or message-driven systems benefit greatly from asynchrony and flow control in their components. This way, you can make sure the system throttles the producer if it outputs messages faster than the consumer processes them. You can find this in libraries like Akka Streams, Pivotal Reactor, and Vert.x that create reactive components. It is important to know that these components must all be chained together for the system to have reactive properties. If a component in the middle of the chain does not have flow control, messages will be lost, some components will halt, or both.

B.2.2   *Architectural patterns*

Event-driven architectures that treat transitions as a source of truth are called *event sourcing* (ES). This approach has many advantages, such as performance. Most databases are optimized for append-only. Another advantage is traceability: because all events are stored, you can prove—by replying to them—that your system behaved as prescribed, which is a legal requirement in many organizations. Another major advantage over in-place replacement is the flexibility to have multiple representations of the same set of events.

Imagine you have a data structure that represents the status of a shopping cart, and you write in it the number of items, their ID and descriptions, and the price for each change in the cart. If you use a CRUD approach and delete an item from the list while a user is shopping, that item disappears forever. And losing traceability limits your options. It is possible, for example, that after some time in production, the marketing team might get the idea to focus on the things that have been removed from the shopping cart as a sign that the buyer is interested in the product but not convinced. In response, the company would make special offers to those customers. With a state approach, where you replace in situ, that wouldn't be possible if you didn't add a specific field for those deletes, which adds complexity.

Another example is how to deal with bugs. For example, let's assume that an error occurred while calculating the price in the shopping cart. A discount should be applied to a certain product, but the program has a bug and applies the wrong discounts. If you have stored only the values but not the events in your database, you have to do a lot of work to correct each wrong value. You must find every value in the database and apply the correct discount. On the other hand, if you keep the events, such as products added, you can feed your program with those events once the bug is fixed, and that will be sufficient. Each cart will end up with the correct discount. An event sourcing system allows you to fix the code and replay the events.

Reading the history of events lets you look at the same events in retrospect from different perspectives. It gives you the opportunity to travel through time, not only to prove that the system is correct but also to replay it if it is not. However, sourcing events comes at a cost: namely, the cost of reading the data. The events are stored as a list of data structures, usually as tuples, with an ID associated with each event.

Representing the current state in event sourcing is an expensive operation. You have to iterate over all the events, although there are some optimizations. A common optimization is snapshotting, where the account's events are summarized from time to time so you don't have to read the entire list, just the snapshots. But even in these cases, the model is not optimized for different queries, and organizations often need to look at the data from different angles. And every time you need to group the data differently, it's very expensive. For example, you may need the balance of each account by customer and office, then by office and country, and so on. There's no SQL you can use for that. The data is stored in events, not rows where the individual fields are arranged. For each query, you have to iterate and extract. To solve this problem, you can use a good, old-fashioned solution called a *projection.*

A projection is nothing more than a materialized view. You take the logs, group them as needed, and store them—exactly what Pat Helland said: "A database is the cache of a subset of the log." You can create a new model from the event log by reading the individual entries, grouping them appropriately, and saving them somewhere. This way, you get data that already has the form you want to query and decouple the logs from the view so they can be scaled separately. The downside is that the projection is *eventually consistent* with respect to the logs. However, since you are only using it for reading and not writing, this usually is not a problem. If you're writing, you probably need stronger consistency guarantees. This brings us to the separation of read and write, the query side and the command side.

Command Query Responsibility Segregation (CQRS; http://mng.bz/rdzj) is based on the idea of Bertrand Meyer's command and query separation (CQS) principle. This states that each method should be either a command that performs an action or a query that returns data to the caller, but not both. In other words, asking a question should not change the state of things. More formally, methods should return a value only if they are referentially transparent and therefore have no side effects. It has been argued that while CQRS is a useful principle, it is not sufficient when dealing with data structures such as stacks or queues because when reading from a stack, the element must be removed, causing side effects.

Even if CQS is not always applicable, it is a powerful idea to which CQRS adds even more. The basic idea is that these commands and queries should be executed not on one but on two different objects—one for the write side and one for the read side. For this, you need different models that exist in different places. For example, the optimization for writing can be a ledger or table normalized to the NF3 degree, and the optimization for reading can be a table normalized to the NF1 degree.

The CQRS abstraction plays well with event sourcing. When you combine the two, the models are no longer stored in two places; only the events are persisted. But you still have two places: one to send queries and another to send commands. For example, with Akka Persistence, there is an entity that you send commands to that keeps its state in memory, and the entity produces events that are persisted in the journal to which you send the queries.

B.2.3   *Business abstractions*

DDD's abstractions give you clarity about how to define the boundaries of the data as it relates to the business. Perhaps the most fundamental idea of DDD is the bounded context. To map a part of the business domain—the subdomain—it makes sense to draw a boundary that allows you to talk and write about it clearly. The language you use to talk about the entities or events within a subdomain should not be used outside it.

Even if the concept of the customer can be considered as one and the same entity in a company, it is almost certain that different departments will only deal with certain aspects of the customer that are relevant to that particular department. Therefore, you should not treat it as the same entity. Different facets of the customer form different entities. Abstracting these different entities into one customer reduces precision, ultimately reducing the concept's usability in its different contexts. Abstracting several things into one entity forces each department to deal with attributes that are irrelevant to its particular business. The right level of abstraction should be found by business experts who have developed their concepts from experience. A *bounded context* is a subset of the business domain with the specific language used to refer to its parts.

There are many great ideas in DDD, but this is not the place to introduce them. A lot has been written, starting with the books *Domain Driven Design* by Eric Evans (Addison-Wesley Professional, 2003, http://mng.bz/VpJx) and *Implementing DDD* by Vaughn Vernon (Addison-Wesley, 2013, http://mng.bz/AlJQ). I encourage you to take a look if possible. Integration through SOA and MOM; isolation in time, space, failure, state, and deployment; microservices; CQRS; event-driven architectures; and DDD are ideas widely used in Akka. They will help you better understand this book and distributed systems in general.

index

A

accrual failure detector 152
action 204
actor programming model and actors 18–22
  Akka gRPC 233–235
  Akka HTTP communicating with actors
    225–228
    transforming requests 226
    transforming responses 226–228
  as hierarchy 44–64
    adapter 48–49
    asking and expecting replies 52–63
    coding 46–47
    guardian, coding 47–48
    overview of 45–52
    workers 49–52
  asynchronous model 18–19
  betting-house example application 239
    bet 248–258
    market 243–248
    wallet 239–243
  components 22–26
    ActorRef 24
    ActorSystem 23–24
    dispatchers 24–25
    mailboxes 24
    network communication 26
  connecting streams to actors 334–336
  effects 67–70
  implementing actors 30–31
  implementing router patterns using actors
    123–125
    content-based routing 123
    state-based routing 123–125
  instantiating actors 29

  multiple actors 70
  operations 19–22
    create 21
    send 20–21
    supervise 21–22
    swapping out behavior 21
  overview of 4–5
  protocol of actors 28
ActorFlow class 335
ActorRef 24, 74
ActorSystem 23–24, 45, 265, 273
ActorTestKit class 66
adapters
  function of 49
  protocol with message 49
  sending messages 48
AddCargo class 231
AddCargo events 202
addCargo gRPC call 231
addCargo method 231
AddedCargo class 231
AddedCargo response message 230
afterAll method 73
Akka 1–64
  actor programming model and actors 18–22
    asynchronous model 18–19
    components 22–26
    operations 19–22
    overview of 4–5
  betting-house example application 238–263,
    306–324
    configuration 317–321
    deployment 321–324
    projections 307–317
  business chat application example 18–22
  clustering 138–170, 264–283

Akka *(continued)*
  Akka Cluster Bootstrap 265–269
  Akka Management and cluster HTTP
    extension 153–157
  cluster subscriptions 156–157
  clustered job processing 157–166
  joining clusters 141–143
  Kubernetes API 269–277
  leaving clusters 148–150
  minimal example 143–145
  overview of 138–139
  resilience 166–169
  shutting down nodes 151–153
  Split Brain Resolver 277–281
  starting clusters 145–148, 166
  unreachable nodes 150–151
  work distribution in master 162–166
configuration 126–137
  configuration library 127–132
  in tests 135–137
  of multiple systems 133–135
  overview of 132–133
connectors 284–305
  Alpakka CSV 300–305
  Alpakka Kafka 285–293
discovery and routing 108–125
  balancing load using built-in routers 114–123
  built-in integration router pattern 112–114
  implementing router pattern using
    actors 123–125
  receptionist 109–112
fault tolerance 82–107
  overview of 83–91
  signals 91–100
  supervision hierarchy alternative design
    101–106
  supervisor hierarchy initial design 100–101
  using actors 89–91
  using plain old objects and exception
    handling 85–89
overview of 2–4
parser example
  adapter 48–49
  asking and expecting replies 52–63
  coding 46–47
  guardian, coding 47–48
  overview of 45–52
  workers 49–52
persistence 180–185
  available effects 184–185
  combined with sharding 184
  customizing persistent entities 186–189
  ingredients for 180–184
persistence queries 198–203
ports 217–237

  Akka gRPC 228–236
  Akka HTTP 217–228
projections 204–212
sharding 171–191
  persistence combined with 184
  stateful systems and 172–179
streams 193–198, 325–349
  adding elements dynamically 346–348
  connecting to actors 334–336
  exceptions 337–345
  processing elements through services
    326–334
wallet application example 28–33
  complete code 31
  creating applications and instantiating
    actors 29
  implementing actors 30–31
  keeping state 33–40
  overview of 28
  protocol of actors 28
  running applications 32–33
  scheduling messages 41–42
  sending messages 29–30
  solution in Git 32
  terminating system 31
Akka Cluster Bootstrap 265–269
  local clusters 265–267
  starting two-node clusters 267–269
Akka extensions 23
Akka gRPC 228–236
  plugin and .proto files 229–231
  Protocol Buffers 229
  RPC 229
  shipping container application example
    231–233
  actors and 233–235
  running example 236
  running service 233
Akka HTTP 217–228
  communicating with actors 225–228
    transforming requests 226
    transforming responses 226–228
  directives 220
  marshalling and unmarshalling 224–225
  route directives 221–224
    complete method 221
    failing 223–224
    traversing route 221–222
  server path 218–220
  servers 218
Akka Management, cluster HTTP extension
  and 153–157
Akka test kit 65–81
  approaches to 66–67
  asynchronous unit testing 72–80

fishing for messages 75–77
log capturing 79–80
log testing 77–79
probes 72–74
synchronous unit testing 67–72
effects 67–70
log testing 71–72
more than one actor 70
AKKA_CLUSTER_BOOTSTRAP_
SERVICE_NAME option 273
akka-cluster module 143, 265
akka-discovery transitive dependency 153
akka-discovery-kubernetes-api module 269
akka-http-core library 330
akka-http-spray-json library 224
akka-http-spray-json method 224
akka-management default configuration 153
akka-management library dependency 153
akka-management module 265
akka-management-cluster HTTP module 156
akka-management-cluster library dependency 138
akka-projection-jdbc module 311
akka-remote module 140
akka-serialization-jackson library 167
akka-testkit module 66
akka.cluster.failure-detector section 153
akka.cluster.type.Down message 151
akka.remote configuration 160
AkkaManagement module 266
alive probe 274
Alpakka CSV 300–305
mapping by column 302–303
reading and writing with FileIO 303–305
Alpakka Kafka 285–293
auto-commit 290
committable sources 290–293
consuming from Kafka 287–288
detecting consumer failures 290
pushing to Kafka 293–298
at-least-once delivery guarantee 295–298
at-most-once delivery guarantee 293–295
effectively-once delivery 298–300
apply function 60
apply method 60, 242, 245
architectural principles 361–364
architectural patterns 362–363
business abstractions 364
event-driven systems 361–362
ask method 57, 60
ask signature 56, 59
asking 52–61
coding manager 55
coding worker 58–59
overview of 56–58
protocols 56

signature 59–61
simple question 53–55
using context 59
with payload 61–63
asynchronicity
asynchronous decoupling 16
asynchronous nature of actor programming
model 18–19
asynchronous unit testing 72–80
fishing for messages 75–77
log capturing 79–80
log testing 77–79
probes 72–74
asynchronous programming model 18
AsyncLogSpec test 79
at-least-once delivery guarantee 295–298
at-most-once delivery guarantee 293–295
atomicity, problem of 360
auto-down-unreachable-after setting 152
AWS CLI, installing 351

B

BDD (Behavior Driven Development) 65
BeforeAndAfterAll trait 73
Behaviors factory 74
Behaviors functions 89
behaviors, keeping state with 37–40
Behaviors.stopped factory 78
bet actor 248, 258
BetProjection projection 315
BetRepository SELECT query 311
bets, in betting-house example application
248–258
events and event handler 254–255
initialization 251–252
Open command 252–253
private protocol 250
public protocol 249–250
Settle command 257–258
states 250–251
validating market and funds 255–257
betting-house example application 238–263,
306–324
actors 239
bets 248–258
market 243–248
wallet 239–243
configuration 317–321
Kubernetes clusters 319
local clusters 319
persistence 317–318
services, sharding, and projections 320–321
deployment 321–324
running in Kubernetes 322–324
running locally 321–322

betting-house example application *(continued)*
    ports 259–263
    projections 307–317
        database projection 307–312
        entry point 316–317
        Kafka projection 312–316
blueprints
    function 194
    materialization of 196–197
    overview of 195–196
bootstrap.servers Kubernetes configuration 321
bounded context 364
business abstractions 364
business chat application example
    asynchronous model 18–19
    components 22–26
    operations 19–22
    overview of 5–7
    scaling
        Akka approach 12–17
        traditional approach 7–12
Byte class 224

C

callback hell 25
Cancel market 259
Cap actor 336
CapturedLogEvent type 72
CapturedLogEvent(level:Level, message:String)
    class 71
Cargo class 227, 231
Cargo request message 230
CargoAdded envelope 206
Cargos actor 235
Cargos case class 234
Cargos message 234
CargosPerContainerProjection class 208
CargosPerContainerProjection
    projection_name 215
carl actor 79
case class 60
catch exceptions 97
ChildFailed signal 98, 102
childInbox method 70
childTestKit method 70
chroot command 357
class 52
close() method 260
CloseMarket market 259
cluster definiton 140
Cluster extension 169
Cluster module 141
cluster singletons 281–282
Cluster states 278

Cluster.MemberUnreachable unreachable
    event 278
ClusterBootstrap module 266
ClusterCommand messages 148
ClusterDomainEvent messages 156
ClusterEvent 278
clustering 138–170, 264–283
    Akka Cluster Bootstrap 265–269
        local clusters 265–267
        starting two-node clusters 267–269
    Akka Management and cluster HTTP
        extension 153–157
    betting-house example application
        Kubernetes 319
        local 319
    cluster singletons 281–282
    cluster subscriptions 156–157
    clustered job processing 157–166
    joining clusters 141–143
    Kubernetes API 269–277
        creating Docker images 269–271
        deployment 271–274
        roles and role binding 275
        service accounts 276–277
        setting Java options 274
    leaving clusters 148–150
    minimal example 143–145
    overview of 138–139
    resilience 166–169
        serialization 167–168
        testing 168–169
    shutting down nodes 151–153
    Split Brain Resolver 277–281
        strategies 280–281
        unreachable nodes 277–280
    starting clusters 145–148, 166
    unreachable nodes 150–151
    work distribution in master 162–166
clusters
    job processing
        overview 157
        work distribution using routers 166
    membership
        joining 141
        leaving 148
ClusterSharding reference 234
commit settings 299
Committable type 292
CommittableMessage type 291
committed position 289
committing the offset 286
complete method 221
concat operand 222
concurrency for scalability 2
configuration 126–137

betting-house example application 317–321
  Kubernetes clusters 319
  local clusters 319
  persistence 317–318
  services, sharding, and projections 320–321
configuration library 127–132
  defaults 130–132
  order 127–128
  substitutions 129–130
  subtrees 128–129
  in tests 135–137
  of multiple systems 133–135
  overview of 132–133
  rebalancing 178–179
connectors 284–305
  Alpakka CSV 300–305
    mapping by column 302–303
    reading and writing with FileIO 303–305
  Alpakka Kafka 285–293
    auto-commit 290
    committable sources 290–293
    consuming from Kafka 287–288
    detecting consumer failures 290
    pushing to Kafka 293–298
consistency 360–361
consistent hashing 120
ConsistentHashing router logic 116
ConsumerPlainSource application 288
ConsumerPlainSource output 288
Container actor 234
container-tag-0 tag 201
container-tag-1 tag 208
container-tag-2 tag 201
ContainerService gRPC service 230
content-based routing 123
convergence of nodes 150
Conversation actor 13–14, 16–17, 20–21
Conversation object 7–8, 16
Conversations actor 21
CORBA (Common Object Request Broker
  Architecture) 353
CQRS (command query responsibility
  segregation) 361, 363
CQS (command and query separation_
  principle 363
create operations 21
CreateChild message 68
createProjectionFor method 208, 211
createRequest parameter 62
createRequest signature 60
CSNET (Computer Science Network) 353
CSV 300–305
  mapping by column 302–303
  reading and writing with FileIO 303–305
CsvFormatting.format() method 304
CsvToMap.toMap() method 302

CsvToMap.toMapAsStrings() method 303
CsvToMap.withHeaders() method 302
curl, installing 351
current queries 198
currentEventsByPersistenceId interface
  methods 199
currentEventsByTag interface methods 199
currentPersistenceIds interface methods 199
currying technique 62

D

DAOs (data access objects) 8
data-processing application example
  Akka Management and cluster HTTP
    extension 153–157
  cluster subscriptions 156–157
  clustered job processing 157–166
  joining clusters 141–143
  leaving clusters 148–150
  minimal example 143–145
  resilient job 166–169
  shutting down nodes 151–153
  starting clusters 145–148
  unreachable nodes 150–151
  work distribution in master 162–166
database MyAppl property 127
DBaseConnection class 128
DbBrokenConnectionException exception 105
DbWriter actor 105
DCOM (Distributed Component Object
  Model) 354
DDD (domain-driven design) 358
deadLetters actor 54–55, 78
deciders 338–339
def parsingDoc(doc:String): String method 326
Delegate message 48
Deregister message 112
directives
  Akka HTTP 220
  route directives 221–224
    complete method 221
    failing 223–224
    traversing route 221–222
discovery and routing 108–125
  balancing load using built-in routers 114–123
    changing strategies 117–118
    consistent hashing strategy 120–123
    group router 118–119
    pool router 116–117
  built-in integration router pattern 112–114
  implementing router pattern using actors
    123–125
    content-based routing 123
    state-based routing 123–125
  receptionist 109–112

discovery method 265, 267
dispatchers 24–25
Distributed Component Object Model
    (DCOM) 354
divertTo 340–341
Docker
    creating images 269–271
    installing 350
dockerBaseImage parameter 270
dockerExposedPorts parameter 270
DockerPlugin 270, 322
Domain Driven Design (Evans) 364
Done type 292
Down state 153
downstreams 193
Dr. Dobb's Journal (Sutter) 2
durability
    Akka scaling approach 13–15
        keeping changes as sequence of events 14
        sharding conversations 14–15
    traditional scaling approach 7–10

E

EAI (enterprise application integration) 354
EditMessage message 20
effectively-once delivery 298–300
enable-http2 configuration 319
encapsulation 20
entity directive 227
eos-commit-interval property 300
errorkernel package 46
ES (event sourcing) 362
ESB (enterprise service bus) 354
ETL (extract, transform, load) processes 203
Evans, Eric 364
event sourcing 14
event-driven systems 361–362
events and event handlers 254–255
eventsByPersistenceId interface methods 199
eventsByTag interface methods 199
eventsByTag method 204
eventsByTag stream 202
exactly-once delivery 204, 298
example.countwords.CborSerializable trait 168
exceptions 337–345
    deciders 338–339
    divertTo 340–341
    modeling exceptions as data 339–340
    restarting sources 341–345

F

failure
    Akka scaling approach 16

detecting consumer failures 290
    persistent entities 186
    route directives 223–224
failure detector 152
Failure option 52
fake text 163
fault tolerance 82–107
    log-processing application example 100–106
        supervision hierarchy alternative design 101–106
        supervisor hierarchy initial design 100–101
        using actors 89–91
        using plain old objects and exception handling 85–89
    overview of 83–91
    signals
        overview of 91–92
        supervision strategies and 92–97
        watching from actors 98–100
faulttolerance1 package 100
faulttolerance2 package 101
FileIO, reading and writing with 303–305
FileWatcher actors 102
filterAndGetValues function 304
finite streams 194
fire-and-forget style 20
flexiFlow stage 295
Flow 195
follow method 343
Follow service 341
FundsAdded event 239, 242
FundsReservationDenied event 239
FundsReserved event 239
futureValue method 302

G

GC (garbage collector) 150
GC pause state 153
GET command 222, 224
GET methods 218
Get Programming with Scala (Sfregola) 61
getBetByMarket method 310
GetCargos RPC call 234
GetState command 248
GetState market 259
Git, wallet application example 32
goldenKey 109
gossip protocol 150, 277
graph function 194
group router 118–119
GrpcClientSettings Akka gRPC module 342
grpcurl, installing 351
guardian, coding 47–48

H

handleCommands method 242, 245
handleEvents method 242
HOCON (Human-Optimized Config Object Notation) format 128
HOST_NAME specified property 129
hotel registration application example 109–112
HotelConcierge actor 109
HTTP cluster extension 153–157
hyperthreading 328

I

IDL (interface definition language) 229, 354
ignore function 67
Implementing DDD (Vernon) 364
implicit keyword 224
implicit variable 207
include option 133
infinite streams 197–198
INFO level 78
init method 262, 315
insertClient method 67
Int class 224
Int parameter 224
interactivity
    Akka scaling approach 15–16
    traditional scaling approach 10–11
internal behavior 66
invalid option 252
isolation.level property 299
isolations 359–361
    atomicity 360
    consistency 360–361
    jailed services 357–359
    sessions 359–360

J

jailed services 357–359
JARs (Java ARchives) 322–323, 357
Java
    installing 350
    setting options in Kubernetes API 274
Java EARs (Enterprise Application aRchives) 357
JavaAppPackaging plugin 322
JDK
    installing 350
    Java 350
    SDKMAN! 350
job processing
    overview 157
    work distribution using routers 166
job processing, clustered 157–166

J (right column)

JOIN message 141
Joining state 148
journal 14
JsonFormat formatter 224
jsonFormat1 formatter 226
jsonFormat2 formatter 224, 226
JVM (Java virtual machine) 1

K

Kafka
    auto-commit 290
    betting-house example application 312–316
    committable sources 290–293
    consuming from 287–288
    detecting consumer failures 290
    pushing to 293–298
        at-least-once delivery guarantee 295–298
        at-most-once delivery guarantee 293–295
        effectively-once delivery 298–300
kcat, installing 351
Kubernetes API 269–277
    betting-house example application 322–324
        clusters 319
        creating images with JAR 322–323
        starting application 323–324
    creating Docker images 269–271
    deployment 271–274
    roles and role binding 275
    service accounts 276–277
    setting Java options 274

L

Leaving state 151
let-it-crash principle 82–83
lifting
    in tests 135–137
    with fallback 133–135
List class 224
List type 227
load function 131
load method 132
local option 143
localhost 144
Location elements 341
location transparency or mobility 358
Log message 78
log-processing application example 100–106
    supervision hierarchy alternative design 101–106
    supervisor hierarchy initial design 100–101
    using actors 89–91
    using plain old objects and exception handling 85–89

LogCapturing property 80
logEntries method 70
logging
   log capturing 79–80
   log testing
      asynchronous unit testing 77–79
      synchronous unit testing 71–72
LogProcessingGuardian actor 100
LogProcessingGuardian monitors 102

M

mailboxes 24
Main betting-house application 316
Main class 127, 151
main executable method 270
main method 212
manager, coding 55
mapAsync 327–328
mapAsyncUnordered 329
mapResponse function 61
Market.Close event 312
MarketCancelled event 314
MarketClosed event 314
MarketConfirmed event 256
MarketOpened event 314
MarketProjection projection 315
markets, in betting-house example
      application 243–263
MarketServiceClient class 260
marshalling and unmarshalling 224–225
master, work distribution in 162–166
master.conf file 161
materialized values 195–196
membership, cluster
   joining 141
   leaving 148
Mentions actor 20
Mentions component 10, 16–17, 21
Mentions object 16, 20
merge function 164
MessageAdded event 13–14
messages 92
   asking and expecting replies 52–61
      ask signature 59–61
      ask with payload 61–63
      asking 56–58
      coding manager 55
      coding worker 58–59
      protocols 56
      simple question 53–55
      using context 59
   fishing for 75–77
   pushing 15–16
   scheduling 41–42

sending and receiving 13–17
      keeping changes as sequence of events 14
      sharding conversations 14–15
      wallet application example 29–31
microservices 352–361
   characteristics of better services 356–357
   development of distributed systems 353–356
   isolations 359–361
      atomicity 360
      consistency 360–361
      jailed services 357–359
      sessions 359–360
middleware 353
Minikube, installing 351
MOM (message-oriented middleware) 353
monitor method 74
MVP (minimal viable product) 6
MyAppl node 127
MyAppl.description property 135
MyAppl.name property 127

N

name MyAppl property 127
name property 127
nine nines reliability 20
nodes
   shutting down 151–153
   unreachable 150–151, 277–280
NotifyUser actor 21
NotifyUser component 16

O

objects 12
offset for groupId 286
Offset.noOffset object 199
Open command 252–253
Open market 259
Open messages 245
open method 246, 253
open(state, command) method 245
Opened event 246, 253
OpenState state 245
Option class 224
org.apache.kafka.clients.consumer.Consumer-
      Record objects 288
OTP (Open Telecom Platform) 20
OutlookContacts actor 22

P

PaaS (Platform as a Service) 2
parameter extraction 226
.parameters directive 226

parameters directive 226
Parse message 50–51, 56
ParseException type 105
parser example
  adapter
    function of 49
    protocol with message 49
    sending messages 48
  asking and expecting replies 52–61
    ask signature 59–61
    ask with payload 61–63
    asking 56–58
    coding manager 55
    coding worker 58–59
    protocols 56
    simple question 53–55
    using context 59
  coding 46–47
  guardian, coding 47–48
  overview of 45–52
  workers
    coding 51–52
    delegating to 49–51
    protocol with commands and responses as
      traits 51
partition points 141
partitioning 15
passivation 179
persistence 180–185
  available effects 184–185
  betting-house example application 317–318
  combined with sharding 184
  customizing persistent entities 186–189
    failure 186
    recovery 186–187
    serialization and schema evolution 188–189
    snapshotting 187
    tagging 188
  ingredients for 180–184
persistence queries
  overview of 198
  shipping container application example
    202–203
persistenceIds API method 200
persistenceIds interface methods 199
PhotoProcessor actor 119
poisoned mailbox 91
polling 10–11
pool router 116–117
port parameter 160
PORT variable 145
port variable 212
ports 217–237
  Akka gRPC 228–236
    plugin and .proto files 229–231

Protocol Buffers 229
    RPC 229
    shipping container application example
      231–236
  Akka HTTP 217–228
    communicating with actors 225–228
    directives 220
    marshalling and unmarshalling 224–225
    route directives 221–224
    server path 218–220
    servers 218
  betting-house example application 259–263
    market 259–263
PostStop signal 94–95, 156
PreRestart signal 95–97
probes 72–74
Process message 165
process method 206
processor 195
ProducerRecord type 294
projections 204–212, 363
  betting-house example application 307–317,
    320–321
    database projection 307–312
    entry point 316–317
    Kafka projection 312–316
  creating 207–209
  main method components 212
  reading 205
  ShardedDaemonProcess 209–211
  shipping container application example
    211–216
  writing 205–207
.proto file 229–231
proto objects 314–315
protobuf library 314
Protocol Buffers 229

Q

questionwithpayload package 62
queue.offer method 348

R

RandomRouting router logic 116
ReadJournal interface 198
ready probe 274
.receiveSignal method 95
receptionist 109–112
recovery, persistent entities 186–187
Register message 109
registerOnMemberUp method 161
remote procedure calls (RPCs) 229
Removed state 150

repeated notation 234
replyTo parameter 62
Report message 55
repository implementation 308
requestFundsReservation validation 256
RequestWalletFunds command 257
Response type 51
Resume message 76
role parameter 160
RootJsonFormat formatter 224
RoundRobinRouting router logic 116
route directives, Akka HTTP 221–224
    complete method 221
    failing 223–224
    traversing route 221–222
route statement 222
routees 114
router patterns
    balancing load using built-in routers 114–123
        changing strategies 117–118
        consistent hashing strategy 120–123
        group router 118–119
        pool router 116–117
    built-in integration router pattern 112–114
    implementing using actors 123–125
        content-based routing 123
        state-based routing 123–125
routers 108, 112
    work distribution among clusters using 166
routing strategies 115–116
RPCs (remote procedure calls) 2, 229

S

Sacred Balance, The (Suzuki) 44
SAs (service accounts), Kubernetes 276–277
SBR (Split Brain Resolver) 277–281
    strategies 280–281
    unreachable nodes 150, 277–280
sbt, installing 350
scalability, definiton 2
scalapb library 231
ScalaTest library 302
ScalikeJdbc library 333
scaling
    Akka approach 12–17
        durability 13–15
        failure 16
        interactive use 15–16
        overview of 16–17
    business chat application example 5–7
    traditional approach 7–12
        durability 7–10
        interactive use 10–11
        transactions 11–12

scheduleOnce method 69
scheduling messages 41–42
SDKMAN!, installing 350
seed nodes 141, 147
seed.conf file 145
SELECT query 310
SelfUp cluster domain event 161
send operations 20–21
serialization
    clustering 167–168
    definition 224
    persistent entities 188–189
serialization-bindings configuration 319
server streaming gRPC 342
servers
    Akka gRPC 228–236
        plugin and .proto files 229–231
        Protocol Buffers 229
        RPC 229
        shipping container application example
            231–236
    Akka HTTP 217–228
        communicating with actors 225–228
        directives 220
        marshalling and unmarshalling 224–225
        overview of 218
        route directives 221–224
        server path 218–220
service accounts (SAs), Kubernetes 276–277
service-oriented architecture (SOA) 352, 354, 356
ServiceKey 109
sessions 359–360
Settle command 257–258
Settle message 257
Sfregola, Daniela 61
ShardedDaemonProcess 209–211
sharding 171–191
    betting-house example application 320–321
    conversations 14–15
    persistence 184
        available effects 184–185
        customizing persistent entity 186–189
    stateful systems and 172–179
        overview of 172–174
        passivation 179
        rebalancing configuration 178–179
        remembering entities 179
        shipping container application example
            174–176
        simplicity of sharded entities 176–178
shipping container application example 189–191
    Akka gRPC 231–233
        actors and 233–235
        running example 236
        running service 233

overview of 174–176
passivation 179
persistence
    available effects 184–185
    combined with sharding 184
    customizing persistent entities 186–189
persistence queries 202–203
projections 211–216
rebalancing configuration 178–179
remembering entities 179
simplicity of sharded entities 176–178
Signal type 92
signals
    overview of 91–92
    supervision strategies and 92–97
        custom strategy 97
        restarting and PreRestart signal 95–97
        stopping and PostStop signal 94–95
        uneventful resuming 92–94
    watching signals from an actor 98–100
SimpleQuestion app 53
simplequestion package 53
SimplifiedFileWatcher logs 98
SimplifiedManager actor 71
SimplifiedManager logs 79
SimplifiedManager.Log message 79
SimplifiedWorker 68
Sink 195
snapshotting, persistent entities 187
SOA (service-oriented architecture) 352, 354, 356
SOAP (Simple Object Access Protocol) 354
Source 194–195
Source.queue queue 346
SourceQueue object 346
spawn method 69
speed camera application example
    balancing load using built-in routers 114–123
        changing strategies 117–118
        consistent hashing strategy 120–123
        group router 118–119
        pool router 116–117
    built-in integration router pattern 112–114
    implementing router pattern using actors
        123–125
        content-based routing 123
        state-based routing 123–125
Split Brain Resolver. *See* SBR
SplitBrainResoverProvider configuration 319
spray-json library 224
SR (sharded region) 208
standard queries 198
Start message 47
state
    betting-house example application 250–251

keeping
    with behaviors 37–40
    with variables 33–37
sharding and stateful systems 172–179
    overview of 172–174
    passivation 179
    rebalancing configuration 178–179
    remembering entities 179
    shipping container application example
        174–176
    simplicity of sharded entities 176–178
    state-based routing 123–125
stop method 69
store command 203
streams 193–198, 325–349
    adding elements dynamically 346–348
    blueprint 195–196
    connecting to actors 334–336
    exceptions 337–345
        deciders 338–339
        divertTo 340–341
        modeling exceptions as data 339–340
        restarting sources 341–345
    finite streams 194
    Flow 195
    infinite streams 197–198
    materialization 196–197
    overview of 194
    processing elements through services 326–334
        CPU-bounded services 326–328
        non-CPU bounded services 328–334
    Sink 195
    Source 194–195
String class 224
String parameter 224
String type 67, 121
Subscribe message 110
subscriptions 156–157
substitutions 129–130
subtrees 128–129
Success Future callback 301
Success option 59
supervise operations 21–22
supervision strategies 92–97
    alternative design 101–106
    custom strategy 97
    initial design 100–101
    restarting and PreRestart signal 95–97
    stopping and PostStop signal 94–95
    uneventful resuming 92–94
Supervisor actor 21, 23
Sutter, Herb 2
Suzuki, David 44
swapping out behavior 21

synchronous unit testing 67–72
  effects 67–70
  log testing 71–72
  multiple actors 70

T

Try 52
tagging, persistent entities 188
target parameter 60
Team object 7
TeamFinder actor 22
TeamFinder object 11, 16
template.metadata.label property 272
Terminated messages 98
Terminated signal 98–99
Terminated(child) message 117
test topic 287, 294
test2 topic 287
test6 topic 287
testing
  asynchronous 72–80
    fishing for messages 75–77
    log capturing 79–80
    log testing 77–79
    probes 72–74
  clustering and 168–169
  configuration in 135–137
  lifting in 135–137
  synchronous 67–72
    effects 67–70
    log testing 71–72
    more than one actor 70
text parameter 62
Tick message 163
time decoupling feature 358
Timeout class 52
.toMat method 196
totalWeight variable 202
traditional approach 5
transactions 11–12, 360
typeahead 11

U

UI (user interface) 7
UnexpectedColumnsException exception 105

unreachability, in clusters 280
unreachable event 278
Unreachable state 150
unreachable tag 278
unreachable, definition 277
Up state 148, 151, 279
Update market 259
upserts 203
upstreams 193
user property 128
UserMentioned messages 16

V

Validated(accepted:Boolean) class 331
variables, keeping state with 33–37
Vernon, Vaughn 364
version MyAppl property 127

W

wallet application example
  complete code 31
  creating and instantiating actors 29
  protocol of actors 28
  receiving messages 30–31
  running 32–33
  sending messages 29–30
  solution in Git 32
  terminating system 31
wallets, in betting-house example
    application 239–243
Watch message 98–99
watching actors 92
withBroadcastPredicate router logic 116
.withHeaders method 303
.withMaxRestarts option 343
worker.conf file 161
Worker.Parse function 60
Worker.Response message 49
WorkerDoneAdapter message 49
workers
  coding 51–52, 58–59
  delegating to 49–51
  protocol with commands and responses as
    traits 51
WSDL (Web Service Definition Language) 354